'Building on her brilliant cultural analysis in *A Jungian Inquiry into the American Psyche*, Burnett now brings together fifteen authors to reflect on a wide range of American topics, from political polarization to intergenerational trauma to capitalism and patriarchy. With rigorous research, imagination, kaleidoscope insights, and heartfelt expression, this collection confirms depth psychology's potential to contribute to social responsibility. Interdisciplinary in nature, timely and timeless at once, this is a great contribution to Jungian studies and beyond.'

Andrew Samuels, *author of* The Political Psyche

'America is on the couch as never before in this splendid collection of essays edited by Ipek S. Burnett. The remarkable success of the collection is to achieve coherence *with* diversity and wide coverage of topics *with* depth of analysis, and to combine different depth psychological lenses *with* ancient myth and twenty-first-century suspicion of patriarchal and religious apologies. However, perhaps the most remarkable achievement of *Re-Visioning the American Psyche* is to make the good old U.S.A. into a case study of contemporary philosophical and political crises. Can democracy exist in systemically repressed psyches? Can the psyche exist if history is systemically falsified and social justice denied? Truly, this book demonstrates that Jungian psychology is a valuable critical lens across multiple social and humanities disciplines. *Re-Visioning the American Psyche* is essential reading for anyone in America or who wants to understand Americans.'

Susan Rowland, *core faculty at Pacifica Graduate Institute and author of* C.G. Jung in the Humanities

'*Re-Visioning the American Psyche* cannot be engaged with the mind alone but through the pores of our skin. Ipek S. Burnett has collected and arranged a number of essays that are designed to liberate us from traditional narratives about America that have permeated our psyche. The still quiet voice of care is awakened as we ask ourselves not only what it means to be a citizen of a differentiated humanity, but how can caring manifest into collective action?'

Robin McCoy Brooks, *co-Editor-in-Chief of* International Journal of Jungian Studies *and author of* Psychoanalysis, Catastrophe & Social Action

Re-Visioning the American Psyche

The United States is at a crossroads: Moving away from the stalemate of political polarization and culture wars requires reflection, critical thinking, and imagination. This book of collected essays brings together leaders in Jungian and archetypal psychology to forge this path by offering a comprehensive look at the American psyche.

Re-Visioning the American Psyche examines the myths, images, and archetypal fantasies ingrained in the collective consciousness and unconscious in the United States. The volume tends to manifest symptoms in political institutions, social conflicts, and cultural movements. Using various interpretative processes—from psychoanalytic to literary and to participatory—it reflects on the meaning of democratic participation, the psychological cost of wars and violence, intergenerational trauma due to racism, the emotional dimensions of political polarization, deep-seated oppositional thinking in patriarchal structures, frailty of the American Dream, and more.

With its rich scope, interdisciplinary scholarship, and critical engagement with historical and current affairs, this book will be of great interest to those in Jungian and depth psychology, as well as sociology, politics, cultural studies, and American studies. As a timely contribution with an international appeal, it will engage readers who are invested in better understanding psychology's capacity to respond to social, cultural, and political realities.

Ipek S. Burnett, PhD, is the author of *A Jungian Inquiry into the American Psyche: The Violence of Innocence* (Routledge). Based in San Francisco, she works with human rights and social justice organizations and writes novels in her native language, Turkish.

Re-Visioning the American Psyche

Jungian, Archetypal, and Mythological Reflections

Edited by Ipek S. Burnett

Routledge
Taylor & Francis Group

LONDON AND NEW YORK

Designed cover image: © Getty Images

First published 2024
by Routledge
4 Park Square, Milton Park, Abingdon, Oxon OX14 4RN

and by Routledge
605 Third Avenue, New York, NY 10158

Routledge is an imprint of the Taylor & Francis Group, an informa business

British Library Cataloguing-in-Publication Data
A catalogue record for this book is available from the British Library

Library of Congress Cataloging-in-Publication Data
Names: Burnett, Ipek S., editor.
Title: Re-visioning the American psyche : Jungian, archetypal, and mythological reflections / edited Ipek S. Burnett.
Description: Abingdon, Oxon ; New York, NY : Routledge, 2024. | Includes bibliographical references and index. | Identifiers: LCCN 2023021538 (print) | LCCN 2023021539 (ebook) | ISBN 9781032351926 (hardback) | ISBN 9781032351889 (trade paperback) | ISBN 9781003325765 (ebook)
Subjects: LCSH: Collective memory—United States. | United States—Social conditions—21st century. | United States—Civilization—21st century. | Jungian psychology. | Archtype (Psychology) Classification: LCC HN59.3 .R42 2024 (print) | LCC HN59.3 (ebook) | DDC 306.0973—dc23/eng/20230712
LC record available at https://lccn.loc.gov/2023021538
LC ebook record available at https://lccn.loc.gov/2023021539

ISBN: 978-1-032-35192-6 (hbk)
ISBN: 978-1-032-35188-9 (pbk)
ISBN: 978-1-003-32576-5 (ebk)

DOI: 10.4324/9781003325765

Typeset in Times New Roman
by Apex CoVantage, LLC

Dedicated to Andrew Samuels

Contents

Editor

Ipek S. Burnett, PhD, is the author of *A Jungian Inquiry into the American Psyche: The Violence of Innocence* (Routledge). Based in San Francisco, she works with human rights and social justice organizations and writes novels in her native language, Turkish.

Contributors

Rebecca Armstrong has graduate degrees from the University of Chicago Divinity School and Chicago Theological Seminary. She worked as the International Outreach Director for the Joseph Campbell Foundation for 12 years and has been teaching courses at Indiana University since 2010, including the class "Myth, Movie, and the American Soul."

Gustavo Beck, PhD, is a Jungian and archetypal psychotherapist with a private practice in Mexico City, and a translator of books and essays on psychology and the humanities. He received his PhD in Mythological Studies from Pacifica Graduate Institute, in Santa Barbara, California, and has published several essays on the work of James Hillman and the archetypal school of thought. He has taught in the Psychology Department at Universidad Iberoamericana in Mexico City and at Pacifica Graduate Institute. His interests revolve around Jungian and post-Jungian thought and archetypal theory, particularly regarding their relationship with contemporary social, cultural, and environmental issues.

Andrew P. Grant is a Quaker peace activist with a recognized concern for Indigenous relations. He holds degrees in theology (MDiv) and information science (MLIS). Fifteen years ago, he exited a career as an ordained United Methodist minister and now works as a sociocracy trainer. He lives in western Massachusetts, on Nonotuck/Pocumtuck homeland. He recently served on the board of the Nolumbeka Project, an organization that preserves Native sites and enables cross-cultural understanding. He is organizing a land justice affinity group to facilitate agreements with local tribes. With fellow Quakers, he is conveying a formal letter of apology to Native Americans as an opening gesture of peacemaking.

Claudette Kulkarni, PhD, is a retired Jungian psychotherapist living in Pittsburgh, PA. She was awarded a PhD in Depth Psychology from the Union Institute, Cincinnati, OH. Over her career, she has served as clinical therapist/supervisor in several non-profit agencies, including a local LGBTQ mental health center. Her writings include *Lesbians and Lesbianisms: A Post-Jungian Perspective* (Routledge, 1997).

Thomas Moore, PhD, is the author of the number one New York Times bestseller *Care of the Soul*. He has written 24 other books about bringing soul to personal life and culture, deepening spirituality, humanizing medicine, finding meaningful work, imagining sexuality with soul, and doing religion in a fresh way. In his youth, he was a Catholic monk and studied music composition. He has a PhD in Religious Studies from Syracuse University and was a professor for several years. He is also a psychotherapist, influenced mainly by C.G. Jung and James Hillman. In his work, he brings together spirituality, mythology, depth psychology, and the arts, emphasizing the importance of images and imagination.

Ronald Schenk, PhD, is a Jungian psychoanalyst practicing and teaching in Dallas. He originally trained in theater and voice, received his master's degree in Social Work from Washington University, St. Louis, and his initial training in psychoanalytic psychotherapy in New Haven, CT. He lived and worked with the Navajo Native Americans before receiving a PhD in Phenomenological Psychology from the University of Dallas. He trained in Jungian analysis with the Inter-Regional Society of Jungian Analysts, where he acted in several administrative capacities, most recently serving as president in addition to serving as president of the Council of North American Societies of Jungian Analysis. In addition to numerous essays on a variety of clinical, cultural, and theoretical topics, he has published four books—*The Soul of Beauty: A Psychological Investigation of Appearance*; *Dark Light: The Appearance of Death in Everyday Life*; *The Sunken Quest, The Wasted Fisher, The Pregnant Fish: Post-Modern Reflections on Depth Psychology*; and *American Soul: A Cultural Narrative*. His recent work has focused on cities, anger, language, complexity theory and Jung, the "Trump" phenomenon, the COVID-19 pandemic, technologically mediated analysis, whiteness, and the criminal justice systems.

Kwame Scruggs, PhD, is the founder and director of Alchemy, Inc., a national award-winning non-profit organization in Akron, OH, which uses myth to transform the lives of urban youth. Kwame holds a PhD and MA in Mythological Studies with an emphasis on Depth Psychology from Pacifica Graduate Institute.

Jordan Shapiro, PhD, has an academic background in archetypal psychology and phenomenology. In addition to teaching at Temple University, Shapiro is Senior Fellow for the Joan Ganz Cooney Center at Sesame Workshop and Nonresident Fellow in the Center for Universal Education at the Brookings Institution. His Forbes column (2012–2017) on global education, learning through digital play, kids, and culture was read by over 5 million people around the world. He is an international speaker and consultant whose fresh perspective combines psychology, philosophy, and economics in unexpected ways. His book *The New Childhood: Raising Kids to Thrive in a Connected World* (Little, Brown Spark, 2018) changed the cultural conversation about parenting and screen time and has been translated into 11 languages. In *Father Figure: How to Be a Feminist Dad* (Little, Brown Spark, 2021), Shapiro offers a norm-shattering perspective on fatherhood, family, and gender essentialism.

Thomas Singer, MD, is a psychiatrist and Jungian psychoanalyst practicing in San Francisco. He is the editor of a book series exploring cultural complexes in Latin America, Europe, Asia, Australia, and North America. His interests include studying the relationship between myth, politics, and psyche in *The Vision Thing* and the Ancient Greece, Modern Psyche series. He is currently the president of National ARAS, an archive of symbolic imagery.

Michael P. Sipiora, PhD, was a professor and associate chair of Pacifica Graduate Institute's doctoral Clinical Psychology Department and taught in the Mythological Studies program. As a tenured professor at Duquesne University, he was an award-winning teacher in both its APA approved clinical program in Human Science Psychology and in the School for Leadership and Professional Advancement. Sipiora is the author of numerous peer-reviewed articles and book chapters and an edited book. He earned a BA and MA in Philosophy at San Jose State University. His graduate studies in psychology, with a concentration on literature, were carried out at the University of Dallas. A licensed clinical psychologist, he has a wide range of clinical experience in private and community mental health settings.

Glen Slater, PhD, has degrees in Religious Studies and Clinical Psychology and has taught for over two decades at Pacifica Graduate Institute in Santa Barbara, California, where he is currently co-chair of the Jungian and Archetypal Studies Program. He has written numerous articles and book chapters for Jungian publications and edited the third volume of James Hillman's Uniform Edition *Senex and Puer*, as well as the essay collection *Varieties of Mythic Experience*. He writes on Jung and film, the psychology of religion, and depth psychology and technology.

Dennis Patrick Slattery, PhD, is Distinguished Professor Emeritus in Mythological Studies at Pacifica Graduate Institute where he has taught for the past 27 years. He is the author, co-author, editor, or co-editor of 33 volumes, most recently *The Way of Myth: Stories' Subtle Wisdom*. He conducts "Writing Personal Myth" retreats in the United States, Canada, and Europe, including Ireland. He also teaches inmates at a prison in California using Joseph Campbell's *The Hero with a Thousand Faces*. He is also a core faculty member at the Jung Platform in Salt Lake City, directed by Machiel Klerk.

Edward Tick, PhD, is a psychotherapist, author, poet, international journey guide, and activist. Dr. Tick has been working to heal the invisible wounds of war and violent trauma in veterans, families, society, and the world for over 40 years, is a leader in the field of holistic healing of violent trauma, and maintains an active private practice. He is Director Emeritus of the non-profit Soldier's Heart, Inc., and currently consults with several veteran non-profit organizations. Dr. Tick is the author of four nonfiction books, including the groundbreaking war-healing books *War and the Soul* and *Warrior's Return*, as well as two books of poetry and hundreds of clinical and popular articles. For a decade, he served as subject matter expert on healing post-traumatic stress disorder and moral injury for the U.S. military. A specialist in the Vietnamese and Greek traditions, he has been leading annual healing and reconciliation journeys to these countries since 1995. His most recent books, *Coming Home in Viet Nam* and *Soul Medicine*, were published in 2021 and 2022, respectively.

Mary Watkins, PhD, is a leading voice in liberation psychology and an early member of the archetypal psychology movement, a co-author of *Toward Psychologies of Liberation, Up Against the Wall: Re-Imagining the U.S.–Mexico Border*, and *Talking with Young Children about Adoption*, and the author of *Mutual Accompaniment and the Creation of the Commons, Waking Dreams*, and *Invisible Guests: The Development of Imaginal Dialogues*. She is Professor Emerita and co-founder of the Community, Liberation, Indigenous, and Eco-Psychologies graduate specialization at Pacifica Graduate Institute.

Luigi Zoja is an analytical psychologist in private practice in Milan who lectures internationally. He is a former training analyst at the C.G. Jung Institute in Zurich, past president of CIPA (Centro Italiano di Psicologia Analitica), and former president of IAAP (International Association of Analytical Psychology). He has taught at the University of Insubria and Beijing Normal University, and his books have been published in multiple languages.

Acknowledgments

The idea of putting together an edited volume on the American psyche was planted in my mind during the early phase of the COVID-19 pandemic. Perhaps naively, I had expected this global crisis to be a catalyst for solidarity, common struggle and sacrifice, collective mourning, and social responsibility. Yet, instead, I witnessed the fault lines deepening, political polarization, and culture wars worsening everywhere I looked. My previous book, *A Jungian Inquiry into the American Psyche*, had just been published by Routledge, urging reflection, critical thinking, and imagination, and, as I beheld the daily manifestations of fear, anger, and anxiety, I found myself longing to continue these conversations in the community.

I reached out to Glen Slater and shared with him the idea for a book which would invite a diverse community of Jungian and archetypal scholars and mythologists to bring psychology's unique perspective to social, cultural, and political matters. Glen's thoughtful feedback and generous support have been instrumental in making this book a reality. He was not only the first one to agree to write for the volume, but also personally introduced me to many of the other authors. I'm particularly indebted and grateful for his efforts.

I wish to thank all the authors for their dedication, critical insights, heartfelt accounts, openness, and hard work. Their contributions to this book and the field of Jungian and archetypal studies are paramount. I am honored to call them my colleagues and look forward to future collaborations.

I would like to extend a special thank you to Andrew Samuels. I have always felt deep respect for his teachings and leadership. Receiving his guidance and support for my books is truly an honor.

I want to express my appreciation for the Routledge team, starting with Alexis O'Brien, who I had the privilege to work with in the early phases of this book. Her questions and comments helped this project expand and strengthen in numerous ways. I also want to thank Katie Randall for her timely, thoughtful correspondence and assistance throughout the process.

I want to take this opportunity to also thank Daniela Blei for all her diligence. She has been an ideal reader and editor. I'm grateful for her partnership, as well as friendship.

So many dear friends, fellow authors, and artists have accompanied me during this journey, lending an ear, offering inspiration, being present, and working alongside me. A special thank you to Holly Mae Haddock, Zoë Dearborn, Mimi Lok, Kaitlin Solimine, Sarah Moore, Minna Dubin, and Maryrose Smyth. A big thank you to the Ruby in San Francisco for providing such a peaceful working space and beautiful community. I'm always touched by the care and enthusiasm of my friends and colleagues at the Human Rights Watch San Francisco team and Executive Committee. Thank you to all.

I certainly would not be writing these lines if it were not for the constant, unwavering support of my family. My mother, Handan Saraç, and father, Hasan Saraç, who always believed in me and my work. Their love is my life force. My husband, Christopher Burnett, who is my rock; I feel blessed to share this life with him. And my sons, who at their very young age are already mighty booklovers. I'm overjoyed to be reading, writing, and learning beside them each and every day.

And finally, here is to James Hillman, who once wrote, "Our wrestling with ideas is a sacred struggle, as with an angel." May we continue, in his footsteps, this sacred struggle, wrestling with ideas.

Introduction

Ipek S. Burnett

On the American psyche

"America has probably the most complicated psychology of all nations," C. G. Jung wrote in 1930.[1] His statement still resonates today: without a doubt, the American psyche is vast and varied. Think of the many immigrants, races, and religions that meet under one flag, each contributing its own ancestral inheritance, folklore, creed, language, and history. It is an ever-changing, dynamic collective. And yet even in diversity and fluidity, the power of particular myths, images, and ideas— such as the American dream, the city upon a hill, freedom, progress, the pursuit of happiness—endures. In shaping ideals and sustaining ideologies, these ideas and images define Americans' experiences as members of the nation and the global world.

To understand and honor this complexity requires embracing a view of the psyche that is invested in examining how it operates in culture and society. Analytical psychologist Joseph L. Henderson defines "the living reality" of the cultural unconscious as an "area of historical memory that lies between the collective unconscious and the manifest culture pattern."[2] Accordingly, the American psyche encompasses American history, political traditions, and culture, alongside the myths, images, and fantasies that are inseparable from them. This living reality transcends the mental subjectivity of the individual. It manifests in various facets of social and public life. Whether in presidential campaign speeches abundant with visions of a new world, a chosen people, or Manifest Destiny, or Hollywood movies that tirelessly retell rags-to-riches stories that underscore promises of prosperity and upward mobility, the fantasies of the American psyche are easily discernible in everyday discourse.

The American psyche resembles a kaleidoscope in some respects. While each shift in time—epoch, or even just a decade—may reveal new patterns featuring social events, wars, heroes, technological innovations, and literary or artistic movements, the contents (myths, images, and ideas, such as those mentioned above) are archetypal and constant. With the mirrors within, these contents are reflected and amplified in patterns that emerge in particular historical moments. For example, starting in the seventeenth century, the myth of the frontier, which identified a

DOI: 10.4324/9781003325765-1

boundary between regions occupied by pilgrims and the wilderness, fueled the acquisition of western lands and America's rapid territorial expansion. With time, urbanization and industrialization spread across the continent, and the wilderness began to disappear. And yet the American frontier had already assumed an essential meaning for politics and identity in the United States as a signifier of unlimited opportunity. Once associated with land, the myth of the frontier now became a driving force for capitalism, technology, and science. It powered political objectives across borders, from spreading democracy in the Middle East to nation building in Vietnam, and even traveling into space and planting the American flag on the moon. This expansion in meaning was accomplished through industrial, technological, and military enterprise, and ideological processes. Meanwhile, in the shadow of the glorified frontier myth lurked the troublesome realities of conquest and colonization, massacres of Indigenous Peoples, the extinction of species, environmental degradation, imperialism, oppression, and exploitation.[3]

Building an awareness of the images, myths, and archetypal fantasies that thrive in the American psyche and uphold its collective narratives and ideologies is imperative. Otherwise, a society blind to their influence is unconsciously controlled by these myths and ideas, and it fails to understand their dark and dangerous aspects. My previous book, *A Jungian Inquiry into the American Psyche: The Violence of Innocence*,[4] unpacks dominant narratives in the United States that often project noble ideals. These narratives begin with the promised land, a paradise, a new world for new beginnings, a city upon a hill. On this stage, the founders unveil the Declaration of Independence, which speaks eloquently about the self-evident truths of equality and the rights to life, liberty, and the pursuit of happiness for all. Interwoven into the narrative is also the American dream of opportunity, success, and upward mobility. These ideals transcend borders in a self-professed effort to redeem the world. This quixotic narrative is, of course, not absolute. In its shadow fester contradictory realities that haunt the national consciousness, contradictions that undermine a simplistic, solipsistic narrative that resounds with goodness, purity, and pride in its enclosed chambers. Difficult realities, while renounced and repressed, produce ample traces of evidence: land theft, genocide, slavery, racism, sexism, xenophobia, mass incarceration, militarism, police violence, immigrant detention centers, border killings, abuse and exploitation of laborers, income inequality, unemployment, poverty, mass shootings, suicide, domestic violence, addictions of all sorts, from alcohol to opioids, materialism and capitalist excess, corporate corruption, environmental destruction, and so on. The chasm between the idealized self-image and current conditions demonstrates an urgent need for critical self-reflection that aims to examine and deconstruct the dominant narratives and ideals that are often taken for granted.

Jungian psychology and archetypal psychology provide analytical tools to become aware of one's unawareness, seek the shadows, recognize and integrate the repressed, split-off, and disavowed parts of a whole. By illuminating the path into the depths to tend to unknowns in an intuitive and purposeful way, they help destabilize, disrupt, and challenge simplistic and reductionist understandings of oneself. When applied to the collective, these methods help build bridges between the past and present, the archetypal and the everyday, and the psyche and the social. Addressing the American psyche with a keen eye for its collective fantasies, memories, and traumas requires nothing short of a creative approach that can accommodate contradictions, paradoxes, and nuance.[5]

On social responsibility

Given current political polarization and raging culture wars across the United States, the task of interrogating the national consciousness and the unconscious has become ever more pressing. The talks I have given since the publication of *A Jungian Inquiry into the American Psyche* in 2020 have offered opportunities to connect with diverse audiences, including human rights activists, journalists, organizational consultants, graduate students, psychologists, and the Jungian community in the United States and abroad. Each talk allowed me to witness the thirst and appreciation for psychological insights into America's current cultural and political problems, as well as a yearning for personal and collective healing.

According to political philosopher Kelly Oliver, the act of witnessing engages a joint responsibility. "Response-ability is never solitary," she writes.[6] Moreover, she argues, this ability to respond is an ethical responsibility. Those working in the field of psychology surely recognize the relational and ethical aspects of responsibility, and yet it is also important that we expand our understanding of responsibility and recognize the ways in which witnessing goes beyond the consulting room. Archetypal psychologist James Hillman is a persuasive advocate for this approach:

> Psychotherapy has been working successfully within its province of psychic reality conceived as subjectivity, but it has not re-visioned the notion of subjectivity itself. And now, even its success there comes in question as the patients' complaints bespeak problems that are no longer merely subjective in the former sense. For all the while that psychotherapy has succeeded in raising the consciousness of human subjectivity, the world in which all subjectivities are set has fallen apart. Breakdown is in a new place—Vietnam and Watergate, bank scandals with government collusion, pollution and street crime, the loss of literacy and the growth of junk, deceit, and show. We now encounter pathology in the psyche of politics and medicine, in language and design, in the food we eat. Sickness is now "out there."[7]

Recognizing psychic realities that thrive beyond the individual self, Hillman commits to taking the world as his patient and understanding its psychopathologies by analyzing social, cultural, political, and environmental conditions. "The world, because of its breakdown, is entering a new moment of consciousness: by drawing attention to itself by means of its symptoms, it is becoming aware of itself as a psychic reality," he reasons.[8] Thus Hillman's writings turn to various subjects, including transportation, urban planning, welfare, and warfare, encouraging us to look at the world again and again, to read each event for its metaphorical and symbolic significance, and deeper meanings.

For those in psychology, whether a Jungian analyst, clinical psychologist, scholar, or student, this call to step out and tend to the world identifies a new kind of social responsibility. Because, while honoring civic duties is paramount, social responsibility goes beyond jury duty and the ballot box. If it is an ethical and relational matter of being in service to community, extending psychology's imaginative and critical perspective to larger cultural, political, social, and environmental realities must also be recognized as social responsibility in practice.

This edited volume seeks to answer a call of duty. By bringing together a diverse group of Jungian and archetypal scholars, including Americans, immigrants to the United States, and citizens of Mexico and Italy who have previously lived in the United States, it represents a collective effort toward joint social responsibility. When I first reached out to potential contributors, my inquiries were met with enthusiasm, hope, and professed desires for solidarity. As the chapters progressed and the book solidified, I was moved and honored to observe how working as a community toward psychological understanding and healing was a gift in its own right. Even our correspondence about possible topics, or the meaning of the term "American psyche," proved to be deeply stimulating and inspiring and highlighted the importance of open dialogue and discussion as we each embrace our social responsibilities and become engaged witnesses in the wider world.

A re-visioning

Honoring the breadth, depth, and complexity of the inquiry at hand, this book of collected essays by leaders in the fields of Jungian and archetypal psychology and mythology offers a close look at the American psyche. Together, the authors deliver a rich psychological and cultural collage. They examine myths, images, and archetypal fantasies ingrained in the collective consciousness and unconscious. They attend to symptoms as they manifest in American history, political institutions, social struggles, and cultural movements. They reflect on many pressing matters: intergenerational trauma due to racism, the psychological cost of wars and violence, the emotional dimensions of political polarization, deep-seated oppositional thinking in patriarchal structures, the frailty of the American dream, and more. As the authors raise questions regarding the meaning of democratic participation, community engagement and wellbeing, the mainstream and the marginalized, and the idealized and the oppressed, they use various interpretative processes—from psychoanalytic, to literary, to participatory—taking a distinct perspective for re-visioning the American psyche.

What is implied here by re-visioning is not an act or process of revising; this book's goal is not merely to propose a diagnosis or treatment plan to eliminate or suppress undesirable symptoms, or to re-write American myths. The *telos* of this work is not to cure and eradicate pathos or discard old myths and replace them with new ones. Rather, it is to behold the chaos, tensions, and complexity of the American psyche to illuminate the eclipsed corners and unconscious realities within it—the repressed, disowned, dissociated, and projected-out elements—and provide insights into the narratives, voices, and images that are often overlooked by dominant ideologies. It is appropriate that re-visioning invokes the metaphor of vision. Hillman, who introduces *psychologizing* as a method of seeing, namely "seeing through," writes:

Psychologizing goes on whenever reflection takes place in terms other than those presented. It suspects an interior, not evident intention; it searches for a hidden clockwork, a ghost in the machine, an etymological root, something more than meets the eye; or it sees with another eye. It goes on whenever we move to a deeper level.[9]

Re-visioning, in this context, emphasizes the prefix "re-" and calls upon verbs that invite psychological deepening: to remember, recover, recognize, reflect, review, rethink, relate. Each analyst, psychologist, and scholar who contributed to this book picks up the kaleidoscope with curiosity and intention, holds it to one eye, and points it toward the light, which is essentially psychological awareness. As they look through the mirrors, they contemplate and see through fascinating patterns. In kaleidoscopic fashion, each chapter represents a slight rotation, offering a unique reflection.

The book contains five parts: the first on politics, power, and polarization; the second on colonization, war, and violence; the third on cultural trauma, racism, and social justice; the fourth on gender, sexuality, and the patriarchy; and the fifth and final part on psychotherapy, citizenship, and cultural movements. An editor's introduction can be found at the beginning of each part, preceding the contributors' essays to provide a theoretical background for the following discussion and an overview of all the essays under the umbrella. These introductions also explain how each part contributes to the re-visioning goal of the book as a whole by projecting different social, cultural, and historical patterns while shining a light on recurring images and myths within them.

As applied in these pages then, re-visioning is about perspective. It is about deepening. It is about the roots: images and memories. It is about psychological truths and imaginative possibilities. It is about empathic resonance and aesthetic responses. It is about critical thinking and imagination in the service of collective self-knowledge and transformation. It is about the relationship between the psyche and the social. It is about the ability to respond, which is an ethical responsibility.

Notes

1 C.G. Jung, "The Complications of American Psychology," in *The Collected Works of C. G. Jung*, vol. 10, trans. R.F.C. Hull (Princeton: Princeton University Press, 1970), 514.
2 Joseph L. Henderson, "The Cultural Unconscious," *Quadrant*, 21, no. 2 (1988): 7.
3 For more on the American frontier, see Richard Slotkin's triology: *Regeneration Through Violence: The Mythology of the American Frontier, 1600–1860* (Norman: University of Oklahoma Press, 2000); *The Fatal Environment: The Myth of the Frontier in the Age of*

Industrialization, 1800–1890 (Norman: University of Oklahoma Press, 1998); *Gunfighter Nation: The Myth of the Frontier in Twentieth-Century America* (Norman: University of Oklahoma Press, 1998).

4 Ipek S. Burnett, *A Jungian Inquiry into the American Psyche: The Violence of Innocence* (New York: Routledge, 2020).

5 Ibid., 4–6, 112–113.

6 Kelly Oliver, *Witnessing: Beyond Recognition* (Minneapolis: University of Minnesota Press, 2001), 90.

7 James Hillman, *The Thought of the Heart and the Soul of the World* (Woodstock: Spring Publications, 1982), 95–96.

8 Ibid., 97.

9 James Hillman, *Re-Visioning Psychology* (New York: HarperPerennial, 1992), 135.

Part I

Politics, power, and polarization

Introduction

Following the 2016 U.S. presidential election, 27 psychiatrists, psychologists, and mental health professionals collaborated on *The Dangerous Case of Donald Trump*, a volume dedicated to assessing the mental health of the newly elected U.S. president. Although the book ignited debates about the ethics and legitimacy of diagnosing a non-patient, its contributors maintained that a moral and civic "duty to warn" the nation and the world of the perils of Trump's presidency outweighed their commitment to professional neutrality. Writing the book was a matter of social responsibility, according to the authors.

Thomas Singer was the only Jungian analyst featured in *The Dangerous Case of Donald Trump*. Rather than focusing on the traits and character of the president, his essay focused on the "collective" nature of responses to Trump's leadership.[1] It is therefore apt that Singer authors the opening chapter of this edited volume, which also is born from the conviction that bringing psychology's unique perspective to historical, social, and political matters is a necessity.

Singer's piece here, "A personal meditation on politics and the American soul,"[2] exemplifies how psychological analysis, with its intuitive and imaginative approach, can provide critical insights while evoking empathy and compassion. Setting out to explore the living interface between the experiences of the individual soul and what Singer calls the national soul, he shares memories of a personal journey and reflects on the Mississippi River and the American landscape. Through Walt Whitman's verses and Toni Morrison's prose, he turns to the depths of the American soul. In the second half of the essay, Singer provides an outline for potent cultural complexes that are underpinned by archetypal patterns and give American political life its dynamism and content. Considering America's relationship to money, progress, speed, nature, spirituality, and more, Singer speculates, sees through, and empathizes, while always beholding the psyche's complexity.

In the next chapter, "Violent hearts: America's divided soul," Italian psychoanalyst Luigi Zoja offers a foreigner and outsider's perspective, also spotlighting the psyche's inherent complexity. Using Odysseus as a starting point, he underscores the importance of recognizing and honoring the realities of internal division,

DOI: 10.4324/9781003325765-2

contradiction, and ambivalence in life to make space for the creative possibilities they yield. Next, Zoja turns to the American soul, examining how a culture of unity that disregards complicated psychological realities—including those mentioned above—can become a one-sided negation of shadow. Surveying the settlers' western expansion, the Civil War, the Monroe Doctrine, and the Cold War, Zoja points out that the United States, driven by puritanical and missionary ideals since its inception, has disowned its self-interest, imperialistic motives, and repeated acts of violence. The country has projected these onto others, including the British monarchy and the Roman Catholic Church, the Native tribes, Latin American regimes, Russia, and beyond. Seamlessly traveling through literature, depth psychology, history, and international policy, Zoja argues that an unchallenged belief in purity and exceptionalism is not only simplistic but also dangerous, as unconscious splitting and division always give way to violence.

Violence continues to be the focus in mythologist Dennis Slattery's essay, "Captain Ahab and Donald Trump: False claims, the fragility of belief, and the perilous ship of America's soul." Considering Herman Melville's *Moby-Dick*, Slattery compares the grievance and rage of the captain, whose leg was severed by a white whale, to those of Donald Trump who lost a presidential election. Drawing on literary analysis, biographical accounts, and psychoanalytic interpretation, Slattery analyzes how both leaders seek to endorse and inflame violence to take revenge, thereby exposing their narcissistic wounding. Paradoxically, their stubborn claim to power lays bare underlying weakness, while a sense of entitlement exposes inevitable vulnerability.

What does it mean to be democratic? What does it mean to be united? What does it mean to be powerful? What does it mean to be exceptional? What does it mean to be a leader? What does it mean to be just? Singer, Zoja, and Slattery wrestle with these questions and, searching for answers, tend to "the fantasies of the political world and the politics of the fantasy world," to borrow Andrew Samuels's words,[3] who then writes:

> The political tasks of modern democracy are similar to the psychological tasks of modern therapy and analysis. In both areas, there is a fight between consciousness, liberation and alterity on the one hand and suppression, repression and omnipotent beliefs in final truths on the other.[4]

The authors step into a liminal space between struggles for critical consciousness, liberation, and social and political change on one hand, and suppression, repression, and fundamentalist inclinations on the other. Probing Homer, Melville, Whitman, and Morrison, they gaze at the kaleidoscopic American psyche. They observe the bright visions—ideals of freedom, unity, democracy, and purity—as well as the accompanying realities that remain in shadows cast long ago. Slavery and tyranny. War and insurrection. Deceit and self-deceit. Discord, division, dismemberment. Disillusionment. Rage and grief. Wounds and losses.

And boundless fantasies, all in relationship with one another, all of them relevant and part of the American psyche.

Notes

1 Thomas Singer, "Trump and the American Collective Psyche," in *The Dangerous Case of Donald Trump,* ed. Bandy X. Lee (New York: St. Martin's Press, 2017), 281–297.
2 Originally published in *Spring Journal* 2007 issue *Politics and the American Soul* (78).
3 Andrew Samuels, *The Political Psyche* (New York: Routledge, 1993), 4.
4 Ibid.

Chapter 1

A personal meditation on politics and the American soul

Thomas Singer

From *Spring Journal* 78, 2007:[1]

In 2007, I was invited by Nancy Cater of *Spring Journal* to contribute an article on politics and the soul of America to a special edition she was publishing. With the 2008 US presidential elections on the horizon, I approached the subject by suggesting that the emerging theory of cultural complexes on which I was elaborating might be one way to think about how the soul of America gets forged in the crucible of the interactions between psyche and politics. I outlined seven potent cultural complexes that stream through the American collective psyche from generation to generation. These same currents are at the core of the new 2020 Routledge book, *Cultural Complexes and the Soul of America*.

An invitation to write about politics and the American soul should cause anyone with common sense to turn and run in the opposite direction in the same way that seeing an advertisement for the "soul of a BMW" or hearing Cadillac's newly trademarked slogan—"Life. Liberty. And The Pursuit."—induces nausea. The language of soul and politics has been so co-opted by a vast public relations machine, which instantaneously turns everything, including soul, into a marketable commodity, that there are probably only a handful of us foolish enough to tackle the subject.

The purpose of this essay is to be more impressionistic and evocative than precisely descriptive of the relationship between the American soul and politics—partly because it is so hard to give specific definitions to such essentially indefinable realities. It may be helpful to think of soul as having both a function and a content. As a function and not a specific content, we experience soul as emotional, embodied psychic movement. Soul, as a function of psychic movement, can legitimately attach itself to various contents—landscape, people, events, eras, values. We can think of our individual and collective souls as being that psychic function which creates and contains the playing fields for the endless encounters between instinct and spirit. And, because of the elusive nature of soul as a function or a content and the essential unknowability of whether there is even such a thing as a collective soul, our topic begs to find a hook in a specific time and place.

DOI: 10.4324/9781003325765-3

Such a hook presented itself to me in 2004 when I was asked to moderate a conference on the theme of "The Soul of America" at the San Francisco C.G. Jung Institute. The topic was as overwhelming to me then as it is now. At the time, a deep divide in the American political psyche took on simplistic but potent symbolic form in the image of the Red and Blue States. It was natural for the conference's topic of "The Soul of America" to veer toward a discussion of "the political fight for the soul of America."

As a Northern Californian for the past 35 years, with deep roots in both the Midwest and East Coast, I chafe at the one-sidedness of most characterizations of members of one political, religious, ethnic, racial, or regional group by another. Living in a liberal region with progressive politics, I did not want to get up and pro-claim that the Democrats had an inside track on the "real" soul of America or that Bush was an "idiot." Both were too easy, because those were the opinions of almost everyone in the audience, and, for that matter, of almost everyone I know. The fact is that no one group in the United States has an exclusive claim on either the "soul of America" or on being "idiots," even though one side will usually claim soul for itself and idiocy for its rival. (In the political rhetoric of the last few decades, the right has been most effective at staking out "the soul of America" for itself and far less stupid than most on the left have claimed.)

It is very easy to project soul into politics and politics into soul. Indeed, I be-lieve it is the first task of an inquiry such as this to try to differentiate soul from politics. This differentiation begins with the acknowledgment that soul and poli-tics get mixed up with each other all the time in the collective psyche and in the intermingling of myth, politics, and psyche in our cultural unconscious.[2] With the goal of differentiation in mind, the first part of this paper will address the topic of "The soul of America," and the second part will address "Politics and the soul of America."

Part 1: What is the soul of America?

George Seferis's poem "Argonauts" tells us that to know our soul we must look in the mirror at both the stranger and enemy.[3] I believe that each of us discovers different bits and pieces of "the soul of America" as the personal journeys of our individual lives interface with the unfolding story of our nation's soul journey. When we inquire about the soul of America, I think we need to keep in mind that we are talking about a living interface between the experience of our individual souls and that of the national soul. And, if looking into the depths of our personal souls often reveals mysteries, ambiguities, and contradictions, how much more complex is it to reflect on the nature of our American soul? We should begin this inquiry with the recognition that we discover the soul of America only as we discover the story of our own souls. If the Hindus speak of Atman and Brahman, perhaps we should think about an intermediary zone and speak of the individual soul and the group soul.

Let me give you a brief example that illustrates the importance of this semipermeable membrane or interface between personal soul and collective soul. John Perry, a well-known Jungian analyst of an earlier generation, once told me the story of his meeting, as a young man, with Jung in 1936. On one of his journeys to the United States, Jung had visited the house of John Perry's father in Providence, Rhode Island. Perry's father served there as a bishop in the Episcopal Church. Conversation with Jung at the Perry house touched on the Native American Indian's role in the story of America and the need for "modern man" to connect with the "archaic man" inside. Jung expressed his opinion that to connect with the soul of America one needed to connect with the American Indian. That night a young John Perry dreamt that *he was standing by the fireplace in the living room with his hand on the mantelpiece. A bare-chested American Indian appeared in the fireplace and threw a tomahawk directly at him. In a startled response, Perry managed to catch the tomahawk in his hands.*[4] One way to think about this dream is to say that the soul of John Perry was introduced to the soul of America in his meeting with a Native American.

Not all of us have such extraordinary meetings between our individual soul and the soul of our country, but each of us is certainly startled when some aspect of America's soul appears to us in our own psychic house. In this context of the encounter of personal soul with national soul, I want to relate a story of my own unexpected personal soul meeting with a part of our nation's soul.

In July 2004, just a few months prior to the national elections later that fall, I traveled with my family from San Francisco to Alton, Illinois. This journey helped give me an inkling of how to speak about what the phrase "soul of America" evokes in me without falling into the easy trap, at a time of presidential elections, of identifying soul with one political group or another. It is no accident that my own musings about "the American soul" began with a personal physical journey halfway across the country, since so much of what we think of as "the soul of America" is embedded in journey—whether it be from a foreign land to the United States, or the journey from East to West to open the continent, or from West to East in search of our roots. The "journey" is at the heart of the "soul of America," and my journey to the Midwest in July 2004 was no exception.

Alton sits on the bluffs of the Mississippi River, just below where the Mississippi and Missouri rivers come together (see Figure 1.1). It is a proud old river town that celebrates its history of having been a safe haven for abolitionists in the pre-Civil War era, as well as having been the site of the famous Lincoln–Douglas debates. I had traveled to Alton with my wife and children in order to bring home the ashes of my mother-in-law, Agnes, who had died in the San Francisco Bay Area earlier in the spring. Alton was the home of Agnes's ancestors, her childhood home, and the home where she had raised her own family. Such homecomings remind us that the soul connects the material and the spiritual realms just as the Mississippi River connects North and South, East and West in the heart of the country.

Figure 1.1 A view of Alton, Illinois, across the Mississippi

Color images at https://aras.org/vision-folly-american-soul

If you grow up in the Midwest, as I did, the Mississippi River reflects the soul of the country. The river's journey is the soul's journey as Huck Finn and Tom Sawyer taught us in our youth. The grandeur of the river and the fertile valleys surrounding it make it a real, symbolic, and spiritual heartland all at the same time—a flowing source of vast generosity and security. It is not an exaggeration to compare the coming together of the Missouri and Mississippi with the confluence of other great rivers of the world, such as the Tigris and Euphrates. Proud civilizations flourish in the fertile valleys and lowlands at the confluence of great rivers, and we were returning Agnes to the generous source of her origins, where her personal soul might join the American soul in its return to the origin of all souls.

On July 3, 2004, having carried Agnes's ashes halfway across the country to her homeland beside the river, we traveled to the Alton Cemetery for a memorial service to honor this profoundly kind and decent woman. Agnes was widely known as "Saint Agnes" because she was like the river—vast in her giving and compassion, both to her family and friends in her personal life and to her patients in her professional life as a nurse. From the photo I took that day in the sublime cemetery (Figure 1.2), you can see why I began to get fleeting recollections and

Figure 1.2 The cemetery in Alton, Illinois

Color images at https://aras.org/vision-fully-american-soul

intimations of Walt Whitman's *Leaves of Grass* as we placed Agnes's ashes in the grave next to her husband's. The cemetery's green canopy of trees and carpet of grass were both a soothing balm and a clear call to my soul, which felt deeply linked to the soul of my mother-in-law and, as Walt Whitman put it, the souls of "black folks . . . White, Kanuck, Tuckhoe, Congressman." I felt my soul resonating to the soul of the river and the soul of the town and the soul of my mother-in-law, all participating in the uniquely Midwestern incarnation of the American soul. Here is how Whitman wrote about leaves of grass, the death of old and young alike, and the meeting of individual soul and the American soul in his poem "Song of Myself":

1

I celebrate myself, and sing myself,
And what I assume you shall assume,
For every atom belonging to me as good belongs to you.
I loafe and invite my soul,

I lean and loafe at my ease observing a spear of summer grass.
My tongue, every atom of my blood, form'd from this soil, this air,
Born here of parents born here from parents the same, and their parents the
same,
. . .

6

A child said What is the grass? fetching it to me with full hands;
How could I answer the child? I do not know what it is any more than he.

I guess it must be the flag of my disposition, out of hopeful green stuff woven.

Or I guess it is the handkerchief of the Lord,
A scented gift and remembrancer designedly dropt,
Bearing the owner's name someway in the corners, that we may see and
remark, and say *Whose?*
Or I guess the grass is itself a child, the produced babe of the vegetation.
Or I guess it is a uniform hieroglyphic,
And it means, Sprouting alike in broad zones and narrow zones,
Growing among black folks as among white,
Kanuck, Tuckahoe, Congressman, Cuff, I give them the same, I receive them
the same.

And now it seems to me the beautiful uncut hair of graves.

Tenderly will I use you curling grass,
It may be you transpire from the breasts of young men,
It may be if I had known them I would have loved them,
It may be you are from old people, or from offspring taken soon out of their
mothers' laps,
And here you are the mothers' laps.

This grass is very dark to be from the white heads of old mothers,
Darker than the colorless beards of old men,
Dark to come from under the faint red roofs of mouths.

O I perceive after all so many uttering tongues,
And I perceive they do not come from the roofs of mouths for nothing.

I wish I could translate the hints about the dead young men and women,
And the hints about old men and mothers, and the offspring taken soon out of
their laps.

What do you think has become of the young and old men?
And what do you think has become of the women and children?

They are alive and well somewhere,
The smallest sprout shows there is really no death,
And if ever there was it led forward life, and does not wait
at the end to arrest it,
And ceas'd the moment life appear'd.

All goes onward and outward, nothing collapses,
And to die is different from what any one supposed, and luckier.
. . .

31

I believe a leaf of grass is no less than the journey-work of the stars.[5]

In Section 21 of "Song of Myself," Whitman proclaims himself the bard of the American soul when he writes: "I am the poet of the Body and I am the poet of the Soul."[6] He is writing of the Body and the Soul of America, which he likens to a blade of grass whose very existence mirrors the "journey-work of the stars" in its immortality. At Agnes's service, "a blade of grass" allowed me to participate for a moment in the immortality of her soul and the American soul.

On July 4, the day following Agnes's memorial service, my family went down to the Mississippi River to join in the holiday's festivities. We were at peace with ourselves and open to participating in the celebration of our nation's birth in the knowledge that we had truly accomplished the purpose of our ritual journey home. If you have not celebrated the Fourth of July by the banks of the Mississippi, I urge you to do so before you become a leaf of grass. Quite unexpectedly, I discovered there another forgotten part of Whitman's "Song of Myself" whispering to my soul as I wandered among the day's celebrants—adults guzzling beer and listening to rock 'n' roll music as the children danced and played and jumped up and down by the river's edge.

32

I think I could turn and live with animals, they are so placid and self-contain'd,
I stand and look at them long and long.

They do not sweat and whine about their condition,
They do not lie awake in the dark and weep for their sins,
They do not make me sick discussing their duty to God,
Not one is dissatisfied, not one is demented with the mania of owning things,

Not one kneels to another, nor to his kind that lived thousands of years ago,
Not one is respectable or unhappy over the whole earth.

. . .

52

The spotted hawk swoops by and accuses me, he complains of my gab and my
loitering.

I too am not a bit tamed, I too am untranslatable,
I sound my barbaric yawp over the roofs of the world.[7]

Figure 1.3 is an image from that celebration that got me musing about the meaning of the "Barbaric Yawp." You might find yourself wondering about my choice of
this image and find it repulsive, vulgar, or simply of little relevance to this journal's
noble topic of "Politics and the American Soul."[8] But, on this particular Fourth of
July, the day after the moving memorial service for Agnes, I was fascinated by this
couple as I secretly circled around behind them in an effort to capture the image of

Figure 1.3 Biker couple at the Fourth of July celebrations in Alton, Illinois
Color images at https://aras.org/vision-folly-american-soul

what struck me at once as so "other" and as so "barbaric." In their unabashed celebration of their own animal force, this couple evoked some primitive connection in my psyche to Whitman's "barbaric yawp."

I too am not a bit tamed, I too am untranslatable,
I sound my barbaric yawp over the roofs of the world.[9]

What is a "barbaric yawp?" Why did the quintessential poet of the American soul, Walt Whitman, link the "barbaric yawp" to the American soul? There are two parts to Whitman's phrase, a phrase that now brings up some 110,000 "hits" on a Google internet search. *Barbaric* means "without civilizing influences, uncivilized, primitive," and a *yawp* is a "loud, harsh cry." Neither *barbaric* nor *yawp* suggests a civilized approach to things. Taken together, they signify a primitive enthusiasm in the form of a nonverbal cry from the essential nature of a living being. In Whitman's imagination, the essence of the American soul is neither civilized nor verbal. The "barbaric yawp" is the fierce "voice" of a soul that is essentially unrestrained and exulting in its self-expression.

One senses in my photograph of the Fourth-of-July biker couple an animal force that does not concern itself with, or simply flouts, more conventional norms. Adding this image to the thought that George Bush's Texas swagger and his inarticulate utterances are heard by many in the United States as some sort of cry from our country's "body and soul," one has to accept the fact that they are as much a part of the American soul and its "barbaric yawp" as our more progressive sensibilities. Linking George Bush and this photograph to the "barbaric yawp" is intended to be both ironic and absolutely serious simultaneously. Who are we to know what or who contains the "barbaric yawp"? Who has a legitimate claim on the American soul? Again, what is the American soul?

Steven Herrmann, a Jungian with a deep scholarly interest in Whitman, wrote to me:

Whitman's "yawp" is a *conscious* cry from the soul of America to make the barbarian in American political democracy conscious! The "barbaric yawp" is Whitman's call from the depths of the American soul to awaken the possibility of hope in a brighter future for American democracy.

Hermann went on to say:

The aim of Whitman's "barbaric yawp" was to sound a new heroic message of "Happiness," Hope, and "Nativity" over the roofs of the world, to sound a primal cry which must remain essentially "unsaid" because it rests at the core of the American soul and cannot be found in "any dictionary, utterance, symbol" (*Leaves*, Section # 50). The "barbaric yawp" is a metaphorical utterance for something "untranslatable," a primal cry from the depths of the American soul for the emergence of man as a spiritual human being in whom the aims of liberty and equality have been fully realized and in whom the opposites of love and violence, friendship and war, have been unified at a higher political field of order than anything we have formerly seen in America. His "yawp" is an affect state, a spiritual cry of "Joy" and "Happiness" prior to the emergence of language.[10]

At this point, the reader may be wondering how it is possible to reconcile what might appear on the surface to be two very different aspects of the "barbaric yawp" that I have presented. How can the image of "Biker Dick" be part of the same "barbaric yawp" that sounds "a primal cry from the depths of the American soul for the emergence of man as a spiritual being?" But, as Stephen Herrmann aptly points out, Whitman's image of man's emergence as a spiritual being

> refers to a person that can realize his earthly existence within the context of his total life pattern, including his depths of erotic passion. Whitman's barbarian is both a spiritual and a sexual being. He is not split inside, but whole and conscious of his full instinctive nature and lives it out according to the preference of his Soul.[11]

In contemporary America, Whitman's "barbaric yawp" is as inclusive of the violence found in the television show *The Sopranos* as it is of the unitary vision of Martin Luther King's "I Have a Dream." This suggests expanding our national imagination to embrace the American soul's "barbaric yawp" as both vulgar and compassionate at the same time. It was the genius of Whitman to see in the "barbaric yawp" of the American soul the capacity for an interconnected transcendent unity.

This section on the soul of America would not be complete without mentioning one final example of how glimpses of the American soul come through individual encounters that open up a window or interface between the individual soul and the larger, collective soul of the group. As she was gestating a novel on slavery, freedom, and the black experience, Toni Morrison tells us in her preface to *Beloved*, she met her main character in the following way:

> I sat on the porch, rocking in a swing, looking at giant stones piled up to take the river's occasional fist. Above the stones is a path through the lawn, but interrupted by an ironwood gazebo situated under a cluster of trees and in deep shade.
>
> She walked out of the water, climbed the rocks, and leaned against the gazebo. Nice hat.
>
> So she [Beloved] was there from the beginning, and except for me, everybody (the characters) knew it—a sentence that later became "The women in the house knew it." The figure most central to the story would have to be her, the murdered, not the murderer, the one who lost everything and had no say in any of it.[12]

Like Perry's American Indian with the tomahawk, this is a soul figure that appears out of nowhere, or, as Jungians might say, "out of the unconscious"—personal, cultural, and collective. She emerges out of the water and presents herself to Toni Morrison, who is trying to figure how to create a fiction based on the true story of "Margaret Garner, a young mother who, having escaped slavery, was arrested for killing one of her children (and trying to kill the others) rather than let them be returned to the owner's plantation."[13]

The soul figure with the "nice hat" who greets Toni Morrison becomes the central character in her novel *Beloved*. Beloved is the soul of a murdered innocent, which becomes a conduit for the voices of all the other black people who perished in slavery and its aftermath. These collective voices are as deep a part of the American soul as John Perry's American Indian or Walt Whitman's barbaric yawp. Her novel roars with the sound of the white race's collective projection onto black people. *Beloved* becomes the spokesperson for a part of our American soul that is as much with us today as when Margaret Garner murdered her baby girl rather than return her to slavery.

Like any other soul, the American soul seeks incarnation in a specific place, specific time, specific event, and even a specific person or groups of people. This specificity of incarnation loves location and the right person(s) at the right moment. This very specificity means that many places and times in American history can claim some piece of the American soul as their own. At the same time, the American soul should not be thought of as bound to any particular person or group, any special place on the continent, or any unique time in our nation's history. As a whole, the American soul is much broader than its particularity and specificity, reaching as far back the American Indians' migration across the Bering Straits and as far forward as one can imagine hearing Whitman's "barbaric yawp."

Part 2: How does the American soul express itself in politics?

In the second section of this article, I want to add "politics" to the already fermenting "soul-of-America" brew that I have been stirring. The first ingredient for the political part of this American-soul concoction that comes to mind is a strangely beautiful book by Doris Lessing, *Briefing for a Descent into Hell*.[14] The central part of the novel takes its lead from the Platonic myth that this world is only a veiled shadow of the world of ideal forms. Indeed, the main character, Charles Watkins, leads us on a science-fiction journey of his inner world, in which he discovers that each individual soul is briefed before its descent to Earth and its human incarnation through birth on Earth. Earth itself is described as a "poisonous hell" for which the soul needs to be prepared. This is the "briefing" of the soul, just as birth as a human is the "descent."

For many readers of this journal, the inner world is primary, and participation in the politics of the earthly realm is, in fact, a "poisonous hell." Many Jungians prefer to avoid politics altogether in favor of other "deeper" soul work. We all know something about the soul's disillusionment when it participates in the everyday politics of institutional life—be it in the Jungian community or national presidential elections. In my own personal experience, I came away from intense engagement in Senator Bill Bradley's 2000 campaign for the Democratic Party's nomination for president feeling burned by the "poisonous hell" of earthly politics. Out of that experience (which I am sure is matched by many similar experiences among this journal's readers in the political arena), I would like to share some reflections on how I am currently thinking about the relationship between politics and the American soul.

First, I don't think that the soul of America is located in identification with one party or the other. Neither party possesses the soul of America. Presumably, the soul of a right-wing fundamentalist is as engaged with the journey of the American soul as is the soul of a progressive liberal. Nor do I think the soul of America is located in one specific issue or another, whether it be abortion, immigration, discrimination based on race or other differences, gay marriage, the environment, the war in Iraq, or a host of other compelling issues.

Usually, a discussion of politics focuses on the rough and tumble of political struggle, 95 percent of which is about how to gain and exercise power. But I am going to turn the traditional discussion of politics as it relates to power a bit upside down in this meditation and focus not on Machiavelli but on some basic, recurring collective psychological themes and tensions that have coursed through our political history. These recurring themes embody deep-seated conflicts in our nation's psyche, in which neither side of the ambivalences and tensions has exclusive claim on meaning or correctness. Both sides have legitimate claim to soul.

The psychological form in which these recurring conflicts take shape over generations is what I have been exploring in the concept of "cultural complexes."[15] Each culture has its own version of how to work out basic human tensions and conflicts. The uniqueness of a culture's way of experiencing these basic human problems becomes embodied in its cultural complexes, which then play themselves out in political life. Sunnis and Shi'ites don't have the same way of dealing with their problems as Midwesterners or Southerners.

In speaking about individual complexes as revealed by the word association test, Jung wrote: "Our destinies are as a rule the outcome of our psychological tendencies."[16] Another way of saying this is that our personal complexes are the hand that Fate has dealt us. How we play the hand that Fate has dealt us, or what we do with our personal complexes, determines who we become as individuals. Jung put it rather bluntly: "We all have complexes; it is a highly banal and uninteresting fact . . . . It is only interesting to know what people do with their complexes; that is the practical question which matters."[17] I believe that the same is true of our cultural complexes. What we do with our cultural complexes determines not only who we become as a people, but also the destiny of the American soul. A good deal of our working out (or not working out) of our cultural complexes occurs in the political arena.

Cultural complexes, underpinned by archetypal patterns, form the core of those highly charged struggles that have defined who we are as an American people throughout our national history. Such cultural complexes accrue a memory of their own, a point of view of their own, and a tendency to collect new experiences in contemporary life that validate their unchanging point of view. Cultural complexes also tend to fire off autonomously and with deep emotion when an event triggers them. We know that a cultural complex may well be on the scene when there is a highly aroused emotional reaction to current events. Emotional reactivity of the collective psyche is the calling card of a cultural complex.

For instance, our more than three-hundred-year conflict around race, as mirrored in the clamoring voices of Morrison's *Beloved*, is an example of an entrenched cultural complex that is always ready to detonate in the psyches of white and black people. Don Imus, the well-known radio celebrity, has made a successful career out of intentionally stepping on the landmines of cultural complexes in his toying with the stereotyping of many racial and ethnic groups. But no one individual or group is immune from the destruction of self and/or others that can come with detonating a cultural complex, as even Imus discovered in the national outrage that came on the heels of his racial slurs about black women basketball players from Rutgers University.

My thesis, then, is that the American soul is embedded in our various cultural complexes. Furthermore, our cultural complexes are what give political life its dynamism and its content. Both the energy and the issues of political debate spring from the autonomous, highly charged emotional material of our core cultural complexes. Political life is the natural social arena in which cultural complexes play themselves out. We forge the American soul in our struggle with our cultural complexes. In the political arena, cultural complexes seem mostly to generate heat, division, hatred; they are inflammatory and polarizing; they usually end in a stalemate without any resolution, only to recur in the next election or the next generation; sometimes they are ignored or kept unconscious for decades; occasionally they can be worked out slowly in engagement, compromise, reconciliation, and healing after generations of recurring battle. In short, they behave like complexes.

We might now reframe the question about the relationship of politics to the American soul as follows: "What are we doing with our cultural complexes in political life?" Or perhaps the question may be better phrased, "What are our cultural complexes doing with us in our political life?" In order to explore those questions, we need to ask, "What are our primary cultural complexes?" As a way of answering these questions, I would like to offer a list of themes or "relationships" around which cultural complexes have formed in the American psyche over the course of our nation's history.

As I briefly consider each of these "relationships," I will refer to "soul-making" and whether or not it appears to be happening around specific cultural complexes. I imagine soul-making as potentially occurring when there is a legitimate claim for something of deepest human value on both sides of a conflict that has come alive in the collective psyche and has been engaged in the political arena. I hope that the reader will keep in mind that the seven American cultural complexes that I outline here interweave with one another in a tangled skein and are by no means as clear or as simple as I sketch them.

1. *Our relationship to money/commerce/consumer goods*

   a. Core attitude of cultural complex: One of the highest values in American society has been the accumulation of personal wealth and material goods, often at the expense of or in disregard for the common good. This complex emphasizes individual achievement in the material world. On the positive side of this complex is the promised opportunity for every person to maximize his or her material well-being. The negative side of this cultural complex emphasizes our collective and individual right to eat the world, own the world, amass personal wealth, and continuously increase the "gross national product." In the name of participating in the American Dream, consumerism has become almost synonymous with the highest good.[18]

   b. Specific current political issue: Campaign finance reform, in an attempt to curb the equation of material wealth with the common good, recent attempts have been made to introduce campaign finance reform as a way of equalizing the role of money in a democratic society. These attempts have been "dead on arrival" and have been undermined by both parties. On this issue, there is no "soul-making" occurring in either major political party. There is little meaningful engagement in the political arena with the overemphasis on money and consumerism in our civic life and in our political life. We are soul-dead with regard to active, conscious engagement with this cultural complex. Our collective psyche is consumed by its consumerism. (Al-Qaeda was very conscious of this when it attacked the World Trade Center.)

2. *Our relationship to the natural environment*

   c. Core attitude of cultural complex: Historically, we have been a country of vast and seemingly unlimited natural resources. This has fostered a cultural complex based on the belief that this blessing entitles us to everything we want and that we own everything in the natural world. A growing number of people have come to understand that "stewardship" is the responsibility that goes along with the privilege of vast but dwindling natural resources.

   d. Specific current political issues: There are a host of ongoing political debates related to the environment that suggest soul-making is going on with regard to this cultural complex. These include policy conflicts about global warming, clean air and water, the limitation of natural resources, and the desire to use those limited resources wisely.

3. *Our relationship to the human community, including family life, social life, and the life cycle from conception to death*

   a. Core attitude of cultural complex: This country was built on a belief in the inalienable rights and freedoms of the individual as much as it was on utopian communalism. A core American cultural complex spins out of the unending dynamic tension between the myth of the self-sufficient individual in opposition to the welfare of the community as a whole and the reality of the community's responsibility to the individual. The good of the whole and all of its members is endlessly challenged by the rights of the individual.

b. Specific current political issues: This cultural complex is ubiquitous in our political debates and makes itself known in all sorts of issues that range from the right to bear arms and taxation to national health-care policy and how to fund pensions and social security. Again, national soul-making appears to be going on in the engagement of this cultural complex. The debate over the rights and responsibilities of the individual in relationship to the needs of the collective and its responsibilities to all its members engages citizens across the political spectrum.

4. *Our relationship to the spiritual realm*

a. Core attitude of cultural complex: Our Puritan heritage launched our country both in dissent and in a tradition of strict belief in moralistic behavior. The belief that America has a special relationship to God fuels our sense of national entitlement, which is matched only by our strong tradition of religious dissent, which drives our national skepticism about privileged authority, divine or otherwise. Out of these twin foundational attitudes grew our tradition of separation of church and state. Inclusive pluralism and dogmatic fundamentalism are the vying poles of a uniquely American cultural complex that is the psychological inheritance of our religious traditions. As in many other countries, the archetypal split between good and evil in our collective psyche projects itself onto many political issues, from the clash over abortion to the debate about the war in Iraq.

b. Specific current political issue: Abortion. Perhaps about as much soul-making has been going on around this issue as around any in recent political history. Although the issue has generated murderous heat, it has also raised fundamental questions about the nature of soul and life, which, to my mind, are part of any healthy debate in society. The clash of religious fundamentalism with the rights of a woman to make choices about her own body in a society that values the separation of church and state cuts across so many of our cultural complexes that I think it forces everyone to sort out what he or she believes on an incredibly difficult series of issues. That is soul-making. It has turned many things upside down in our society. For instance, conservatives most often align themselves with the rights of the self-sufficient individual, and progressives side with the needs of all in the community. But, on the issue of abortion, progressives uphold the right to individual choice, whereas conservatives argue for a community value that applies to all.

5. *Our relationship to race, ethnicity, gender—all the "others"*

a. Core attitude of cultural complex: There have been two distinct poles in the American cultural complex with regard to race, ethnicity, and gender. As much as in any other country in the world, inclusiveness in terms of race, ethnicity, and gender has been part of our national character and its proud "melting-pot" history. But, ever since the nation's inception, the radioactive background behind the apparent embrace of diversity has been the premise that white, Anglo-Saxon, heterosexual men were destined to dominate the nation.

b. Specific current political issues: Same-sex marriage, immigration. The powerful unconscious hold of the cultural complex of discrimination on the basis of sex, race, ethnicity, and age has been challenged on multiple levels simultaneously in the past several decades. Indeed, the assault on the established complex has been so thorough that the new cultural complex replacing it—"political correctness"—has itself become the dominant persona of the collective, behind which lurks the shadow of stereotyping on the basis of differences. In a sense, white male dominance and the embracing of diversity can be thought of as two sides of the same coin of this cultural complex. But, most importantly for our discussion, soul-making in the collective psyche is occurring at unprecedented speed with regard to the active engagement of this complex in such potent current political issues as same-sex marriage and immigration, and in the fact that, for the first time in American history, a black man, a woman, and a Mormon are running simultaneously for the presidential nomination.

6. *Our relationship to speed, height, youth, progress, celebrity*

a. Core attitude of cultural complex: As the "new land," America has always been identified with what is new—a new land with new people and new ideas, faster, higher, younger, ever progressing, ever renewing itself. The wedding of celebrity, charisma, and ingenuity is forever the hope of the American Dream and American politics. The "new land" gave substance to the belief in our nation's unique destiny, poignantly portrayed in John Gast's *American Progress* from 1872 (Figure 1.4). This wonderful illustration

Figure 1.4 John Gast's *American Progress* (1872)

Color images at https://aras.org/vision-folly-american-soul

shows an archetypal anima figure who serves as a symbolic image of the American soul's identification with "Progress." "She"—the American soul as Progress—floats at the core of a national cultural complex of entitlement, exceptionalism, and the "American Dream."

b. Specific current political issue: Stem cell research. This political debate has tremendous potential for soul-making in the collective psyche because it pits what is "God-given" against what is "new." Surely, there is soul on both sides of the debate. Our addiction to creating something new, quicker, easier, better is a source of American ingenuity and prosperity. It endlessly challenges what has existed for a long time, if not forever. For many, what has existed forever is good enough, and for some it is even God's will. In John Gast's *American Progress*, a diaphanously and scantily clad woman, representing America, floats westward through the air with the "Star of Empire" on her forehead. She has left the cities of the East behind and the wide Mississippi, and still her course is westward. In her right hand, she carries a schoolbook, a testimonial to the National Enlightenment, while in her left she trails the slender wires of the telegraph, which will bind the nation together. Fleeing her approach are Indians, buffalo, wild horses, bears, and other game, all of which disappear into the storm and waves of the Pacific Coast. They flee the wondrous vision—the star "is too much for them."[19]

7. *Our relationship to the world beyond our borders*

a. Core attitude of cultural complex: The theme of the freedom of the individual versus the individual's responsibility to the whole is writ large in the cultural complex of our relationship to the broader world beyond American borders. In this case, our nation arrogates to itself, as a nation, the same rights as the individual, whose freedom it sees as paramount. As an "individual" nation, we place our economic and security interests for the most part above our responsibility to the global community as a whole. The tension between the freedom of the individual and the individual's responsibility to the whole in this complex joins forces with another cultural complex—our sense of entitlement, which comes from our view of ourselves as exceptional and therefore as knowing what is best for the world. These two cultural complexes get acted out in peculiar ways—we wage war in other parts of the world in the name of individual freedoms just as easily as we retreat from broader engagement in the world in the name of individualistic isolationism, which renounces responsibility to the broader whole.

b. Specific current political issues: The American-led war in Iraq is a horrific contemporary example of how a cultural complex (or more than one cultural complex) can seize the collective psyche and come alive in politics. Part of the motivation for waging this war grows out of a deep-seated American belief that affirms the unique destiny of our people as guardians of democratic principles and therefore as exceptional, blessed by God with endless opportunity, perhaps even eternal youth and immortality as a nation. The conduct of the Iraq War has revealed the flaws in a cultural complex that puts the nation's rugged individualism ahead of a sense of responsibility to and participation in the global community. The experiences of the wars in Vietnam and now Iraq have begun the slow process of challenging these core beliefs that sit at the heart of those fundamental American cultural complexes in which our fierce individualism joins forces with our sense of entitlement and exceptionalism. As the deflation of bankrupt policies settles into the collective psyche, one hopes that this terrible misadventure has had its soul-making impact on the body politic.

Conclusion

In each of the broad areas that I have characterized as cultural complexes, a set of specific issues take center stage at any given time in the political life of our country. In the great crucible of politics, where our core cultural complexes enter the political life of the nation, the American soul gets forged and crucified—made, remade, unmade, made again—over and over. These autonomous psychological clusters of memory, affect, and repetitive historical behavior seize our collective psyche in an endless round of racial strife, economic striving, gender warfare, and unending worship of technology, progress, speed, height, information, youth, innocence, moral simplicity, heroic achievement, and insatiable consumerism, all of which have addicted the entire nation—Democrats, Republicans, independents, and the uncommitted alike. It is the "barbaric yawp" of the American soul embodied in political life.

Signs of soul life can clearly be detected in the growing conflict around our relationship to the natural environment. Such signs can also be detected in the intensifying struggles and rapidly changing collective attitudes to race, gender, and sexual identity. In these particular cultural complexes, the American soul seems to be transforming itself through highly engaged political activity. On the other hand, our country is so addicted to money, to speed, to youth, to consumerism, and to progress that our collective soul seems lost or invisible in our possession by these complexes. Our national politics with regard to these possessions seems hopelessly unengaged and unconscious. Lively debate on the current political issues generated by these underlying cultural complexes that course through our history like an underground river is essential to the continuing growth of our collective psyche and our individual souls as well.

The politics of the day that challenge our more entrenched cultural complexes are met with the same kind of fierce resistance from groups that an analyst encounters when asking a patient to take on or confront a personal complex—or that the ego faces when it encounters the unconscious resistance of an entrenched complex, which does its best to keep from being known or made conscious. Frankly, I was surprised, in taking this most approximate inventory of our cultural complexes, that I reached the conclusion that soul-making activity is taking place in so many areas of our political life. At the outset of writing this article, I would have said that there was little happening in our political life that suggested soul. Of course, many readers may disagree with my conclusions.

Many in our country would prefer that the sound of our national soul be less of a yawp and closer to the "Om" of Hinduism. "Om" evokes compassion, peace, reverence, unity. To make a bad pun, "Om" is a far cry from Whitman's primal "barbaric yawp." But the reality is that the sound of the American soul is messier than "Om," and, when the barbaric yawp sounds its discordant note in politics, it is rarely unifying or resonant of deep compassion. Rather, at its best, it vibrates with dynamism, energy, and the promise of renewal. Perhaps we should be most afraid of the time in our country when the mix of politics and soul has left us so deadened by disillusionment and distrust that we are unable even to hear the barbaric yawp.

Notes

1 Thomas Singer, "A Personal Meditation on Politics and the American Soul," *Politics and the American Soul* 78 (2007), was originally published in 2007 in *Spring Journal*.
2 Thomas Singer, ed., *The Vision Thing: Myth, Politics and Psyche in the World* (London and New York: Routledge, 2000).
3 George Seferis, "Argonauts," in *Collected Poems: 1924–1955*, ed., trans. and intro. Edmund Keeley and Philip Sherrard (Princeton: Princeton University Press, 1967), 9.
4 Personal communication with John Perry.
5 Walt Whitman, "Song of Myself," in *Leaves of Grass*, Project Gutenberg, www.guten berg.org/ebooks/1322.
6 Ibid.
7 Ibid., my italics.
8 This is a reference to the essay's original publication in *Spring Journal*'s Politics and the American Soul issue (2007).
9 Ibid.
10 Personal communication with Steven Herrmann.
11 Ibid.
12 Toni Morrison, *Beloved* (New York: Vintage Books, 1987), xviii. Excerpt(s) from *Beloved* by Toni Morrison, copyright © 1987 by Toni Morrison. Used by permission of Alfred A. Knopf, an imprint of the Knopf Doubleday Publishing Group, a division of Penguin Random House LLC. All rights reserved.
13 Ibid., xvii.
14 Doris Lessing, *Briefing for a Descent into Hell* (London: Vintage Books, 1981).
15 See Thomas Singer, "The Cultural Complex and Archetypal Defenses of the Collective Spirit: Baby Zeus, Elian Gonzales, Constantine's Sword, and Other Holy Wars," *The San Francisco Library Journal* 20, no. 4 (2002): 4–28; Thomas Singer, "Cultural Complexes and Archetypal Defenses of the Group Spirit," in *Terror, Violence and the Impulse to Destroy*, ed. John Beebe (Zurich: Daimon Verlag, 2003), 191–209; Thomas Singer and Samuel L. Kimbles, eds., *The Cultural Complex: Contemporary Jungian Perspectives on Psyche and Society* (London and New York: Routledge, 2004).
16 C.G. Jung, *The Collected Works of C.G. Jung, vol. 4, Freud and Psychoanalysis* (Princeton: Princeton University Press, 1961), 309.

17 C.G. Jung. "The Tavistock Lectures, Lecture 3," in *Analytical Psychology: Its Theory and Practice* (New York: Vintage Books, 1968), 94.
18 Jack Beatty, *Age of Betrayal. The Triumph of Money in America, 1865–1900* (New York: Alfred Knopf, 2007).
19 Adapted from a contemporary description of Gast's painting, written by George Crofutt, who distributed his engraving of it widely. Source: www.esubak. edu/~gsantos/img0061.html

Chapter 2

Violent hearts

America's divided soul[1]

Luigi Zoja

Division

Why is Odysseus called unique, timeless, and modern in every age? Not, according to the commonplace, because he is intelligent. Are modern people always bright and the ancients dimwitted? Not because he is a hero; every age enumerates this theme to the point of tedium. And not even because he is, in contemporary terms, an ordinary man, an antihero. Thersites, a common man, antiheroic in knowing the shadow of destiny but also the light of common sense, is already present in the first episodes of the premier poem of the West. In fact, it will be Odysseus himself, in the second book of the Iliad, who castigates this figure for daring to stir up the battle-weary Greek army against the king's authority.

The answer to our question turns out to hinge upon our theme. That is, Odysseus is ageless because of internal division or splitting. He is hardly compromised by that fact; indeed, he thrives on it.

Odysseus is at home in every era because, in his complexity, many personalities belong to him. Each character in Homer is allotted a fixed set of adjectives which elaborate a single quality and which are meant to help the oral performer of the poem by supplying rhythmic promptings and supporting his imagination during oral performance. But Odysseus is an exception. No single focus exists for his characterization, such as physical prowess. Instead, a whole array of qualities is present, forming a complex whose parts intermingle: *poly-tlas* (he can bear many things), *poly-tropos*, *poly-metis*, *poly-mechanos* (he can cleverly invent or create many things, he can think his way through anything, he can travel anywhere)— which is to say, he has many identities.

He is fierce and destructive like the ancient heroes; in fact, we know that his name means "that which hates."[2] In the end, however, once he has conquered, he shows a surprising respect for the dead[3] and for survivors.[4] This sensitivity toward external enemies is a mirror reflection of his respect for internal adversaries. Odysseus battles opponents but also fights with himself, in that way opening a door onto a psychic dimension. While the masterworks of many national literatures ignore the soul's complexity, and the Hebrew and Christian scriptures enlist the soul in the service of the divine, the first great Greek author, who as a man of the eighth

DOI: 10.4324/9781003325765-4

century bc did not know the written medium, already tried to describe what today we call a psychological process. Perhaps because of such early attempts, we still use the Greek word *psyche* to designate the inner dimension.

Naturally, Homer did not carry out a psychological analysis as we understand it today. If he had employed modern psychological terms, imaginatively impoverished as they are, most likely his narrative poems would have been entirely forgotten. He makes direct use of symbols, which say far more than do the abstractions which explain them. In that sense, the novelty of Ulysses is situated in the very language of human contradictions—the "I" that would but cannot, the compromises among internal pressures—2600 years before psychoanalysis.

The author whom we call Homer must have been an extraordinary poet and psychologist. He devoted fully half of his work to describing a single character—Ulysses—most likely attributing to him qualities that must have been his own: introspection and the ability to identify himself with others. He made the first attempt to tell the story, not of a war, a myth, or a god, but—to use the first word of the *Odyssey*—a man: *ándra*. And the man he described was not a unified being.

Confronted with mortal danger, not every Homeric hero goes on the attack as do the figures in modern action films. Some of them, given to reflection, hang back. In the decisive duel of the *Iliad*, Hector failed to confront Achilles. Consulting his own heart, he asked himself if he might make peace with his enemy. Imagining that this would mean loss of honor, he tried to change his mind. But, giving in to fear once again, he turned back to beleaguered Troy, finally rebuking his heart and forcing himself to wait for Achilles. Odysseus, however, behaves this way not only in the face of death but rather consistently. In contrast to the ancient heroes, who immediately look for some way to impose themselves on an adversary, Odysseus knows how to listen for the voice of the other man—the other within you, the other you have before you—to make his acquaintance. And, based on that new knowledge, he knows how to gain new opportunity.

To accept the soul's inherent division, to elaborate on it and turn it into a rich resource, is the new super-weapon. Odysseus is one figure and many figures (*poly-*) in one.

The fact that Odysseus disguises himself and presents himself under names that are not his own is therefore not simply a narrative expediency. Odysseus in fact invents the "capacity to put on another man's clothes," sometimes to elicit his sympathy, at other times to psych him out and beat him at the first opportunity. This capability is the necessary presupposition either for the organization of a non-tyrannical society—like that of the Greeks—or for winning calculated victories over an enemy. This very characteristic has awarded the advantage to the West over millennia.

If a shadow happens to fall across the street, the dog either barks or does not bark. If a scare likewise befalls a man, he either cries "Help!" or does not. But the man who has cried for help will go on asking himself, with one part of his mind, if that was the right thing to do. Only the stupid or the fanatical fail to realize that the inner voices which contradict each other are a great gift from the psyche.

The fact that twentieth-century psychiatry has given rise to both psychoanalysis—which constantly reveals the existence in us of a counter-position, the unconscious—and the diagnostic system of classification is one of the paradoxes of modernity. These classifications would have us believe that everything is simpler: that the person is the category rather than, as psychoanalysis would say, the person is the category but also, in their unconscious, something else.

One of the most debatable psychiatric classifications is precisely the one that takes up pathological ambivalence. Naturally, any psychic condition has its exaggerated expression, and the exaggeration of ambivalence is paralysis. But ambivalence is not only an ordinary human condition; it can also express the highest degree of creative capacity. I have written elsewhere seeking to show how the greatest harm coming from mass entertainment is due precisely to its loss of the ambivalence, the insolubility of the most important human dilemmas, that was the strength of tragedy. Mass entertainment replaces this strength with the predictable Hollywood hero.

Our major works of art tell us in various ways about our absurd ordinariness: only the gods are absolutely beautiful or entirely good. The superiority of human beings to the ingenuous gods of antiquity rests, in a certain indefinable way, with a single attribute, being torn between opposite modes of being. Something of the same kind of superiority is true of artistic representation—its indefiniteness—next to the common kind, which is definite. Leonardo's *Mona Lisa* is a masterpiece in part because it expresses happiness and sadness at the same time, indistinguishably. As is Euripides's *Medea* for being simultaneously heroic and perverse, and Goethe's *Faust* for describing an ambivalent soul, a force that wills evil but works goodness. Truly great creations are embodiments of the intricate profundity of the human being.

Therefore let us draw the following inference. The world of the machine "wants" to supplant the human world. Being operational seems more important than being. For the operation of a machine, whether it is with the lever for forward or reverse, there is only one way. We are surrounded by devices which condition us to think that this is the only possibility. But the human soul is exactly the combination of both levers, of the two functions—going back and forth—engaged at the same time. This makes it a little slower and more cumbersome than a machine, but infinitely more interesting.

Homer's figures are among the best known of all, even if no religion or powerful nation has adopted them. They are known because they are human; in their simple mental processes we can still recognize ourselves. We take part in their dramas not only because of their staying power but also, as Bruno Snell has said, because of *recognition*. In line with Snell's idea, Jacqueline de Romilly has observed that Odysseus's admonition "Be patient, my heart!" initiated what today we call psychology.

Odysseus has returned to Ithaka, among the parasitical suitors who deplete its wealth and lie in wait for his wife. Furious to the core, he would like to grab the bow and revenge himself immediately: he is a *violent heart*. But he knows that this would be suicidal. His heart yelps like a mother hound defending her young. Like the dog's master, Odysseus forces it to be quiet. He does not stop at simply chiding it. He knows that it is right, but that its rightness is only one among many good reasons for acting. Motive determines the objective; prudence decides on the timing. He orders his heart to sustain him.[5] Odysseus differs from conventional heroes because he listens, and also waits. Homer describes his thinking as being like a ball that volleys back and forth continually "between head and heart" (*kata phrena kai kata thymon*).

In the Western tradition, division within the soul has been literally demonized; European languages define evil with terms derived from the Latin *diabolus* (devil), in its turn derived from the Greek *dia-ballo*, that which divides things. However, a conscious psychic division, accepted by the ego, is also our richness and humanity. It is the fertile field in which our ambivalence grows, our complexity, and, finally, our creativity. *Di-vision*—separation into two parts—is the necessary earth for *dis-course*—the word that runs or flows between two parties. The prefix here, *dis-*, is Latin for separation. Only that earth which has been divided by the plowshare can receive any seed.

Vertical division, those passages from one level of the soul to others less profound, may also correspond to *horizontal* divisions, over time.

In this respect too Odysseus is the forerunner of Western vitality. His life is made up of radical shifts in activity and changes of place. After growing up on Ithaka, he endured ten years of war at Troy. Ten years of return voyaging came after that. Finally, his reign on Ithaka was to be followed, according to prophecy,[6] by another long voyage and another return. His life with Penelope was interrupted by a long bachelor phase, during which he spent one year with Circe and seven with Kalypso before returning to Penelope. He went from being a king to being a wanderer and beggar, then king once more and again a wanderer, at long last making a definitive homecoming.

A prefiguration of Western man? Better yet, a prefiguration of the West's own West, the United States of America, where the courage and insatiable curiosity of Odysseus became the national soul: a way of being with no geographical or historical precedents. Inheriting the command to "Go West!" the new man has stayed on the move. With arrival at the Pacific Ocean, the *West* was finished, but the *Go!* went on living, becoming a commandment, a mission. Not a journey, but America's stable essence—so much so that a foreign visitor on American highways is most likely to hear the police say, "Keep moving!"

The typical American citizen nowadays changes his place of residence more often than any other person in any other country or era, and not only location: marital status, sexual orientation, religion, and profession are changed more often as well. These changes occur because of a belief in improvement or betterment, faith in a future greater than the past, a faith inconceivable to a Greek or an Italian but obligatory to the Pilgrim Fathers and their descendants.

To accomplish this mission, however, one must divide up time: one must close the door to the past and vault the fence of the future. The search for purification from evil has driven Americans to eliminate the internal "other." But this liquidated factor returns as the "other" in time. The search-mission abandons England as impure in order to build a pure society, but it also leaves a filthy past for a less polluted future. *Time* divides itself into separate *times*. In the United States, life can be diced up into very different periods, such that one cannot come to grips with them. The extraordinary legibility of spaces and times, into which the American soul adventures at the behest of its original commandment, is a possibility without equal, but also—something less talked about—an anxiety without definition. To pull up stakes, leave it all behind for the new thing, and with it every time to secure rebirth, also becomes a violence, a death for the former life. It is an endless revolution. And revolutions are always violent; the old king, the outworn condition, must die. The anxiety of separation or division is therefore the absolute American anguish: an inner panic about losing identity, about taking on too much change, of falling into the void that rises from having lived in too many spaces. Of discovering that a country that has crumbled on every side no longer occupies any place.

At the origins of Western history, the Greeks were divided into independent city-states. They frequently made war on each other, but little happened in these wars. The conquering city did not incorporate the defeated one, and the dimensions of cities did not grow very much. Having invented democracy, the Greeks passed the better part of their time in the civic square discussing the nature of life in society, with each citizen advancing his own opinion. Every four years, the Greeks gathered themselves at Olympia; like champion duelists from armies, they gave themselves over to literary and athletic contest. Unity and division were two faces of Greek identity. Sustaining that tension within the city-state framework, Greeks very well knew that society, if it grew too large, risked becoming ungovernable and ceding power to a tyrant.

Once Greek society had grown in scale, democracy was abandoned for monarchy (*monos* meaning not just one but *only* one). Much the same thing happened to the Roman republic. Western history had to wait until the American and French revolutions to see dualisms, and differences in general, fully recognized again. History, however, has brought the two continents to deal with the problem of division in different ways. Europe was always divided into nations that were strong rivals. Infant French democracy immediately resisted internal squabbles, suppressing them with terrorism or projecting them outside, contributing to a paranoid nationalism. Wars among the nation-states continued through the first half of the twentieth century. At that point, Europe plunged itself without any illusions into a massacre bloodier than all the rest of human history. Thereafter it began to construct a federation that was post-national, post-ideological, post-religious, and post-heroic.

The United States, by contrast, did not meet up with genuine external threats; consequently, the first phase of its history did not lend itself to aggressive nationalism. The single mortal risk was internal division. The struggle against division has remained an absolute priority, continuing uninterrupted until today.

Such a fundamental American word as "divisive" is not translatable into the European languages; it simply is not to be found in dictionaries. Another difficulty encountered by Europeans who explore the American language is the discovery that the substantive plural *The United States* is followed by verbs in the singular number—*is*, and not *are*. History has less logic than grammar does; it was after the Civil War that the singular number became the correct form.

The USA and Europe have therefore marched off in opposite directions. While from the beginning the States so United were less aggressive and more tolerant than Europe, in a certain sense their positions today have changed places. The turning points are the Civil War in the United States and the two World Wars in Europe.

Today, concepts such as *federal* and *federation* (from Latin *foedus*, oath) arouse different emotions in the European and American unconscious. For Europe it connotes a secular concept, contractual in the way of civil marriage. It is a freely chosen union, which in the same free manner can be dissolved again. (Compare Article 60.1 in the projected EU Constitution.) The American concept of federation instead remains quasi-religious, absolute like Catholic marriage. The preamble to the Articles of Confederation for November 15, 1777, speaks of *perpetual union*. The preamble to the Constitution for September 17, 1787, speaks of *a more perfect union*. For the post-religious European, qualities such as *perpetual* and *perfect* are not human but divine. From that viewpoint, therefore, the American Constitution contains no provisions which allow for exits from the Union, because it is a religious document—and, like Catholic marriage, is religiously integralist.

Psychodynamics, let us remember, function by reproducing oppositions. If consciousness accepts only one aspect of a polarity, the other aspect sets up a clamor in the unconscious, until repression no longer works, and there will be some kind of explosion. Issuing from the death of Greek democracy, the equilibrium between unity and division has suffered throughout the West, first in Europe and now even more so in America.

America was born out of two originating traumas—the religious separation first from Rome and then from London, and the separation of the 13 colonies from the English monarchy—and then from two historical fractures—the Civil War and an ethnic mix composed of three hostile races. Because of these facts, America, in its own collective unconscious, has chiseled into stone the motto, *Never again division!*

Over time, this culture of unity at all costs has transformed itself into a one-sided negation of shadow, that is to say, of divisiveness or divisions, which are an ordinary human reality. Being further along into a future that no one can escape, America is experimenting for the first time with new kinds of division. It has met up with the war between the sexes, which had not existed before, and new rivalries among ethnic groups, and differentials between social classes which are growing with explosive speed, and a divide between free persons and persons in prison which has no historical precedent—indeed, proportionally eight times the number jailed in Europe. Analytical psychology has this to say about the situation: that whoever refuses to accept the presence of opposites is destined to meet up with them in pathological forms.

Perhaps it is no accident that the most typical new syndrome to come along in America is that of multiple personality disorder.[7] It prohibits the psyche from dividing within itself. Since many people are not going to be following orders, at some point they will definitely be calling in sick.

Even in war, the real winner is probably the unconscious, which manifests a crude, sarcastic irony. The major preoccupation of politicians is that a war, which bit by bit kills people, is going to be *divisive*. Yet, as time goes on, a war not only brings about death and division, it piles up literally divided corpses, blown to bits. In modern war, fewer and fewer victims are killed by conventional weapons, and always more by bombs. It is said that human tools are extensions of the human being. So too are weapons the extensions of tools: if the shovel is an extension of the arm, the rifle is an extension of the shovel. But a bomb strikes at random because it has lost even this shred of meaning: it is simply the extension of hatred. The American preference for bombing, which also serves its preferred denial of contact with shadow and its will to *eliminate* opposition (my concerns in the next section), compounds this sarcastic irony of the unconscious: the *indivisible* nation delivers the indiscriminately pulverizing blow.

To the dead blown into a hundred pieces, it is simply impossible to offer even the proper rites of burial. While this outcome is not peculiarly American, American denial of radical division renders it peculiarly potent. The dignity of such ritual, even in Homer's day, was still more sacred and inviolable than the respect for life itself. Having made it a priority to multiply our terrifying violence by technological means, we are stripping ourselves of those burial customs which not even the Neanderthals did without.

From *E pluribus unum* to *Ex uno plurimi*: The generation of opposites

If Odysseus is the character who best prefigures the American spirit, the epic poem which most influenced the founding fathers was not the *Odyssey* but the *Aeneid*. In contrast to Odysseus, who has nourished a myth, the figure of Aeneas—who is probably mythic in his own right—already came equipped with a historical and ideological mission. The success of Aeneas's mission put down roots for a tree that has grown through the millennia. The twin criteria of mission and success story have been an excellent match for the intentions of the founding fathers and correspond to the development of American spirit throughout its history.

The *Aeneid* is the first example of a convincing and coherent construction of national history. Its program expresses the history and ideology of Octavian Augustus's program, the founder of the Roman Empire and the most enlightened of the emperors, who promoted literature. As often noted, it also offers an epic model for the birth of the American nation. Surviving the Greeks who would have exterminated them and trusting in the gods who protected them, the Trojans of Aeneas carry out an adventurous westward voyage, with no other compass than faith in the divine mission entrusted to them. They arrive on the coast of Italy, the land promised to them by the gods. When they encounter native peoples they conquer them by force of arms, but end by making a compromise and an alliance. The love of the founding fathers for the *Aeneid* was such that they inscribed, on the Great Seal as well as on the dollar bill, three phrases in Latin instead of English, two of which they freely drew from Virgil.

As we know, if the political history of the United States begins in 1776, its cultural history begins much earlier, with the arrival of various radical Protestant groups on the coast of New England. In their own eyes, this advent already marks a radical demarcation between themselves and other colonizers of the Americas. Ships from Spain and Portugal carried only men to America's shores. These men killed off the native males and forced the women to become slaves and concubines, as well as the mothers of their bastard sons, only sometimes making them their legitimate wives. Giving birth to a legitimate society into which illegitimate children were born was the rule. This foundational contradiction has subjected Latin America to inferiority in the view of the northern hemisphere, more than either military or economic domination. This stain has made the presence of sin and darkness—already accepted with resignation out of Catholic tradition—as customary and inevitable as the change of the seasons.

How different were the Anglo-Saxon immigrants to the New World! Fleeing the corruption of the Roman Church and the British monarchy, they were dedicated to re-establishing both society and religion. They arrived as families and chose to keep sexuality in the channels laid down by God. The colonists' founding spirit and westward conquest, their subjugation of native peoples on new territory for a divinely ordained mission, echoed the Trojan–Augustan program but at the same time inaugurated a grandiose political experiment: a system of government made up of free and equal individuals, who did not accept the dictates of external tyrants. But they were also trying out a grandiose *psychological experiment*, a system of government for the soul which eliminated the corresponding internal tyrant, evil itself, which they left behind with the rulers of Europe.

The foundational project of the United States was not only political, as it was for most other countries, but also missionary and puritanical. It was the project which today is called *civil religion* and its continuation. From the viewpoint of analytical psychology, the project of a radical elimination of evil—that is, the definitive separation and negation of the so-called shadow—is unavoidably dangerous. Omnipotence sooner or later meets up with impotence. It feels constrained to take measures which become ever more radical and more violent and, in the end, to introduce, under the forms of violence, precisely that evil which it wanted to do away with.

In a simple society, one is better able to cultivate the need for purity. This the colonists understood very well, and so, in contrast to the Spaniards, they sought to keep themselves distinct from the natives, out of motives that were moral rather than political. The original geographic and demographic circumstances of the USA differed from those of all other conquering peoples known to history. Over time, Americans were able to incorporate new territories into the Union without any apparent compromises, placing the native peoples on reservations. The political enterprise and the psychological project went hand in hand, confirming each other in perfect alternation. It was possible to push the collective shadow ever farther off in the process of exclusion, just as it happened with the Indians.

This process gave birth to more than just a new society. It also brought into being the first collective soul that would not compromise with the shadow.

However much the American founders did not flee from the fact that the Union could victoriously compete with the European powers, they preferred to avoid the question. Contact with power games would only soil their hands.

No other people that came before them had thrust the contaminating shadow so far away from themselves. First evil was projected on England and its monarchy. Then—continuing the English tradition of the "Black Legend," by constructing a negative myth shored up by gossip as much as by history—a black shadow was cast onto Spain, gradually spreading itself over the Spanish-speaking Catholic countries at large. America's political officialdom sought to construct a geography that suited this projection. The Monroe Doctrine (the annual message to Congress of December 2, 1823) has been analyzed numberless times as a political manifesto. What ought to interest us as well is its psychological manifesto, in which the tendency toward purity becomes global. The Americas will remain democratic, while the rest of the world will fall under the shadow of geography and history. Without an Iron Curtain (the ocean supplied a wall), this doctrine anticipated the psychology of the Cold War.

But the Americas embraced many peoples, whom it was not possible to "purify" by relocating them like the tribes of Native Americans. The relationships with these peoples could not be avoided. The Big Stick of Teddy Roosevelt had not yet been named, but it already leaned against the frame of the Open Door. The success of foreign policy in an expansive political program came along with a failure in political psychology; that failure followed from the psychic tendency toward "purity" which had given shelter to splitting and division.

In a certain sense, American armed forces—in accord with America's absolute historical exceptionalism—have always carried out "police actions." An army can either be victorious or suffer defeat. A police battalion, on the other hand, has no plans for anything except victory. Its only contingencies concern the different possibilities for timing and the measures to be taken. This view of the American military has stripped its enemies of legitimacy and transformed military campaigns into attempts at destroying the shadow: the dark wilderness of the Native American tribes, the darkness that has corrupted many Latin-American regimes, the imperial blackness of international Communism. Ultimately the two World Wars were wars for the Europeans, but for the USA they were first of all global police actions aimed at defeating outlaw regimes explicitly defined as such.

Only the Civil War was a military undertaking in the full sense of that term: it was witnessed and endured directly by the civilian population, and it called the country's boundaries into question and placed the country in mortal danger. While the outcome was not the defeat of a national enemy, but rather the preservation of the country's original unity, memory of the war has not nourished the myth of a good nation that defeats evil ones, but instead a myth of *the unity that vanquishes division*.

The psychological history of the tendency to purify oneself of shadow accounts for several current events better than political history does. In contrast to all other countries, the United States has carried out the greater part of its territorial expansion by monetary purchase, even when this was apparently unnecessary because it already had taken them by conquest. There is no need to explain this as a calculated move. Naturally the payment corresponds to a contractual acceptance of new frontiers, and makes it more difficult to put them back into question. But from the psychological point of view the donation of payment enhances the tendency to purify the soul; even if the conquest was accomplished through violence, that act get projected into the distance, into a past that is already over with, which is replaced by a present based on economic relationships. If a particular affair has been tidied up and finished, it is better for both parties. At the price of *dividing time into distinct epochs*, division is foisted off onto the enemy.

In recent years the mass media frequently have presented Colin Powell as an exponent of the strategy of "overwhelming force:" a commander who has prepared not so much for a single military campaign as for total supremacy, a way of fighting that leaves no other options. In reality this massive superiority is simply the military tradition of the USA. Other conditions being equal, the Puritan tradition is hostile to engaging in any war, once victory has been secured, that continues the confrontation with the enemy in the form of a protectorate, an occupation, or in political arrangements which link victors and vanquished in contentions over maintenance of control. In this respect, the unconscious of the radical Protestant tradition fears anything that brings about contamination through continuous contact with the shadow. The adversary—whether military or internal—will not be conquered but *eliminated.* Let us not forget how the initials in General U. S. Grant's name came to be read: *Unconditional Surrender* Grant. The two World Wars were no exceptions, and the American delay in entering them can be explained, among other things, as the need to take care of having maximum superiority—not only in military but also in moral terms—when doing so.

All this comes with a manifest advantage and a hidden cost. If the American tradition unwillingly wishes—at the expense of using either military or economic force—to avoid contamination by shadow, in time it will allow itself to be contaminated by force. Force will become part of the collective shadow; few countries have had as many former generals become president as has the USA. The fact that this has not led to the destabilization of democracy constitutes one of the miracles of American life. The United States, however, has defended itself against internal division at the price of the accumulated envy and ill will of many other countries.

We have in mind not the political but the psychological program, which has been beautifully expressed in the remarkable propaganda from the Second World War, *Why We Fight*. At the beginning, after having shown the territories held by the fascist regimes, the camera pulls away into a wide-angle view that finally takes in the whole earth. The viewer is left with a luminous American hemisphere, in contrast to the dark Old World, in every sense immersed in shadow. The story is one of global conflict, but the myth is that of the Monroe doctrine, an archetype of purity nearly unaltered by time.

The internment of American citizens of Japanese origin in detention camps during the Second World War, removing them from the three western coastal states, was a continuation of the need to repel the shadow. Very simply, the Japanese are more easily identified as a group, and the psychological cost of constantly seeing the shadow near oneself seemed intolerable. One must distinguish, however, between internment and relocation camps. The actual number of internees included a modest majority of German and Italian Americans, with others of Eastern European descent, next to a large minority of Japanese. The Old-World enemy shadow, then, apart from the racial shadow, was sent to barracks in Crystal City, Texas and Fort Lincoln, North Dakota, and even detained at Ellis Island for nearly two years after the war.

In Europe, and particularly in the Catholic countries, it is difficult to understand how America's practice of capital punishment could have enjoyed such widespread support in a democratic country. One comes to think that state-sponsored violence has habituated people to view violence as a normal, daily fact. But the historical experiences of the two continents are quite different. In America, capital punishment has been the expression of local seats of power, individual state governments, or even sheriffs in small outposts where they were supposed to represent the only law at hand. In taking that route, the collective unconscious plays out, although in a juridical fashion, the ancient ritual of the scapegoat and its corresponding expulsion of the shadow. In Europe, however, capital punishment has represented the maximum form of deterrence and arbitrary jurisdiction by non-democratic power. One of the typical formative texts read by my generation was called *Letters from the Resistance by Those Condemned to Death*. For years, the European continent was sealed off by the forces of Nazi-Fascism, and those condemned to death were condemned politically. In the collective unconscious of Europe, the abolition of capital punishment and the abolition of tyrannies are one and the same thing. At the dawn of the modern West, these positions were reversed. In representing the American Revolution, Thomas Paine gave two speeches (on the 15 and 19 of January 1793) at the French National Assembly, futilely pleading that the former king Louis XVI not be put to death.

This rapid survey of the relationship between violence and the Puritan splitting-off of the shadow would not be complete without a brief nod toward the power given by the United States to the idea of Social Darwinism and the concept of Manifest Destiny. Social Darwinism was one of the most dangerous of all ideologies (its final fruit in Europe was Nazism), but it attained great popularity in being presented as a *science* which anticipated sociology, anthropology, and genetics.

These two ideological gods were able to sink roots into the American collective unconscious because they were, in several respects, a secular and extremist transformation of Puritanism. Those who are destined to be God's Elect become the darlings of both nature and history. In this fashion, the idea of superiority was no longer placed in check by Judeo-Christian compassion. The problem of the shadow became more intricate through social complexities; immigration brought into the USA ever fewer Anglo-Saxons and ever more people from Eastern and Central Europe, and over time has brought even more non-Europeans. The Puritan distortion did not really disappear, but slid into the unconscious, while the new "science" inherited the responsibility for housecleaning and decontamination. Evolution seemed to guarantee that the "inferior" races would be wiped out. Assisting in this transformation had nothing to do with moral choice, because the sheer weight of possible conditions was to blame. No individual was violent—no, it was "natural" evolution, with which one could collaborate.

It led people to believe that things were arriving at a stage very near the summit of progress, so that social progressives, paradoxically, were often pushing in this direction more than were conservatives. One example would be those who, following the Civil War, wishing to provide a solution to the problem of the Afro-American population, promoted the return of the blacks to Africa. On the one hand they were looking for some kind of generous action, one that would alleviate guilt for the institution of slavery. On the other hand, the unconscious fantasy probably was that of freeing themselves from the African shadow (therefore the unconscious double meaning in the name "Liberia").

As one moves through the various levels of exclusion or removal of the weakest, one finally comes to twentieth century eugenics. During the first few decades of the century this practice underwent a powerful expansion throughout the West, but made a particular name for itself in America, whence it would return to Europe, supporting the birth of Nazi ideology.

Psychology and a new ethic

Jung's disciple Erich Neumann, observing that the victors over Nazism were mounting the threat of nuclear weapons, wrote a short book in 1948 that proposed a *new ethic*. The grounds for this step span several boundaries. The Judeo-Christian tradition appeared to be increasingly less adapted to a technological mass society; the distinction between good and evil had passed directly from religion over into politics. The refusal to recognize that evil was a part of one's own psychology, and the projection of this rejected evil onto the opposing group, transformed the moral distinction into one more instrument of intolerant and implacable struggle. Technical progress—and ideology, which as Solzhenitsyn has said becomes in its turn the multiplier—changed conflict into extermination.

The only real alternative to catastrophe was the way of psychology. This means two things. First of all it was necessary to confront the problem of good and evil on individual terms; condemnation of the group is not a distinction between good and evil but an evil in itself. Second, if a good intention produces violence, conscious understanding of one's intentions is not enough. The responsibility for violence cannot be suppressed. If the responsible party among two adversaries is always "the other," that other is not to be found in the enemy but in the unconscious. The new ways of proceeding along this path—into the individual person and into what is unconscious—render evaluation and judgment much more difficult. But there is no other alternative. Collective justice has executed far too many injustices.

We have returned to what we proposed at the outset. The opponent, the adversary, the enemy is within us. The recognition of that truth makes one sad.

Walter Benjamin has described the experience of melancholy as the suffering of history. History is a carpet woven out of devastations and assassinations, along which rides the chariot of the conqueror in triumph. Whoever wishes to understand Carthage must go into mourning. In an act of prudential wisdom, the Romans stood another man next to the triumphant conqueror in his chariot, a double or "other," whose task it was to whisper into his ear that he was mortal, and that successes come and go like the wind.

In the history of my own country, the Roman Empire declared a *Pax Romana*, paid for with slavery and massacres. What followed was a drunken binge from which we have had to purify ourselves. The voice of the shadow in the chariot was right. During the fourteen centuries that followed the empire, we were divided and subject to foreign domination. It is time to get used to feeling the weight of history and its responsibility, time to grow sad and a bit reasonable.

Could it be that one of America's problems is that the carpet of victims beneath its wheels is still too fresh, that its triumph is still rolling along, and that the excitement arising from all this has not had a chance to subside into melancholy? The heart of America is submerged in the center of history. And so we come to the impossible question: is it possible to be powerful and just at the same time?

From the psychological viewpoint, the ideas of Social Darwinism and Manifest Destiny are attempts to escape the horror of history and the necessity of struggle. Just as there came a time when people cried *It's God's will!* while sharpening their swords for the Crusades, so these ideas proclaimed that *Science has spoken!* which is at once the modern god and the new sword.

Should we be at ease because these things took place in the past? I don't know. One important book, *American Mania: When More is Not Enough*, analyzes the tendency—global, but particularly advanced in America—always to want more while obtaining less satisfaction. This addiction is related to the one we call consumerism, but is especially visible in relation to food because its leads to obesity. The analysis of this pathology—and of the business that exploits it—is persuasive. The causes, however, can all be explained entirely by way of genetics. or so runs the author's argument: today's Americans are descendants of particularly audacious people, passionate about new things and remarkably insatiable, so much so that they chose to make the great leap across the ocean. In Darwinian terms, these characteristics have been selected, being passed down to their descendants.

Since I am not a biologist, it is not my place to make authoritative comment. But it seems to me that Afro-Americans have a tendency to obesity no different than that among whites, even though they do not descend from anyone who crossed the Atlantic by choice. I ask myself whether our author does not submit to that fear of history which is a trademark of the modern collective unconscious. When we look at ourselves in the mirror, we can scarcely believe what we have become as individuals and peoples, and we prefer to flee from psychological and cultural responsibility into biological explanation.

Just as with the assignment of capital punishment to a single person, so too with war (which condemns a collective to death): in Europe it could be decided by rulers, while in the United States it has had to gain public approval. A book like *Just and Unjust Wars: A Moral Argument with Historical Illustrations*[8], is therefore profoundly American and civic, in its aim of discussing when a war is moral. But can war, today, be moral?

The ethic that sets out to talk about a just war—and not *inevitable* war, or war *justified by the absence of alternatives*—is, unfortunately, still the old collective ethic, seeking some kind of collective punishment. Technical progress has multiplied atrocity almost beyond limit. At the end of the nineteenth century, war unavoidably killed civilians, but at least 90 percent of the dead were soldiers. Things rapidly reversed themselves between the First and the Second World Wars: in the First War, 8.6 million soldiers next to 6 or 7 million civilian victims, and in the Second War, 17.1 million soldiers compared with 20 to 27 million civilian dead. Today the majority number reverses the earlier ratio exactly: 90 percent of the dead in our wars are civilians.

The American military today has the ability to avoid, and indeed a preoccupation with avoiding, civilian casualties, more than any military organization in human history. Notwithstanding this, if we are mindful of the massacres in Iraq, we must conclude that in modern warfare the slaughter of innocents is no longer a chance or collateral occurrence, but the unavoidable essence of conflict.

A central criterion for evaluating war is the proportionality between war aims and human costs. If the human costs of war today cannot be controlled by the authorities who decide to wage war, then we must reconsider the very idea of the just war, because whoever makes the decision can no longer know what he is doing, or evaluate it properly, and therefore cannot actually authorize it. What Erich Neumann has called a new ethic demands of anyone a personal assessment, and Odysseus already knew that this calls for *time*. The psychic processes of the unconscious cannot be accelerated.

In this respect the memoirs of Traudl Junge—who was Hitler's personal secretary from 1942 until his suicide in 1945—are instructive and excruciating. What she learned little by little during the years following the war, and narrates, is already frightening. But she had to live through another half century in order for the most tremendous thing to come home to her; that much time was required to fully portray to her the evil that she had encountered and with which, even if in a minimal way, she had collaborated. Her adversary, the person she most despised, was not some crude Nazi, but the girl whom she herself had been. Slowly, Traudl Junge had accomplished the ethical *personalization* that Neumann describes.

She was trying to forgive herself for saying to herself that she was too young at the time and that she did not know what was going on. One day, on the street, she saw a monument to Sophie Scholl, one of the young people martyred in the White

Rose resistance to Hitler. Reading the inscription on the monument, she found out that she and Sophie had been the same age, and that on the very day when she began working for Hitler, Sophie had been sentenced. She realized that the fact of not being informed about evil and not consciously choosing it do not take away responsibility. She discovered another person within herself, an accomplice to assassination by omission. She also discovered that we are morally divided within ourselves over the course of time. Perhaps this fact already invalidates capital punishment: even the worst criminal, given time, is able to become a just man. By taking such a man's life, we also kill that just man who probably began to grow in him but might still be in the infant stage.

Hitler, Jung tells us, was directly moved when he sensed that certain of those who carried out his orders felt compassion for the victims. "You understand," he told them, "that it is necessary to sacrifice one's feelings for the common good. When everyone comes to see the results, they will understand that it was worth the suffering. In the meantime, you must not feel guilty, I assume the responsibility." These are the collective norms of the old ethic. Someone takes on the charge of evaluating things for us. Of deciding if war is just, or if eugenics—of which genocide is the extreme manifestation—is a good thing. Naturally, war and eugenics are collective operations and demand collective judgments; but the assessment is collective because it is functional, not because it is moral.

I go in fear of that adjective "just." It is something far too lofty to be pressed into service by something as base as war. It becomes dangerous, like an explosive device. It transforms a murderous impulse into something acceptable. What a strong temptation that is, just as strong as the one to obey those people who say they know what the collective good is and take responsibility for it. They seem generous twice over, because they busy themselves with the good of the collective and even offer to carry the charge of our conscience. They offer us inner calm, untroubled by division.

It becomes easier to kill when this kind of inner agreement prevails. And still easier, if one can say—with Shakespeare's King Richard III—that even one's enemies

> Had rather have us win than him they follow.
> . . . If you fight against God's enemy,
> God will, in justice, ward you as his soldiers.
> If you do sweat to put a tyrant down,
> you sleep in peace, the tyrant being slain.[9]

I do not know with any certainty whether killing is ever justifiable. I do know, however, that no one ought to sleep in peace after having taken a life.

Notes

1 This essay was originally published in *Spring Journal*'s 2007 issue, *Politics and the American Soul,* 78.
2 Homer, *Odyssey*, Book XIX, II. 406–409.

3 Ibid., Book XXII, II. 411 ff.
4 Ibid., Book XXII, II. 371 ff.
5 Ibid., Book XX I. 18.
6 Ibid., Book XXIII II. 264–284.
7 *Diagnostic and Statistical Manual of Mental Disorders IV*, 300.14.
8 Michael Walzer, *Just and Unjust Wars: A Moral Argument with Historical Illustrations* (New York: Basic Books, 2006).
9 Shakespeare, *Richard III*, Act V.198–210.

Chapter 3

Captain Ahab and Donald Trump

False claims, the fragility of
belief, and the perilous ship of
America's soul

Dennis Patrick Slattery

In thinking about creativity and the role of the artist, C.G. Jung commented on Herman Melville's *Moby-Dick*. In "Psychology and Literature," he distinguished psychological fiction from visionary fiction. The former is created "with materials drawn from man's conscious life" then "assimilated by the psyche of the poet, raised from the commonplace to the level of poetic experience, and expressed with a power of conviction,"[1] whereas visionary fiction emanates from a deeper place in the psyche. Its material "is no longer familiar. It is something strange that derives its existence from the hinterland of man's mind . . . . It is a primordial experience which surpasses man's understanding."[2] Jung then identified *Moby-Dick*, published in 1851, as a poetic creation of the visionary mode, which he considered "to be the greatest American novel, in this broad class of writings."[3]

In *Moby-Dick*, through Melville's narrator, the marginalized figure of Ishmael, we learn of the primal presence and force of wounding—of the individual, of those who are different, and of the ultimate wounding of the Earth through the slaughter of whales. In the novel, one enormous white whale, a rich metaphor for the world soul (*anima mundi*), is marked for slaying because of its confrontation with the captain of the *Pequod*, Ahab. In this confrontation of the afflicted captain with the white whale who dismembered him, Jung recognized a primal encounter both universal and deeply symbolic.

In this essay, I wish to focus on the correlations between the leader of the whaleship *Pequod*, Captain Ahab, and the former president of the United States, Donald Trump, and demonstrate how Melville's novel touches on our own national myth whose impulse is to slay, absorb, and swallow differences and to favor a uniformity in thought and behavior that contradicts the diversity that is part of our democratic spirit.

Wounded grievances and the need for revenge

As I see it, what animate both Captain Ahab and Donald Trump are a shared sense of grievance as a response to their respective wounds and a relentless deployment of the role of victim chafing for revenge. Ahab's surface wound is inflicted by the white whale's attack and dismemberment of his leg during a battle at sea; it is

DOI: 10.4324/9781003325765-5

followed by the interior steaming wound of resentment he carries on board and through which he weaves a false narrative that seduces the ship's 30 whalers into complicity with his baseless slandering of what the white whale is. This plot and ploy have a through-line that runs from the publication of *Moby-Dick* in 1851 to a similar plot—the meticulously planned insurrection at the United States' Capitol on January 6, 2021, by Trump and his followers, who capsizing all facts to the contrary, executed the defeated former president's fantasy that he had won reelection absent any facts to bolster his claim. Trump's obsessive need not to be seen as a loser brokered a shared fantasy as true, with a consequent attempt to be reinstated as president, in violation of federal law. In developing his engineered victimhood, Trump exaggerated what was already deeply ingrained in America's soul: that the rugged individualism of the American male character does not stand for any consequence except being a winner, supreme and uncontested.

A general agreement on board the *Pequod* to attack and slay the white whale as their primary mission was activated by a false narrative that the *Pequod*'s captain advanced when he gathered the entire crew on the quarterdeck: that Moby Dick was the embodiment of evil; further, Ahab proclaims, "be the white whale agent, or be the white whale principal, I will wreak that hate upon him."[4] Trump advanced a similar false claim, with an equally heated and wounded rhetoric, that the election was stolen and must be redeemed, through violence if necessary, to reinstall him as "legitimate leader" of the United States; in such a strategy, he positioned himself outside the directives expressed clearly in the Constitution on the peaceful transfer of power as a result of the will of the voters who chose another candidate for the presidency, Joseph R. Biden.

But first, to the rise of untruth in both Ahab's and Trump's wounded narratives. It is compelling to imagine the correspondence between the two events and the strategies leading up to them. The legitimacy of what was proven to be true was and continues to be diminished in favor of what the aggrieved loser wished to believe was true, which is central to the insurrection against the truth, both on the quarterdeck of the *Pequod* and in the strategy rooms of a hotel near the nation's Capitol. There, the elaborate, well-orchestrated plot to overthrow a fair election was birthed and fed. To violate the Constitution is to dismember the myth of Democracy, which serves as the psychic infrastructure that organizes and expresses what our national identity believes in, is supported by, and is worth defending from evisceration. Democracy bestows on our national and personal life a world of values that enrich our continued existence as a unified collective. Furthermore, as a myth, Democracy aids us in ascribing significance to the contents of our lives within a shared national context; it prescribes meaning for the patterns and purposes we tacitly agree to live by.

The grievance in both Ahab's and Trump's worldview shifts our focus as a nation from participating in the overarching myth of Democracy to the cult of the individual. Such a shift signals an invasion of the tenets of Democracy, which now suffers an unravelling of its weakened fabric by forces that seek power for its own sake.

In a nuanced study, Jungian analyst Ronald Schenk returns to some of the insights written by French political philosopher and historian Alexis de Tocqueville when he visited the United States in 1830. Schenk highlights the dangers Tocqueville realized as he studied our country: "When the utopian ideal upon which the nation is founded loses the right understanding of 'self-interest,' its 'window on the world,' an 'ignorant and coarse shadow presents itself and the ideal becomes transformed.'" Schenk further cites Tocqueville's observation that "It is difficult to foresee to what pitch of stupid excess their selfishness may lead them."[5]

Trump's desperate scheme to regain power echoes psychologist Robert Karen's insight:

> We are all haunted to some degree by a smallness and a mortality we wish to deny. To cope, we seek applause, power, diversions, obsessions . . . Is it any wonder that threats to power can, much like rejection, sexual betrayal, or public humiliation, engender an unforgiving rage of infantile proportions?[6]

In his fury at being a loser in the election, which is also a psychological and emotional dismemberment for him, Trump signaled his faithful acolytes, including elected officials in both federal and state offices, to go into battle. When Bob Woodward interviewed Trump for his book *Rage*, he cited the former president's relation to such a potent emotion: "I bring rage out. I do bring rage out. I always have. I don't know if that's an asset or a liability, but whatever it is, I do."[7]

Both Trump and Ahab suffer similar forms of humiliation when dismasted of elements of their power; both sense in their respective impotencies that, through violence, they can restore themselves to former formidable conditions. Ahab deployed an attack on nature, while Trump deployed an attack on a people's guiding cultural and political mythology.

There exist as well dramatic analogies between the violent hunt for the white whale and the fierce insurrection against the heartbeat of Democracy: the Constitution. Both events were perpetrated by repetitions of untruths. Ahab unfurled his fantasy on the quarterdeck of the *Pequod*, his public podium, while Trump signaled his shipmates through the media and reinvigorated rallies. Both figures carefully crafted their accusations of being violated while claiming their own innocence and victimhood. Psychologist Rollo May writes that "In this country, the Garden of Eden myth, along with the open denial of power, has continuously coexisted with a great amount of violence."[8] He furthers his insight in suggesting, *"primarily, the violence and, second the tenderness is connected with our conscious denial of power and the pseudoinnocence that accompanies the denial.* Violence comes from powerlessness . . . it is the explosion of impotence."[9]

Returning to Melville's epic, it is told in the first person by an "isolato" who asked of his audience, "Call me Ishmael,"[10] in his introduction. He too suffered from his own fractured life and wobbled on the brink of despair. Ishmael chose to go to sea (and to see) to escape the suffocation of the land and its cities. After meeting with his savage Other, Queequeg, son of an island chief, who Ishmael soon clearly saw as his brother in spirit, together they sought a whaling ship to begin their adventure. Given three ships to choose from, Ishmael selected the *Pequod*, named after a native American tribe, the Pequot nation. From one of the Quaker owners, Captain Bildad, Ishmael heard the story of the *Pequod*'s captain and his dismemberment by the white whale.

Sometime later, after the ship sailed from Nantucket Island, Ahab emerged from his cabin to the quarterdeck for the first time to address the entire crew; his narrative of unjust dismemberment, mentioned earlier, framed him as a victim of the evil leviathan. Ahab trumpeted his rallying cry, his initial call-to-arms. He conjured a narrative through the aperture of feigned innocence, a "pseudoinnocence" in May's word.

What Ahab and Trump share at this juncture include: (1.) a sense of being an innocent victim of a demonized other; (2.) a call for retribution to right a (fictitious) wrong; (3.) the use of violence to reinstate a manufactured sense of justice; (4.) a promise to lead their followers to fulfill this task. Most importantly, however, these four elements are housed in a fabrication, a fiction, that abandoned any factual foundation. In both instances of Ahab's and Trump's false narratives, a fantasy *of* reality morphs into a belief *about* reality, which then evolves into a fact about reality as well as a solution to this injustice: violence.

Ipek S. Burnett's insightful study leads us into the history of such narratives that demonize others, whether the story is based on a truth of history, or a belief, or an assumption, or the voice of violence and the wound that suppurates from it. Writing of the Puritans' response to the Indigenous peoples in America, she observes their literal reading of the Bible:

> The Puritans did not just perceive the Native Americans as not-chosen, inferior people, they demonized them. Seeking to apply the Old Testament's narrative to their own lives, they maintained that they were called by God to come to his new promised land and dispel the tyranny of Satan with the gospel.[11]

Gospel becomes weapon, a harpoon that will erase Native American presence.

Tightly wrapped in what Eckhart Tolle calls a "victim identity,"[12] Ahab, as a seasoned rhetorician with a skill in creating and expressing his own version of reality, pushes his false metaphysic a bit further. In response to his first mate Starbuck's challenge of his definition of the white whale, Ahab declares that Moby Dick is like a wall that keeps the wounded captain from penetrating behind the "pasteboard masks" of the visible world. The leviathan, in Ahab's imagination, represents qualities that he finds abhorrent:

> To me, the white whale is that wall, shoved near to me. Sometimes I think there's naught beyond . . . He tasks me; he heaps me; I see in him outrageous strength, with an inscrutable malice sinewing it. That inscrutable thing is chiefly what I hate.[13]

Melville scholar Andrew Delbanco refers to Ahab as "a brilliant personification of the very essence of fanaticism."[14] Such a claim is not outside the bounds of describing Trump's own extremism, witnessed in the four years of his presidency and then accelerated in his fixated intent to overthrow the truth of the Constitution with the barbs of lies. It is also noteworthy that both Ahab and Trump function inside an equally powerful prevailing myth of the United States: capitalism itself and the power of money to enflame greed, avarice, and the further rapacious hunger for power that financial incentives often breed. As part of the overarching theme of values that define a myth's purpose, capitalism represents the power of economics that places economic worth above the intrinsic value of people and professions. Capitalism bestows worth on what it values; it shapes the American psyche's desire to be a success, which often translates as "making money." The myth of capitalism tells us what to value, not exclusively but largely, in the American psyche. Choosing to work at something primarily to make money rather than nourishing one's soul through work that creates meaning and purpose in one's life is its dominant desire.

Delbanco's biography reveals how much closer Ahab is to Trump when he writes: "The *Pequod* becomes a replica of the American ship of state; its thirty-man crew ('isolatoes federated along one keel') matched in number the thirty states that constituted the Union in 1850."[15] He further clarifies Melville's political inflections in the epic: "Melville made of the *Pequod* a mirror of America rushing westward, poisoning itself by eating up a continent."[16] The epic lays bare America's self-consuming folly as it slays, butchers, boils in the try-pots, and then barrels whales for consumption as fuel in American cities to light their streets.

Ahab, like Trump, turns his position of authority to exclusively self-serving ends through distortion, deceit, and depravity toward the truth. Today there appears an intensifying presence of a hyperbolic imagination to sensationalize its messages as it severs itself from its anchors in historical accuracy. Being outrageous and off the grid of a common shared reality is often the ticket to national recognition and fame.

Cultural critic Kurt Andersen keenly identifies tendencies in the American soul; he tracks American society's fascination with conspiracies, with exaggerated distortions of reality, and its disposition as a people "to believe exciting untruths."[17] *Fantasyland* is a landmark study of what forces have borne down on American culture to shape its myths, torque its beliefs, and prey on Americans' fever for the fantastic. That fever has now metastasized into full-blown violence with nothing to support it but fallacies masquerading as facts. For a growing number of citizens, the distinction becomes more irrelevant.

Americans continue to learn of new revelations that italicize the deepening complicity of so many accomplices in and out of public office, and how keenly orchestrated this almost-successful coup was in its formulation. As citizens, most are gaining a fuller composite of how deeply and broadly this insurrection had become a full-blown infection even before the actual attack on January 6, 2021. Its intent was to unravel the country's fundamental identity as a nation and to place the cult of personality of one man over the electorate's clear choice of Joe Biden. If the white whale may be understood as an emblem or analogy of the divine in Nature, then the assault on it is a secular attack on the sacredness of Nature. For Trump, his white whale's dismemberment focuses on a system which allows *all voters* to easily and fairly cast their preference as citizens in a functioning democracy.

No one myth stands alone: each connects with, and entangles itself in, other belief systems, other assumptions and engineered points of view on values and aspirations, as well as memories within the webbing of history's large design. Observing the mythic structures of Ahab's and Trump's narratives, one who sails across the unfathomable waters of the unconscious on a ship of state, the other at the heart of America's government, we can discern patterns that, while not exclusively American, nonetheless carry many of America's lineaments.

Ahab–Trump field of influence

Fields, whatever their brand, always include psychological, mythical, intellectual, emotional, political, and racial contents, as well as categories of class and gender, depending on the intentions of the fields' creators. Fields most often comprise some mix of subjectivity and objectivity. They might also be understood as interpretive pockets of influence. One purpose of any myth, be it individual or collective, is to establish a field which one enters and is influenced by. The field holds the values and beliefs that establish that myth and give it credence.

From a Jungian perspective, these fields may fit under the rubric of what Jung terms "*archetypes of transformation*. They are not personalities, but are typical situations, places, ways and means, that symbolize the kind of transformation in question."[18] The field is not created instantly; it requires one person's strong presence, or a community's effort, to craft and construct it, to gather its psychic and emotional energy, to be affective—that is, to gain or evoke affect—an emotional and imaginal response to the field's terms and conditions. That field may be boarding the *Pequod* and sailing with the crew and its fanatical captain, who is governed by a wound he struggled to name and then acts to avenge.

A healthy field does not seek to breed absolute conformity, but it does arc toward some form of consensus or alignment. However, a field that produces cult-like worship can persuade its adherents to accept a reality severed from established facts. Fields can be amplified by a scapegoat that strengthens the infrastructure of beliefs, as writer and cultural critic Toni Morrison makes clear. She asked, 20 years ago, "How did the founding writers of young America engage, imagine, employ, and create an Africanist presence and persona?"[19] Her response continues to be an indictment of Americanism today:

> Africanism is the vehicle by which the American self knows itself as not enslaved, but free; not repulsive, but desirable; not helpless, but licensed and powerful; not history-less, but historical; not damned, but innocent; not a blind accident of evolution, but a progressive fulfillment of destiny.[20]

Morrison's list of ingredients gathers and creates a recipe for prejudice and the desperate need to keep the Other at bay; one of its culminating events is the insurrection of January 6. Trump stoked fear in the hearts of white supremacists losing out to minority groups, whose voices and influence would nurture a truer and more inclusive democratic republic.

After a discussion in which she noted, how such a "strong affinity between the nineteenth-century American psyche and gothic romance has been much remarked,"[21] Morrison introduced one of Melville's observations:

> There is no romance free of what Herman Melville called "the power of blackness," especially not in a country in which there was a resident population, already black, upon which the imagination could play; through which historical, moral, metaphysical, and social fears, problems, and dichotomies could be articulated.[22]

Today, one might add to her list: immigrants, ideas that make students uncomfortable when taught in schools, book-banning from schools and libraries, the alarming increase of antisemitic and anti-Muslim words and deeds that deny the integrity of entire peoples, as well as successful gerrymandering that pushes minority voters to the sidelines and strips them of their political power. Morrison's discussion highlights the same proclivities to violence we see today, especially with the battle cry of "freedom." "We are fighting for freedom!" was shouted by white supremacists scaling the walls of the Capitol Building. Morrison observed: "The concept of freedom did not emerge in a vacuum. Nothing highlighted freedom—if it did not in fact create it—like slavery."[23] Today, more alarming distortions of freedom carried out by individuals who believe the propaganda and become violent against minorities in shopping malls, supermarkets, and houses of worship attest to the growing destruction of Democracy's promise of equality.

Most important here is the way that the American psyche has responded to the field of theft Trump carefully crafted—through fantasies untethered from the truth—to bring about a literal insurrection. It served only one end: to put the wounded narcissist back into power, with no agenda, no platform, and no benevolent uses of that leadership position but his own appetites. Left to gestate and infect the national imagination with its cruel and tyrannous divisiveness, it has for millions become a corrosive worldview that weakens the larger mythic infrastructure of Democracy itself.

Another dimension of the Ahab–Trump complex is that they share a field of "castration and male rage," as Jungian analyst Eugene Monick describes these conditions in his book by the same title. Both share a sense of deep dismemberment in their respective woundings. Monick lists and discusses six forms in which castration can occur. I would call them *fields of castration*, and each occasions male rage to avenge the wounded. These include: (1.) the castration of one male by another; (2.) castration inflicted by a female; (3.) a man's castration of himself; (4.) a societal castration: men destroyed by patriarchal structures; (5.) castration as an imposition of fate; and (6.) ontological castration, where a man's very being is called into question.[24] Ahab is "dismasted" by a whale that embodies the soul of nature, itself violated by a form of industrial capitalism that turns nature into commodified matter to be bought and sold. For Trump it is "a societal castration," which Monick outlines as: "men destroyed by patriarchal structures that are oriented around dominance and submission."[25]

Further, what both figures share is a degree of "ontological castration, where a man's very being is called into question, where the meaning of his existence, his deepest sense of himself, is denied."[26] Their respective dismemberments create intolerable suffering for both leaders, which are then projected onto a scapegoat to absorb their rage as well as to infect all those willing to carry this wounding into violent action.

Melville scholar H. Bruce Franklin identifies a critical passage in *Moby-Dick* that adds to the internal chaos suffered by the deep archetypal wound that originates rage. What Franklin believes to be "the most important passage in *Moby-Dick*" describes "the psychological truth of the White Whale":

> Ever since the fatal encounter, Ahab had cherished a wild vindictiveness against the whale, all the more for that in his frantic morbidness he at last came to identify with him, not only all his bodily woes, but all his intellectual and spiritual exasperations. The White Whale swam before him as the monomaniac incarnation of all those malicious agencies which some deep men feel eating in them, till they are left living on with half a heart and half a lung . . . all evil to crazy Ahab, were visibly personified, and made practically assailable in Moby Dick. He piled upon the whale's white hump the sum of all the general rage and hate felt by his whole race from Adam down; and then, as if his chest had been a mortar, he burst his hot heart's shell upon it.[27]

Franklin goes on to discuss how Ahab's madness combined "with the whaleman's imagination . . . to create a myth which determines the fate of both captain and crew."[28] This crucial moment is one shared by Trump as well, who, in the madness of losing the election, and to shore up his own fragility, was desperate to create a myth as a counterweight to the facts of the national election's results. He formulated "the big lie" that asserted Joe Biden stole the election from the aggrieved former president and that widespread voter fraud contributed to his victory; only by reinstating Trump as president for a second term would justice be served, yet no court of law that heard the complaint by Trump's attorneys found any evidence of fraud, except in Trump's charge of a fraudulent election. The fantasy was born out of the fevered rage of Trump in order to reestablish himself in a position achieved by violence, a position he initially won by the very political system he now attacked as an enemy of his identity as a winner, not a loser.

In an earlier essay, I suggested a comparison between the story of Jonah swallowed by a whale and Ahab's rage toward Moby Dick that swallows his entire being into its vortex: "Jonah's denial of God's command is in direct contrast with

Ahab's making his own woundedness his God, and it is the cry of vengeance that controls him."[29] The infection spread from there to those so willing to give themselves over to a counterfeit that they have promoted it with increasing ferocity ever since.

One must grant to Ahab and Trump the reality that both are myth-makers; both create fields of belief in undeserved afflictions while proclaiming their identities as innocent victims. The response in both cases is violence. For Trump more specifically, he successfully cocooned himself in a field of affluence as a self-proclaimed multibillionaire by which he manufactured a field of influence. He tapped into another potent myth of America mentioned above, perhaps through a fiction of wealth—capitalism itself.

All of the counternarratives based on facts were, for millions of Americans, less persuasive than beliefs conjured out of thin air: that Trump was an innocent victim of a deplorable theft and that the Constitution itself must be harpooned. I use that word because many of the weapons used by a host of insurrectionists were the long poles holding both confederate and American flags that, like harpoons, were hurled by the invaders at police, at windows of the Capitol, and at Democracy itself, as if to impale the life of our national myth, in service to one's man vindictive vengeance.

Words, dramatizations, innuendos, and repetitions of slanderous attacks, when deployed within a field created by media, rallies, classrooms, school board meetings, pulpits, or any other venue of influence, can unleash dark recesses of the human psyche to inflict harm. They can also bring a feeling of justification that someone they like, respect, and listen to for guidance has given them *carte blanche* to behave in ways that, in more sober moments of reflection, would be reined in. Now, however, they reign. But, if the field of influence is less interested in reflection and thought among its members and more in enflaming emotions through outrageous invectives and comparisons, then the wound is given credence through the fictions that dismantle any shared reality that promotes coherence.

Enter once more Ahab on the quarterdeck and Trump in the public space of the media. Both carry and seep their respective wounds through the aperture of fake claims to elicit both loyalty and violence to salve the wounded. Writing of Ahab specifically in his mythic study of the epic, Christopher Sten asserts that "Ahab is a universal figure, an image of the infantile rage, and hunger, deep within us all."[30] He further cites Ishmael's observation that "the 'moody stricken' Ahab carries the look of a 'crucifixion' in his face, emblem of the would-be redeemer who has lost faith and feels himself forsaken by his God."[31]

By referring to such a soul wound, Sten offers that Ahab degenerates into "a ruler who forsakes his public duty for his private need and is thus transformed into a tyrant."[32] Trump follows suit in assuming the same tyrant archetype. Both men realize their fundamental challenge: to alter beliefs in their recipients and adherents such that violence is an inevitable consequence.

Tyranny-creating is often a subtle form of myth-shaping, as Timothy Snyder's recent book reveals. In his valuable list of "Twenty Lessons from the Twentieth

Century," Snyder offers sober warning signs that indicate the rise of the tyrant and the demise of freedom in thought and action. He continually excavates moments in history from around the globe to reveal patterns that many, in their innocence and incredulity, often fail to see because, perhaps, they do not want to believe it. Hence the sluggish response to signs that other nations may alert us to watch for. One of these "lessons" is "Listen for Dangerous Words," even encouraging one to "be angry about the treacherous use of patriotic vocabulary."[33] Other examples may include "Hoax," "stolen election," "take back America," "evil," "Make America Great Again." Psyche lives in linguistics; words carry power; wounds have their own anguished and vitriolic rhetoric. The words used in the public sphere can shape, distort, and so breed distrust toward a world the collective assumed that they were all were invested in. Both Ahab and Trump are accomplished rhetoricians. Both seek to keep their respective wounds open, raw, and suppurating because of the energy that seeps from them and the persuasive effects that perpetuate them.

The Ahab complex and its opposition

Herman Melville's epic, published when he was only 32 years old, is prominently an exploration of America's founding myth, offered in mythopoetic language, of the American soul's being shaped by a democratic mythos, to which Ishmael draws attention:

> Men may seem detestable as joint stock-companies and nations: knaves, fools and murderers there may be . . . but, man, in the ideal, is so noble and so sparkling, such a grand and glowing creature, that over any ignominious blemish in him all his fellows should run to throw their costliest robes.[34]

Ishmael goes on to praise the inherent dignity of man, which one can discern in the worker who "wields a pick or drives a spike; that democratic dignity which . . . radiates without end from God; Himself! The great God absolute! The centre and circumference of all democracy! His omnipresence, our divine equality!"[35] We keep in mind that this ideal, however imperfectly realized in fact, is a goal to strive for, even as epic stories such as Melville's reveal their shortcomings; the striving is what gives such a pursuit nobility and mythic certitude.

Yet behind such praise lurk shadows of the myth no less powerful and darkly ominous—the shadows of retribution, vengeance, woundedness, unyielding predatory self-righteousness—all poignantly expressed in cult-like rhetoric by the captain to persuade others to follow his maniacal lead. He dramatizes his obsession with bravado by hammering a gold doubloon into the main mast as economic incentive to the one who first sings out the white whale's appearance; he then demands non-negotiable fidelity to his mission: to eradicate what he believes is the source of evil incarnate. Sten offers that "The evil he sees in Moby Dick is a projection, mainly, out of the hell of his own psyche."[36] That ominous evil to be eradicated, which is a centerpiece of both Ahab's and Trump's grand designs, is always out there in an Other, never within. This projective way of dealing with both wounding and evil is another form of innocence, either contrived or authentic.

In *Myths America Lives By*, religious scholar Richard Hughes offers, "The history of the myth of innocence almost invariably reveals that it finally transforms itself into its opposite. Indeed, it typically encourages those who march under its banner to repress those they regard as corrupted or defiled." He then reveals

> the dynamics of this paradox . . . illumined by two Christian traditions . . . the Latter-day Saints (Mormons) and the Disciples/Churches of Christ. These two streams of beliefs take us to the heart of America's mythic self-understanding; both embraced the recovery of pure beginnings (primitive church) as the means to usher in the golden age at the end of time (millennium).[37]

Hughes further observes a major point relevant to my thesis:

> because they [the two traditions mentioned above] had leapfrogged over human history, both traditions imagined that they had achieved a level of purity and innocence denied to those earthlings still rooted in the messy ambiguities of ordinary time and space.[38]

Trump's slogan "Make America Great Again" seems to point to history, but it is actually an empty phrase expressing an ahistorical fable. Not coincidentally, Trump came into power and then to the presidency as one of the most historically ignorant figures in American history. From that perch, his intention was to show that he embodied the archetype of the Fixer but that such an honorific was "stolen" from him unfairly. If we imagine the sleeve of a coat that has a lining in its invisible interior, then myth is the inner sleeve of history, represented by the outer fabric. The invisible but substantial myth gives shape and form to the outer world of history while remaining out of sight until and unless it is challenged. Myth is history's inner sleeve.

When an individual or an entire population becomes unmoored from a common shared history, the invisible myth supporting it begins to unravel, losing both its effectiveness and its intimacy in history. The Fixer archetype may then find a significant tear in the fabric of history to enter and claim, without any anchor in reality, that it can fix the problems if only it is given power to do so in return. Such seemed to have worked with Trump as the Fixer archetype, yet it has not delivered on its promise.

By the same sleight of hand and mouth, all on board the *Pequod*, even lowly and wise Ishmael, succumb to the captain's demands of loyalty. Yet no credible explanation or proof from the dismembered captain ever shows up to prove or support the claim of Moby Dick as evil agent, much less its principal; all on board simply accept it as fact, so powerfully and persuasively has Ahab's paternal and iron-clad screed framed the hunt as well as the final destiny of its harpoons. No casualties or pleas from other whaleboat captains for assistance dissuade the fanatical leader from his singular course of action: to slay in vengeance the source of his wound, one which seems to give his life a purpose it did not possess until the instant of dismemberment. Running within his ideology is the myth of purity against the myth of pollution. To be unfettered by the messiness of history is to enjoy a condition of angelism, a commanding purity that helps acolytes to accept as credible the fabricated narrative with no anchor in the past, and thus no accountability in the present.

Wounded Ahab then sets up a sequence of seductions orchestrated to extend his fantasy of evil into his crew's soul. Their collective journey is now a mythic one. Robert Karen speaks directly to the shared conditions of Ahab and Trump: "What cannot be successfully mourned remains like an indigestible lump in the psyche, a place of unbearable, irreparable loss that mars the self." He concludes, "It is as if the original wound is surrounded by electrified barbed wire and warning signals that blare, 'Do Not Come Near,' as in 'Do not question this wound of resentment but fight like hell to avenge it.'"[39]

Whaling's purpose is to hunt and slay whales, then dismember them into commodities. They are transformed from their natural state to cultural merchandise, then packaged and distributed throughout the towns of America. This process is a complex and revealing metaphor for how a tyrant can infiltrate the natural state of others and persuade them to accommodate one's fabricated version of reality. How often such a project begins with the display of a wound, a grievance, as the tyrant-as-victim assumes the role in the drama of one who suffers unfairly.

Let's return briefly to Ahab's declaration cited earlier, when Ahab proclaims his grievance to the crew. With all gathered around him, the captain allows his wound to bleed onto the quarterdeck:

"Aye, Starbuck, aye, my hearties all round; it was Moby Dick that dismasted me; Moby Dick that brought me to this dead stump I stand on now. Aye, aye" he shouted with a terrific, loud animal sob, like that of a heart-stricken moose . . . "And I'll chase him round Good Hope, and round the Horn, and round the Norway Maelstrom, and round perdition's flames, before I give him up. And this is what you have shipped for men! to chase that White Whale . . . till he spouts black blood and rolls fin out."[40]

This is news to the crew, who originally assumed they signed on to a particular "lay," or percentage of the profits, for hunting and slaying as many whales as possible. But now their profits take a less important position than Ahab's prophecy.

The pattern we see most commonly is that, if there is resistance to a tyrant's manifestoes, it will be from a minority corner of the conspiracy. His first mate, Starbuck, challenges his captain with what is now also considered an erroneous image of the natural order: "'Vengeance on a dumb brute!' cried Starbuck, 'that simply smote thee from blindest instinct! Madness! To be enraged with a dumb thing, Captain Ahab, seems blasphemous.'"[41] Starbuck too misses the point of the white whale as representative of the natural order, created by God and manifesting divinity's presence; his is another reductionist reading of nature as dumb and blind, which has been a central part of the American soul for centuries in its assertion of ultimate superiority of humankind in the great chain of being.

As his wound continues to entangle the crew in its web, Ahab proclaims his position in the universe: "Who's over me? Truth has no confines . . . . The crew, man, the crew! Are they not one and all with Ahab, in this matter of the whale?" He passes grog around and commands all the crew to drink from "the heavy flagon."[42] Then he calls his chief harpooneers forward: "'Cross your lances full before me. Well done! Let me touch the axis.' So saying, with extended arm, he grasped the three level, radiating lances at their crossed centre," passing his own "same fiery emotion accumulated within the Leyden jar of his own magnetic life. The three mates quailed before his strong, sustained and mystic aspect."[43] The seduction is complete; the force of the individual promoting his vision of reality in the crew has successfully morphed *his* fantasy into *their* belief to cement the base of his self-absorbed pursuit.

Heinz Kohut, writing on narcissistic rage, believes that "human aggression is most dangerous when it is attached to the two great absolutarian psychological constellations; the grandiose self and the archaic, omnipotent object." Underneath the narcissistic wound is the rage for revenge, "for righting a wrong, for undoing a hurt by whatever means and a deeply anchored, unrelenting compulsion in the pursuit of all these aims."[44]

In my book on *Moby-Dick*, I noted that "wounds themselves seem at times necessary in order for us to deepen into who we are"; however, "relentlessly kicking against the feelings that bubble up from the violence may be far more debilitating, Wounds can take the shape of a chrysalis to encase us or liberate us."[45] Like myths themselves, wounds can carry several meanings at once. Kohut suggests that there exists almost superhuman power around this form of woundedness. The one seeking vengeance has no regard "for reasonable limitations" and feels a "boundless wish to redress an injury and to obtain revenge."[46] His observation encompasses both Ahab's and Trump's respective rages and the fallacious stories determined to give them plausibility.

Sadly, and at times maliciously, splinters of the American psyche are all too primed to join the ship of rage and sign on board for a destructive voyage toward their own destiny. By calling attention to the sources of this unravelling of the fabric of our democratic myth, there is hope for arresting its greed for power and control.

Jung's insights in "Psychology and Literature" reveal how badly we need to be nourished by visionary fiction and to realize that we can be easily deluded into a belief "that we possess and control our own psyches."[47] Isn't the psyche, he asks, "rather a door that opens upon the human world from a world beyond, allowing unknown and mysterious powers to act upon man and carry him on the wings of the night to a more than personal destiny?"[48] An imagination of depth is now a necessity for retrieving the best elements of the myth of Democracy under attack and to share a profound vision of the deeper layers of the archetypes that propel this invasion forward as well as counterforces that carry the energies of redeeming what is valued.

Notes

1 C.G. Jung, "Psychology and Literature," in *The Collected Works of C. G. Jung*, vol. 15, trans. R.F.C. Hull (Princeton, NJ: Princeton University Press, 1950), 89.
2 Ibid., 90.
3 Ibid., 88.
4 Herman Melville, *Moby-Dick; or, The Whale* (Norwalk, CT; Easton Press, 1977), 174.
5 Ronald Schenk, *American Soul: A Cultural Narrative* (New Orleans: Spring Journal Books, 2012), 18.
6 Robert Karen, *The Forgiving Self: The Road from Resentment to Connection* (New York: Anchor Books, 2001), 67.
7 Bob Woodward, *Rage* (New York: Simon & Schuster, 2020), xii.
8 Rollo May, *Power and Innocence: A Search for the Sources of Violence* (New York: W.W. Norton, 1972), 52.
9 Ibid., 53–54. Original italics.
10 *Moby-Dick*, 3.
11 Ipek S. Burnett, *A Jungian Inquiry into the American Psyche: The Violence of Innocence* (New York: Routledge, 2020), 33.
12 Eckhart Tolle, *Stillness Speaks* (Novato, CA: New World Library, 2003), 31.
13 *Moby-Dick*, 174.
14 Andrew Delbanco, *Melville: His World and Work* (New York: Alfred A. Knopf, 2005), 163.
15 Ibid., 158.
16 Ibid., 161.
17 Kurt Anderson, *Fantasyland: How America Went Haywire. A 500 Year History* (New York: Random House, 2017), 105.
18 C.G. Jung, "Archetypes of the Collective Unconscious," in *The Collected Works of C. G. Jung*, vol. 9.1, trans. R.F.C Hull (Princeton, NJ: Princeton University Press, 1971), 38. Original italics.
19 Toni Morrison, *Playing in the Dark: Whiteness and the Literary Imagination* (Cambridge, MA: Harvard University Press, 1992), 51.
20 Ibid., 52.
21 Ibid., 36.
22 Ibid., 37.
23 Ibid., 38.
24 Eugene Monick, *Castration and Male Rage: The Phallic Wound* (Toronto, Canada: Inner City Books, 1991), 78.
25 Ibid.
26 Ibid.
27 H. Bruce Franklin, *The Wake of the Gods: Melville's Mythology* (Redwood City: Stanford University Press, 1963), 59–60.
28 Ibid.
29 Dennis Patrick Slattery, "The White Whale and the Afflicted Body of Myth," in *The Wounded Body: Remembering the Markings of Flesh* (Albany, NY: SUNY Press, 2000), 152.
30 Christopher Sten, *The Weaver God, He Weaves: Melville and the Poetics of the Novel* (Kent: Kent State University Press, 1996), 68.

31 Ibid., 163.
32 Ibid., 164.
33 Timothy Snyder, *On Tyranny: Twenty Lessons from the Twentieth Century* (Berkeley, CA: Ten Speed Press, 2021), 91.
34 *Moby-Dick*, 123.
35 Ibid.
36 Sten, 163.
37 Richard Hughes, *Myths America Lives By: White Supremacy and the Stories That Give Us Meaning*, 2nd ed. (Urbana, IL: University of Illinois Press, 2018), 202.
38 Ibid.
39 Karen, 49.
40 *Moby-Dick*, 173.
41 Ibid., 174.
42 Ibid.
43 Ibid., 176.
44 *The Wounded Body*, 149.
45 Dennis Patrick Slattery, *Our Daily Breach: Exploring Your Personal Myth Through Herman Melville's Moby-Dick* (Cheyenne, WY: Fisher King Press, 2015), 105.
46 *The Wounded Body*, 149.
47 C.G. Jung, "Psychology and Literature," 94.
48 Ibid., 95.

Part II

Colonization, war, and violence

Introduction

"War is first of all a psychological task," writes James Hillman, underscoring the need for understanding and imagining this collective force.[1] The same is true regarding violence. Once reframed as a psychological task, it is important to remember that war and violence do not just equal bullets, bombs, and blood. War and violence have many dimensions and manifestations, including ideological and spiritual ones. Slovenian philosopher and cultural theorist Slavoj Žižek speaks to the need to step back from obvious and subjective examples of violence—such as crime, terror, and international conflict—to recognize the invisible, objective violence inherent in everyday life. He asserts that systemic violence in the socio-political and capitalist ideologies that rule the world must be taken into account to be able to make sense of acts of subjective violence.[2]

The first essay in this part, "Frontierism and the American psyche" by Glen Slater, assumes the psychological task of tending to visible and invisible violence in history by examining the American psyche's orientation to the frontier. Slater remarks that, with the "discovery" of the New World, expansion through the Great Plains, and the push toward the Pacific Ocean came a psychological propensity for relentless horizontal movement, most conspicuously displayed in a spiritual quest to expand colonial settlement, an ideology known as "Manifest Destiny." He shows that, whereas geopolitical expansion found its limits on the shores of California, psycho-cultural frontierism lives on in a fixation with possibility, opportunity, innovation, and growth. According to Slater, this extroverted stance has come at the cost of impoverished introversion. He surmises that this is why America looks to the horizon, is absorbed in the relentless production of new goods, and struggles to absorb the tragedies of the past, including, but not limited to, genocide, slavery, and war. This turn from the past and the lack of self-reflection have become central to the national character, fueling religious fundamentalism, anti-intellectualism, paranoid fantasies, and conspiracy theories in the cultural imagination. It is thus not enough to reveal a dark history, claims Slater. Rather, the shadow-making apparatus of the frontier mindset must be understood and mitigated.

The next essay comes from psychotherapist Edward Tick, who specializes in military, violent, and developmental trauma. In "The American way of war," Tick

DOI: 10.4324/9781003325765-6

also takes up the shadow as a theme. He observes that war not only wounds the individual's body, spirit, and morality, but also breaks open a society, cracking its social containers so that the cultural shadow leaks out. He invites a descent into the Underworld to recount the ways in which the American shadow has been revealed, released, and expressed in wars from Wounded Knee to Viet Nam, and to recent battles in Iraq and Afghanistan. Through personal accounts of veterans, Tick unpacks how their suffering—alienation, nightmares, flashbacks, violent behavior, drug and alcohol abuse, and intimacy and employment problems—reflects a cloud of despair and a moral stain on American society, remarking that PTSD must be considered not only as post-traumatic stress disorder but also post-traumatic *social* disorder. From colonization to present-day international conflicts, in tracing the violent history of the United States, Tick argues that American wars are repetitions of traumatic experiences and wounds in the nation's founding and early development, and that, as long as the shadow side of the American psyche remains unacknowledged and in the dark, war and violence will continue to haunt the nation's future.

In "Hate, rage, and cultural war: The truth of America's big lie," Jungian analyst Ronald Schenk addresses the wars in Viet Nam, Afghanistan, and Iraq, as well as cultural wars within the United States. He observes that deep divides in the country—targeting race, ethnicity, religion, age, political beliefs, and economic status—stem from deep-seated insecurities and a pervasive need for power and identity. From mob violence in the Colonies before the Revolution to the aftermath of the Civil War, and from American warfare in Viet Nam, Afghanistan, and Iraq to the January 6 insurrection at the U.S. Capitol, Schenk demonstrates how a hunger for power has always resulted in reckless, reactive violence and exposed the warlike nature of American politics. After reflecting on the psychodynamics of rage and hate as displayed in tribalism and populist reactionary nationalism, Schenk turns to Greek mythology and the divinities of revenge, the Furies, discussing how cultural splits can only be mended through psychological integration.

Jung comments, "No noble, well-grown tree ever disowned its dark roots, for it grows not only upward but downward as well."[3] Though invisible to the naked eye, it is the gnarled and tangled roots reaching deep down into the dirt that keep a tree grounded and upright. To "under-stand" is to "stand beneath," to get to know the roots. Hence, to understand the place of violence and war in the American psyche, the three authors in this section—Slater, Tick, and Schenk—descend to the Underworld, the Kingdom of Hades, to witness what dwells underneath upper-world claims to divine virtue, power, justice, and pride. There they discern the blood-stained realities of self-interest, hostility, tyranny, and insecurity, which all run counter to patriotic self-narratives. They discern the American shadow waiting in the dark, generation after generation, to be recognized and integrated.

Notes

1 James Hillman, *A Terrible Love of War* (New York: Penguin Press, 2004), 2.
2 Slavoj Žižek, *Violence* (New York: Picador, 2008).
3 C. G. Jung, *The Collected Works of C. G. Jung*, vol.12, trans. R.F.C. Hull (Princeton: Princeton University Press, 1993), 114.

Chapter 4

Frontierism and the American psyche

Glen Slater

Few things shape American life more than the pursuit of progress, and nothing has shaped this pursuit more than the image of a boundless frontier. To be American, to partake of what has united its states and forged its dominance in the world, is to be marked by this image. Whether present to the literal horizons of migratory behavior and colonial strategy, or to the metaphorical horizons of innovative thinking and economic growth, the frontier image has defined the national character. From Atlantic crossings to a new world, to the push across the central plains, to the search for California gold and the projection of power across the Pacific, the actual movement west and the aggression associated with this movement configured the nation's birth and early development. From its Declaration of Independence to its bold experiment in democracy, from industrial and military prowess to winning the early space race, from the mesmerizing entertainments to the technological creations of its western edge, the nation's culture has always focused on pushing envelopes and building new worlds. In such ways, frontierism[1] lies at the core of a myth that has pervaded American consciousness and outlived its geographical realization.

From the beginning, however, the one-sided and divisive character of this horizontal movement and the outlook accompanying it has left strife and destruction in its wake. Being oriented to life on an always renewing edge has also entailed a narrow focus as well as a resistance to looking back. Such an orientation, cemented by the perception of divine imprimatur, has also involved a fierce individualism, first named by French nobleman turned political scientist Alexis de Tocqueville nearly two centuries ago,[2] which has all too often licensed a disregard and devaluation of broader human sensibilities. A vast and largely unexplored psycho-cultural terrain is thus also part of this frontierism—a roiling unconsciousness that both defines the American character and divides its peoples. At regular intervals, this unconsciousness has taken the upper hand and turned life on the edge into living on the brink. Working its way beneath and behind the nation's espoused ideals, everything suppressed by the great movement west and all it implies has returned to induce frequent episodes of destabilization, the remnants of which have accumulated more than dissipated.

DOI: 10.4324/9781003325765-7

After going beyond the literal terrains once identified with the western reaches of what has become the United States, and after its extension via the accumulation of material wealth, the turning of nature into resource, the projection of power across the globe, and the spirit of invention, American frontierism has more recently come into contact with a series of formidable limitations. These limitations, which are redefining global existence, pose a threat to the nation's activity and a challenge to its thinking. Here I am pointing to the implications of collapsing ecosystems and depleted natural resources, which have made clear pending limits of industrialization and consumption. A turn to multiculturalism and the associated recognition of minority values have also taken hold, alerting America to the prospect that, externally, its mythos may no longer be widely lauded and, internally, its racial and economic divisions can no longer be cast aside. In both geopolitical and psycho-social ways, the world has become smaller. Whether actually or virtually, people everywhere are exposed to different worldviews. Nations and regions are also awakening to their interdependence and the need for cooperation that stems from this. In the face of these developments, the lone cowboy riding into the sunset seems to have lost his way.

With the obstruction of its frontierism, the American psyche is forced back on itself. As when an individual confronts a midlife crisis and finds their psychic energy can no longer be channeled into old habits, forcing its flow back into the unconscious, this energy ignites what has lingered beneath the surface. Underlying cultural complexes are thereby activated, impressing their configurations upon collective awareness, forcing an adjustment of maladaptive attitudes and a careful accounting of the sins and wounds of the past. This is a fraught time, however, and the prospect of creative renewal is in no way assured. Whereas pockets of conscious reckoning can be detected, America is prone to defensiveness and escapism. Such tendencies, evident in everything from adamant denials of changing planetary realities, to paranoid and conspiratorial scapegoating, to regressive reconstitutions of anachronistic ideals, and to futuristic fantasies of transcending existential and earthly bounds, are themselves woven into the national mindset.

The American psyche thus finds itself sandwiched between the obstacles and limitations confronting its constant forward striving on one side and the unconscious and semi-conscious territory this striving has put aside on the other. A crisis of identity is the result, which socio-political events unfolding over the past decade appear to underscore. In his book of the same title, the historian Greg Grandin has argued we may be facing *The End of the Myth* and contends phenomena such as Trumpism are exploiting this perilous situation.[3] If it is to avoid the pathways of denial or escape that are gathering around these new circumstances and instead come to terms with itself, America will need to engage a process of self-reflection and create institutions dedicated to such reflection. Yet even if its ingrained tendencies can finally be redirected and the nation can avoid imploding in the face of inner and outer pressures, this reflective process and institutional change will likely take generations and the embrace of altogether new paradigms of knowledge—"a present and future period of prolonged liminality and deep restructuring," according to

Murray Stein.[4] What follows in this chapter attempts to follow at least one critical line of reflection along which such a process might unfold.

Archetypal elements

Understanding the grip of American frontierism begins by recognizing the archetypal promise of a New Eden. This promise has been passionately if not desperately embraced by European migrants and their progeny, generating storied events that extend from Puritans stepping off their ships to astronauts stepping on the moon. These events, fixed in collective memory, have determined patterns of behavior and reinforced habits of mind, resulting in a subterranean configuration in the national psyche some Jungians would describe as a cultural complex.[5] To the extent this is so, however, it is also a configuration that overlaps the nation's very character, configuring an identification with an ultimate value, making the challenges associated with it characterological—a complex of identity. We need only consider the following distillation by Founding Father John Adams:

> I always consider the settlement of America with reverence and wonder, as the opening of a grand scene and design in Providence for the illumination of the ignorant, and the emancipation of the slavish part of mankind all over the earth.[6]

Here we see the fantasy of settlement guided by divine hand, purposed with spreading the precepts of the Enlightenment, all wrapped up in a numinous vision. This fantasy, restated and reinforced on many occasions throughout American history, is a statement of divinely ordained destiny and calling. If, as C. G. Jung argued, the meaning of life ultimately comes down to a relationship with the God image in the psyche,[7] America has, from its very beginnings, cultivated a potent mythic formula for its very being.

By fusing providence and progress and reinforcing this fusion through the self-evident blessings it generates—the accumulated wealth of many, the fortune-making of some, the expansion of political power, the increased control over nature—American frontierism also unites spiritual guidance and material gain, providing ultimate justification for this gain. This fusion is the basis of *Manifest Destiny*, the term coined in the middle of the nineteenth century to convey the notion that America's movement west, with all it entailed, was destined by God. Manifest Destiny was, just as it sounds, God's plan realized in the most concrete ways. If frontierism is the outer shell of America's identity complex, Manifest Destiny describes its archetypal core.

Even to the extent the overt religiosity of Manifest Destiny has waned, however, its covert presence has waxed, with supreme significance attached to prosaic and profane undertakings, turning matters such as economic expansion into a godly business. This very fusion, the recognition of which is primary in any conscious reckoning with the nation's story, is also the departure point for coming to terms with the main source of division in the national psyche. Following God's plan of expanding ownership and wealth without turning back is also the reason the historical and ongoing costs of this form of progress and its blessings have been, and continue to be, obscured. For when the divine mandate is to keep looking and moving in the same direction, questioning this direction is anathema. In this way, a profound one-sidedness and resulting unconsciousness are also part of the frontier vision, complete with their own built-in resistance to critical examination.

Disregard for the history of Indigenous and Black Americans, the killing and enslavement of whom empowered the national expansion, both territorially and economically, constitutes the most glaring dimension of what the frontier vision has obscured. As Stein puts it, "A kind of naked power shadow therefore is woven deeply into the fabric of our original identities."[8] European purveyors of frontierism dehumanized peoples and despiritualized places, imposed utilitarian and instrumental values on other ways of life, and disregarded a starkly contrasting vision of the sacred in which being and earth are bonded. By undoing these bonds, frontierism, true to the transcendent God of light at its core, reduces plants, animals, and the lands they depend on to resources to be harnessed. Lakota Indian Russell Means describes the connection between this attitude toward the earth and toward those peoples who happen to live closer to it, noting that "the European materialist tradition of despiritualizing the universe is very similar to the mental process which goes into dehumanizing another person."[9] Recalling the beginnings of American culture, the poet Robert Bly makes a parallel observation: "most Puritans did not distinguish darkness from Satan. They feared swarthy Indians, probably were suspicious of dark-feathered turkeys, and walked uneasily in the pitchy pine woods of Massachusetts."[10] Bly relates this lacking reverence for the natural world to a "hatred of the Yin side of the circle" and notes that "hatred of Yin at the start gave New England a fierce energy; but three hundred years later, the same hatred drains people and leads to some sort of spiritual death."[11] Means connects "the European's arrogance of acting as though they were beyond the nature of all related things" to the "belief that man is God,"[12] and a God of a certain kind.

In her book on the American psyche, Ipek S. Burnett draws out the key parallels between the Puritan encounter with Indigenous tribes and the Israelite meeting of "heathen tribes in the promised land,"[13] described early in the Old Testament. Addressing the Puritan posture, she notes, "they inferred that the American wilderness and tribal people of this land were governed by Satan."[14] In terms of the violence that then ensued, Burnett offers, "it was their faith that helped them understand these murderous acts as sanctified deed."[15] This recapitulation of biblical themes points to both the image of a jealous, intolerant God and to the deep one-sidedness and associated splitting and projection that have accompanied the trajectory of Western consciousness, especially in the fantasy of embracing the one God and his revealed word over pagan ways of seeing—or any other way of seeing. The suspicion of efforts to preserve wilderness, engage wider environmental concerns, address climate disruption, and the reverence for the natural world at the heart of such things is strong to this day among American Evangelicals.

In *American Soul*, Ronald Schenk examines in detail the biblical background of the nation's mythic heritage. After observing the fundamental divide between the nation's idealistic identification with "democracy, egalitarianism, and humanistic concerns"[16] and the long list of darker attitudes and behaviors, he poses the question: "How can one explain the sheer ubiquity and vastness of the discrepancy between ideal and practice in many different aspects of American life that has occurred throughout its many decades?"[17] His answer points to "a fundamental narrative or myth as indicator of core character lying latent in the rhizome of the psyche," which is "predominantly derived from the Judeo-Christian tradition, especially the first five books of the Old Testament and the book of Revelation in the New Testament."[18] This source then shapes the national narrative according to "motifs" such as "the chosen people, presumed innocence, the journey, the Promised Land, God's blessings and protection, the privileged elite, travail, ambivalence towards the law, and the role of dominance."[19]

Each of these motifs offers a way into the myth of America and the cultural complex that configures the national character, particularly in terms of how they have initiated existential and psychological divisions. The theme of innocence, central to Burnett's understanding of the American psyche, stems from the paradisal and providential elements of this religious backstory. She writes, "paradisiacal innocence not only produced corruption and cruelty but also whitewashed the colonizer's memories so they could remain in denial of their wrongdoings."[20] However, she also recognizes how this pattern must eventually play out:

> Although paradise may imply perfection, innocence, wholeness, and totality, even such archetypal ideas are no absolutes; they cannot exist without their opposites. Just like light and dark, good and evil, and high and low depend on one another, perfect rests upon the ground of the imperfect, and completeness can only be fulfilled through incompleteness. If fulfilling paradise's destiny of wholeness necessitates its opposite—living through sin, loss, guilt, and shame—then this is exactly what happened in the history of America.[21]

Innocence and other biblical motifs noted above are also present in Grandin's descriptions of the frontier orientation: "Facing west meant facing the Promised Land, an Edenic utopia where the American as the new Adam could imagine himself free from nature's limits, society's burdens, and history's ambiguities."[22] Further, "True religion moved east to west with the sun, believed early America theologians, and if man could keep pace with its light, perhaps historical time itself could be overcome and decline avoided."[23] To apply Burnett's meditation on archetypal opposition to these descriptions, we must concede that the "limits," "burdens," and "ambiguities" from which America has attempted to escape have simply followed its frontierism and been deeply etched into its historical record across time.

As much as frontierism attempts to maintain its front, it's the divide from its back that now impresses itself upon us. Both sides of frontierism have become more than evident. The question is how might America bring these sides into something resembling a meaningful dialogue? How might it not only behold the fullness of its character, but in so doing discover a more fitting stance toward the conditions now confronting it?

Tocqueville and Jung

A number of collective habits of mind offer themselves as entry points into understanding how frontierism as a complex of identity maintains its grip on the American psyche. In the course of his analysis of the national character, prominent in the second part of his extensively researched *Democracy in America*, Tocqueville notes that "in no country in the civilized world is less attention paid to philosophy than in the United States," and that, "each American appeals only to the individual effort of his own understanding."[24] As a result, "Every one shuts himself up in his own breast, and affects from that point to judge the world."[25] Tocqueville eventually relates this inclination to what has become more readily recognized as American "individualism," a term he coined in this work.[26] As philosophy was, at the time of Tocqueville's observations, the field by which reflection on the mind occurred, he was describing a way of being that eschewed self-knowledge or self-reflection—in other words, an avoidance of introspection. Written in 1840, this is also one of the earliest descriptions of American anti-intellectualism, which is still present in many parts of the country.

Schenk, in his turn to the writings of Tocqueville, makes this characteristic central to his analysis of the American psyche, particularly as its qualified conception indicates where the nation's future development may lie. As Schenk sets out, Tocqueville writes of a "principle of self-interest rightly understood,"[27] wherein "rightly understood" points to "keeping open a window of accessibility to the world."[28] This is the means by which self-interest avoids becoming blind and is thus a pivot point upon which America might correct its one-sidedness. Schenk also refers to the theme of innocence, which takes on another valence in this context, arguing that the shift from "'self-interest rightly understood' to an enclosed vacuum where the individual is 'shut up in the solitude of his own heart' is a paradise of innocence protected by an invisible parental power."[29] He goes on to refer to "the American character as a Disney World . . . the ubiquitous simplification of the mind through systematic banishment of the other."[30] The habit of mind that would thus be the most enlightening were it developed is *self-understanding through contemplation of the other*.

Tocqueville also observes a people who "readily conclude that everything in the world may be explained . . . denying what they cannot comprehend; which leaves them but little faith for whatever is extraordinary, and an almost insurmountable distaste for whatever is supernatural."[31] Such one-sided attitudes in the conscious sphere are typically compensated by rudimentary and reactionary expressions of their opposite. In this case, an appetite for the "extraordinary" and "supernatural" aspects of life accumulates in the American unconscious only to surface in unwieldy and sometimes possessive ways. The implications of this penchant for easy explanations are many, including the way Americans are so easily taken in by tribalism, zealotry, snake-oil salesmen, and side-show hucksters.

The pervasive embrace of religious fundamentalism, with the so-called Bible Belt exerting considerable socio-political influence to this day, is but one manifestation of this odd combination of mental habits, with some of the nation's leading clergy frequently turning out to be both salesmen and hucksters. It is no accident this part of the country, which stretches from the Carolinas to Texas, is not only where anti-intellectualism is strongest, it is also most associated with the history of slavery. Fundamentalism is a style of religion that thrives on a lack of intellectual discernment and philosophical acumen, a style that is more explanatory than inspirational, especially as it is defined by literalism and dogma and leaves little room for the questioning curiosity and mental dexterity that characterize mature expressions of religious thought. It is a form of what has been called rational Christianity, wherein mythos gives way to logos, and there is an accompanying loss of the symbols and rituals that provide a bridge to the depths and generate a sense of soul. The worldview that results functions as form of psychological defensiveness that keeps the American unconscious most at bay.

It is therefore not difficult to see how this rigid religiosity prevents soul-searching when it comes to the myth of America. Instead, it functions as a vehicle for the myth's unexamined perpetuation. The so-called "Prosperity Gospel,"[32] for example, often preached at highly influential mega churches, has become a dominant strand of Evangelical worship and continues to provide religious support for policies and laws that disenfranchise minorities and widen the gap between rich and poor. That this belief runs directly counter to a central strand of Christianity matters not. The American way, defined by frontierism and Manifest Destiny, functions as the ultimate value, the actual religion, and the texts and teachings of the nation's churches are regularly molded around this. In the American psyche, the ordinary and extraordinary, the natural and supernatural, the rational and irrational are combined in a volatile concoction that evades reflection and normalizes duplicity.

The result of this confluence of rationalism and religiosity is that much of America enacts a myth without knowing it is in a myth. Instead, its attitudes and actions reflect a reductive, formulaic belief in the God-given nature of its bearing, resulting in a national character with little inclination to relativize its egotism. Rather than seeing itself in terms of the whole—the rest of the world, its peoples, and nature-at-large—it both consciously and unconsciously usurps the whole—or at least conceives of itself being at the center. It thus suffers from a habitual state of inflated self-assurance if not fanaticism, in which the extraordinary and supernatural unconsciously infuse the worldliest things, from golf to guns, from cars to baseball, from fame to notoriety.

On his third visit to America, in 1912, Jung gave an interview to the *New York Times* magazine in which he offered a number of startling observations about the

American psyche, seeing a lack of self-awareness and an associated split between the upper and lower levels of the psyche. There he says,

> It seems to me that you are about to discover yourselves. You have discovered everything else—all the land of this continent, all the resources, all the hidden things of Nature which can serve you in the building of your Nation.[33]

However, to make proper use of these things, he suggests "you will have to study your own self-control" and "analyze your own consciousness."[34] "You will have to admit," he goes on, "that you have been hiding from yourselves ever since the Puritans and Huguenots came to this country."[35] The pressing nature of this project, he offers, has to with a polarization in the American psyche between self-control and emotion, or what he refers to as "prudery" and "brutality."[36]

Jung perceives the American mind as "very direct . . . very logical," spending "much of its time with what we call reality . . . in order to bring forth . . . great enterprises."[37] He goes on to call the style of thinking he observes "abstract" and "mechanical," clearly building a similar case to Tocqueville's for the lack of self-reflection and philosophical sophistication. For Jung, this amounts to a lack of introspective thinking, which is accompanied by widespread symptoms of "nervous disease" or "neurasthenia," the somatization of psychological disturbance.[38] As he puts it rather simply, "You are uncomfortable. But you do not know that you are unhappy."[39] Although Jung perceived a dawning capacity for psycho-cultural development, more than a century later his confidence seems misplaced.[40]

American self-interest requires American self-knowledge, without which a polarity of egoic concern and unconscious disturbance take hold. This is where the advice offered by Tocqueville and Jung converges. Although Tocqueville made a deep study of the nation over several years, and Jung's observations were derived mainly from a handful of short visits and a small group of American patients, the depth of Jung's understanding of the human psyche, which focused on the ill-effects of psychological one-sidedness, lends equal weight to his insights.

Contemporary conditions

The paranoid style, described by Richard Hofstadter in 1963 as a recurring phenomenon in American politics,[41] is also a recurring expression of America's failed self-reflection. As an externalization of the unconscious knock on the door of the mind, paranoia is the result of deploying psychological defenses against the burden of inner conflict. The conscious outlook ends up dogged by the conviction that hidden forces are at work to derail the American way and then reinforced in the face of a perceived enmity. Having always been a feature of frontier mind (recall Bly's quip about the Puritan suspicion of wilderness), this inclination reached a peak after World War II when the projection of power across the globe was swiftly followed by the "Red Scare" on the political front and film noir in the cinema. Dark forces seemed suddenly afoot and in a way that was disproportionate to the objective dangers of the Cold War. Arguably, this was also a period in which an idealization of everyday American life took place, with the baby boom, economic expansion, the start of rock 'n' roll, and the new wonder of time-saving devices. Once again, the American psyche seemed deeply split, and a vicious psychological circle was evident: The more frontierism takes hold, the more it is haunted by the ghosts of the past; the more haunted it is, the more subject it becomes to paranoid projections; the more paranoia it experiences, the more the hold tightens. The horizonal outlook then becomes either short-sighted or overreaching. The resistance to civil rights was the short-sightedness; Vietnam was the overreach. Inside and outside, the world becomes more threatening. Obstacles, both actual and conjured, seem to multiply, crises unfold, leaders oscillate between attempting to face prevailing conditions and trying to reinstate the frontier. President Carter attempted the former and seemed to fail; his penchant for moral reckoning became tangled in the new global complexities. President Reagan tried the latter and seemed to succeed; his cowboy countenance, Hollywood persona, and Cold War "win" met the mythic expectations. But the division in the national psyche continued on.

After starting the third millennium with the deep national wound of 9/11 and deploying the manic defense of control, contempt, and triumph, flexing its military muscle rather than searching its soul, America's frontierism has been continually hampered. The neatly packaged "War on Terror" brought little control and triumph, and the contempt only squandered opportunities for new levels of international cooperation. During this period, the online world also began to serve as a hothouse for viewpoints that might otherwise be left out in the cold, with the defensive postures multiplying in a desperate attempt to deny prevailing conditions and reinstate the frontier posture. But this virtual frontierism soon revealed a realm of gathering darkness. Enter Donald J. Trump and the spectacle of self-interest entirely stripped of right understanding.

Whereas volumes have been written, are being written, and will be written about the rise and fall of Trump, few recognize that it has been this divisive figure's posture—his attitude toward conditions arising inside and outside the country—that secured his power. Vast numbers of Americans have failed to see through his narcissism because they too are prone to grandiose fabrications that compensate for an absence of soul. Trump promised to keep everything moving forward, toward a restoration of a threatened ideal—to Make America Great Again. Whether there was ever a time when America was great is beside the point, because its greatness has always been ahistorical and without the complexities and ambiguities that surround sober accounts of actual events. In this way, Trump managed to extract the promise and the peril of frontier orientation and create compelling if caricatured renderings of both.

There can be little question that Trump deepened the chasm between the American ego and the American unconscious, not only through constant lying but through the uncanny ability to model and induce states of dissociation, so that the disconnect between what he said and did was of little immediate consequence. As Schenk wrote, even before the rise of Trump, "If America's mythic gaze is perpetually caught on the horizon, drawn toward a promised land of plastic images, and the spin of artificial language weaves an obfuscating veil, then the actuality of what is at hand inevitably becomes lost."[42] Again and again in American history, plastic images triumph and actuality is lost.

It is thus entirely fitting that Trump's rise would coincide with another phase of profoundly paranoid thinking, this time in the form of outlandish conspiracy theories, which buoyed his presidency all the way through to the January 6, 2021, insurrection. Trump's main ploy, to run for office as an outsider, promising "to drain the swamp" of Washington, DC, required turning institutions and processes of government into a source of distrust and suspicion and aligning his political enemies with this source. With the help of some imaginative political operators and right-wing commentators, he conjured the ominous perception of a "deep state" aiming to keep the liberal elite in power, frequently implying it was operating with the aid of America's traditional international allies rather than its enemies. Suspicion could thus be cast in all directions. This fantasy came from the same mold Hofstadter identified decades before, naming "the central perception of the paranoid style—the existence of a vast, insidious, preternaturally effective international conspiratorial network designed to perpetrate acts of the most fiendish character."[43] As simply pulling the strings of government was not fiendish enough, the orchestrators of the movement that became known as QAnon added the finishing touches: Trump's opponent, Hillary Clinton, and other leading figures on the political left were at the center of an international pedophile ring and Satanic cult. As bizarre and "supernatural" as this movement turned out, it epitomized the broadly paranoid posture Trump embodied: If he wasn't playing the music, he was whistling the tune.

Like his narcissism, Trump's own paranoia, as well as the splitting, projection, and demonization that were a constant feature of his rhetoric, lent credibility to the whole socio-political disaster, encouraging millions to think the way he did. Hofstadter's description of the paranoid style as exhibiting "qualities of heated exaggeration, suspiciousness, and conspiratorial fantasy"[44] alongside "the feeling of persecution"[45] could not be more fitting.

Grandin argues that Trump's wall was something of a response to the frontier myth meeting its end—"a monument to disenchantment,"[46] as he puts it. But it is, at the same time, a potent symbol of Trump's defensive psychology, which, I would argue, is perfectly matched with the defensive thinking that ignites every time the frontier is at risk of discovering its limits or the duplicity its preservation needs to maintain is threatened. Trump's sixth sense for attacking everything that could be perceived as a challenge to the frontierist faith—gun control, immigration, liberal media, climate change, identity politics—has made him a cult figure, even in the face of political defeat. The kind of thinking and worldview he embraces casts aside anything containing the barest hint of the American shadow, even as he enacts that shadow. From the top down, any real insight into the American psyche is thwarted. What Tocqueville observed almost two centuries ago has thus only become more ingrained: Alongside American sophistication lies a pervasive epistemological naivete and a resistance to consensus views of reality that only invites wild fantasy—the "extraordinary" that thrives just beneath the surface.

To work backwards then, to get to the kind of "self-interest rightly understood" that Tocqueville named as the pivot for authentic growth of the American character, to take up Jung's challenge of national introspection, to go deep enough to expose the archetypal roots of its frontierism, the nation must begin by peeling back the layers of its defensive, fundamentalist-style thinking. There it might discover a deeper kind of religious pursuit, one that involves recollecting rather than dissociating, making room for the known and the unknown, and realizing the only viable way forward is one that can join the future and the past, the immediate and the universal.

Ultimate horizons

Following the complete mapping of the Earth, the external manifestation of the frontier has moved to outer space, where prospective exploration and possible exploitation have given rise to two distinct fantasies. In the *Star Trek* fantasy, the extraterrestrial realm assumes the role of the "the final frontier" and carries forth an "end of history"-style ethos that bears witness to democratic values going beyond the heavens and seeking a harmonious integration of human, alien, and artificial life. While no longer absorbed by imperialist intentions, other critical challenges of contemporary civilization are projected onto this futurist undertaking. One involves the collision of humanism and rationalism, and, by extension, humanism and "technologism," initially portrayed in the series-defining Kirk–Spock relationship. Another, present in later installments of the series, concerns the allure of the hive mind in the shape of "the Borg," a cyborg race who assume the role of arch-enemy and refer to themselves as "the collective." In this *Star Trek* fantasy of the extended frontier, we thus find a reflection of the shadow dynamics present in Jung's early warnings about the modern mind, struggling with rationalism, the mass mind, and the way these proclivities threaten psychic integrity.

The other fantasy associated with this futuristic extension of the frontier involves imagined encounters with hostile alien species who range from being hell-bent on human destruction to resisting our attempts to colonize other worlds. I have written elsewhere about how the insect alien figure in particular shows the unconscious face of human greed and ecological manipulation turning to thwart us.[47] The consistently associated motif in this fantasy is technological overreach. In essence, the destructive, devouring alien thus appears to be a monstrous omen from the unconscious in response to the prospect of a boundless technocracy.

Among other reflections on the expansionist dimensions of American myth, Schenk notes that America has "a quasi-religious faith in technology itself."[48] The religious dimensions of post-industrial technologies in particular have also been thoroughly laid out by others.[49] As one might expect, the split between light and dark, the creative and the destructive, pervades this largely Americanized religion of technology and its dreamscape, just as it has in the forms of frontierism that have already played out. Jung had already observed early last century that America "does not understand it is facing its most tragic moment: a moment in which it must make a choice to master its machines or to be devoured by them."[50] That moment has now stretched across the late modern era.

Yet it is not just the venture beyond the Earth that has given rise to revealing if fantastical scenarios. Our turn to the new frontiers of cyberspace and artificial intelligence has found another vast terrain to mine and commodify—our very own natures. The new horizon for the post-industrial entrepreneur and corporation, whose concentrated efforts are fittingly housed along the far edge of the American West, concerns minds and bodies and falls under the broad heading of posthumanism, which has been called "the worldview that is ascendant" in American culture.[51] This extension of the frontier involves nothing less than the redirection of the evolutionary process, a remaking of ourselves as cyborgs, whether functionally or literally, according to our own willful desires. Among posthumanists, here we also find the notion that God has provided us with the tools and resources to complete what biological evolution started.

As we might expect, tropes of self-destruction and techno takeovers also haunt this imagined future, with rogue robots and other diabolical extensions of artificial intelligence playing the same role as the invading aliens. Here, too, we find the motif of creating a New Eden, always forged through the transcending of natural bounds. Some extrapolations of current innovation already influential in technology circles, such as neural implants and nanotechnology, have us eventually abandoning the flesh and thriving as immortal beings in cyberspace, spreading whatever kind of intelligence exists at this point throughout the universe—a fantasy of ultimate colonization.

In their compelling book *Projecting the Shadow: The Cyborg Hero in American Film*, Janice Rushing and Thomas Frentz make the case for creating a "transmodern frontier,"[52] a transformation of the modern frontier at the heart of American identity, which suffers from "the attempt to separate understanding from valuing"[53] and from an ego that "can only perfect itself by controlling the Other."[54] To this end, in their grappling with the American shadow, they "tie together three myths—the Indian hunter (the premodern), the white hunter (the modern), and the technological hunter (the postmodern)"[55]—and show that, in many science fiction films in particular, the technological hunter (our present-day posture), by aiming to extend the frontier, only ends up becoming the hunted—that is, the victim of their own creations. This occurs because of a failure to learn the lessons of the past, especially the way the hubris of colonialism and industrialization has cast aside premodern sensibilities, enacted to the extreme in the white hunter's decimation of the more holistic and ritually contained hunting practices of the Indian. Among recent nightmarish renderings of this theme, the cultural imagination has produced *Westworld*,[56] a television series that overtly unites the ideal of the Wild West with the recurring motif of the humanoid beings we dare to create eventually turning on us. The enantiodromia repeated in these tales may be construed as the return of the Titans in a world that fails to recognize the gods, or as the return of the id following a failed psychological initiation and maturation. But the essential dynamic is the same: A psychic division occurs in which a raw drive for power eventually upends the utopian vision. Such images of the future are extrapolations of American frontierism pursued to its psychotic end, fully dissociated from the realities gathering before us.

Conclusion

I end these reflections on prospective journeys beyond both Earth and human to underscore just how far American frontierism could extend and to highlight the ultimate implications of failing to shed light on the American unconscious. Following Jung's formulation, this unconsciousness has already begun to be lived out as fate, not only in the collisions with the limitations and sensibilities an interconnected and multicultural world generates, but in inner divisions and their production of leaders who exploit rather than engage prevailing conditions. Whether a more conscious turn to this unconsciousness begins by recognizing the histories of America's Indigenous and Black peoples, contemplating the manic movement toward environmental self-destruction, grasping the dangers posed by the unmitigated horizontality of the online world, or glimpsing the escapist extension of utopianism into fantasies of a post-Earth, posthuman future, what these efforts share is the goal of cracking open America's identity complex enough to allow the cultural imagination to find new forms—forms better able to unite the future and the past, what lives in the land and beyond it, and what may generate and preserve an axis of understanding that joins America's spiritual reach to its psycho-cultural reality. Only such a marriage of action and idea will bring about a more conscious way forward.

The soul of America, its deep character and all that turns around its psychic core, exists somewhere between its frontier consciousness and what it keeps putting behind it. Yet only now is it being forced to account for all it has excluded. From the perspective of its egoic interests, this has been perceived as a painful defeat and undoing of its usual way, which is to meet each crisis with heroic overcoming. What it must learn, by contrast, is that regression is often purposeful and, properly tended, can precipitate a growth of character and an expansion of consciousness. If it is to grasp the current state of humanity and its power to determine the course of existence more widely, it must also grasp the necessity of such a development.

It was Heraclitus, a founding father of depth psychology, who formulated the relationship between character and fate. If I am correct in aligning frontierism with the American character, it will be its fate to either reconcile the two sides of this configuration or be torn apart by them. While reconciliation would involve a more complete understanding of itself, which may also create enough consciousness to navigate the prevailing changes to human experience and knowledge, further division would be the basis of its eventual demise. In this regard, we may only speculate as to whether America's confrontation with its shadow, which would awaken it to the one-sided nature of its Manifest Destiny, might in some way coincide with

Jung's perception of an emerging myth involving the completion of the Christian God image.[57] In other words, at the core of America's complex of identity we may also locate a concentration of the mythic change unfolding in the deeper reaches of the Western psyche.

In the end, America's destiny may be driven by God, but its fate has everything to do with the image of God that actually guides its actions. Whether this God image continues to be construed as an unmoving dogma or is recognized as a force that works through the collective psyche and thus constitutes a co-created reality that integrates the nation's actual experience will be the makeweight. In this regard, Jung's compelling definition of God, which he provided Americans in an interview with *Good Housekeeping* magazine in 1961, may provide a fitting prompt:

> To this day God is the name by which I designate all things which cross my willful path violently and recklessly, all things which upset my subjective views, plans and intentions and change the course of my life for better or worse.[58]

This definition fits the overall trajectory of American frontierism, but, for America to take up such a view, it would need to make a full manifest of how it has so far embraced its destiny and come to see ultimate value in accepting this more complete reality.

Notes

1 American frontierism was first described by the historian Frederick Jackson Turner in 1893, who put forth the "Frontier Thesis," also known as the "Turner Thesis." See Frederick Jackson Turner, *The Frontier in American History* (New York: Holt, Rinehart & Winston, 1920).
2 Alexis de Tocqueville, *Democracy in America and Two Essays on America*, trans. Gerald E. Bevan (New York: Penguin Books, 2003), 223ff.
3 Greg Grandin, *The End of the Myth: From the Frontier to the Border Wall in the Mind of America* (New York: Metropolitan Books, 2019).
4 Murray Stein, "On the Politics of Individuation in the Americas," in *The Cultural Complex: Contemporary Jungian Perspectives on Psyche and Society*. Thomas Singer and Samuel L. Kimbles, eds. (New York: Brunner-Routledge, 2004), 263.
5 Singer and Kimbles, eds.
6 Ronald Schenk, *American Soul: A Cultural Narrative* (New Orleans: Spring Journal Books, 2012), 83–84.
7 See, for example, C.G. Jung, *Aion: Researches into the Phenomenology of the Self*. CW 9ii (London: Routledge and Kegan Paul, 1959).
8 Stein, 262.
9 Russell Means, "Fighting Words on the Future of the Earth," in *Questioning Technology: A Critical Anthology*, John Zerzan and Alice Carnes, eds. (London: Freedom Press, 1988), 73.
10 Robert Bly, *A Little Book on the Human Shadow*, William Booth, ed. (San Francisco: Harper, 1988), 11.
11 Ibid.
12 Means, 78.

13 Ipek S. Burnett, *A Jungian Inquiry into the America Psyche: The Violence of Innocence* (London: Routledge, 2019), 33.
14 Ibid.
15 Ibid.
16 Schenk, xiii.
17 Ibid.
18 Ibid., xiv.
19 Ibid.
20 Burnett, 13.
21 Ibid.
22 Grandin, 2.
23 Ibid., 3.
24 Tocqueville, 163.
25 Ibid., 164.
26 Ibid., 223ff.
27 Schenk, 13.
28 Ibid., 15.
29 Ibid., 19.
30 Ibid.
31 Tocqeville, 164.
32 See Sarah Posner, *God's Profits: Faith, Fraud, and the Republican Crusade for Values Voter* (Sausalito, CA: PoliPoint Press, 2008).
33 C.G. Jung. *C. G. Jung Speaking: Interviews and Encounters*, William McGuire and R.F.C. Hull, eds. (London: Thames & Hudson, 1978), 14–15.
34 Ibid., 15.
35 Ibid.
36 Ibid., 14.
37 Ibid., 22.
38 Ibid., 17–22.
39 Ibld., 22.
40 It must be noted here that, while Jung attributes the brutality he observes to the history of colonization and slave ownership, he fails to question the impetus toward these things in the first place. He appears to rationalize this stance by stating, "I am a psychoanalyst. It is for me to try to understand, and where one understands one cannot judge." Nonetheless, his perspective strikes our contemporary grasp of these matters as one of privileging colonialism.
41 Richard Hofstadter, *The Paranoid Style in American Politics and Other Essays* (New York: Vintage Books, 2008).
42 Schenk, 39.
43 Hofstadter, 14.
44 Ibid., 3.
45 Ibid., 4.
46 Grandin, 272.
47 Glen Slater, "Aliens and Insects," in *Varieties of Mythic Experience: Essays on Religion, Psyche and Culture*, Dennis Patrick Slattery and Glen Slater, eds. (Einsiedeln, Switzerland: Daimon Verlag, 2008), 189–207.
48 Schenk, 18.
49 See Erik Davis, *Techgnosis* (New York: Harmony Books, 1998); Richard F. Noble, *The Religion of Technology* (New York: Penguin Books, 1999).
50 Jung, *Speaking*, 18.
51 Leon Wieseltier, "Among the Disrupted." *The New York Times*, January 18, 2015.

52 Janice Hocker Rushing and Thomas B. Frentz, *Projecting the Shadow: The Cyborg Hero in American Film* (Chicago: University of Chicago Press, 1995), 29ff.

53 Hocking and Frentz, 31.

54 Ibid., 40.

55 Ibid., 48.

56 *Westworld*, 2016–. Created by Lisa Joy and Jonathan Nolan. HBO Entertainment.

57 See, especially, Jung, *Aion*.

58 C.G. Jung, Interview. *Good Housekeeping*, December 1961, 64, 139–141.

Chapter 5

The American way of war[1]

Edward Tick

The mythic arena and archetypal dimensions of war

When bombs fall, bullets fly, and guns rattle, men charge and scream and grapple, forests and mountains burn, villages and cities are destroyed, when the earth fragments beneath us and the air is thick with poisons, surely, we are in an extreme and merciless arena. During combat, the heart beats too hard. Adrenaline pumps too fast. Muscles, bones, and mind strain beyond capacity and still perform. Sensations bombard too quickly to be processed. Thoughts and feelings fly by and disappear unrecognized.

Then, suddenly, the system still in overdrive, all is still. We try to awaken from the trance-like experience. Where there was a forest or a village, fire and devastation. Human bodies, or perhaps just parts, are scattered around. We look for friends. Some, with whom we were just talking, groan in pain. Others lie at our feet and will never respond again. The world has returned, but it is different forever, and we helped make it so. And we too are different forever.

Nor do we have time to figure out who or what we have become. Waiting and watching start again. Still on edge, days may pass with nothing but routine tasks to perform. Boredom reaches an extreme and can be worse than combat. We long to break the tedium that has no outlet but through the gun. Finally, we crave battle.

The war zone is an arena of elemental conditions. We stand on the knife edge of life and death, good and evil, preservation and destruction. Human beings against whom we are arrayed have been rendered "enemy" and "other," so different and threatening that they must be irradicated. Simultaneously, life on our side must be protected at all costs.

General Sherman famously said, "War is hell." He wrote,

I confess, without shame, that I am sick and tired of fighting—its glory all moonshine; even success the most brilliant is over dead and mangled bodies, with the anguish and lamentations of distant families, appealing to me for sons, husbands, fathers . . . It is only with those who have never heard a shot, never heard the shrieks and groans of the wounded and lacerated . . . that cry for more blood, more vengeance, more desolation.[2]

DOI: 10.4324/9781003325765-8

In war, literally and archetypally, we are in horrific real-world conditions creating a hell on earth. We are simultaneously in the mythic Underworld where the human shadow and existential conditions dominate. Some people may behave with great courage, self-sacrifice, and kindness. Yet with the dictum "kill or be killed" ruling survival, others display madness, violence, cruelty, or cowardice. And always there is suffering, pain, anguish, despair, and loss of meaning.

War destroys ordinary categories of existence. It blasts the participant with experiences of supernatural intensity, projecting each participant into a mythic dimension of cosmic power. There only such ultimates matter as keeping your socks dry while you and your neighbor survive one more day. World War II correspondent Ernie Pyle wrote from the front lines, "War makes strange giant creatures out of us little routine men who inhabit the earth."[3] We become both miniscule and gargantuan.

In combat, the soul's container and patterns are shattered. As James Hillman writes, "Some accidents swamp the boat, bust the form. For example, 'shell shock,' as post-traumatic stress disorder was called during the First World War."[4] In *The Iliad*, Homer relates that, during the Trojan War, Aphrodite the goddess of love was wounded by the fierce warrior Diomedes and fled to Olympus for safety. Here is a mythic representation of how love and the soul itself are wounded by savagery and try to flee connections with this world.

War breaks open a society's forms as well, cracking our social containers so that the cultural shadow floods out, revealing the best and worst in a culture and society as well as in its participants. From the Afghanistan War, a Marine declares,

> The war was a decade too long. It lost its mission, pursued meaningless objectives, killed civilians, lost hearts and minds, and was in the wrong place against the wrong people. But helping their women achieve freedom and rights, trying to build schools and end child abuse, and rescuing allies we left was correct. I can't resolve the ways my own and our country's worst and best clash in my mind.[5]

As a willful activity chosen by their society, civilized people believe that war is, or ought to be, the final strategy used under extreme and threatening conditions when other options have failed. "I am a pacifist until they break into my house and try to kill my family," declared Jason Moon, an Iraq combat veteran in 2003–2004.[6]

Clearly, war is rarely a last resort. Many small, traditional cultures used it regularly as a rite of passage for youth, with rituals before and after, containment of conflict, and casualties kept to a minimum. In contrast, in the history of mass civilizations from ancient times to the present, it appears regularly, usually with patriotic exuberance at its advance and, to the shock of young, innocent troops, destruction and death in its wake.

War invites all that is primitive, suppressed, denied, rationalized, or disguised in a culture to display itself in force and savagery on that part of the globe chosen, with endless political rationalizations, to be its arena. It reveals, releases, and expresses the cultural shadow.

War, mass psychology, and the repetition compulsion

After fighting fascism in World War II, Jean-Paul Sartre focused on racial violence in the United States. His play *The Respectful Prostitute* was produced in 1946, shortly after the war's end. A black man is accused of raping a white woman on a train in the American South. To protect the society's power structure and prejudices, the white accuser who was the actual attacker and local authorities pressure the woman to falsely accuse an innocent man. The accuser argues,

> The first Clarke [family name] cleared a whole forest . . . killed seventeen Indians with his bare hands . . . his son practically built this town; he was friends with George Washington and died at Yorktown for American independence. My great-grandfather was chief of the Vigilantes in San Francisco.[7]

After reciting his ancestral history, the character argues, "We made this country, and its history is ours . . . I have the right to live; there are things to be done and I am expected to do them."[8]

In addition to exposing social ills, Sartre presents the thought-world of power figures who stand on their conqueror's version of history to justify their manipulation of the law, the truth, and the underclasses. Here, as throughout history, are enacted versions of: "the ends justify the means," "might makes right," "shoot first and ask questions later," "to the victor go the spoils," "the winner writes the history." Embedded is the belief that "my family earned these rights, powers, and privileges by generations of service and sacrifice." Such transgenerational factors commonly inspire youth to enter military service. Many families trace their service history generations and centuries back. Many Americans carry a sense of entitlement to victories and spoils, no matter its impact on other peoples or cultures. Countless enlistees want the war experience, regardless of the cause, mission, purpose, or place of a particular conflict. These matters operate unconsciously in individuals and collectively drive a culture.

A culture and a society are not independent entities, but a conglomerate of individuals, each carrying a psyche that inhabits us all. In Jung's words, "society is the sum total of individuals in need of redemption,"[9] that is, still unconscious and not spiritually awake. Thus, societies act as do individuals, out of a collective mass consciousness that is largely unconscious and conforms to what Jung called "unreflected belief," a generalized, publicly accepted and transmitted mythological, cultural, historical system. These beliefs represent the popular mythology rather than the true story. "Unreflected beliefs" turn individuals into droplets of the mass. Their beliefs represent the collective ego creating a national persona, an acceptable public story that disguises or hides the shadow and its harmful actions. From this base, the society acts out its hidden dimensions. Vietnam War navy veteran Lawrence Markworth served offshore on the USS Castor from 1963 to 1965. He testifies:

> At the time I enlisted, during the Cuban Missile Crisis, I believed as a nation we had to stop the spread of Communism. Years later I realized that I joined

because I wasn't safe at home. But the American belief system sustained me until . . . near the end of my deployment I visited the ground zero museum in Nagasaki. That visit was the beginning of my unraveling of my belief that America could do no wrong. Six months after discharge I switched to the other side, a radicalized student vehemently protesting. The best words to describe my feelings then were betrayal and rage.[10]

Psychodynamic psychology since Freud has recognized the repetition compulsion as a core of neuroses. If our wounds remain unconscious and unhealed, we endlessly repeat actions symbolic of our original transgenerational birth, childhood, and life traumas. In psychoanalyst Theodore Reik's words, we "reproduce a repressed experience instead of remembering it"; we are "compelled to resurrect a piece of forgotten life."[11] Demonstrated in individual life histories, this is equally true of nations, attested in the well-known statement by philosopher George Santayana, "Those who cannot remember the past are condemned to repeat it." Reik observed that the compulsion to repeat conceals darker motives. It fosters a "neurosis of destiny" that enables the development of exceptionalism and a feeling of innocence, as if life were compensating for unacknowledged earlier traumatic experiences. Ultimately, "the unconquered past is recreated in the compulsion."[12]

War and the American birth trauma

The United States has been called "a country made by war."[13] This refers in part to remarkable advances in science, technology, medicine, and other fields achieved out of the difficult necessities of waging wars. Radar, penicillin, sulfa drugs, plastic surgery, synthetic rubber, blood banks, freeze-drying, and computers are just a few of the many innovations useful in civilian life that came out of the two world wars. But "a country made by war" also highlights the endless history of American wars and the fact that, since World War II, the United States has evolved into the dominant world power exerting global influence while operating on a permanent war budget. On the unconscious level, our wars are repetitions of traumatic experiences and wounds in the nation's founding and development. Again, as in individual psychology, difficult truths regarding the nation's founding conflict with the dominant, tolerable, inculcated mass mythology.

By the time of the European arrivals, the continent was not pristine wilderness for the taking and settling. It had long been heavily settled and developed by its native inhabitants. The region around Plymouth Colony settled by the Pilgrim refugees had been the homeland of the Wampanoag peoples for 10,000 years.

The Pilgrims are popularly hailed as first arrivals, and the Thanksgiving story our beneficent founding myth. This disguises the real story. Pilgrims were members of a radical faction of the Puritans known as the English Separatist Church. Separatists were critical of the Church of England and sought independence to pursue their own religious values. In England, their practices were outlawed, and practitioners were persecuted and sometimes imprisoned, tortured, or executed. American children are taught that they were seeking religious freedom but not the degree of intolerance they practiced nor the trauma and oppression they recreated on this continent.

Contrary to grade school mythology, Pilgrims were not the first European arrivals. Native peoples had previously encountered white intruders who had kidnapped some to sell as slaves. The first encounter between Pilgrims and Natives occurred about a month after the Mayflower landed, in December 1616, and was a violent skirmish.

At the first Thanksgiving, held in 1621, Pilgrims shared a harvest feast with the Pokanokets. No turkey or potatoes present—though that is the national meal reinforcing the popular myth. Deer meat was provided by the Wampanoags.

Refugees from England followed the Mayflower. Two more ships arrived in 1621, another in 1623, and one thousand refugees in 1630. The New World was also used by the British as a dumping ground for their prisoners of war, petty criminals, and other unwanted groups. Native and settler factions practiced cordial relations for several decades, but relations deteriorated as arrivals occupied more land, crowded out the regional inhabitants, attempted or forced religious conversion, and spread decimating diseases.

Finally, these collisions exploded in violence. It is popular mythology to think of the Revolution as America's first war, a just uprising for freedom against a tyrannical power. But it was not America's first war. Nor were the French and Indian Wars. They were both world wars involving foreign powers disputing possession of this continent. The British, French, and Germans not only fought with or against Americans, but in proxy against each other. Arguably, the first American war setting the pattern for all to follow was King Phillip's War, also referred to as the Second War of Puritan Conquest.[14]

By the beginning of this conflict, lasting from 1675 to 1678, the Natives had experienced the new colonists as invading, conquering, exploiting people and resources, destroying ancient forests, stealing land, imposing laws they did not understand or conform to, kidnapping, enslaving, and killing their brethren. It included pre-emptive attacks on innocent villages, massacres of noncombatant women, children, and elders, burning and razing villages and food sources, introducing smallpox to cause plague among the inhabitants, breaking alliances and treaties, and turning Natives against each other. Perhaps the worst of these was the so-called Battle of Turner's Falls, fought on May 19, 1676, and more accurately known as the Peskeompscut massacre. About 150 inexperienced settler militia attacked a peaceful sleeping fishing village on the Connecticut River while its warriors were away, slaughtering about 415 women, children, and elderly and looting the camp.

The Native perspective was that the war was their resistance to invasion. Their warriors fought back after this attack and in many other encounters, also killing innocents and committing atrocities. This war left about 5,000 New England inhabitants dead, three-quarters of them the outnumbered and out-armed Natives. It decimated some tribes such that they never recovered. In percentages of population killed, this was America's deadliest war, twice as costly as the Civil War and seven times more costly than the Revolution.

A Seneca chief gave both George Washington and his father the Indian names "town taker" or "devourer of villages."[15] In 1779, when the Iroquois sided with the English, believing it the best alliance to protect their homelands, Washington ordered, "Your immediate objects are the total destruction and devastation of their settlements and the capture of as many prisoners of every age and sex as possible." This led to a ruthless campaign that destroyed 20 villages.[16] This policy, a continuation of that established by the Puritans, raged against the Native peoples to the end in the Ghost Dance Massacre at Wounded Knee in 1890. This makes the "Indian Wars" either a two-centuries-long series of wars of conquest against individual tribal nations or one long war against all Native peoples on this continent.

These wars gave form to American wars since. They were characterized by the invasion of lands not our own; ignorance of the cultures against whom we fight; dehumanization of their peoples; development of highly destructive new armaments; overwhelming influx of peoples and arms; imposition of our ways of life and law; massive exploitation and despoliation of lands and resources, making homelands poisonous and nearly uninhabitable; massive innocent and civilian casualties; massive armaments and firepower to cause "shock and awe" and overwhelm the foe; brutality, enslavement, betrayal, and murder of civilians, causing disease, starvation, destruction, and death of genocidal proportions; stealing, transporting, and kidnapping children and acclimating them into the dominant culture; and more.

In the relations and wars with the original inhabitants of this continent ever since the Indian Wars, and most American wars abroad—Mexico, the Philippines, Hawaii, Cuba, the Spanish–American War, Dominican Republic, El Salvador, Grenada, Vietnam, Iraq, Afghanistan, the many secret wars Americans are hardly aware of, the hundreds of countries around the world today in which we have military bases or secret operations—the conditions that characterized King Phillip's War have characterized American wars since. This country endlessly repeats its birth trauma and the transgenerational trauma settlers carried here.

The Vietnam War: Loss of innocence and shattering of belief

Iraq and Afghanistan, the recent "sandbox wars," were controversial, characterized by the lack of a draft, few threatened with unwanted service, desperation in the employment market, and college funding leading to many enlistments for non-patriotic reasons, and the weakness and quietness of any protest movement. Regarding war, Americans generally practice an "out of sight, out of mind" strategy; our government maintains an all-volunteer force to keep it that way, and civilians are left with the rationalization that the troops "knew what they signed up for"—never true about combat. Thus, civilians and government escape and practice denial without responsibility. Veteran Drew Mewes was a .50 caliber machine gunner in the Iraq surge from 2007 to 2009. He says, "Fighting all over the world keeps war away from our civilians so they don't know."[17]

The Vietnam War reveals archetypal dimensions that America did not then and does not now want to see.

Approximately 2.8 million individuals served in Southeast Asia, 1 million seeing combat, with an average age of 19. As early as 1978, a half million had been diagnosed as having post-traumatic stress disorder,[18] "affecting not only the veteran but countless millions of persons who are in contact with them."[19] The number of diagnosed cases has risen steadily in the decades since the war, and moral injury has more recently been identified as a significant invisible wound. Men and women in their 60s and 70s, many as they face death, find their lives still interrupted by war's aftermath.

Personal testimony from countless sources and decades of psychotherapy work with veterans reveal that few feel, in retrospect, that that war was correct, moral, justified, or honorable. In contrast, they may feel that their service was. They often develop an attitude that stretches conscience and tolerates paradox—"I am proud to have served my country when called but do not believe in the call I had to serve." Here is a Janus-faced psychic division declaring national service to be correct and honorable but service in *this* war for *these* reasons to be immoral and ignoble. Vietnam War marine Pat Guariglia tells younger veterans, "No matter how you judged your service, at least you showed up. Always be proud of that."[20] Whenever military service and its purposes are misaligned, a psychic split occurs in individuals and the nation that is the root of neurosis.

Alienation, nightmares, flashbacks, violent behavior, drug and alcohol abuse, intimacy and employment problems, throwing medals at the Pentagon, refusing to vote or pay taxes, all began before the war was over. The recent sandbox wars have been so prolonged and their generation so outspoken that we had many books, movies, and expressions from veterans even as the wars dragged on. The same issues as from the Vietnam War haunt recent returnees but in lower numbers, which enables the nation to look the other way. Currently, about 1.3 million Americans serve in the military, about 0.5 percent of the population; they are all volunteers, and non-serving citizens are asked for nothing in support of the wars, troops, or returnees. These are some reasons to call "PTSD" post-traumatic *social* disorder.[21]

During the war, massive antiwar protests, demonstrations, and actions indicated overwhelming generational pain and doubt. Not to have adequately addressed the pain of our veterans or generation during the war or since and not to have addressed the despair dominating the psyche of the generation amount to denial of an overwhelming degree. John, a tank corps veteran said, "The main lesson I learned in Vietnam is that Denial is the name of the all-American disease."[22]

What is being denied? That our youth, our families, our own, and an entire foreign nation were in pain. That we cannot participate in warfare without causing pain to ourselves and others. That war is frightening and terrible. That America's prevailing cultural mythology of patriotism, super-heroism, and geopolitical war of good against evil is wrong and misleading in its depiction of history, warfare, its human consequences, and our intentions. That, in modern times, warfare has become especially brutal as it is practiced with devasting advanced technology.

That we do not practice war with the rituals and restraint that aid participants in survival and recovery. That the United States, with democratic ideals it supposedly wants to export around the planet, is an aggressor nation building empire, imposing its military, values, and ways of life on very different peoples, as happened during the European arrival. Nobody can participate in modern warfare and emerge psychologically unscathed. The pain of war does not go away when the bullets stop flying. It gets buried in the culture, covered by false myths, acted out in public violence, and is transferred to the individual survivor to carry alone as a diagnosis of pathology.

One jungle combat survivor wrote, "What you do, you become."[23] What one does in one moment under extreme conditions may define and shape one's life forever. The repetition compulsion to make war will not be resolved or go away through conflicts, politics, or well-meaning social action.

American wars—pursuit and aftermath

As a culture, the United States claims innocence and goodness, as though the country were immune from war's unavoidable truths, paradoxes, and evils. We believe—and behave as if—and some leaders insist to this day that the country is doing God's work when invading other peoples and cultures. Europeans took this continent from its inhabitants by force and within the protective context of a God-blessed mythology. The nation has been repeating this birth drama ever since. We try to conquer other peoples and land "for their own good," for our Manifest Destiny, because "we're number one," we know and do better than other people, it is our sacred task to slay an evil demon incarnate in the foreign other, we are "nation builders," our form of government and way of life can be imposed by force, and we want their resources to continue feeding the ravenous "defense" industry and consumer culture while finding new cheap sources of labor. All within the blessing-curse of having this mythology upheld in World War II.

The Vietnam War was conducted within this mythological context. Many young soldiers who went to war, and Americans at home, believed we were right in fighting the spread of Communism. The Vietnamese people's resistance and willingness to suffer massive casualties and atrocities, the failures of our political and military aims over so long a span of time, the pain, anger, and dysfunctionality of returning veterans did not teach the country to shed innocence. A devastating lesson to many veterans was the discovery that they, as agents of the nation, were not the good cavalry saving helpless settlers from savages. Rather, those we were trying to save saw us as another savage invader needing to be stopped by their painful, heroic sacrifices. This discovery shocked the archetypal foundation on which their psychology of goodness and innocence was based:

> While the Vietnamese family stared at me, I stared out the door of their hut . . . like a picture frame . . . I was staring out through God's eyes. I watched . . . as . . . men I fought with, the good guys, yelled like idiots and pushed these little

people around . . . I watched my buddies walk over to the hut right across from me . . . and torch it.

Suddenly something woke up in me. Good and evil. Honor and dishonor. Right and wrong. They were real, living things. You earned them by torturing yourself with questions until you knew what was right and good and honorable . . . because you saw.

These weren't gooks! They were a helpless mother and her terrified little children! They weren't evil, enemies, or bad guys. We were!

Everything turned around. I wanted to raise my M-16 and blast away at these crazy marauding Americans who were wasting this helpless village.

I walked off in a stupor while they torched my hut with my family in it, where I found my soul, where I figured out the truth. I was in a daze for a long time. Then I went numb. At the very moment my soul woke up and I could see the truth for the first time, at that very second when I knew we were evil, it fled, I lost it.[24]

A cloud of despair and moral stain settled over the American psyche. Archetypally and collectively, the countless veterans in chronic anguish are symptoms of a national soul sickness. The first President Bush staged the Gulf War, in part, to overcome the Vietnam War's aftermath. He wanted a decisive outcome to "finally kick in totally the Vietnam syndrome,"[25] believing that our national soul sickness stemmed from losing the war. "But all the Gulf War proved," one combat veteran said, "was that we Americans don't like to lose." Afterwards, we had the mysterious Gulf War syndrome which, by 1995, afflicted more than 30 thousand of the troops sent to the Gulf.[26] This syndrome ushered in a new generation of veterans suffering a gestalt of soul sickness nobody can explain, officials deny, and is researched as a medical rather than holistic condition. Reclaiming innocence through more warfare does not work.

War can teach its participants that life is short and fragile, its challenges must be met with courage, we are agents of both creation and destruction and should act with wisdom, restraint, and compassion. Further, America claims innocence as its fundamental character trait. "[B]elief allowed them to go forward uncorrupted in the midst of dirty doings, untouched by their own shadow, innocent," James Hillman writes about characteristic American public figures. "[P]recisely this American habit of belief . . . must be the essence of the American character."[27]

The same holds of veterans. As a culture, we believe that young troops should be able "to go forward uncorrupted in the midst of dirty doings" and return home innocent and well. After the Abu Ghraib prison scandal revealing torture and abuse, Donald Rumsfeld said, "No Americans I know would do that." But they were Americans, and they did it. It is a historical straight line from the Turner's Falls massacre to Washington's extermination orders to Wounded Knee to My Lai to Abu Ghraib.

At a movie screening one night soon after his arrival in Vietnam, Preston Stern, a Quaker who volunteered as an infantryman to witness the war as "the defining event of my generation," watched Yul Brynner in *The Magnificent Seven* shoot down evil banditos. Afterwards he declared, "Now I know why I'm here and what my country wants me to do."[28] Many American veterans from all wars refer to John Wayne, in movies the quintessential war hero, as their guiding cultural role model: "I was seduced by World War II and John Wayne movies."[29] John Wayne avoided conscription and never served in war. Yet, through public performance of how we wish war to be, he became a role model for American soldiers. Hollywood consciousness expresses American innocence, replicating through technology the self-creation of the American Adam free to start over on his own terms. As we remake life narratives in the movies, so we believe we can do with our lives.

American servicemen were portrayed as coming home from World War II with no pain. The supposed minority of psychological casualties were hidden in back wards of veterans' hospitals. America was proud of its successful participation in the worldwide battle against evil. It moved on to the good life defined by consumerism, with only nostalgic glances backwards. The GI Bill that treated World War II veterans generously at the conflict's end is the historical exception rather than the rule for treatment of returnees. Perhaps what was unique about the Vietnam War was that so many people, both veterans and non-veterans, screamed out against denial. "The capacity to deny, to remain innocent, to use belief as a protection against sophistications of every sort—intellectual, aesthetic, moral, psychological—keeps the American character from awakening," says Hillman.[30] The severity of veterans' suffering with and symptoms of post-traumatic stress disorder is in direct response to the enormity of our culture's denial of their pain. Post-traumatic stress disorder, in its archetypal sense, represents the anguish, dislocation, betrayal, and rage of the collective soul as it attempts to awaken from such massive denial and neglect.

The destruction of veterans' innocence is not an individual psychological phenomenon, damaging but a component of the passage to adulthood. The war removed many veterans from participating or girding themselves in the archetypal American mystique of innocence. Frank, an air force squadron commander, realized we were the bad guys as he watched the napalm bombing of beautiful, virginal mountains along the Laotian border; Walt, an army machinist, realized it when he was ordered to exhume bodies of enemy dead with his backhoe; Conrad, an artillery observer, when he recovered family pictures off a soldier he had just killed; Art, a machine gunner, as North Vietnamese were throwing themselves at his emplacement. "They had something noble to die for," he reflected. "I just wanted to survive and go home."

Recovering the times, places, and incidents during which the moral character and soul of a veteran awakened in the field is essential. The awakening is Janus-faced, looking simultaneously at both past and present, found and lost, good and evil. In the field, the marine found and lost himself at the same moment. At home and re-experiencing the war imaginally in therapy, he reclaimed his soul along with a truthful moral order.

Veterans with post-traumatic stress disorder are people with their personal and collective belief systems shattered. Such people are no longer innocent, no longer believe that we or our actions, values, or policies are inherently good. Morally and spiritually, they have left, abandoned, or felt banished from the collective mythological context. "I'm not an American," Scott, a helicopter gunner, said. He neither voted, paid taxes, nor obtained a driver's license. "I'm a citizen of the Underground."[31]

Many of the homeless on our urban streets, more than 20 or 30 percent by some estimates, are Vietnam veterans. "On any given night, an estimated two hundred and seventy-one thousand of the nation's 26.4 million veterans are homeless," 55–60 percent of these having served during the Vietnam era.[32]

Homelessness is not merely an economic condition to be remedied by social programs. Homelessness is an archetypal condition in which the state, as *polis*, the essential political body of which we are an integral part, is no longer the proper and fit home for the individual. *Nostalgia* was a name given to the traumatic wound in the Middle Ages. Veterans tell us, with homelessness and post-traumatic stress disorder, that their souls cannot be at home in America. Too many veterans from all American wars since the nation's beginning do not fit into a culture based on the unyielding belief in its own innocence and goodness, and denial of its shadow.

The American shadow at war

With innocence and belief systems shattered by the injustice and brutality of technological warfare, the psychological and cultural containers of the young men fighting were shattered. The shadow leaked, flowed, or exploded through their psychological remnants. Without humanizing restraints, the warrior archetype became free to possess the soldier and sometimes drove him berserk. The archetype itself is not inherently brutal or sadistic and can be honorable and protective. However, sadism in war and life, explains Robert Moore, occurs when the ego has been shattered and the shadow warrior possesses the psyche.[33] Young troops had insufficient ego development and/or experienced it shattered in combat and so became operatives of the shadow. Veterans with post-traumatic stress disorder and moral injury carry the ethical and spiritual stain and archetypal damage of war. They live in the shadow cast by the Shadow. The survivor must become conscious of the mythic dimensions by which his soul was damaged and the shadow dimensions he unwittingly served.

Indian country

Enemy territory in Vietnam was known as "Indian Country," with frightened or incompetent field officers; commanders making bets with soldiers' lives; learning to say "It don't mean nothing" as men looked upon their dead; burning and destroying people's homes, huts, livestock, gardens; poisoning and igniting forests and jungles; prostitution; black marketeering; drugs; rape; torture; body bags; mass executions of villagers; secret assassinations of political figures; fragging and assassinations of our own people. Not John Wayne behavior.

Think of the Vietnam War as the American frontier myth displaced to a virginal Asian forest among a people as different looking as were the Native Americans to European ancestors, reenacted in frenzy, attack helicopters and fighter planes with Indian names serving as cavalry horses, destructive modern weaponry for carbines and sabers. This is how Americans fight when the wounds of our own historical past have not been integrated but instead are given an undifferentiated arena in which to reenact it.

The recent sandbox wars have substituted the terms Taliban Country or Enemy Territory for Indian Country, but attach similar dehumanizing emotions and great threat. Veteran Drew Mewes says, "To the United States, the whole world, even the moon, is Indian Country!"[34]

"Waste them!"

The code word combatants used to indicate killing was "waste." In military slang, to waste was to kill an enemy. It was also applied to any Vietnamese person or live-stock, and to the destruction of huts, homes, villages, and rice paddies. In Vietnam, troops attempted to waste an entire people and country.

Think of the Vietnam War as consumer culture displaced to a jungle among people and a landscape not our own, with no rules or rituals to restrain or humanize it. Immature troops carried the shadow of consumerism—blind, devouring hunger, incessant making and disposing of waste—to its extreme. At war's end, the United States left behind the world's second largest military air force, dumped into the ocean, when Sai Gon was evacuated. This pattern has remained in all conflicts unto Afghanistan, where the United States left behind $7 billion of armaments. Troops in modern wars often find themselves fighting abandoned American weapons. A 14-year army veteran, Chuck Collins, who served in Kosovo, Iraq, and Afghanistan, testifies, "the phrase 'waste them' still exists and I've heard and used it when speaking of killing."[35]

"Waste them" also referred to our own. During the war, minorities and the poor were represented among our troops in numbers beyond their proportion in the population. Draft practices emptied ghettoes and hills. Young men in trouble with the law or disaffected with society were sometimes given the choice of prison or Vietnam. The war occurred at the same time as the Civil Rights Movement and heated up in Asia as did racial unrest at home. Think of the Vietnam War as population control, tear gas and water hoses on the ghettoes. The military has historically been one of the few ways out of poverty and hopelessness in America. Then and now, the way out was through fire while the country wastes its youths.

"Waste them" also refers to the treatment of returnees. No parades or home-coming rituals, spit on at airports—these were surface signs. Long-term neglect and ignorance are more insidious.[36] For decades, Agent Orange complaints were ridiculed by governmental authorities.[37] Veterans are dispensed pharmaceuticals at Veteran Administration hospitals as if they were at candy stores. Vets show computer printouts of their drug dispensation histories that read like chemistry experiments of mad scientists. In hospital, veterans were put in body coffins during flashbacks. By the late 1980s, more than 60 thousand veterans had committed suicide since returning from Vietnam, more than were killed during the entire war.[38] Imagine the Vietnam Memorial Wall in Washington as more than twice its length. Post-traumatic stress disorder is the soul screaming its anguish as America wastes the veterans carrying it. The treatment of veterans since returning from war is an unconscious collective attempt to kill the messenger.

"Shock and awe"

In contemporary times, "shock and awe" is General Colin Powell's doctrine. But it is only his name for how the United States has waged wars since its beginning. Early settlers exterminated entire native villages and poisoned populations with infected blankets. The Indian Wars were fought at the same time as the Civil War. Sherman's March to the Sea was characterized by massive civilian destruction and instituted the "scorched earth policy" that is still used. The United States remains the only nation to have used atomic weapons. In bombs dropped and non-military targets destroyed, the destruction in Vietnam even surpassed World War II. "Shock and awe" has been American fighting doctrine since colonization.

America at war now

America has carried transgenerational trauma from its inhabitants' countries of origin since its beginning. Trauma abroad is reenacted on home soil. American history has been violent and traumatic since colonization. Further, we live in a violent, traumatizing world. Along with the World Trade Center, 9/11 destroyed the country's illusion of security. Traumatized America responds with a raging power that traumatizes others.

> In response to 9/11, America has invaded and occupied two countries, bombed four others for years, killed at least 801,000 people . . . terrified millions more, tortured hundreds, detained thousands . . . create[d] a global surveillance dragnet, disposed of veterans with cruel indifference, called an entire global religion criminal . . . created at least 21 million refugees and spent as much as $6 trillion on its operations.[39]

Veterans from the sandbox wars feel abandoned, neglected, overly medicated, not given what they need for homecoming. Worse, they wonder if their wars were necessary, moral, just, or did any good. They suffer a vacuum of meaning that needs to be filled. Many want to serve in Ukraine, seeing it as a just defense of a sovereign nation against a brutal aggressor. They believe that serving there would heal their moral injury. Many do. We are still the country made by war.

War remains a large part of who we are as Americans, with almost a sixth of our federal budget going to defense, keeping troops deployed in 800 military bases around the world and engaging in counterterrorist missions in 85 countries. And yet, thanks to a series of political and strategic choices, to the average American that's mostly invisible.[40]

Meanwhile, veterans fight for other than patriotic or moral reasons.
  Pat Guarilgia, a Vietnam War marine said,

I stopped believing in the war when I realized I was not trying to defeat the latest incarnation of cruel Nazis. When my best friend was killed, revenge became my purpose. It was fire against fire. My military objective was killing them all.[41]

Marine squad leader Jeremy Latimer, with four deployments in both Iraq and Afghanistan, explained,

I went to war a happy-go-lucky nineteen-year-old. But when my friends were killed, my heart filled with hatred. I developed total concentration on the present situation for safety. I had to manufacture the ability to do violence. My hatred and anger became my greatest strength.[42]

Emerging from the shadow

James Hillman uses the word "accident" for those events that unexpectedly knock our souls off their projected course. Participation in war is a traumatic "accident"— unplanned, unexpected, and cosmological in its distortion and destruction of previous form. The archetypal approach to post-traumatic stress disorder necessitates, in Hillman's words, that we

keep accident as an authentic category of existence, forcing speculations about existence . . . What does it mean, why did it happen, what does it want? Continuing reappraisals are part of the aftershock. The accident may never be integrated, but it may strengthen the integrity of the soul's form by adding to it perplexity, sensitivity, vulnerability, and scar tissue.[43]

The archetypal perspective reveals post-traumatic stress disorder among veterans to be the shape of the soul's broken container due to its participation in unspeakably brutal modern warfare, the soul's cry of anguish, moral injury, the stain the soul carries from being an operative of the cultural shadow. Charles Blocher led the Air Force Missile Communications branch for testing American nuclear armed intercontinental ballistic missiles from 1988 to 1989. He says his moral injury dates from that service, and it is the consequence of "leaving a piece of your essence somewhere outside of yourself."[44] It is the soul's attempts to purge and cleanse. It is the ongoing shock of witness. It is the dislocation at returning to a culture denying such witness and making war on the returned veterans' truths. It is the homelessness of the veterans' souls in a *polis* no longer their own. It is a troubled, incomplete presence in place of a dignified warrior archetype. It is continued possession by the shadow warrior because the returned soldier is supposed to be civilized in a culture that does not grant its veterans a mature warrior identity. The carrier becomes a walking, breathing symptom of the culture's soul sickness—a scar on the streets of a country that denies its shadow and offers no rituals for containing yet expressing it. It becomes the identity of one who has participated in apocalypse and been abandoned there. Justin Sabo, a nine-year U.S. Army veteran who served in the Sinai Peacekeeping Mission, Iraq, and the police force, observed, "When you look into the abyss, it looks back."[45]

Effective psychotherapy for veterans must address these archetypal dimensions. It must include going on patrol with the veteran into the dark corners of the American shadow as they were revealed downrange and at home. It must have the courage to stare into the horror of apocalypse, seek and gather the remnants of soul left there. It must discover how, when, where the soul awakened, protested, betrayed itself, went silent, became terrified, or numb. It must tend to the needs of returning warriors as traditional cultures did, offering the veteran the possibility of developing a new identity as an honorable returned warrior and filling the inner void with meaning. Ultimately, it must affect an imaginal initiation into a new form of warriorhood.

The mature warrior archetype helps an individual serve the community in truth. The mature warrior has witnessed horror and shadow, recognizes them, and helps protect against their pathological outbreak. This is what the accident of war wants of its survivor. Only in this new identity can the soul that has survived modern war regain a necessary and life-affirming form and restore its integrity.

The archetype of the warrior is a necessary component of psyche and culture that cannot and should not be eradicated. Healing for veterans consists not in becoming a civilian again but in purifying, embracing, and maturing the warrior archetype. Healing for our world can occur only with the wisdom, restraint, and dark witness that mature warriors can offer.

Mike Walker served as a marine staff sergeant in several sandbox war deployments. Shattered at home for years, he finally used Native American teachings and practices to recreate his warrior identity. He arrived at a therapy session with a still photo from the movie *Dances with Wolves*. It showed the Lakota medicine man mounted and costumed beside the renegade soldier in cavalry uniform. "Which warrior do I want to be?" Mike asked, pointing to the shaman. "Not the American soldier, but the Medicine Man, can lead me home." We give Mike the last word:

In moments of despair answers will illuminate themselves. Sometimes we are so blinded by our own self-loathing that we ignore them. I was at the precipice, driving my truck contemplating how I would end my life, when I awoke to a new path. Listening to an audio book of *Warriors Return* by Dr. Edward Tick, as a half- ass attempt to stay in the fight, a passage engulfed my heart, forcing me to pull over and weep with an overwhelming release of emotion making it hard to breath. Dr. Tick spoke of the Lakota and how they modeled their treatment of warriors on the bison herds of the plains. The protected were accountable for the role of healing the wounds and strengthening the legacy of the warriors who had protected them.

This one passage sent my heart into agony and flooded my eyes with tears. I was longing for a world where it was okay to hurt, to feel, to be supported in healing emotional wounds from battle and still maintain the identity of the fearless warrior I wanted to believe I am. The tribe treating their returning warriors to ensure a lifelong warriorhood spoke to me with a depth that I desperately needed to hear. There was a lens to my life that could make sense.

The Lakota ask their young warriors: are you willing to take on the lifelong battles that ensue in the life of a warrior? I needed to know that these battles in my mind were part of living a lifelong legacy of warriorhood. It did not end when I took off the uniform, but merely transformed. The wins and losses on the battlefield, the mourning and legacy of those who perished, the guilt, shame, sense of pride in glorious triumph and passing them on to future generations had meaning, provided a purpose to the pain. I needed to know that both identities—the fearless warrior, and the gentle compassionate man—could exist in the same entity. It was important that both exist; one without the other is dangerous.

Not blessed with being a member of the Lakota tribe, I could create a similar environment for myself. By finding likeminded warriors on a similar path as well as people who understand and support those who have seen war, I immersed myself in a community of true support. I have embraced both the warrior and the poet that exist within me. I live the warrior life through physical training, combat sports, and educating others on leadership and resilience. I embrace the poet by taking time to play and write music and stories and experiences both old and new, and embracing love and companionship. I did not banish the warrior but strengthened the duality within me. It has opened more avenues to heal and grow within my newfound community. I am now on a path to enjoy peace yet always be ready for war.[46]

Notes

1   Portions of this manuscript appeared in an earlier and shorter article focusing on the Vietnam War as "The Vietnam War and the American Shadow," *Spring: A Journal of Archetype and Culture*, 62 (1997): 71–86. This expansion is based on 20 more years of research and warrior-healing work with veterans of all American wars since.
2   William T. Sherman, Letter, May 1865.
3   David Nichols, ed., *Ernie's War: The Best of Ernie Pyle's World War II Dispatches* (New York: Simon & Schuster, 1987), 87.
4   James Hillman, *The Soul's Code: In Search of Character and Calling* (New York: Random House, 1996), 87. Richard Lattimore, tr. *Greek Lyrics* (Chicago: University of Chicago Press, 1960), 61.

5 Anonymous (Marine veteran, Afghanistan War). In discussion with the author, spring 2022.
6 Jason Moon (Army veteran, Iraq War, 2003–2004). In discussion with author, 2006.
7 Jean-Paul Sartre, *The Respectful Prostitute* in *No Exit and Three Other Plays*, trans. S. Gilbert (New York: Vintage, 1949).
8 Ibid.
9 C.G. Jung, "The Undiscovered Self," in *The Collected Works of C. G. Jung*, vol. 10, trans. R.F.C. Hull (Princeton: Princeton University Press, 1970), 276.
10 Lawrence Markworth (US Navy, Vietnam War, 1963–1965). In discussion with author, January 2022.
11 Theodore Reik, *Curiosities of the Self: Illusions We Have about Ourselves* (New York: Farrar, Straus & Giroux, 1965), 125–126.
12 Ibid., 127–128.
13 Geoffrey Perret, *A Country Made by War* (New York: Random House, 1989).
14 Francis Jennings, *The Invasion of America: Indians, Colonialism, and the Cant of Conquest* (New York: Norton, 1976).
15 Gerald Carbone, *Washington* (New York: Palgrave Macmillan, 2010), 11.
16 Joseph J. Ellis, *His Excellency, George Washington* (New York: Vintage, 2005), 123–124.
17 Corporal Drew Mewes (Iraq War combat veteran, 2007–2009). In discussion with author, May 2022.
18 Goodwin, 6–7.
19 Ibid., 8.
20 Sergeant Pat Guariglia (US Marine, Vietnam War). In discussions with author, spring 2022.
21 Edward Tick, *War and the Soul* (Wheaton, IL: Quest Books, 2005).
22 John Haker (US Army Vietnam War veteran). In Edward Tick, *War and the Soul* (Wheaton, IL: Quest Books, 2005), 154.
23 Gustav Hasford, *The Short Timers* (New York: Bantam, 1980), 55.
24 Edward Tick, "Satori in the Hut," *Pilgrimage: Psychotherapy and Personal Exploration*, 19, no. 3 (Summer, 1993): 24–26.
25 George Bush, *Presidential Diaries*, quoted in Herbert Parmet, *George Bush* (New York: Scribner's, 1997), 479.
26 Eric Schmitt, "The Gulf War Veteran: Victorious in War, Not Yet at Peace." *The New York Times*, May 29, 1995.
27 Hillman, 268.
28 Preston Stern (US Army Vietnam War combat veteran). In Tick, *War and the Soul*, 156.
29 Mark Baker, *Nam: The Vietnam War in the Words of the Men and Women Who Fought There* (New York: William Morrow, 1981), 33. This quote is notable not for its uniqueness but for its commonality. Echoed by a majority of Vietnam veterans, it is a mantra of a media generation.
30 Hillman, 268.
31 Scott Wolf (Vietnam War combat veteran). In discussion with author, 1995.
32 Schmitt.
33 Robert Moore and Douglas Gillette, *The Warrior Within: Accessing the Knight in the Male Psyche* (New York: William Morrow, 1992), 132ff.
34 Corporal Drew Mewes (Iraq War combat veteran, 2007–2009). In discussion with author, May 2022.
35 Charles "Chuck" Collins (US Army veteran, multiple deployments). In discussion with author, June 2022.
36 For a fuller treatment of the symptoms and consequences of such neglect, see Edward Tick, "Neglecting Our Vietnam Wounds," in *Voices: The Art and Science of Psychotherapy*, Spring, 22, no. 1 (1986): 46–56.

37 For an early yet definitive examination of the Agent Orange problem, see Fred A. Wilcox, *Waiting for an Army to Die: The Tragedy of Agent Orange* (New York: Vintage, 1983). For a recent personal exposé by two veterans dying of Agent Orange cancers, see Sandy Skull and Brenton MacKinnon, *Agent Orange Roundup: Living with a Foot in Two Worlds* (Morgan Hill: Bookstand, 2020).

38 W.H. Capps, *The Unfinished War: Vietnam and the American Conscience* (Boston: Beacon Press, 1982).

39 Spencer Ackerman, *Reign of Terror: How the 9/11 Era Destabilized American and Produced Trump* (New York: Viking, 2021), 210.

40 Phil Klay, *Uncertain Ground: Citizenship in an Age of Endless, Invisible War* (New York: Penguin, 2022), vi.

41 Sergeant Pat Guariglia (US Marine, Vietnam). In discussion with author, April–July 2022.

42 Sergeant Jeremy Latimer (US Marine, multiple deployments in Iraq and Afghanistan). In discussions with author, 2021–August 2022.

43 Hillman, 207.

44 Charles Blocher (US Air Force veteran 1987–1993, Missile Communications Branch 1988–1989). In discussion with author, April 2022.

45 Justin Sabo (Marine and Police Force veteran). In discussion with the author, June 2022.

46 Sergeant Mike Walker (Marine staff sergeant in several deployments in Iraq and Afghanistan). In discussion with author, May–June 2022.

Chapter 6

Hate, rage, and cultural war

The truth of America's big lie

Ronald Schenk

On January 6, 2021, an event occurred that was uniquely paradoxical—as predictable as it was unimaginable, as psychological as it was literal, as primitive and barbaric as it was an emergent reflection of a complex interaction of systems—the storming of the national Capitol Building in Washington, DC, by 8,000 rioters intent on disrupting and undoing the constitutional electoral process of Congress. Although most of the country would not have been able to imagine such an extreme encounter, for decades the country had been moving toward more and more extreme political action and rhetoric. Prior to January 6, despite several official and unofficial alarm signals, blatant indications in social media, and warnings by the FBI, the Capitol Police were unprepared. The riot was fomented by President Trump who, in direct opposition to his primary task of upholding the Constitution, perpetrated the falsehood that the election was fraudulently managed in certain states, actively engaged himself in attempting its undoing, and refused to call in the National Guard. The rioters were claiming to "take the country back" while striving to destroy the literal structure which housed one of its primary bases of operation and dismantle the machinery of one of its fundamental governing structures. Although a great deal of planning and coordination between extremist white-nationalist militia groups and Republican members of Congress in conjunction with the White House had gone into preparation for the riot, the majority of those arrested were not affiliated with any group. For the most part disaffected individuals, representative of a broad swath of the electorate, independently chose to answer the call of the president to bring about the undoing of the election through reactive violence.

In this essay, I indicate how each of the elements that went into the January 6 uprising were, in fact, not aberrations, but rather an extension of the underside of the weaving that makes up the fabric of the American psyche. I suggest that the mindless but self-certain, violently reactive rhetoric and physical force in the name of a blatant falsehood perpetrated on January 6 were an expression of a primary, albeit concealed, orientation in the national character which ultimately gave rise to a form of atmospheric cultural warfare. To elaborate this theme, I dwell on the last three major wars in which the U.S. has played a primary role, focusing on their disastrous handling by political and military leadership not so much as a matter of

DOI: 10.4324/9781003325765-9

calling out individual inadequacies, but as an illustration of leadership reflecting the cultural character out of which it arises and which its effort reinforces. In addition, I attempt to indicate underlying political and religious influences leading to a warlike orientation and then explicate the psychological dynamics that underlie these themes. Finally, I show how the event has an archetypal basis founded in the Greek myth of Orestes, the Furies that plagued him, and the goddess Athena's decision to bring about an overlay of civilized order through the integration of kinship revenge.

Mob violence in the U.S.

Despite the dominant narrative of the country as one which welcomes immigrants, looks with compassion outside itself, and addresses its problems through peaceful means for change, the resort to reactive vigilantism, mob violence, and warfare in service to perceived injustice at the hands of an Other holds a substantial place in the history of the country. The Puritans of the seventeenth century lived a lifestyle on the one hand in service to entitled privilege as the "Latter Day Children of Israel," as well as enmeshed in violence in the name of God and enacted by groups to remind the individual of God's ultimate power. Their actions included genocidal atrocities committed against tribes of Native Americans and police state tactics of banishment, torture, and killing of individuals in the community for committing "sins" as reported by fellow community members.[1] Mob violence occurred frequently in the Colonies before the Revolution, bringing about destruction in the countryside and the closing down of cities. Conflict within the colonial population grew increasingly intense as the Revolution became more probable, with the country dividing into thirds—loyalists, patriots, and the indifferent. Historian Arthur Schlessinger wrote, "Mass violence played a dominant role at every significant turning point in the events leading up to the War of Independence."[2] Mob practices included torture, hanging, scalping, and rape. The civil unrest exemplified by the infamous Boston Tea Party pointed the way toward the Declaration of Independence and Revolutionary War, to be followed by citizen insurrections against taxation policies such as Shays Rebellion in Western Massachusetts, which indicated the need for a constitution, and the Whiskey Rebellion in Pennsylvania during George Washington's term, an event which contributed to the formation of rival political parties.

In the pre-Civil War nineteenth century, slave patrols combed the southern countryside, and justice in the west was brought about by vigilante committees through means characterized by one observer as "savagery." The Eisenhower Commission described the perpetration of violence upon Native Americans, much of it by groups of civilian frontiersmen formed into posses taking scalps and slaughtering defenseless women and children. Gangs used by corrupt politicians were the main source of justice in urban areas, and historian Richard Brown referred to the urban violence of the period relative to anti-immigration sentiment as some of the most intense in the country's history. In 1838, Abraham Lincoln wrote of "the increasing disregard for law which pervades the country—the growing disposition to substitute the wild and furious passions in lieu of the sober judgement of courts, and the worse than savage mobs, for the ministers of justice."[3] Mob violence by abolitionists and slavery proponents alike, in addition to weaponized physical fights on the floor of Congress, led up to the Civil War, and, during the war, white civil unrest against blacks broke out in New York and other northern cities as a result of the Enrollment Act legalizing inscription.[4]

For decades after the Civil War, domestic right-wing groups such as the Klan as well as white mobs engaged in the lynching of over 2,000 black males. In the latter part of the nineteenth century and early twentieth century, as the country moved into the age of exploitation of workers, vigilante groups, backed by industrialists, openly attacked labor movement activists, often with the blessing of government officials. With the onset of World War I, ethnic nationalist militia groups such as the American Protective League were formed with the backing of big business to carry out intimidation and sabotage of groups and individuals suspected of disloyalty. After the war, African Americans migrated to northern urban communities, only to be met with violent opposition from white mobs, fearful of losing jobs, resulting in riots against blacks in several cities across the country during the 1920s. At this time, the Ku Klux Klan organized itself around the theme of white nationalism and anti-immigration, and the Klan held sway in several state legislatures.

This history of mob violence in the U.S. is revealing of central tendencies oriented around the theme of warfare. It is conducted with a sense of self-righteous entitlement in relation to an Other cast as enemy. It is fueled by a rageful or vengeful countenance which finds its expression in violence and is triggered by a single-minded, zealous form of "tribal" identification operating in service to power. The atmosphere of embattlement and the tone of warfare permeating the January 6 rioters were manifested in the descriptions of the scene itself as a "war zone," rife with "carnage and blood" and overtaken by an atmosphere of chaos. The rioters were armed with primitive weapons and body armor and stormed the Capitol in a militaristic fashion. The sense of war was prefigured in the post-election rhetoric on social media and at prior rallies as well as manifested in the war cries of the rioters themselves: "There's gonna be a war!" "Trial by combat!" "Take the country back by force." "You gotta go to the streets and be . . . violent." "I am willing to give my life for this fight."[5]

American warfare

The trope of "war" catches the American psyche as a particularly expedient way of thinking and a mode through which to address what appears as problematic: War on Poverty, War on Drugs, War on Terrorism, War on Cancer, War on Crime, and the militarization of police, not to mention historically questionable military invasions of such countries as Mexico, the Philippines, the Dominican Republic, and Granada, in addition to the most recent catastrophes in Korea, Vietnam, Afghanistan, and Iraq. Since the country's inception, there has been scarcely a year that has past where there has not been an American military presence on foreign soil.[6] Between 1990 and 2017, the U.S. intervened militarily on foreign, sovereign soil 122 times, in addition to imposing violent regime change in 11 countries. The idea of war for America is carried by a messianic national narrative of heroic involvement, "answering the call," charismatic leadership, a unified front, an identified enemy, the use of exceptional means relative to clear goals, all backed by limitless resources leading to ultimate victory and the establishment of a new community in the image of Judeo-Christian, democratic, capitalistic ideals, all of which provides a renewed, solidified, self-certain identity for the country.

A review of America's three most recent military wars—each of them carried out in support of corrupt, compliant governments, at tremendous cost, through deceitful accounts of justification for commencement and subsequent progress, involving an unimaginable scope of death and destruction, all conceived out of blind ignorance and motivated by self-interest, hunger for power, hubris, and fear, and ultimately resulting in abject failure and humiliation soon to be forgotten by the country as a whole—illustrates strains in the country's character which can be seen as giving rise to the January 6 riots. The riots and ethos of cultural warfare emerged out of the same rhizome as these military wars, and at the same time the wars served as causal factors for the distrust and disillusionment that played a great part in the causality of the cultural war leading to the riots.

Vietnam

The war in Vietnam was brought about after years of flawed secret actions by the U.S. and was based upon faulty assumptions on the part of the American political and military establishment, commenced under deceitful circumstances, was protracted over several years with full knowledge of its unsustainability without clear goals for victory, and utilizing practices of torture and genocide.[7] The war could have been avoided or brought to a close at many steps along the way but for fear of humiliation based on the Cold War delusion that the loss of Vietnam meant the takeover of Southeast Asia by China.[8]

President Johnson initiated American armed involvement by lying to the country that an American ship had been attacked in the Bay of Tonkin, after which a gullible and fearful Congress gave him overwhelming support to carry out war to the extent he desired. The war was fought without clear military goals except that of "war by attrition" in which as many as possible of the enemy were to be killed; hence "body count" became the standard measure for success, a matter of numbers to be manipulated at each level of reporting all the way to the top ranks. When General Westmorland received accurate, but disappointing, reports from military intelligence regarding numbers of Viet Cong, he then proceeded to give Secretary of Defense McNamara what he knew McNamara and Johnson wanted. The "anything goes" attitude from the top ranks, in denial of the fact of losing the war at the cost of tremendous loss suffered by American troops, led to a depletion of morale on the ground. Torture, indiscriminate wiping out of entire villages with gunfire and

Agent Orange, throwing of prisoners from helicopters, mutilation of women, and sabotage of officers became commonplace in some areas. Hundreds of thousands of soldiers returned to the U.S. suffering permanent mental and physical trauma.

McNamara and Johnson, Kissinger and Nixon, the Pentagon and the CIA, all knew the war was unwinnable and the allied South Vietnamese government, corrupt and unsustainable, while at the same time perpetuating the war's death and destruction at enormous cost—58,000 American soldiers, 2 million Vietnamese civilians, and 1.4 million Vietnamese fighters dead (not including countless casualties from leftover unexploded bombs), millions of acres of forest and countryside laid to waste or poisoned, hundreds of villages and cities decimated, all at a cost of $1 trillion and all based upon deceit in service to hubris and the preserving of personal image on the part of leadership indulging the fantasy of innocence, invincibility, and divine sanction on the part of the majority of the population.[9] These same dynamics would be enacted 40 years later in Afghanistan and Iraq.

Afghanistan

During the summer prior to 9/11, the Bush administration was repeatedly presented with briefings warning of imminent attack by al-Qaeda.[10] In May 2001, George Tenet, CIA director, presented a plan to undermine al-Qaeda's stronghold in Afghanistan along with a warning of its imminent strike. In July, Condoleezza Rice was informed at a meeting with CIA officials of a "spectacular attack" by al-Qaeda, and, on August 6, President Bush was given information warning that bin Laden was determined to strike the U.S. Rice and Bush chose to give no heed to these warnings.[11]

After 9/11, in an emotionally laden reactive mode, the U.S. Congress gave the Bush administration unlimited military power with which to respond, as well as the ability to consider any citizen an enemy combatant, resulting in the haphazard rounding up of hundreds of Muslims in the U.S. homeland itself.[12] U.S. forces immediately started bombing Taliban-ruled Afghanistan in retaliation for harboring the terrorists who were in charge of the attack on the Twin Towers, specifically Osama bin Laden, leader of al-Qaeda. In the face of American bombing, the Taliban quickly became a spent force and sent signals to U.S.-backed Afghan leaders. "The Taliban were completely defeated, they had no demands, except amnesty," reported Barnett Rubin, UN observer. Defense Secretary Donald Rumsfeld shot down the offer, responding, "We don't negotiate surrender," confident of the capture of the Taliban leader, Mullah Omar.[13] Omar was never captured, and the result of this act of hubris was a war against the Taliban that was predictably unwinnable. Meanwhile, bin Laden fled into the mountain region of Torah Bora, but Rumsfeld inexplicably declined the request of the CIA Special Forces in command on the ground in the area to utilize adequate numbers of forces at the ready, choosing instead to bomb caves where the terrorists were thought to be hiding and, at cost of $70 million, to farm out the job of capturing bin Laden to corrupt warlords who couldn't come close to completing the task.[14]

What amounted to an American military occupation of Afghanistan resulted in the willy-nilly rounding up of hundreds of Afghans as terrorist suspects. Money was given out for the reporting of individuals who were then taken into custody without evidence. Attempts by NATO agencies to create trust, work with civilians, and stabilize areas were undermined by U.S. soldiers invading homes, questioning occupants under duress, taking bystanders as prisoners, and killing innocent suspects. Once in custody, hundreds were in fact tortured at foreign country "black sites" or Guantanamo prison in Cuba. The Bush administration, led by Vice President Cheney and Rumsfeld, took the position that accountability and holding to international law were not necessary, so that "enhanced interrogation procedures" concocted on the spot by behaviorist psychologists became the action of choice.

The themes that emerge from the beginning of the U.S. engagement in Afghanistan would mark its failure throughout its 20-year duration. The war was conducted without clear goal and with little knowledge of the culture, the enabling of endemic corruption on a massive scale, and a vast underestimation of the resources, resolve, and capability of the Taliban. In terms of an overall cultural goal, there was considerable ambivalence as to whether the U.S. was "nation building," inevitably in its own image. The related goal of military victory over the Taliban was also unclear in terms of what would be considered victory and the "end" of the war. Ultimately, each aspect of the two-sided involvement, cultural and military, was characterized by half-hearted attention, a moral void, and clueless policy based on the power of the U.S. dollar, all of which resulted in failure.

In terms of cultural rebuilding, over $145 billion was spent on construction, of which 40 percent went to the hands of Western corporations.[15] The remaining amount went into the private hands of various Afghan officials, warlords, and contractors. Corruption and bribery were generally known to be the primary way of doing business in Afghanistan, and, during the period of American involvement, it was estimated that $2.5 billion was spent annually in bribery across the country.[16] Additionally, humanitarian aid was customarily given on condition of return intelligence regarding the Taliban, putting recipients in danger of reprisal. In sum, what was presented as a moral principle of rebuilding a nation (a notion which was officially denied) did achieve a fragile improvement in education, especially for women, but, overall, accomplished little more than the enrichment of certain Afghan individuals and American corporations.

Could the military ever eradicate the Taliban, given the mountainous terrain of the country, the tribal loyalty of the culture, and the never-ending supply of available recruits motivated by an ideology demonizing the Western world and perpetuated by misguided American actions? The question of whether or not the war was truly winnable was never really addressed by the U.S. Both the nation building and the military projects in Afghanistan were conducted with an overall ambivalence, nonchalance, and lack of clear purpose and were rife with lies, corruption, ignorance, and criminal behavior, with the result being a $2 trillion war in which 2,500 Americans and over 200,000 Afghans were killed, the country was torn apart by civil war, and the Taliban was back in control, with ties to al-Qaeda as formidable as ever.

Iraq

For years, a group of neocon politicians in the Republican Party, disappointed by the refusal of President George H.W. Bush to dismantle the government of Saddam Hussein during the Gulf War, had been pushing for the removal of Hussein and a takeover of the Iraqi government and oil (the world's second-largest supply). A memo sent to then President Clinton advocating the need to establish power in the Middle East through the overthrow of Hussein, signed by Dick Cheney, Donald Rumsfeld, Paul Wolfowitz, and others, gives testimony to their desires. This letter advocates a strategy of securing "the interests of the U.S . . . (through) the removal of Saddam Hussein's regime of power," while noting the possibility of Hussein's "producing weapons of mass destruction [WMD], thereby threatening the world's supply of oil."[17] When George W. Bush came into office and appointed these individuals to positions of power, the mindset and the structure were in place for them to follow through with their agenda.

Long before 9/11, Bush was determined to find a way of taking out Hussein as a means of countering his father's resistance to total victory over Hussein in the Gulf War.[18] Terrorism gave him an enemy against which to become a "wartime President" winning "freedom" in the Middle East as a liberating redeemer acting to "rid the world of evil," as he declared days after the 9/11 attacks.[19]

Hours after 9/11, Bush requested evidence of Saddam's involvement in the attacks, and, despite evidence to the contrary and under Cheney's prodding, taking out Hussein became a "fixed idea" in Bush's mind.[20] In the ensuing months, the Bush administration arrived at the tactic of painting a picture of Iraq as gathering chemical weapons and nuclear armaments while in association with terrorists, particularly al-Qaeda. Cheney worked on George Tenet, director of the CIA, and Rumsfeld secretly set up his own intelligence system within the Pentagon, both projects for the purpose of *soliciting* intelligence ("data mining"), however false, to fit the administration's purposes. Regarding intelligence reports, a CIA official testified, "They knew what would please the White House. They knew what the king wanted."[21] A CIA memo stated boldly, "WE HAVE TO SAY IRAQ HAS WMD."[22] In November 2001, Rumsfeld ordered military planning for an invasion of Iraq, and, in the summer of 2002, Bush secretly siphoned off $700 million from aid to Afghanistan for the purpose of planning the war in Iraq.[23]

In March 2003, under false pretenses engendered by manufactured data for the purpose of aggrandizing American power in the Middle East, the United States invaded Iraq with what turned out to be no planning by Rumsfeld and the Bush administration for handling the predictably chaotic aftermath of the invasion. U.S. forces easily captured Baghdad but did nothing to maintain order, with the result being vast destruction of property, the wiping out of social institutions, and massive loss of life. The ruling bureaucracy and the standing army were disastrously disbanded, creating massive unemployment, leaving the culture without facilities, and engendering inevitable secular civil war and eventual insurrection.

Fourteen years of continuous warfare ensued against an "enemy" with goals that remained elusive and undefined; its course consisting of a cyclical rhythm of surge and withdrawal. The torture of detainees was conducted at the same prison where Saddam had tortured his prisoners, Abu Ghraib ("where the crows gather") with techniques imported from Guantanamo, as directly ordered and approved by the Bush administration.[24] Villages were wiped out by American forces, and surviving farmers were forced to buy seeds from American interests. Billions of dollars went to contracts with American corporations such as Halliburton and Bechtel, with no means of accountability, and billions of unaccounted-for U.S. dollars were siphoned off via corruption within Iraq.[25] In the chaotic political conditions in Iraq, the terrorist organization ISIS was established and flourished, creating a direct threat to American homeland security, incurring the hatred of the Muslim world and loss of trust by its allies and enhancing Iranian power and influence in Iraq—all at the cost of 4,000 American lives, 200,000 Iraqi lives, and trillions of dollars. The Iraq War was not a preemptive war or a preventive war; it was plainly a war of exploitation and self-interest, two fundamental aspects of the American character, in the name of "freedom" abroad and "security" at home. The result has been precisely the opposite—chaos abroad and insecurity at home.

Mark Twain wrote, "History does not repeat itself, but it rhymes."[26] The etymological root of the word "culture" is "the tilling of the soil." We can understand the notion of culture, then, as the ground of underlying assumptions and values giving rise to habitual modes of action which are at work in a given population. The culture wars of the U.S., culminating in the January 6 riots in the Capitol, have a common ground of style and orientation with recent military failures as well as being partially derived from them. These military wars were marked by a void in memory of similar situations, ending up in deceitful manipulation in entering illegal warfare; occupation of an unwilling sovereign nation; misrepresentation in reporting "progress"; ignorance of foreign culture and character; inability to grasp the nature of guerilla warfare conducted in service to secular and national interests; and overestimation of the effectiveness of American military tactics involving the raw use of air power and manipulation of numbers on the ground, together with an underestimation of the enemies' capacity to perpetuate engagement.

Military failure was in service to a political mindset that identified with a sense of America as a redeemer nation whose God-sent mission was to foist its own values, its own image, founded on an idealized notion of democracy in conjunction with capitalistic enterprise, onto sovereign foreign countries perceived as in need. This mindset in turn was in service to a fear-based perception of threat from cultures and movements representing values opposed to those of mainstream America. This underlying fear, in turn, gave rise to a cultural orientation based upon entitlement, "anything goes," hubris, domination, manipulation, dishonesty, hypocrisy, singlemindedness, and reckless and reactive action—in short, any means necessary to justify power-based ends, as illustrated and evidenced by the cultural warfare at home leading up to the January 6 assaults. The result in terms of recent wars was loss of the war, catastrophic destruction, and death, at the cost of trillions of dollars, with the consequence of the physical and psychological death and the wounding of millions of American individuals and families as well as the splitting of the nation. The conclusion can only be that a colonizing power operating through ignorant, authoritarian, and corrupt means at home cannot establish a society and government abroad in the image of democracy.

Politics

Carl von Clausewitz has famously written, "The only source of war is politics."[27] Just as politics is the "womb"[28] of war's development, so politics is also warlike itself, especially on the American front. This was made explicit on January 6 as well as by subsequent revelations that Republican members of Congress were involved in planning the event. Recent history of the warlike nature of the American political scene goes back to 1994 when, after the defeat of Democrats for seats in Congress, Newt Gingrich and Tom DeLay began an assault on democratic conventions with a no-holds-barred quest for power for the Far Right and exercised gloves -off measures such as bringing the government to a halt through legislative manipulations of budget approval as part of a "Contract with America." Republican manipulations continued during the G.W. Bush administration as state legislatures in which Republicans were in the majority began a countrywide movement to gerrymander voting districts to their advantage such that, in a great deal of the country, the largest portion of the population is represented by the lowest number of representatives. As districts became more slanted in their base, they also became more extreme, enhanced by the wildfire social media commentary, partisan reporting of some news networks such as Fox and evangelistic far-right radio talk shows.

In addition, the Supreme Court began making blatantly partisan decisions, beginning with deciding the election for Bush in *Bush v. Gore* (2000), continuing with Citizens United (2010), which essentially gave the moneyed interests of corporations free rein in influencing elections, *Shelby County v. Holder* (2013), which took away protections for black voters, and finally a 2019 refusal to end extreme and rampant partisan gerrymandering. Each of these decisions went against the time-honored practice of jurisprudence which brings about change by honoring precedence through recognizing and then altering prior decisions. The political power-mongering of Republican politicians taking advantage of Trump loyalism in the party reached its apex when Mitch McConnell manipulated the selection of three Supreme Court members such that they would be selected by Trump (all three of whom lied about their willingness to adhere to precedence regarding abortion). The politicization of the Supreme Court was completed, and its power could be used as a weapon in the cultural/political wars of the country, as became evident in the Court's continued political assault on legal precedence and majority rule in 2022 via its decisions to end *Roe v. Wade*, to restrict the federal government's ability to regulate to protect the environment, to disempower separation of church and state, and to limit local government's ability to control use of guns.

The cultural mode of reckless action has given rise to the spectacle of the warlike mode of the executive, legislative, and judicial branches of government, thus, along with the control of government by lobbyists and corporate money, giving lie to the ideals of democracy. The Hamiltonian privileging of manufacturing turns to the domination of corporate over individual interests. The received Jeffersonian narrative is revealed to rest upon mutually exclusive notions of liberty and equality. The pursuit of happiness in a competitive culture where fear and power hold sway turns into a desperate craving in service to self-interest at the expense of others.

Religion

Militant force in conjunction with Christian ideology has been an aspect of American culture since its inception with the Puritans, as noted above. Much of mob violence, such as has recently been carried out in attacks on abortion clinics, has historically been based on Christian themes in which the Other as evil is a foe to be vanquished in God's name. The Ku Klux Klan of the 1920s prefigured the January 6 mob in that it was nationalistic, white supremacist, and evangelistic in its orientation. The Great Awakenings of Christian zealotry in the eighteenth and nineteenth centuries can be seen as anticipating January 6 in that they set up the model of ecstatic, revivalist celebration, which can easily turn to violence under the goading of a charismatic speaker.

In the wake of the January 6 riots, there has been an emergence of the blending of Christian faith and extremist political action that has gone so far as to challenge the very notion of the separation of church and state. George W. Bush, as a born-again Christian, justified the war in terms of God's punishment of "evil" and cast himself as the recipient of God's message to go to war against terrorists and tyranny, a latter-day reflection of medieval crusades. Three days after the 9/11 attack, he told an audience, "our responsibility to history is already clear, to answer these attacks and rid the world of evil."[29] Bob Woodward came away from interviewing Bush with the sense that he had "cast his mission and that of the country in a grand vision of God's master plan."[30] In a 2016 report, it came out that, in 2003, Donald Rumsfeld had been feeding Bush cues relating to the war in Iraq with Biblical passages accompanying photos of the war as a cover sheet for daily briefings on the war.[31] We are left with the insidious sense of American spiritualized hypocrisy in Bush as the personification of Christianized homogeneous mediocrity, the affable "good guy" called to war by his God and relying on blind faith as motivator. Meanwhile, he enabled an underbelly of deceit, corruption, and power-driven violence to dominate and brought about vast swaths of death and destruction through lending the power of his station to the manipulations and machinations of key members of his administration to carry out a war manufactured by that very administration for self-serving, power-grabbing purposes.

Archetypal psychologist James Hillman[32] has gone to great lengths to show that religion, especially a monotheistic religion such as Christianity, as a matter of belief, inevitably leads to war or a warlike attitude. Belief gives rise to identity: I am what I believe; any other belief therefore is a threat to my identity, and I become martial. Hillman particularly focuses on the effects of Christianity on the American

character and America's history of movement into domination and subsequent oppression of the Other, rendered as evil, through warfare. He sees America's Christian heritage at work in its turn to literalism in service to faith, its clinging to a
self-image imbued with innocence and virtue, its singleness of vision, its insistence
upon the mission to foist its values on the Other, and its tendency to rely on a reactive volatile mode through unreflected violence. America becomes unassailable
in the image of Christ as Warrior carrying out God's martial plan.[33] Hillman goes
on to note that the false narrative that this engenders—America as Christian (two-
thirds of country claims to be Christian), therefore peace-loving, versus the actuality of America as Christian, therefore warlike in its nature—is a hypocrisy that is
necessary for the American way of life to endure—church and military-industrial
complex side by side.

The psychological dynamics of cultural warfare

The rage and hate manifested in the cultural warfare of the country and acted out in
the riots of January 6 can be analyzed through the lens of the French psychoanalyst
Jacques Lacan. To oversimplify: For Lacan, the seminal trauma of being human is
the castrating discovery of the subjective "self" by the infant when it realizes its
separateness from a womblike "at-oneness" with an all-gratifying Mother (the ultimate signified to which all objects of desire as signifiers point). This discovery sets
up a perpetual unconscious sense of "Lack" and subsequent desiring or yearning
that finds different objects as signifying gratification. Lack carries with it an undifferentiated mass of grief, betrayal, rage, and hate (the Real), which is defended
against by the system of narrative (the Symbolic), the unconscious being structured
as language. It is language that both protects from chaos and its pain through its
falsification and allows for involvement in life through sublimation of fundamental
unconscious desire into contrived narratives of conscious fulfillment (the Imaginary). The narrative of conscious desiring takes the form of a manufactured story,
a fiction, because the gratification of one desire will only give rise to desire for another object owing to the fundamental lack in psychological being. In other words,
conscious life is lived through a web of deceit, and what is left is the reality that
we are perpetually desiring beings. The moment the fabrication of wellbeing in the
desired object is broken, there emerges an upwelling sense of betrayal, deprivation,
or dispossession with accompanying affects of hate and rage.

In recent years, psychoanalysis has focused on group attachment as a source
for the creation of self-identity as well as physiological inheritance and historical experience of environmental influences.[34] We are always "belonging" in one
way or another such that "I am" exists according to that which I feel I belong to.
In the Lacanian sense, a group or cultural narrative or fiction forms my being in
that, through my adherence to the group image, I am *seen*. "I am" as I am formed
through the gaze of an Other as substitute for the gaze of the all-seeing eye of the
original Mother. The shared qualities, assumptions, beliefs, and expectations—in
short, the group psychology which I share with others—form a matrix with which

I can identify and be recognized, serving as a form of Mother. By the same token, that which my group dissociates itself from will be located in another group. "I am" as that which is *not* of those qualities, assumptions, beliefs, and expectations of the Other. A fabrication of belonging is thereby created which involves a radical differentiation of Self from Other. Belonging legitimates Self as separate from Other through recognition of this separation and recognition of sameness with the group of identification. Self and Other thereby become interdependent, each needing the other and the power that co-dependence brings. At the extreme of fragility of identity, a hierarchy of value is fashioned with the Other as either superior or inferior. It follows, as Hannah Arendt has indicated, that totalitarianism emerges from a collective that is lonely.[35] When the tenuousness of the false narrative brings about its collapse under pressure, hatred and rage are evoked.

Hate and its expression through rage serve identity. Hatred serves the function of complete disavowal, the total denial of qualities that are undesirable and, hence, psychologically relocated in an Other as object or fetish, now the container for all that is rejectable. Disavowal is the clinging to belief in something that is opposite of which one *knows*, albeit at a different level of consciousness. Through disavowal, validity of difference is obliterated. Relocation of undesirability reinforces both the qualities that make up identity ("I am as I am this") and, at the same time, those qualities that allow for identity through disassociation ("I am as I am not that"). The rageful expression of self demands further recognition of self and reinforced identity formation, while at the same time serving to discharge painful feelings experienced as toxic. Following Lacan, it is as if the underlying powerlessness, fragmentation, and lack resulting from the original realization of separate subjectivity and resultant yearnings have come too close to the sun, too near to consciousness, and extreme defensive measures taken for reconstitution take hold. Knowledge has come to threaten belief. Through hatred, there is renewed clarity to the narrative of identity, albeit ultimately deceitful, and rehabilitated focus to its mission, albeit ultimately misguided and in vain.

American rage

Contrary to received narrative, America has always been an angry and violent nation, its history marked by split sides engaged in conflicts dealt with through violence. From the internal strife brought on by the Revolution, the genocidal obliteration of Native American culture, the enslavement of Blacks, the Civil War, the carnage wrought against the labor movement, the brutality perpetrated against immigrants, and the hostile acts against those labeled as "communists" and then "terrorists" to the rage of the Trump phenomenon and the emergence of a cultural rupture in several areas, America has shown its dark underbelly. In a country overtly based on the idea of equal opportunity, a pervasive fear of dispossession and fundamental distrust of authority have formed the underlay. A perfect storm of conditions—heightened economic competition, deceitful wars, political power plays, fraudulent corporate practices, the movement toward more diverse cultural values, and the increased threat to whiteness as the predominant mode of being—has led to the emergence and enactment of rage as the predominant mode of civic interaction.

For most Americans, the ideals of democracy have not been manifested, resulting in a slide into the historical split between those focused on singularity of being and those oriented to the welfare of the community.[36] In relation to the former, any government regulation, corporate or personal, such as COVID-19-related mask wearing and vaccination, gun control, immigration access, or equal opportunity for minorities, is an intrusion on personal self-interest, as is the invasion of belief systems which allows for abortions and freedom of gender choice or sexual orientation. The result has been the emergence of the reality that America is an aristocracy primarily oriented around the notion of self-interest which is then manipulated by the few. This realization acts as a flame to the atmosphere of competitive striving for individual power that envelops the country, evoking hate crimes, riots, and polarized legislation and judicial decisions.

The turn of those experiencing mistrust of government institutions looked to as protecting a father figure or fearing dispossession of opportunity or belief system engendering disenfranchisement of identity (expressed as being "forgotten," "left behind" or "replaced," "real pain uncared for," or "interest not taken into account") is then toward tribalism and loyalty to a charismatic leader. This figure promises instant empowerment through violence in the name of reinstating source values (whiteness, freedom from accountability, self-interest protected, spiritual beliefs advanced, patriarchal and misogynistic hierarchy secured) as a means of validating and reinforcing fragile identity.[37] Not only in the continued overt calls for violent retribution and warfare from Trump loyalists, but in the Supreme Court's extreme aggression in dismantling accepted judicial tradition can this be evidenced. From a Lacanian view, tribalism as populist reactionary nationalism is a display of yearning to cover the experience of the void by those feeling betrayed by the perceived promise of democracy. The writer Julia Kristeva would call this the emergence of the state of abjection.

> There looms, within abjection, one of those violent, dark revolts of being, directed against a threat that seems to emanate from an exorbitant outside or inside, ejected beyond the scope of the possible, the tolerable, the thinkable . . . the abject has only one quality of the object—that of being opposed to "I."[38]

The war cry of those rioters who followed Donald Trump's instigation to take back their country by violently undermining the transfer of power was that the election itself was a "Big Lie" and that Trump had won. Although this assertion was clearly refuted over and over and shown to be baseless, one can look to the dynamics of the country and see that, indeed, there is a "Big Lie"—that is, that America can live up to its narrative as a democracy with ideals of equal opportunity, freedom of choice, and the right to pursue personal wellbeing. A psychological view of the culture would see that the primary vision of the country is self-interest, and that the opportunity for a return on investment of self for most is quite limited, while, for a few, it is quite large. This view would reveal that power is the primary driving force in the culture, and the availability of power is a zero-sum game to which only a few have access. The offense to the Mother then is the Big Lie of the all-embracing promise of democracy. As this deceit is revealed, America turns out to be not the land of the free and the home of the brave, but rather the land of corporate hierarchy and the home of fear. A Greek myth gives us a model for this condition which is enacted in the cultural wars symbolized in the events of January 6.

Trump's Furies

In Greek myth, the paradigmatic image of the spilling of the Mother's blood is that of Orestes killing his mother, Clytemnestra, in revenge for her killing of her husband, his father, Agamemnon (avenging, in turn, his killing of their daughter as a sacrifice). Orestes is pursued by the Erinyes (Furies, in some translations), ancient divinities of revenge related to kinship murder. Ovid describes them as soaked in gore, garments stained in blood, draped in snakes dripping with venom, representative of grief, fear, and madness, and the very personification of curses. They were rage incarnate, daughters of the night, emanations of the underworld, all that was most repulsive to the higher gods and humans, driving their victims to madness with their venom. In Aeschylus's play *Orestes at Athens*, the ghost of Clytemnestra's exhortations to the sleeping "virgin crones" to take revenge upon Orestes are very much ancient echoes of Trump's words to his followers on January 6 to "Take back the country!"

> Get up, I tell you!
> . . .
> Feel stabbing in your guts from my reproaches,
> Blast him with your bloody breath,
> And shrivel him with scorching from your womb.
> Go after him, once more pursue, and bleed him dry.[39]

When Orestes arrives before Athena to be judged, the Erinyes proclaim

> A mother's pulsing blood
> Once spilled upon the ground
> Can't be fetched up again;
> It soaks in and gone
> . . . eagerly we gulp
> From your veins the sour syrup.
> Once we've drained you hollow,
> We shall drag you down below.[40]

However, Athena ultimately rules against them in favor of Orestes, and they explode.

Deprived of rights and full of rage,
I'll blight this earth
With poison, poison from my heart
To pay back grief.
I'll drip it on the soil to make
foul cankers sprout,
mildews to bring children to death
and foliage blight—
O Justice!—make plagues sweep the land
And rot the soil,
Rot human flesh.[41]

Athena is patient with the anger of the Erinyes and offers them a temple of their own, seeking to integrate their energy into the community so that they may receive honor and privilege as being called upon to bring prosperity to each household. In order for this to happen, however, they must give themselves over to persuasion as a means of coming to terms rather than to raw fury in the name of vengeance. Here, Athena is enacting a psychological truth, that what is experienced as abhorrent must be integrated in order for a being to pursue its wholeness. The Other must be recognized as part of the Self and through interaction be integrated. The Erinyes, as carriers of underworldly forces, are necessary within community life to uphold boundaries of social structuring from the deepest parts of the psyche. The whole can then take its form as a disparate unity greater than the sum of its parts.

Extending the myth, the January 6 storming of the Capitol by the rioters was a form of assaulting the temple of Athena representing justice through the civilizing influence of persuasion as democratic ideal versus justice through revenge. From the Lacanian standpoint, the riot was an expression of need for identity through recognition of the yearning desire for an original state of wholeness associated with the Mother, as expressed in the ideals of personal wellbeing through democracy. The rioters, as representative of the Furies, were dishonored by a nonegalitarian, exclusionary culture, and a sense of betrayal was the result.

The ancient myth presents the psychological mode of *inclusion* of the discounted as the in-tension of the drama, an idea which holds as well for today. From the standpoint of depth psychology, when there is a dream in which a monster is trying to get into the house, the indication is that there is a repressed element in the psyche that is repugnant and terrifying to habitual consciousness now calling for integration into the whole. How might we recognize the Furies of the cultural psyche by giving them a place, with the understanding that such a transformation would be ultimately psychologically beneficial? First, it would seem that we need to understand the working of the psyche as being through an autonomous life of its own, and that our willful desiring (which Lacan would consider illusory), as only one of the players in the game, has a limited effect on the overall emergent outcome. It would have to be acknowledged that, in a power-driven culture dominated by self-interest, the values of democracy would have a limited place. Violence would then be seen as inherent in a country whose functioning through hierarchical systems is founded in competition. Anger and rage would then be given a place as the natural offspring of inevitable distrust and fear. All of this can then be seen in terms of the emergence of the dark, but necessary, underside of the received narrative of the culture as white, Christianized descendant of the Enlightenment. What form this creature takes, slouching toward the center, has yet to gather its shape.

Notes

1   Danial Buchannan, "Taves in Wheat—Puritan Violence," *Religion and American Culture: A Journal of Interpretation*, 8, no. 2 (1998): 205–236.
2   Arthur Schlessinger, "Political Mobs and the American Revolution, 1765–1776," *American Philosophical Society Proceedings*, XCIX (1955): 244.
3   Harry T. Williams, ed., *Selected Writings and Speeches of Abraham Lincoln* (New York: Routledge, 1980), 5–6.
4   Joanne Freeman, *The Field of Blood: Violence in Congress and the Road to Civil War* (New York: Macmillan, 2018).
5   Luke Mogelson, "The Storm," *The New Yorker*, Jan. 25, 2021. Mark Danner, "Be Ready to Fight," *The New York Review of Books*, Feb. 11, 2021.
6   Michael Ignateff, "Why Are We in Iraq?" *The New York Times Magazine*, Sept. 7, 2003.
7   President Truman ignored Ho's request for support leaving him to resort to Chinese support. President Eisenhower supported the French against the Vietnamese with billions of dollars of support (80% of the cost to the French). President Kennedy gave the go-ahead for the Diem coup which only perpetuated Vietnamese political instability in the south, leading to America's taking over the war. Lulls in the fighting during President Johnson's term gave him the chance to back out, as also was the case with President Nixon who had, before his election, sent word to South Vietnam to back out of peace talks because he could give them a better deal.
8   Ironically, in 1979, Vietnam went to war with China.
9   For full accounts of the flaws and deceits that the Vietnam War was based upon, see: *The Vietnam War*, directed by Ken Burns and Lynn Novick (Arlington, VA: PBS, 2017); Max Hastings, *Vietnam: An Epic Tragedy* (New York: HarperCollins, 2019); Daniel Ellsberg, *Secrets: A Memoir of Vietnam and the Pentagon Papers* (New York: Viking, 2003); H.C. McMaster, *Dereliction of Duty: Lyndon Johnson, Robert McNamara, the Joint Chiefs of Staff and the Lies That Led to Vietnam* (New York: Harper Perennial, 1997).
10 See Richard C. Clarke, *Against All Enemies: Inside America's War on Terror* (New York: Free Press, 2004), and Steve Coll, *Ghost War* (New York: Penguin, 2004).
11 Mark Danner, "Donald Rumsfeld Revealed," *The New York Review of Books*, Jan. 9, 2014; Tim Dickerson and Jonathon Stein, "Chronicle of a War Foretold: Truth Was a Casualty Long Before We Invaded Iraq," *Mother Jones*, September/October 2006.
12 Only one Representative in all of Congress, Barbara Lee of Oakland, California, voted against the measure, calling instead for a response of measured reflection.
13 Alissa J. Rubin, "U.S. Passed on Taliban Surrender, and 20 Years of War Followed," *The New York Times*, Aug. 23, 2021.
14 Bob Woodward, *State of Denial: Bush at War* (New York: Simon & Schuster, 2006).
15 Farah Stockman, "The War on Terror was Corrupt," *The New York Times*, Sept. 15, 2021.

16 Fintan O'Toole, "The Lie of Nation Building," *The New York Review of Books*, Oct. 7, 2021.

17 Project for the New American Century, "Statement of Principles," Jan. 26, 1998.

18 Dickerson and Stein, "Chronicle of a War Foretold," and Russell Baker, "Condi and the Boys," *The New York Review of Books*, April 3, 2008.

19 Mark Danner, "Taking Stock of the Forever War," *New York Times Magazine*, Sept. 11, 2005.

20 Joan Didion, "Fixed Opinions, or The Hinge of History," *The New York Review of Books*, Jan.16, 2003.

21 Sidney Blumenthal, "Bush Knew Saddam Had No Weapons of Mass Destruction," *Salon*, Sept. 6, 2007. See also *A War Uncovered: The War in Iraq*, directed by Robert Greenwald (Brave New Films).

22 Fred Kaplan, "Why Did We Invade Iraq?" *The New York Review of Books*, July 22, 2021.

23 Charlie Savage, "Bush Challenges Hundreds of Laws," *The New York Times*, April 30, 2006.

24 Mark Danner, "Torture and Truth," *New York Review of Books*, June 10, 2004.

25 Ed Harriman, "Where Has All the Money Gone?" *The London Review of Books*, July 7, 2005; Joseph Stiglitz and Linda Bilmes, *The Three Trillion Dollar War: The True Cost of the Iraq Conflict* (New York: Norton, 2008).

26 In Brian Adams, "The History Doesn't Repeat, but Often It Rhymes," *Huffington Post*, Jan. 18, 2017, www.huffpost.com/entry/history-doesnt-repeat-but-it-often-rhymes_b_6 1087610e4b0999d2084fb15

27 Carl von Clausewitz, *On War*, ed. and trans. Michael Howard and Peter Paret (Princeton: Princeton University Press, 1984).

28 Secretary of State Condoleezza Rice extended the trope of pregnancy and war by couching the sound of bombs going off in the chaotic aftermath of the American invasion as the sound of birth pangs of freedom.

29 Danner, "Taking Stock of the Forever War."

30 Arthur Schlessinger Jr., "Eyeless in Iraq," *The New York Review of Books*, Oct. 23, 2003.

31 Countdown with Keith Olbermann, "George W. Bush: God Told Me to Go to War," YouTube, Feb.15, 2016, www.youtube.com/watch?v=WKt56ztXSK0

32 James Hillman, *A Terrible Love of War* (New York: Penguin, 2005).

33 See my chapters on "Puritan Consciousness and American Soul" in *American Soul: A Cultural Narrative* (New Orleans: Spring, 2012), 49–62, and "The Soul of Violence" in *Dark Light* (Albany: SUNY Press, 2002).

34 See Francis Fukuyama, *Identity: The Demand for Identity and the Politics of Resentment* (New York: Picador, 2018); Lynne Layton, "Racial Identities, Racial Enactments and Normative Unconscious Processes," *Psychoanalytic Quarterly*, 75, no. 1 (2006): 237–269. Gillian Straker, "Race for Cover: Castrated Whiteness, Perverse Consequences," *Psychoanalytic Dialogues*, 14, no. 4 (2004): 405–422. Farhad Dalal, "Racism: Processes of Detachment, Dehumanization, and Hatred," *Psychoanalytic Quarterly*, 75, no. 1 (2006): 131–161. Ryan N. Parker, "Slavery in the White Psyche," *Psychoanalytic Social Work*, 26, no. 1 (2019): 84–103.

35 Hannah Arendt. *The Origins of Totalitarianism* (New York: Harcourt, 1968), 317.

36 The split between individual and community orientation can be traced back to the Puritans when the conflict was a matter of belief—that God favored those with a community orientation versus those oriented toward God's grace through personal wealth—echoed in the contemporary culture in the split between rural and urban populations, red and blue political areas.

37 See Sarah Longwell, "What Makes Trump Supporters Believe in the Big Lie?" *The Atlantic*, April 8, 2022. Neil Vigder, "Survey Looks at Acceptance of Political Violence in U.S.," *The New York Times*, July 20, 2022; Alan Ferrer, "As Right Wing Rhetoric Escalates, So Do Threats and Violence," *The New York Times*, Aug. 13, 2022.

38 Julia Kristeva, *Powers of Horror: An Essay on Abjection*, trans. C. Louis Ferdinand (New York: Columbia University Press, 1982), 1.

39 Aeschylus, *The Oresteia: Agamemnon, Women at the Graveside, Orestes in Athens*, trans. Oliver Taplin (New York: Liveright, 2018), 127.

40 Ibid., 134.

41 Ibid., 154.

Part III

Transgenerational trauma, racism, and social justice

Introduction

"We know, in the case of the person, that whoever cannot tell himself the truth about his past is trapped in it, is immobilized in the prison of his undiscovered self," writes author and civil rights activist James Baldwin. "This is also true of nations."[1] Collective national self-knowledge, attained through historical consciousness, undoes blind patriotism and begets a different kind of love for one's nation—an ethic of love[2] that is founded upon honest, critical social consciousness.

This is an ethic of love that does not attempt to repress that which is problematic or turn away from contradictions, but embraces complexity, paradox, and even uncertainty. As feminist philosopher Kelly Oliver argues, "This process of loving, but with critical interpretation, opens up the possibility of working through rather than merely repeating the blind spots."[3] Self-knowledge grounded in an ethic of love, with a commitment to critical consciousness, honesty, and wisdom, can help the American nation see through its dominant narratives and rhetoric to distinguish realities that are overshadowed by national ideals, name the unfulfilled promises of equality, freedom, and justice, and thus embark on a new path of personal and collective healing.

Guided by an ethic of love, the three authors in this section offer intimate accounts that reveal the ways in which the personal is always political, and psychic suffering and public struggles belong together. They break with silences and bear witness to transgenerational trauma. They tend to ancestral wounds. Only after mourning injustices, losses, and injuries, do they begin to share their dreams of liberation, reconciliation, and healing.

This witnessing and mourning process begins with Quaker peace activist Andrew Grant. In "Defiant remembering: A quest for transgenerational healing," Grant presents an epigenetic case study that reflects historical, cultural, and environmental colonization. Immersing himself in multiple research modalities, from historical and placed-based research to active and embodied imagination, Grant breaks through collective amnesia and acknowledges the dark past of his Nantucket whaling family. Wrestling with repressed fears, sorrows, regrets, guilt, outrage, and the shame of generations, he atones for harmed and lost lives—whales, trees, and,

DOI: 10.4324/9781003325765-10

harder to admit, whole Indigenous communities. For Grant, the shadow work he undertakes is about awareness, responsibility, and, ultimately, respect for all relations.

Cultural mythologist Kwame Scruggs's work is situated at the intersection of storytelling and social justice. In "Life from the shadow's point of view," he describes his engagement with urban youth, addressing anti-Black racism and coping with collective shadow projections. Unflinchingly honest and deeply personal, Scruggs shares his profound pain and the sense of isolation, paranoia, and insecurity inflicted by centuries-old systemic racism in the U.S. His story is about resonance as well as restoration. It is about honoring ancestors and preparing the future for the young generations. Through storytelling, Scruggs illustrates how critical consciousness and compassion can—and must—go hand in hand in unraveling social and psychic oppression.

In "Toward 'splendid cities': The thirst for the imaginal in the life of community," liberation psychologist Mary Watkins critiques a predominantly individualistic American culture by calling attention to how people are accustomed to turning toward dream and image to address their personal woes and wellbeing, while often failing to understand how intimately these are tied to cultural pathology and community wellbeing. Underscoring the interdependence of the personal and communal, as well as psyche and culture, Watkins beckons the reader to accompany her on a "moral pilgrimage" from the Montgomery of the Civil Rights Movement to the U.S.–Mexico border and migrant settlements there. Citing public artworks—murals, music, and poetry—she shows that participatory practices of liberation psychology, such as community dreaming, imaging, and visioning, can be instrumental for social and psychic decolonization, reconciliation, and restoration.

Profoundly personal and simultaneously socially aware, these three essays offer a powerful testament to an ethic of love that goes beyond individualism by consciously making space for community. Kelly Oliver attests, "The loving eye is a critical eye in that it demands to see what cannot be seen; it vigilantly looks for signs of the invisible process that gives rise to vision, reflection, and recognition."[4] Because the loving eye understands relatedness and interdependence, it grants not only courage but also determination to remember and mourn history with all its horrors and trauma. With a loving eye, Grant, Scruggs, and Watkins skillfully demonstrate that social justice requires American citizens and society to face history—slavery, slaughter, ecological destruction. Only then can the wisdom, humility, compassion, and resilience for collective healing and transformation be attained.

Notes

1 James Baldwin, *The Price of the Ticket: Collected Nonfiction 1948–1985* (Boston: Beacon Press, 2021), 324.
2 For a discussion of an ethic of love, see: bell hooks, *All About Love: New Visions* (New York: Harper Perennial, 2000).
3 Kelly Oliver, *Witnessing: Beyond Recognition* (Minneapolis: University of Minnesota Press, 2001), 218.
4 Ibid., 219.

Chapter 7

Defiant remembering

A quest for transgenerational healing

Andrew P. Grant

This chapter serves as an epigenetic case study demonstrating the impacts of historical, cultural, and environmental colonization rippling through both native peoples and relative newcomers to the North American continent, as well as efforts we can make to heal that transgenerational trauma.

My methodology—historical place-based research and embodied learning—includes reading primary texts, storytelling, journaling, bodywork, and active imagination. Walking meditation, solo or accompanied, with attention to the wisdom of the land itself, has been essential. Guidance has come from various sources, including a traditional Abenaki elder and advisor, a succession of two archetypal psychotherapists, my Quaker community, and healing practitioners. This self-directed learning has been accelerated by involvement in the Nolumbeka Project, "where the histories, cultures, and persistence of Northeastern Indigenous Peoples are recognized and celebrated, and where all beings coexist in balance and reciprocity."[1]

> The bird fights its way out of the egg.
> The egg is the world.
> Whoever will be born must destroy a world.[2]

Confrontation

My family of origin was eerily silent about the people of the land—variously called Native Americans, Indigenous Peoples, or American Indians, among other names—who were here before our arrival. We hardly spoke about their ongoing presence or experiences in the place we call home. To me, our silence is a subtle indication of our complicity in genocide as defined by international conventions:[3]

- Killing members of the group;
- Causing serious bodily or mental harm to members of the group;
- Deliberately inflicting on the group conditions of life calculated to bring about its physical destruction in whole or in part;
- Imposing measures intended to prevent births within the group;
- Forcibly transferring children of the group to another group.

DOI: 10.4324/9781003325765-11

As an act of conscience, I refuse to continue participating in the collective amnesia about what happened here. Rather than repressing our family history, I intend to look for my ancestors, embrace them, see them in context, and stand with them beyond good and bad, even if I find their deeds repugnant. Why would I lock them in the cell of an unremembered past? In the words of C. G. Jung: "Then turn to the dead, listen to their lament and accept them with love."[4]

Referring to archetypal psychologist James Hillman, Ipek S. Burnett writes, "If innocence in America is about 'not knowing and not wanting to know, either' . . . then trying to understand the significance of this innocence in the American psyche puts us on a quest for knowledge—self-knowledge in particular."[5] I accept this charge.

My quest has led me to encounter human-on-human atrocities. Perhaps incongruously, it has also led me to revisit the mass slaughter of whales.

I consider that moral injury—the consequence of overriding conscience to commit acts of violence—may be woven into my family tapestry. Archetypal psychotherapist and author Edward Tick, a contributor to this volume, asserts that moral injury is now recognized as a critical component of military wounding and must also be seen as a wound passed on through the generations, even to distant offspring of the original transgressors.[6]

The resolution of transgenerational trauma, metabolizing a violent past by addressing it, causes a shift that I feel almost at a cellular level. When I register the traumatic encounter and let the shudder—sorrow, outrage, pain, regret—run through me and pass cleanly, I am changed. Allowing waves of grief clarifies my vision. Digesting hard truths energizes me in surprising ways.

To illustrate, on a walking meditation last year, I stood at the opening of a trail in the woods and paused to give thanks and introduce myself as Abenaki elder and educator Grandmother Strong Oak had recently taught me. The words, "I am Andrew, son of Puritans," popped out, and I chuckled with surprise. These are words I had never uttered, and they rang true. Yet, with this naming, something shifted as if fetid layers of shame and guilt loosened above me, allowing more air and light to enter.

Coming to America

As far as I can tell, my ancestors came *en masse* from England to "New England" in the seventeenth century, initially as part of the Great Puritan Migration—or invasion, depending on your point of view.[7] They claimed the land where I now live, displacing the people who were already at home here.

Quaker author Shirley Hager states, "We were the houseguests from hell."[7] Though the native people initially welcomed us and offered to share space, they were ready to send us packing within a generation. Relentlessly pursuing land acquisition, we incited a campaign of violence and terror in which we spread disease, coerced land deeds, compelled religious conversions, introduced alcohol and trade debt, sold people into slavery, committed massacres targeting women, children, and elders, proclaimed bounties for scalps, separated children from their families and sent them to remote schools that ultimately became assimilation camps, forced sterilization, and more. In the words of gkisedtanamoogk (Mashpee Wampanoag), "Your people's every action was meant for the destruction of my people."[8]

"We are still here" is the resounding message from Indian Country today. As far as I know, I am one of the first people in my lineage to attend to this message.

Remembering Nantucket

Since childhood, I was aware that I descended from a Nantucket whaling family. We had a heroic view of Captain Cash, my third great-grandfather.

Growing up, I learned that Nantucket is an island off the coast of modern-day Massachusetts, in the North Atlantic, that was an epicenter of the nineteenth-century whaling industry. Candles, lamp oil, and lubricants were the main products, but there were curiosities such as the baleen used in constructing umbrellas and corsets or scrimshawed whales' teeth. Ambergris, a waxy substance retrieved from the intestines of whales, was prized by perfumiers as a pungent additive.

However, no one taught me that the island was home to the Wampanoag for millennia; in their language, Nantucket means something like faraway place; the island was a refuge from hostilities on the mainland; the Wampanoag numbered about 3,000 people before the English claim on the island in 1641.

This not telling is part of my general experience as a white settler descendant. The omission illustrates the myth of "the vanishing Indian,"[9] as if the land was empty and free for the taking. In reality, along with dozens of distinct tribes in the Northeast, the Wampanoag people are still here. I have found that it is possible to meet and know each other by name and to form relationships built on trust and mutual regard. There are people of Wampanoag lineage dispersed in the general population, and many are maintaining a foothold on small patches of unceded land elsewhere (but not on Nantucket).

Encounters

This quest has brought me to thin, ephemeral spaces where I have had significant encounters with my ancestors. Imaginally, I have picked up their tools, the ax and the killing iron.

In retrospect, I see that I spontaneously flexed my mind and spirit in a way consistent with the Jungian practice of active imagination and gravitated toward healing. As analyst Terrill L. Gibson explains,

> Many believe this in-between liminal realm, this vast, ripe emptiness within our understandings of conventional time and space, is where our primal wound is healed by the only ultimate balm there is—relationship and love, or what alchemists call *relatio*.[10]

The ax

"To feed the ironworks' insatiable appetite for fuel, men felled entire forests." In these triumphal tones, the narrator of a U.S. National Park Service documentary film extols the ingenuity and grit that went into Hammersmith, the first European iron production on these shores and the start of the American steel industry. The engineer situated the plant in modern-day Lynn, Massachusetts, on the Saugus River, "in a place," the narrator declares, "where Native Americans had lived, fished, and hunted for ten-thousand years," assigning the Wabanaki (people of the dawn) to the remote past but not the present or future.[11]

Peter Grant—my eighth great-grandfather—landed at Hammersmith along with at least 36 other Scottish prisoners of war, including his brother James.

As my direct paternal ancestor and the only Scot I have met in my family tree, Peter is important to me. He arrived in the Massachusetts Bay Colony on the ship *Unity* with about 150 prisoners in late December 1650 after suffering at the hands of the English one of the worst defeats in Scottish history. Having seen the brutality of war, he was brought here against his will, sold into seven years of indentured service, and put to work to generate profits for the owners. He was also caught up in a larger plan to occupy the land and extract its riches.[12]

White passing (or the myth of whiteness)

Curiously, at the time of his arrival, Peter would not have thought of himself as being of the white race. In the words of healer and author Resmaa Menakem, "Our concepts of whiteness, Blackness, and race were invented in the seventeenth century. While they seem self-evident to Americans today, these concepts would have appeared foreign and bizarre—even outright addled—to an American colonist in the early 1600s."[13] If anything, the English would have seen Peter as of the Scottish race and, therefore, inferior.

However, with the rise of "white body supremacy," as Menakem and others call it, the later descendants of Peter Grant had an easy pass into the white racial category. They likely saw themselves as separate from their Black and Indigenous counterparts. According to educator Mishy Lesser, "settler society and its colonial overlords deliberately tried to fracture their potential opposition by using the practice of divide and conquer to maintain their domination."[14]

We arrived here more than 350 years ago, and yet I am as light-skinned as my Scottish ancestor and, ironically, whiter culturally. Curating my whiteness, I acknowledge, has come at a terrible cost. Menakem writes: "Race is a myth, but a myth with teeth and claws. Institutions, structures, beliefs, and narratives have been created around it. Until we recognize it for the collective delusion it is, it might as well be real."[15]

My ability to write a detailed account of my ancestry in itself is evidence of whiteness: Our story, including the once-disparaged Scots, was privileged and well recorded. In contrast, others were neglected, suppressed, or even bashed and trampled underfoot. My people tried to expunge the actual native culture and the very people of the land.

It is conceivable—and my gut says probably true—that, over the generations, some of my family members were "Indian hunters." According to the Upstander Project research team, colonial authorities in New England issued no fewer than 79 official "scalp" or bounty proclamations, the declaration of a cash reward, in descending value, for the scalps of men, women, and children.[16] Yet this family knowledge, if actual, is deeply buried in shadow, effectively erased from conscious memory.

Encounter at the Gathering of Pines

In 2020, I set the intention to greet the sun on the Pocumtuck Ridge along the Connecticut River in Western Massachusetts at least once a week. I was determined to listen for the wisdom of the land itself, remembering the original people of the land and their experiences in this place. The Woolman Hill Quaker retreat center, present stewards of the land, hosted me. This weekly walking meditation practice and reading and journaling continued for nine months.

One January morning with light snow, I was drawn to a cathedral-like opening in the forest I called the Gathering of Pines. I stopped in my tracks to acknowledge a large, straight white pine, contemplating how five hundred years ago, in the well-groomed native forest, the trees were twice as tall.

In a mode of reflection, I imagined what it would be like to cut down such a life force, remembering my conjecture that Peter Grant's job was to fell trees that the collier would convert to charcoal for the blast furnace. I tested my muscle memory for the ax striking the tree. I contemplated how it felt, and what Peter might have thought of these actions. Moreover, I speculated about who was observing him and what they might have thought and felt. What did it mean to see a tree unceremoniously chopped down? In this rumination, I felt compassion for all my relations: my human and more-than-human kin.

I conveyed the thought to my ancestor: "I do not blame you." Then, continuing up the path in a waking dream, I suddenly found myself accompanied by Peter Grant, a twenty-something Scottish prisoner of war in these strange environs.

Amazingly, he replied in an agitated tone with a wall of words I could not understand; it seemed he was remonstrating in some archaic Gaelic dialect. Then we were joined on the path by an interpreter. I entreated, "Please say, 'I do not blame you.'"

Then, through the interpreter, these words tumbled out:

> They ripped me away from my homeland.
>   They took me from my bonnie bride and our wee bairn.
>   They made me do this—my labor or my life.

I replied: "I understand," and felt a new empathy for the man.

Since that encounter, I have yearned to return to my roots, to the place where my people were indigenous. Ripped away, forbidden from speaking a native tongue or practicing the traditional ways, breaking the tribal circle—these are resonant themes and give me a surprising point of connection with my American Indian associates.

The killing iron

My family history necessitates that I also confront the myth of dominion and the characterization of whales as dumb brutes to be mined for their riches or, worse, as mortal enemies to annihilate without remorse. My people engaged in what mythologist Dennis Slattery calls "the ultimate wounding of the earth through the slaughter of whales."[17]

For countless generations, native people who lived near the coast harvested whales traditionally, receiving them as a gift from the sea and sharing the abundance. By contrast, my family pursued the whale to the ends of the earth—their ships, owned mostly by Quakers, were floating factories.[18]

To intensify my identification with my ancestors, I visited whaling museums in the two centers of American whaling: Nantucket and New Bedford, Massachusetts.

Nantucket displays a sperm whale jaw that my ancestor brought back as a trophy from his final voyage on the bark *Islander*, 1862–1865. The more than 15-foot-tall specimen is from a massive bull whale with an estimated length of 88 feet, nearly 30 yards. I touched the jawbone and wondered what it was like to take such a life. It must have required courage and physical skill. But what else? To act in this way, how must one conceive of a whale?

At New Bedford, the lance, or "killing iron," drew my attention—a wooden-handled implement with a long metal shaft and a spade tip that was kept razor sharp on all edges. Whalers used shorter, barb-tipped harpoons to latch onto and tire the whale, then brought out the lance at the end of the chase to finish off the exhausted creature. They reserved the "honor of the kill" for the captain or other officers who were answerable to the ship owners.

My paternal ancestor William K. Cash was born on Nantucket before the American Revolution and raised in an English household. In 1796, he embarked on a whaling voyage aboard the *Leo*. At 31, this was at least his fourth command as ship's captain, having risen through the ranks of the whaling fleet. Captain Cash got as far as the Sulawesi Sea in Indonesia, where he raised the killing iron for the last time. Contemporaneous reports simply state that William was "killed by the whale."

William S. Cash was born in 1816, the grandson of the captain. I speculate young William heard the story about his namesake and was nursed on the myth of the man and the whale. In time, young William became a highly proficient Nantucket whaler. Like his grandfather before him, he raised the killing iron. In 1844, at 28, William attained the rank of ship's captain aboard the *Milton*. I imagine he kept count of the kills in his career. How high the score, we can only guess.

Aboard the *Columbia* on one of these whaling voyages, Azubah Bearse Cash joined the captain as a "petticoat whaler," a term for wives who went to sea.[18] On this four-year journey to the Pacific hunting grounds, the Cashes had their ten-year-old son Alexander with them and conceived two more children, William Murray and Fidelia Coan Cash.

Murray, as he was known, was delivered in Hilo, Hawaii, and Fidelia was born once they returned to Nantucket. Azubah famously kept a baby book of Murray's escapades on the journey. My family tells how Murray repeatedly fell the first time he tried to walk on land because he had learned to walk on board a rocking ship. The toddler and his older brother also witnessed first-hand the pursuit and slaughter of whales.[19]

Over his lifetime, William S. Cash participated in no fewer than ten whaling voyages on a succession of ships—*Catherine, Peruvian, Edward Quesnell, Ganges, Milton, Gideon Howland, Columbia, Citizen,* and *Islander*—first as a deckhand, then officer, but ultimately as the commander of a vessel he co-owned. As mentioned, he set sail for the last time in 1862 and, three years later, brought back 2,400 barrels of sperm oil (a pure oil from the head of the whale), 560 barrels of whale oil (rendered from fat), and 1,800 pounds of baleen. In that voyage alone, he and his crew were responsible for slaughtering at least 30 sperm whales and an assortment of other species.

Only through a series of external events did Nantucket cease to be a viable whaling center: The Gold Rush drawing away would-be sailors, the development of railroads with access to new markets for mainland ports, the psychological blow of the Great Fire of 1846, and the Civil War wrecking the whaling fleet. Whaling under sail moved to other ports and was eclipsed by global industrialized whaling, with harpoon cannons mounted on chase ships, that continues to this day.[20]

I hold the truth that my ancestors rode the wave of commercial whaling as long as they could until the local economy crashed around them. Archetypally, for generations, they participated in an all-out war on whales, a massacre of global proportions.

Instruments of destruction

It is possible that the instruments of destruction used by my ancestors—the ax and the killing iron—were forged in the same blast furnace. At what cost were they used? With what consequences? What about this willingness to destroy, annihilate, wipe out—trees, whales, and, harder to admit, other humans? What stories must we tell ourselves to commit such acts of violence?

In his book *Mayflower*, historian Nathaniel Philbrick describes the Pilgrims literally walking over the bones of members of the local tribes whom the plague had mowed down, leaving a scar and loss that Indigenous communities feel to this day.[21] The pious newcomers took this as a sign of divine favor, but there is a maleficent reading of these events to consider.

In this quest, I have joined an original research effort to demonstrate, among other topics, that "The Great Dying," as remembered by native people, was not accidental, a simple case of virgin soil exposure and pandemic death. Rather, there is evidence, still unproven, to suggest that the colonizers understood germ warfare technology and orchestrated a series of exposures to soften the ground for a takeover by the English.

A key actor in this alleged scheme was Sir Ferdinando Gorges, who was adjacent to King Charles I and is lauded as "the father of English colonization in America."[22] Gorges never came to these shores but was instrumental in assigning patents—royal land claims—for the area where many of my people settled, including modern-day southern Maine and Nantucket Island, where the ax and the killing iron were employed.

According to historian David A. Price, at Gorges's direction, the English made several "trials" to establish a foothold on these shores.[23] In 1615–1616, Gorges's agents made expeditions to the northeast coast. These included "four good ships" under the command of Thomas Dermer, along with Richard Hawkins and Richard Vines arriving later in their own ships.[24] The Great Dying immediately followed, running its course in 1615–1617. Explorer John Smith, also employed by Gorges and the first person to label this region "New England," described the results:

> [I]t seemes God hath provided this Country for our Nation, destroying the natives by the plague, it not touching one Englishman, though many traded and were conversant amongst them; for they had *three plagues in three yeares* successively neere two hundred miles along the Sea coast, that in some places there scarce remained five of a hundred.[25]

Transformations

Truth coming home

Traveling with my mother this summer, we made a side trip to the cemetery in southern Maine (Abenaki territory), where my late father is buried in a family plot. Along the way, we stopped at the York County Courthouse and held in our hands the last will and testament of ancestor Peter Grant, probated after his 1713 death. Outside the courthouse, I was confronted with a sign that reads:

YORK COUNTY COURTHOUSE
HERE ARE OLDEST CONTINUOUS COURT
RECORDS IN UNITED STATES. GOING
BACK TO 1636 THEY INCLUDE PATENT
CONVEYING THE LAND BETWEEN
PISCATAQUA AND KENNEBEC RIVERS
FROM CHARLES I TO SIR FERDINANDO
GORGES.

We were there too. At the end of his indenture, my ancestor Peter Grant purchased land from James Emery of Kittery, granted to him by Sir Ferdinando Gorges—land that again had recently been "cleared" of its original inhabitants, the Abenaki.

I have concluded that the X-factor in the American economy is the taking of lives, land, and labor by whatever means, and that this is a collective truth hidden in plain sight. I feel this not as an abstraction but as a weight of responsibility.

Such awareness calls for a response in solidarity with people still impacted by these actions. How can I, how can we, put this right? Abraham Joshua Heschel wrote, "Few are guilty, but all are responsible."[26]

Synchronicity: Hilo

My journey includes synchronicity, a term coined by C. G. Jung to characterize "the significance of the simultaneity of events that could not be causally linked."[27]

In the last year, Hilo, Hawaii, has come into focus. Here are four instances:

First, Hilo was the birthplace, as mentioned, of my grandmother's grandfather, Murray. He was born during a whaling voyage in the home of Christian missionaries Titus and Fidelia Coan. Pregnant, Azubah had disembarked at Hilo while Captain Cash continued the hunt for whales. After nine months of perilous whaling—the ship's rudder broke in the frozen Arctic—he returned to the news of Murray's birth, and they continued on the voyage as a family of four.

Second, on the island now called Martha's Vineyard, I attended a gathering hosted by the Aquinnah Wampanoag tribe on Indigenous Peoples Day 2021. There, I met a tribal member who had just returned from supporting the grandmothers defending Mauna Kea in Hilo from further desecration.[28] When I told her briefly about my origins and quest for ancestral healing, she remarked, "You have to go there."

Third, Hilo was significant in developing boarding schools to "civilize and Christianize" Indigenous Peoples.[29] Titus Coan, the same missionary who hosted our whaling family, helped found a boarding school to assimilate native Hawaiians. The Hilo School was an early prototype for the more than four hundred "boarding schools" in the U.S. and Canada, including Kamloops, where investigators found a mass grave of 215 native children in the spring of 2021.

Fourth, near my home, I attended an intimate workshop with a Hawaiian Kahuna, a master of healing arts. He was from Hilo and a practitioner of *Ho'oponopono*, a traditional way of reconciliation and forgiveness.

Healing the wounder

In a spiritual rendering, aided by this Kahuna, I had a mystical encounter with my whaling ancestor. What I saw was striking—a duty-bound, lonely, and depressed man. On his last voyage, Captain Cash surpassed his peers in the number of barrels returned. Yet I saw that he felt let down because excelling in the whaling industry and generating monetary wealth did not bring him closer to the pulse of life—quite the opposite. He carried an unmet sorrow and gravity born of violence. He had command but lacked joy and ease.

This psychological portrait contrasts sharply with a sunnier view written about Cash not long after his death:

Captain Cash entered heartily into the interests of his home, becoming a director of the Savings bank, and serving as a selectman of the town for several years. He died February 8, 1882, respected by all who knew him, for his sterling qualities of head and heart, his directness, courage, honesty and industry, and for the brave manner in which he had fulfilled every duty that life presented to his hand.[30]

Perhaps light and shadow complete the portrait, a more lifelike rendering.

Muscle memory for violence

I sometimes imagine steering the boat toward the exhausted whale, taking a position in the bow, picking up the lance, avoiding the eye of the distressed creature, and striking at the heart and lungs, jabbing fiercely in and out until the telltale "chimney afire" appeared when blood gushed from the spout. This gruesome physicality of slaughter is part of my accounting for the repeated actions of my whaling ancestors, testing my muscle memory for violence.

As I am learning, people with an indigenous worldview are conscious that taking a life is a sacred act and necessary for life to go on. However, what my ancestors did was wholly different.

Captain William S. Cash documented his whaling voyages down to the last barrel of oil. He was part of a fleet of whalers that originated in the waters off Massachusetts and went to the four corners of the Earth to slaughter whales to generate profits. There was no end in sight. The New Bedford museum displays a wall chart that traces all the voyages from that period by fleets of whaling ships, marking the numbers and types of whales killed. The enormity of the effort appalled me. I stood and grieved. "How could we? Why would we? I am sorry we did."

Cash "cashed in" as part of what was arguably America's first peak oil event. Unwittingly, he helped lay down the rails for the train wreck the global north is perpetrating today.

Herein we join Ipek S. Burnett:

[D]econstructive processes . . . expos[e] the inherent complexities, contradictions, and ambiguities in the American psyche, so we can witness what breathes in the shadow of the presumed innocence and reinforces the vicious cycles of oppression and violence. These revelations can then help us understand that when it comes to self-recognition, nothing stands alone and everything belongs—the light and dark, high and low, good and evil, innocence and violence, and every shade of truth in-between.[31]

What happens when we operate in the field beyond right and wrong?[32] What space opens up when we shed guilt and shame as motivators? I propose that we can then entertain a multiplicity of stories, holding these realities with curiosity, understanding, and compassion.

An alternate view of settlement

Like my father before me, I was trained in theology and ordained as a Christian minister. When I was in my early career as a church pastor, I mused that the baptismal font, the communion table, and the pulpit were the furnishings of my home. While I am no longer in that place, I am still religious. A practicing Quaker, I seek to live in the spirit of truth and follow the essential teachings of Jesus, though I seldom speak that way anymore.

Nonetheless, I am aware that starting on the East Coast and sweeping westward, the Christian church was on the frontier, arguably the blade edge of the bulldozer used to wreck native lifeways. For instance, in the colonial period, a church with a settled minister was required before a town could be established—once the land was "cleared" of its original inhabitants. How many municipalities were set up in this fashion and endure to the present?

In the Northeast, even native people who accepted the English ways and professed the Christian faith were betrayed, most strikingly in an incident known as the Deer Island Tragedy. In the course of King Philip's War—or the Second War of Puritan Conquest[33]—native residents of the so-called praying towns in "New England" were rounded up and left to perish over winter on a small island in Boston Harbor.

Later, Quakers were lead proponents of the so-called Indian boarding schools and, during the Grant administration, worked as agents of the state. So what happens when people seeking to do good perpetuate harm?

A whole mythos developed to justify the settlers' claim to lives, land, and labor. Yet the impacts are unmistakable, most pointedly for Native- and African-Americans. I hear Indigenous elder Alma Brooks's complaint, echoing gkisedtanamoogk, "Consider that all of these bad things that happened to my people were done in the name of Jesus."[34]

Coming out of their own trauma, ignorance, fear, and sense of "not enoughness," my people did these things. Shedding assumed innocence, we can face this; we must.

For whatever reasons, it is apparent that the settler community judged indigenous lifeways as a failure or, more probably, as an impediment. So we sought to appropriate what we could and wipe away the living reality: Song, dance, drum, medicine, spirituality, teachings, hunting and gathering, governance, names, languages, and the people themselves.

Closer to home, I am learning about the settlement of the Connecticut River Valley. The Algonquian word *Kwenitekw* means *a long tidal river* or *water rivering a long way from the sea*. Archeologists are finding that humans have lived here for approximately 12,000 years, since a massive glacial lake drained out and left behind a fertile river valley. Native peoples tell stories that go back that far.

In the seventeenth century, an influx of new people began when expeditionary ships arrived from Europe. Starting with Dutch explorers at the river's mouth and followed by an English takeover in the 1630s, towns—Saybrook, Hartford, Spring-field, Northampton, Hadley, and Deerfield—were established in rapid succession. Settlement reached an inflection point mid-river with the 1676 Peskeompskut Massacre, a pre-dawn raid on a riverside encampment in an intertribal gathering place where, plausibly, peace was sustained for countless generations.

Three military officers—Captain Turner, Lieutenant Holyoke, and Chaplain Atherton—led a militia of about 150 young men. They began by firing their muskets directly into the wetus of the sleeping relatives. In less than an hour, they killed three to four hundred people of all ages. (The site of the massacre, now called Turner's Falls, is less than 15 miles from where I live.)[35]

Ultimately, the English claimed the entire 410-mile course of the Connecticut River, which had been home for thousands of years to a constellation of river tribes and extended kin.[35]

I hold the truth tenderly that the native people I meet in the place we call home—Abenaki, Nipmuck, Narraganset, Nehantic, and Wampanoag, among others—are survivors of attempted genocide. While I embrace my ancestors, I am profoundly sorry for some of their actions. If appropriate, I will apologize. I will work for reparations.[36] However, the main thing native people ask of me is basic acknowledgment, to see them in their life and experience. That, I can offer readily.

As a white settler descendant, I am attending to my healing so that I can better witness and support others who most directly experience the ongoing harms of colonization.

Resurgence

With determination and joy, Indigenous communities are holding fast, even flourishing in the right conditions. Native peoples testify that returning to the tribal circle is a homecoming, a place for healing the many wounds of colonization, especially cycles of addiction and abuse.

The late Cherokee tribal chief Wilma Mankiller said,

> Each time a traditional Cheyenne man engages in a Sun Dance or a Cherokee woman straps on terrapin shells and steps out into the circle to dance, it is practically a revolutionary act, a miracle, a living testament to the enduring spiritual strength of the people.[37]

Tribal groups across Turtle Island, as this continent is known, are continuing indigenous knowledge and lifeways against all odds. They are preserving their languages—nearly two hundred in North America—and teaching them to their children. They are re-accessing land piece by piece through organizations such as the Native Land Conservancy, which says that "all land is sacred in our eyes and worthy of special care."[38]

Despite the dominant culture, children are being born into resurgent Indigenous communities. The federal or state governments recognize nearly six hundred nations and tribes within the United States. Even tribes once declared "extinct" are reorganizing. As I have heard native people say, "When they buried us, they forgot we were seeds."

We in the settler community have responsibilities now to acknowledge the harm and, by grace, to help restore the balance of life or suffer the consequences and adapt to a dystopian future.[39]

Deep shadow

There is, of course, a deeper layer that Carl Jung suggests in "After the Catastrophe," his essay on the psychic brew that made the Nazi period in Germany possible:

> From time immemorial, nature was always filled with spirits. Now, for the first time, we are living in a lifeless nature bereft of gods. [. . .] The mere act of enlightenment may have destroyed the spirits of nature, but not the psychic factors that correspond to them . . . in short, all those qualities which make possession possible. Even though nature is de-psychized, the psychic conditions which breed demons are as actively at work as ever. The demons have not really disappeared but have merely taken on another form: they have become unconscious psychic forces.[40]

New scholarship makes the shocking claim that, for its "Final Solution," the Nazi regime emulated the attempted erasure of American Indians.[41] By not doing shadow work, addressing "the psychic conditions that breed demons," we as a human species invite further catastrophe.

Tearing down the veils

Through direct experience, I have found that these myths—dominion, race, innocence, among others—create veils of separation. By tearing them down, the space has opened up for me to navigate in a more vivid and complex environment, to find people and more-than-human people lost to me.[42]

Jung writes: "Everything about [analytical] psychology is, in the deepest sense, experience; the entire theory . . . is the direct outcome of something experienced."[43]

Seven generations: Re-remembering Nantucket

My children are seven generations from William S. and Azubah B. Cash. I speculate how life would be different if my whaling ancestors and their counterparts had adopted the indigenous worldview of acting in the present with concern for the seven generations, past and future.

What if, instead of the *honor of the kill* as an ultimate sign of domination, they had practiced the *honorable harvest* as a sign of humble gratitude for the gift of life gained by necessity through the death of another being in a web of relationships? Indigenous knowledge keepers teach, "Sustain the ones who sustain you and the earth will last forever."[44]

In our day, free divers report being welcomed into pods of sperm whales and "communing for hours" with animals bearing the planet's largest brain, the whales standing vertically in a circle in the water column. Scientist James Nester is trying to decode their communication. He suggests, "It's going to be a lot harder to kill an animal that can speak its own name."[45]

Grandmother Strong Oak tells me that, according to indigenous knowledge, the whales are our elder siblings here and the memory keepers. So, as the descendant of people who attempted to erase the memory of a living planet, how can I respond?

- With a willingness to feel into, and heal, the fragments of ancestral shadow within me;
- By using my inherited privilege to change the historical narrative of settlers and native peoples to one of honoring, respecting, and learning from one another;
- By interrogating what historical fictions we still rely on for justification and continued celebration of violent colonialism;
- By actively engaging in broader efforts to mend the torn fabric between our cultures;
- By learning from our more-than-human kin, plants and animals who were here first and, as I am told, agreed to teach the two-leggeds how to live well in this place.

I choose defiant remembering—to call to mind and hold in my heart all of our relations.[46]

Sky Paddler

Yesterday, I paddled the canoe north on the Back River.
To Rising Sun, I said, "Good morning," and "Thank you."
Beams of warm light cast onto the island ledge.

Paddling along, I felt the Presence
And looked up to see Eagle gazing down at my approach.
I said, "Oh, good morning."
When I broke stroke and turned around for another look,
Eagle swooped away.

Paddling along the ledge further, I felt the Presence again
And looked up to see Sun's light
skipping off the mirror-like surface of the river
and projecting a moving image

—a blazing silhouette—
high on the rock wall.
Sky Paddler accompanied me, stroke for stroke,
striking a radiant bow wave into eternity.

Paddling along the ledge even further,
I felt the Presence yet again
And looked down to see the inverse
—the Paddler of the Depths—
traveling upside down and under Water
like a miner for hidden truths.

I returned this morning, under a dome of gray,
as if revisiting a sanctuary the day after a wedding.
The place reverberated with the memory
of golden light and deep shadow.[47]

Notes

1 Nolumbeka Project, http://nolumbekaproject.org.
2 Herman Hesse, *Demian: The Story of a Youth*, trans. Thomas Mann (Mansfield Center: Martino, 2011), 112.
3 United Nations Office on Genocide Prevention and the Responsibility to Protect, "Definition of Genocide," accessed February 12, 2022, www.un.org/en/genocideprevention/genocide.shtml
4 C. G. Jung, *The Red Book* (New York: W.W. Norton, 2009), 175 176.
5 Ipek S. Burnett, *A Jungian Inquiry into the American Psyche: The Violence of Innocence* (New York: Routledge, 2020), 4.
6 Edward Tick, *Warrior's Return: Restoring the Soul after War* (Boulder: Sounds True, 2014).
7 For more on this theme, see Francis Jennings, *The Invasion of America: Indians, Colonialism, and the Cant of Conquest* (Chapel Hill: University of North Carolina Press, 2010).
8 Testimony from the documentary film *Dawnland*. https://upstanderproject.org/films/dawnland. gkisedtanamoogk is also a contributor to *The Gatherings*.
9 M.M. Bruchac, "Revisiting Pocumtuck history in Deerfield: George Sheldon's Vanishing Indian Act," *Historical Journal of Massachusetts*, 39, no. 1–2 (2011): 30–77. See also Jean M. Obrien, *Firsting and Lasting: Writing Indians Out of Existence in New England* (Minneapolis: University of Minnesota Press, 2010).
10 Terrill L. Gibson, *The Liminal and the Luminescent: Jungian Reflections on Ensouled Living amid a Troubled Era* (Eugene: Wipf & Stock, 2021).
11 FutureLearn, "Saugus: How to Make Iron," FutureLearn, August 8, 2013, www.futurelearn.com/info/courses/battle-of-dunbar-1650/0/steps/66261. Notice the "View Transcript" link under the video. Quoted material at time marks 3:32 and 5:45.
12 The Scottish P.O.W.s on the ship *Unity* departed from Gravesend, England, on November 11, 1650. See "Aftermath and Prisoners," Scottish Prisoners of War Society, https://spows.org/new-england

13 Resmaa Menakem, *My Grandmother's Hands: Racialized Trauma and the Pathway to Mending Our Hearts and Bodies* (Las Vegas: Central Recovery Press, 2017), 62–63.
14 Mishy Lesser, learning director for Upstander Project, "Review Request," email communication, September 1, 2022.
15 Resmaa.
16 Mishy Lesser, *Bounty Teacher's Guide* (Upstander Project, 2021), https://upstanderpro ject.org/films/bounty
17 See Dennis Slattery's contribution to this volume.
18 Admittedly, the Wampanoag and others also adopted the whaling practices of their Yankee counterparts, with many "Indians" recruited as whalers and a number attaining the rank of captain. They built fleets of ships, some with distinctive red paint on the masthead and deck rails. However, white society soon quashed this commercial success, foreshadowing attacks on African Americans in the Reconstruction period after the Civil War and the 1921 destruction of "Black Wall Street" in Tulsa, Oklahoma.
19 Nantucket Historical Association, "Sometimes Think of Me," Issuu, accessed July 29, 2022, https://issuu.com/nantuckethistoricalassociation/docs/sometimethinkofme2018_ final/74. Azubah also kept a full journal which, because the ship's log was lost, is the remaining account of the voyage of the *Columbia*. Nantucket Historical Association, "Azubah B. Cash Whaling Journal MS220 Log 312 1850–1854," accessed July 29, 2022, https://nantuckethistory.org/permalink/?key=6000_m4069
20 Nantucket Historical Association, email message to author, August 15, 2022.
21 Nathaniel Philbrick, *Mayflower: A Story of Courage, Community, and War* (New York: Penguin, 2006), 79–80. Jonathan Perry, email message to author, October 2, 2022.
22 Leslie Stephen, *Dictionary of National Biography* (London: Smith, Elder, 1887), 241.
23 David A. Price, *Love and Hate in Jamestown: John Smith, Pocahontas, and the Start of a New Nation* (New York: Vintage, 2007), 225.
24 Charles Knowles Bolton, *The Real Founders of New England: Stories of Their Life Along the Coast, 1602–1628* (Baltimore: Clearfield, 1974), 26.
25 John Smith, *Travels and Works of Captain John Smith* (John Grant, 1910), 933; emphasis added. See also John Smith, *A Description of New England: Or the Observations, and Discoveries of Captain John Smith in the North of America in the Year 1614* (Boston: Hanse, 1616).
26 Abraham Joshua Heschel, *The Prophets* (New York: HarperCollins, 2001), 17.
27 C. G. Jung, *The Collected Works of C. G. Jung*, vol.8, trans. R.F.C. Hull (Princeton: Princeton University Press, 2012), ix.
28 Thirteen telescope installations mark the summit of the mountain that traditional Hawaiians consider sacred. The Indigenous Grandmothers are resisting the installation of one more, the Thirty Meter Telescope (TMT). All My Relations Podcast, "For the Love of the Mauna Transcript," All My Relations (blog), Dec. 8, 2020, www.allmyre lationspodcast.com/post/manage-your-blog-from-your-live-site. See also: www.vox. com/2020/8/7/21354619/mauna-kea-tmt-telescope-native-hawaiians
29 The National Native American Boarding School Healing Coalition, "'The Truth and Healing Commission on Indian Boarding School Policies in the U.S. Act' (H.R.5444 and S.2907)," accessed August 4, 2022, https://boardingschoolhealing.org/truthcommission
30 Seelye A. Wilson, "Nantucket and the Whale-Fishers," ed. J.H. Kennedy, *Magazine of Western History*, 10 (1889): 540.
31 Burnett, 8.
32 See Rumi's poem, "Out Beyond Ideas of Wrongdoing and Rightdoing," in *The Essential Rumi*, ed. Coleman Barks (New York: Harper Collins, 1995).
33 Jennings.
34 Shirley Hager and Mawopiyane, *The Gatherings: Reimagining Indigenous-Settler Relations* (Toronto: University of Toronto Press, 2021). From a panel discussion about *The Gatherings* to which Alma Brooks, one of the Mawopiyane, was a contributor.

35 See Lisa Tanya Brooks, *The Common Pot: Indigenous Writing and the Reconstruction of Native Space in the Northeast* (Minneapolis: University of Minnesota Press, 2004); Nolumbeka Project, "Indigenous Voices: From the Connecticut River Valley of Massachusetts," directed by Robbie Leppzer, *Indigenous Voices Film Series* (Nolumbeka Project, May 12, 2022), https://nolumbekaproject.org/indigenous-voices-introduction

36 I am working with fellow Quakers to extend a formal apology to Native Americans in the Northeast U.S. https://neym.org/right-relationship-indigenous-peoples-resources-engagement. In addition, I have helped to organize, guided by Grandmother Strong Oak, a Land Justice Affinity Group to facilitate dialog between landholders and tribal partners. I am also engaged in a research project to report on the Quaker involvement in promoting the Indian boarding schools at the request of Secretary of the Interior Deb Haaland.

37 Excerpt from the "Roots of Injustice, Seeds of Change" workshop led by Paula Palmer. For more context, visit "Toward Right Relationship with Indigenous Peoples," Friends Peace Teams, https://friendspeaceteams.org/trr

38 Native Land Conservancy, accessed July 28, 2022, www.nativelandconservancy.org. To read more about the plight of the Wampanoag on Nantucket, see Nathaniel Philbrick, *Abram's Eyes: The Native American Legacy of Nantucket Island* (Nantucket: Mill Hill Press, 1998), and Frances Ruley Karttunen, *The Other Islanders: People Who Pulled Nantucket's Oars* (New Bedford: Spinner, 2005).

39 Robin Wall Kimmerer, *Braiding Sweetgrass: Indigenous Wisdom, Scientific Knowledge and the Teachings of Plants* (London: Penguin UK, 2020). See the concluding section, "Burning Sweetgrass," and the retelling of the Windigo myth, a cautionary tale about the consequences of greed.

40 C.G. Jung, *The Collected Works of C. G. Jung*, vol. 10, trans. R.F.C. Hull (Princeton: Princeton University Press, 2014), 211.

41 Robert J. Miller, "Nazi Germany's Race Laws, the United States, and American Indians," February 19, 2020, https://papers.ssrn.com/sol3/papers.cfm?abstract_id=3541009, accessed September 3, 2022.

42 Robin Wall Kimmerer, "Nature Needs a New Pronoun: To Stop the Age of Extinction, Let's Start by Ditching 'It,'" *YES! Magazine*, Mar. 30, 2015.

43 C.G. Jung, *The Collected Works of C. G. Jung*, vol. 7, trans. R.F.C. Hull (Princeton: Princeton University Press, 2014), 117.

44 Kimmerer, 183.

45 James Nestor and PROJECT CETI (Cetacean Translation Initiative), www.projectceti.org. CETI TEDx Talks, "Deep Dive: What We Are Learning from the Language of Whales," YouTube, October 18, 2017, www.youtube.com/watch?v=JM77aTk1XyI&t=382s

46 For a book in this genre, consider Louise Dunlap, *Inherited Silence: Listening to the Land, Healing the Colonizer Mind* (New York: New Village Press, 2022).

47 Written by the author, August 4, 2021, in modern-day Boothbay, Maine, Abenaki homeland, as evidenced by a more than 2,000-year-old softshell clam midden excavated on nearby Indiantown Island. See Arthur E. Spiess, Kristin D. Sobolik, Diana C. Crader, John I. Mosher, and Deborah Brush Wilson. "Cod, Clams and Deer: The Food Remains from Indiantown Island," *Archaeology of Eastern North America*, 34 (2006): 141–187.

Chapter 8

Life from the shadow's point of view

Kwame Scruggs

In my sessions working with urban youth, I tell them mythical stories while I play a slow rhythm on a djembe drum. At pivot points during the narration, I stop and invite the youth to comment on what resonates with them. I ask them to think about what decision they might make if they were in the position of the mythical character in the story.

No matter how long I continue this work, the youth never fail to respond in ways that astound me. Through the lens of the myth, the youth feel freer to comment on life's dilemmas than they ever feel when we ask them directly about their own life's dilemmas.

I, along with most of my students, grew up in a black neighborhood in an inner-city environment. We share the common experience of being black in a nation where people of my race are labeled "minority." While it is true we are fewer in number than whites, our minority status is not "minor" by any means. In fact, unless we take great care, the term manifests in ways that go much deeper than the surface meaning.

We are all tattooed with the wounds we receive from the world and our attempts to heal them. To show you what I mean, I will tell you a story:

> Once upon a time, not this time, but another time, there lived a small black boy. He lived in a comfortable home that seemed to hold all worlds. But one day he became curious, and he left the comfortable and expansive home of his parents. He walked down the center of the front walkway and went to a carnival. He had never been there before, so he had no idea where to go. He followed the flow of the crowd.
>
> The flow took him to an area where he was bound and chained to a wall-like structure. Others who were not bound and chained were allowed to throw objects at him. These objects consisted of all the things that the people did not want to own themselves. He noticed that only black children were bound and chained, while all the children throwing the debris were white. Being a child, he expected fairness, and he assumed that they would soon switch places. However—and as I tell my students, there is always a however—he was sadly mistaken. He also

DOI: 10.4324/9781003325765-12

noticed that after the white children threw the debris, they walked away laughing as if nothing had occurred.

Being a child, he could not clean himself, so he had to walk home with his newly acquired stench. Once home his mother comforted and cleaned him. Then he reached for the glass of water she offered him.

He sat down to relax, willing to forget this long, confusing day. He turned on the television, which always entertained him. But now he noticed that all of the children who looked like him were working diligently, while the white children were playing in their nice clean white outfits. He went into the bathroom and put white soap all over his face in order to look like the children who were playing, both at the carnival and on television.

The following day the small black boy again left his home. He walked down the center of the walkway to visit downtown. But on this particular day, he wore the white soap on his face in hopes of having fun. However, again he was sadly mistaken. All of the people, both black and white, noticed his blackness under the mask he was wearing. Again, they started to throw debris at him. He ran back home as fast as he could.

Once home, he cried himself to sleep. While asleep he had strange dreams of evil white men chasing him.

On the following day he left the house again. Being a child, he hoped anew to experience the joy and laughter of childhood. But before long, he realized he had landed in an all-white neighborhood. Initially, he felt uncomfortable, but after some time he realized that this was obviously something he was going to have to deal with.

On his way home, he happened to meet a small black girl who gave him some advice. He hadn't realized he was crying, but when he heard her words, his tears started to subside.

She said: Accept your blackness!

Many black children could tell a version of this story. The opening of "once upon a time" informs us that this happens always, it is timeless.[1] Although I wrote this story only a short time ago, its timelessness shows that it could have been written in the 1800s or even just yesterday—with television standing in for whatever is the cultural entertainment of the day. It could legitimately be argued that, for black children, things have not changed all that much in the past hundred years. At least.

It is a situation that occurs over and over. For black people it seems archetypal. Though the story was written in a time of politically correct language, I chose to describe the boy as black as opposed to African-American. I wished to cast the shadow in its customary color of black.

The image of the color black carries negative connotations. It was, and still is for many, a symbol of evil, filth and repulsion. Since we think in dualistic terms, the color white would then harbor the exact opposite image—one of purity and goodness.[2]

I am deliberately choosing to stay with this metaphor. First, because I have taken the advice of the little girl in the story. "Accepting blackness" means more than accepting only the parts I like. And second, because at the same time I hold a positive view of blackness. It is a view that recognizes the rich possibilities that exist in "prima materia," the base material in alchemy from which all things, including gold, may be forged. This is the way I view my black students.

Like the child in the story, we blacks learn early in life that the negative viewpoint will not go away and refuses to be ignored. It is a projection on black people, whether individual or collective. It is the Shadow.

C. G. Jung defined the Shadow as: "The inferior part of the personality; sum of all personal and collective psychic elements which, because of their incompatibility with the chosen and conscious attitude, are denied expression in life."[3] So, by definition, the Shadow is something we all prefer to avoid. But, despite our best efforts to suppress it, blacks sometimes feel like we encounter the Shadow wherever we turn, even within the walls of our homes when we watch television.

Which brings me back to the story of the small boy who lived in a home that felt large enough to hold all worlds, until he explored outside.

Fall from grace

The description of the home being expanded alludes to inflation of the ego. Early childhood is a time when the child's ego and Self are one. It is a time when all is taken care of for the child; it is an age of paradise. Jungian analyst Edward Edinger elaborates, "In the paradise age, the people are in union with the gods. This represents the state of the ego that is as yet unborn, not yet separated from the womb of the unconscious."[4] In our story, the first day the child interacts with the world outside his home he learns that his expectations are vastly different from what he has experienced inside his home. This discovery is so overwhelming he is not sure he can trust his eyes or ears, or his understanding of what happened.

According to Jung, both the Shadow and the Self are archetypes. Jung wrote: "[The Self] is older than the ego . . . it stands for the essence of individuation, and individuation is impossible without a relationship to one's environment."[5]

The boy's leaving home symbolizes his initial contact with his environment, his reality. It is also his initial contact with consciousness, "the fall."

Everyone's state of paradise is short-lived. For blacks in America, our state of ego-inflation is even shorter. Our relationship with the environment catapults us into a phase where our ego most assuredly becomes separated from the Self. We are reminded on a consistent basis that we are outsiders. We do not belong.

Feelings of stress based on feeling unwanted are well documented. Physician and psychoanalyst Edward Whitmont writes: "The child accepts himself in terms of fitting in. Harmony with the Self and thus with consciousness appears at first to be dependent upon external acceptance."[6] Edinger adds, "Encounters with reality frustrate inflated expectations and bring about an estrangement between ego and Self."[7]

Fortunately, not all blacks feel unwanted; some are very comfortable in any environment. I am not in their company; I personally carry two handkerchiefs with me to wipe the nervous sweat from my brow. Seldom do I walk into any place alone, owing to my paranoia of not feeling wanted.

The following is my attempt at hermeneutics, the art of interpretation. I will explore certain aspects of this shadow story, offering my analysis or amplifying what the symbolism means to me. As we tell our youth, and adults, there are no right or wrong answers to our projections, it is all merely to create discussion and introspection.

Connection with ancestors

The idea of being bound and chained reminds the child of the struggles of his ancestors who were enslaved. This symbolizes the enduring link blacks in the U.S. feel with our ancestors, even though we often do not have much information about them.

This is the child's medium to contact his collective unconscious, the primitive nature of his psyche—primitive in the sense of original and ancient.[8] While the child is chained, he recalls the strength of his ancestors—his ancestors are holding him up—even though his knees buckle under the constant stress of being black in this world.

In my own life, my ancestors have played a significant role in my development. I have always had a great admiration for their sacrifices, courage, and perseverance. All of these traits are true character traits of the hero. It was during my Akan rites of passage process that I became more familiar with the important role ancestors play. This rites process was designed to assist us in recalling our purpose in life, to communicate more with our ancestors and to give back to the community. I was taught that our ancestors exist to assist us in completing our tasks here on Earth. I was taught to call on them when necessary. I was taught, in a playful, yet serious way, that they are just waiting for us to call on them as they become bored in heaven. They are there to open doors for us. I am assuming that the more we do on our end, the more they will do on theirs. I say a prayer to my ancestors every night. I always begin by thanking the Creator and my ancestors for the abundance of blessings they have bestowed upon me.

Not wanted

The debris thrown at the child in the story consisted of objects that the others did not want to own themselves. This debris represents repressed characteristics such as greed, lust, rage, and the inhuman treatment of others. These fall neatly into the category of the Shadow. A Shadow that white men are unwilling to acknowledge and, instead, project onto others. Connie Zweig, a Jungian psychotherapist, and co-author Steve Wolf, a clinical psychologist, talk of the projection of the Shadow: "Our cultural shadow projection—we are light, they are dark—falls upon different groups at different historical moments. In the name of the one right way, whole populations cast their darkness onto others with holy zeal."[9]

The fact that it was only white people that were casting the debris is symbolic of America projecting its dark side onto the "cultural other." Marimba Ani, an anthropologist and African studies scholar, adds to this when stating:

> It is Europeans who define "humanness" in terms of their own self-image and with such intensity that the ethic and rules of behavior that apply to those who are like them do not apply to those who are not. The cultural other is, therefore, the person (object) who can be treated in any manner—with an unlimited degree of hostility and brutality, as is evident when one reviews the history of European's relations to people of other cultures.[10]

As a black man, I feel as if we blacks in America have carried a substantial portion of this projection. If you are not black, try to imagine what it is like for a black man who carries the projection of America's shadow.

I feel as if I live as "the Shadow."

Did that really happen?

In the story, the children laughing as if nothing happened denotes how people who project their shadow onto others have no clue what they are doing. They act like nothing has occurred. They never give a thought to what the "the other" might think or, more importantly, feel. Jung substantiates this with his following comment:

> Western man lives in a thick cloud of incense which he burns to himself so that his own countenance may be veiled from him in the smoke. But how do we strike men of another color? What do China and India think of us? What feelings do we arouse in the black man?[11]

In the story, with this first encounter, the small boy is confused. No one is interested in his reaction to the events, in fact no one responds in a way that makes sense to him. They walk away, and he is left to sort it out alone.

Cleansing

The boy is now walking home with this "stench." He is carrying the projection of the Shadow. Wherever he goes, the odor follows; people now despise him owing to what he "carries." He is looked upon with utter disgust.

His mother is at home to clean him.

This is not only his personal mother, but also the archetypal Mother. She is there to cleanse him and is attempting to bring him back to his original state, representing his longing for redemption.

Now clean, the boy accepts a glass of water from his mother, hoping to transition back to himself.

Water is the sign of life; however, when you are draped in the projection of the Shadow, everything you touch turns dirty, turns black. It is similar to blacks moving into a neighborhood, and the "For Sale" signs popping up in record numbers. The water has become polluted; it can now kill.

Fortunately, the boy is at home and not in an area of Jim Crow where he would be further humiliated by having to drink water from a different fountain. God forbid he should want to visit a larger body of water such as a public pool. He would be forced to get out while they clean the pool of his stench; even more humiliation. The example of "For Sale" signs going up in neighborhoods when blacks move in is not theoretical. This is exactly what my family experienced in the 1970s when we moved into a white neighborhood. When I say "1970s," I do not mean to imply things have changed much. Just like the story, it was "once upon a time."

Temporary relief—trying to forget

The boy's attempt to forget his long, confusing day is symbolic of blacks and our relationship to drugs and alcohol. Amos Wilson, a noted black psychologist, talks of how some blacks increase their intake of drugs and alcohol in an attempt to escape their "black condition," hoping to find temporary relief.[12] Some of us use this as a tool to "help" us mitigate the daily challenges of being black in America.

The boy turns to the drug (television) to relax, but this only causes more confusion. All the people who look like him are portrayed in subservient positions, such as pimps, drug pushers, and clowns. He notices that the white children are in positions of power, having fun, enjoying life.

So now he has two choices: Identify either with those who do not look like him (the hero archetype with white skin) or with the one who looks like him, the evil or inferior one (the Shadow), wearing the black costume. Because it is natural to identify with your own, he becomes what he sees—a pimp, pusher, or clown.

Trust me, growing up and only seeing yourself portrayed in a negative light has detrimental effects on your psyche! Even though I possess a PhD from a prestigious institution, founded a nationally known non-profit organization which was awarded the nation's highest honor for its after-school program, and even though I hold multiple other awards, I still feel "less-than" owing to the color of my skin. Is this my problem? Yes, I thoroughly comprehend this is my cross to bear and I continue to work on it. Is it a common problem among blacks owing to our shared experience? Also, yes.

Arthur Ashe said to be black in America is like having two full-time jobs. Author James Baldwin stated that, "To be Black and Conscious in America is to be in a constant state of rage."[13] To be conscious in this sense is to be aware of one's "blackness," meaning that a black person would have to realize that they are indeed black.

You might ask, how can they not know they are black?

We as a people have been so brainwashed with negative images of "blackness" that many of us disown anything with any semblance of black. For those who have been unwilling to accept their blackness, it becomes a Shadow figure in their unconscious, fighting to be acknowledged.

The boy in the story is headed in this direction. He is now beginning to realize that everything black has a negative connotation. One does not have to search far in Western culture to find examples. There is even a fairy tale titled "The White Bride and the Black Bride," where God caused the woman and her daughter to become "black and ugly," "cursed and made black," while the white bride was made beautiful.[14] Once the boy comes to the realization that being black does not "cut it" and tires of the filth being thrown at him, he chooses to identify with the one who does not look like him. He goes so far as to put white soap on, hoping to make himself white, so now he is wearing a mask.

This symbolizes Jung's "persona," the mask we adorn for the world. As Jung remarks, it is "the individual's system of adaptation to, or the manner he assumes in dealing with, the world."[15] He cautions that the danger arises when we start to identify with the mask, escaping who we really are. In *Pedagogy of the Oppressed*, Paulo Freire writes on oppressed people and our relationship to identification with the mask:

> At a certain point in their existential experience the oppressed feel an irresistible attraction towards the oppressors and their way of life. Sharing this way of life becomes an overpowering aspiration. In their alienation, the oppressed want at any cost to resemble the oppressors, to imitate them, to follow them.[16]

In the past, we saw this in blacks straightening their "bad" hair in order to have "good" hair like whites. We see it today in blacks wearing blue or green contact lenses.

The journey

Despite all the boy has been through, he still leaves the house, walking down the center of the walkway.

Walking down the center and leaving the home represents his unconscious intent to reach completion, to embark on his destiny. Jung speaks of "the almost irresistible compulsion and urge to become what one is, just as every organism is driven to assume the form that is characteristic of its nature, no matter what the circumstance."[17] The boy is imbued with the character traits of the hero.

When the Shadow is white

The small black boy now goes home and cries himself to sleep. While asleep, he has a dream of an evil white man chasing him. The dream represents the entrance of the unconscious. The evil man is the shadow figure. The Shadow has often been portrayed as a dark figure, a negative image ready to wreak havoc on our lives. "In myths and fairy tales throughout time, the human shadow has been imagined as a brutal Beast, an unruly savage whose tireless aggression and bottomless appetites stem from his animal origins."[18]

It was no coincidence that blacks were defined as animals and savages during the early conception of America.[19] Racist attitudes were a continuation of European colonial attitudes. Joseph Arthur de Gobineau, a French aristocrat who was a proponent of the Aryan master race theory in the nineteenth century, commented, "The negroid variety is the lowest, and stands at the foot of the ladder. The animal character, that appears in the shape of the pelvis, is stamped on the Negro from birth, and foreshadows his destiny."[20] In one of Jung's dreams, there was the image of a brown-skinned man, a savage. For Jung, this represented the primitive Shadow. [21]

For myself, a black man, my shadow figure in dreams is often a white male.

Example: I dreamed an overweight white man attempted to kill me, but somehow I was able to escape with relative ease. I have since realized that the evil white man in the dream caused a tension of opposites and thus served as a symbol for my own efforts to suppress or even vanquish the Shadow. I escaped, but so did the Shadow—no doubt to fight another day.

A different kind of neighborhood

The small black boy leaves the house again, only to land in an all-white neighborhood. His initial uneasiness is symbolic of the black man's state of paranoia. This also represents the insecurity and paranoid feeling I encounter each time I enter an area in which I am the only black. This inferiority complex has its origins in my childhood, same as the little boy, who sees only negative images of people who look like him.

Naim Akbar, another esteemed black psychologist, comments that the topic of our inferiority is one of the most frequently discussed topics among psychologists.[22] He goes on to add: "With the image of a Caucasian as God, and with all kinds of images of Africans as dirty and only half human, it was inevitable that a sense of inferiority would grow into the African-American personality."[23] It certainly has a permanent home in my psyche.

Carrying the projection of the Shadow has greatly affected my sense of comfort. To this day I find myself extremely paranoid when I am in an environment populated by whites. I feel like an outsider, as if I do not belong, like everyone is looking at me and wondering, "What is he doing here?" This feeling intensified during my visits to Pacifica Graduate Institute in Santa Barbara, California, and the surrounding areas. I always felt so alone.

During our second quarter at Pacifica, a conversation arose in which we asked each other what was our conscious reason for choosing to attend this institution? In my case, the course of study was exactly what I was looking for, to the extent that it became a personal calling. So much so that I was willing to make many sacrifices to attend, not to mention time away from my family and job.

Next, we asked ourselves to explore our unconscious reason. What had we since learned about the deeper psychological purpose for attending?

For me, my question had been answered the previous quarter on the second day of class. We did an exercise in which we were asked to imagine ourselves in a personal role in the Temple of Asclepius. I was the only black person in the class. To my surprise, even in my imagination I could not see myself in any position other than as a slave. This realization brought me to tears.

When class ended I was in a personal crisis. I finally asked my ancestors, "What am I doing here with all these white people?"

I did not get an immediate response that day, but I have since learned that I was there to confront my Shadow and to overcome my sense of insecurity and paranoia about being black. At times, many times, I found myself literally crying without understanding why. I eventually accepted I was crying the tears of my ancestors. Like the small boy who found himself in the all-white neighborhood, I was learning that I needed to conquer my fear of this all-white environment.

Anima

On his way home, the small black boy meets a little girl who just "happens" to be walking by. Of course, this is no coincidence. This is synchronicity at work. As Jung states, "The view that all things are arranged according to God's will is one that leaves little room for causality."[24]

The girl depicts his anima, his female half or, as Jungian analyst and author Robert Johnson calls it, the *soul-image*. Johnson adds:

> In every man and woman there is an inner image being whose primary function in the psyche is to serve as the *psychopomp*—the one who guides the ego to the inner world, who serves as mediator between the unconscious and the ego.[25]

Therefore, the girl is there to assist the boy in becoming complete. She is his medium to connect him with the spiritual realm and help him return to a higher version of the Self, to lead him to God. She gives him one simple line of advice: *Accept your blackness.*

The comment is a clear instruction to accept his Shadow and his true Self, for he is certainly a black man. He can no longer run from his Shadow, or from the fact that he is a black man in a white man's world. He must face both, which is practically one and the same. Once he faces the dark side, it will diminish in stature.[26] It is not until he can accept his Shadow that he may begin his spiritual cultivation. This is considered essential to start the process of self-knowledge, the introduction to the Self.[27]

If the little black boy refuses to accept his dark side, he will remain in a "child-like" state, compelled to face complex situations in life with only half-understanding at best.

The black man in America is a symbolic wound, a wound that the nation must deal with. However, it is also a wound that we as black people must embrace. Like the boy in our story, it took me a while to embrace my blackness. There is no other color I have ever consciously wanted to be. However, owing to our miseducation of being black, some of us struggle with our fate.

There was a version of a myth we explored with our youth in which a black dwarf and 12 black men are mentioned. The first two times I shared this myth, I refrained from describing the dwarf and men as black. At that particular time it was not a subject matter I wanted to tackle; I was more focused on our youth incorporating the character traits of the hero into their own lives.

The third time I went over this myth, with a different cohort, I shared with them my hesitancy about talking about being black in America. Once the topic was up for discussion, our youth shared their feelings of both pride and shame. There did not seem to be a middle ground.

The youth talked of how powerful we are. They talked of how fragile we are. They discussed how they felt they were judged just for being black. They talked of how they were inspired to prove society wrong about being a black man. Through myth and discussion, we eventually found a middle ground, living in between worlds.

We live the myths while the myths live us. Sometimes we laugh, sometimes we cry. All of the time, we search for better ways to navigate through this world. Sometimes we succeed, sometimes we do not.

What gives me fear is when I see one of our youth, with so much promise and potential, walk down the wrong path. What gives me hope is when I see so many of them become the hero within their own story.

Notes

1 Marie-Louise von Franz, *The Interpretation of Fairy Tales* (Boston: Shambhala, 1996), 9.
2 Winthrop D. Jordon, *The White Man's Burden: Historical Origins of Racism in the United States* (New York: Oxford University Press, 1974), 6.
3 C.G. Jung, *Memories, Dreams, Reflections*, trans. Aniela Jaffe (New York. Vintage Books, 1989), 398–399.
4 Edward F. Edinger, *Ego and Archetype* (Boston: Shambhala, 1991), 8.
5 C.G. Jung, *Aion: Researches into the Phenomenology of the Self*, ed. Gerhard Adler, William McGuire, and Michael Fordham, trans. R.F.C. Hull (Princeton: Princeton University Press 1978), 167.
6 Edward Whitmont, *The Symbolic Quest: Basic Concepts of Analytical Psychology* (Princeton: Princeton University Press, 1991), 162.
7 Edinger, 37.
8 C.G. Jung, "The Undiscovered Self," in *The Collected Works of C. G. Jung*, vol. 7, trans. R.F.C. Hull (Princeton: Princeton University Press, 1977), 66.
9 Connie Zweig and Steve Wolf, *Romancing the Shadow: Illuminating the Dark Side of the Soul* (New York: Ballantine Books, 1977), 54.
10 Marimba Ani, *Yurugu: An African-Centered Critique of European Cultural Thought and Behavior* (Trenton: Africa World Press, 1994), 403–404.
11 C.G. Jung, *The Portable Jung* (New York: Penguin Books, 1976), 473.
12 Amos Wilson, *The Developmental Psychology of the Black Child* (New York: Africana Research, 1987), 14.
13 John Beilenson and Heidi Jackson, *Voices of Struggle, Voices of Pride: A Collection of Quotes of Great African-Americans* (White Plains: Peter Pauper Press., 1992), 26.
14 von Franz, 193–195.
15 C.G. Jung, "The Undiscovered Self," in *The Collected Works of C. G. Jung*, vol. 9.1, trans. R.F.C. Hull (Princeton: Princeton University Press,1990), 122.

16 Paulo Freire, *The Pedagogy of the Oppressed* (New York: Continuum, 1970), 44.

17 Jung, *The Collected Works*, vol. 9.1, 357.

18 Zweig and Wolf, 54.

19 Jordon, 13–18.

20 Marimba Ani, *Yurugu: An African-Centered Critique of European Cultural Thought and Behavior* (Trenton: Africa World Press, 1994), 282.

21 Jung, *Memories, Dreams, Reflections*, 398–399.

22 Naim Akbar, *Chains and Images of Psychological Slavery* (Jersey City: New Mind Productions, 1984), 20.

23 Ibid., 21.

24 C.G. Jung, *Synchronicity: An Acausal Connecting Principle* (Princeton: Princeton University Press, 1973), 75.

25 Robert A. Johnson, *Inner Work: Using Dreams & Active Imagination for Personal Growth* (New York: Harper & Row, 1989), 47.

26 Harry Wilmer, *Practical Jung* (Wilmette: Chiron, 1987), 101.

27 Whitmont, 164–165.

Chapter 9

Toward "splendid cities"

The thirst for the imaginal in the life of community

Mary Watkins

Feeding "a burning patience" with embers of image

When Pablo Neruda accepted the Nobel Prize for Literature, he recalled a line of poetry from Rimbaud: "In the dawn, armed with a burning patience, we shall enter the splendid cities," cities which Neruda said "will give light, justice and dignity to all mankind."[1] In the dark times we are now living in the U.S., it is clear that we must be armed with such patience. What are the seed embers that kindle such patience, and how do we care for them?

Image and dream are potent seeds required to fuel our vision of the possible. Indeed, "the splendid city" and what Martin Luther King, Jr. called "the Beloved Community" are kindred images which express deep longings for communities of peace and justice. They orient us toward the deeply desired and also reveal the gap between how things are and how they could more ideally be.

Paradoxically, such a widening abyss can demoralize us, allowing our fatalism to express itself in a retreat into narrow lives, cut off from rootedness in community and insulated by consumerist preoccupations; lives which breed states of social amnesia and denial. To mitigate this, we must invite images to chart the paths of what King called our "moral pilgrimage," while continuing to sketch our longed-for destinations and feeding our "burning patience."

It is by grace that images not only orient us toward a longed-for future but help midwife moments in the present where what is longed for becomes incarnate, re-freshing the soul. Martin Luther King, Jr. saw America itself as a dream, a dream where men and women of all races, nationalities, and creeds can live together as brothers and sisters, a society governed by love.[2] King believed that the purpose of the Civil Rights Movement was to create the beloved community. Coretta Scott King recalls the hushed silence that fell on a quarter million people, before a crash of applause, as King's "I Have a Dream" speech concluded in Washington in 1963: "The feeling that they had of oneness and unity was complete. They kept on shouting in one thunderous voice, and for that brief moment the Kingdom of God seemed to have come on earth."[3]

DOI: 10.4324/9781003325765-13

King described a similar experience as he visited with protesters in the Montgomery airport after the boycott and march in 1955.

> As I stood with them and saw white and Negro, nuns and priests, ministers and rabbis, labor organizers, lawyers, doctors, housemaids and shop workers brimming with vitality and enjoying a rare comradeship, I knew I was seeing a microcosm of the mankind of the future in this moment of luminous and genuine brotherhood.[4]

An image of the beloved community is an ember that gives rise to such a moment in reality, feeding on the subtle body of desire. Awash in the individualism of our time, we have primarily focused on image and dream for insight into our narrowly defined personal situations, rarely taking into account the interdependence of the personal and the communal, psyche and culture.[5] We have failed to take seriously Jung's insight that "In the deepest sense we all dream not out of ourselves but out of what lies between us and the other."[6]

In more communitarian cultures, dreams feed the symbolic life of the community. They are incubated, remembered, shared, and performed, connecting people through the regenerative spring of imagination so that its waters can feed the roots and vision of the community. In the U.S., we are in continuing need of community dreaming that reflects critical insights about the situations in which we find ourselves and images that remind us of the world we want to create together, allowing us to liberate from their depth the energy for our creative actions.

The work of image in the decolonizing of psyche

Postcolonial scholar Janmohamed says that when we try to step outside of the safety zone of the way our culture and its ideologies have informed our work and structured our relationships to others, we must become "archaeologists of the site of [our] own social formation."[7] I grew up in a commuter town east of New York City in a displaced Southern family, amid other upwardly mobile white families who had become part of the "privileged" and glad of it. There was little criticism of the status quo, because we were trying to be the status quo, identified with Madison Avenue's imagination for us, rendering our own imaginations inert. There was no public artwork, no community visioning processes. The activities of shopping and arranging appearances stood in where critical dialogues did not appear. Desire was channeled into the realms of personal consumption, ambition, and pleasure seeking. No amount of quiet alcoholism, of housewives disappeared to mental institutions, of domestic violence, of restless boredom or feelings of emptiness could move the town to paint, to imagine. The potential metaphors were lived in an unreflected manner. In the morning, the men streamed onto trains to conduct the city's commerce, leaving mothers sorted in neat rows in suburban houses, children in their own rows in schools built on the model of industrial settings. Gates and fences protected each plot from one another. To win remove from one's neighbors was a sign of prestige, worthy of jealousy, not mourning or alarm.

Liberation psychologist Tod Sloan describes the underlying dynamic U.S. society is captive to:

> the state and the market project the existing or near future reality as the ideal, filling the space in which alternative collective and personal ideals could be formulated through ongoing interaction and debate. The individual's task becomes one of adjustment, of "fitting in" rather than individuation or self-realization through intersubjective communication.[8]

While offered more and more choices and options, "the frames within which [we] chose are themselves manufactured to a large extent to coincide with market and state imperatives for social reproduction" of the prevailing economic and political system.[9] Accommodation to these invisible powers colonizes the personality, "replac[ing] symbolic cultural sources of meaning with mere stimulation. Decolonization of this sphere requires ideological desymbolization be countered by de-ideologizing resymbolization." Our own vital capacities for imagining need to replace those of the state and the market, reawakening the springs of our visioning together.

Jungian individuation is understood to entail an ongoing effort to differentiate oneself—one's values and perspectives—from a blind identification with collective norms. Similarly, object relations theorist Winnicott argued that conformity and adaptation to prevailing norms—here he was thinking of the child's relation to the mother—establish the center of the personality in what he termed the "false self," a center that is robbed of connection to psychic vitality and meaning. Such precocious compliance renders our lives tainted with feelings of futility, while working to help guarantee our fitting into—and thus perpetuating—the pre-established order of things. Without any gap between us and the collective images produced for us, there is no public space opened to call forth alternate images or to even create images that reflect back everyday life so that it can be grasped on a more conscious level. Analytic work can open a private space to begin the work of disidentifying and resymbolization necessary to individuation, but, I am asserting, it must take place within a wider community effort to see through dominant ideologies with which we—and even depth psychologies themselves—become compliant and in which we become complicit.

What if, on the wall of the shopping mall in my childhood town, we had seen the following image from *The Great Wall* mural, the longest mural in the world, painted in Los Angeles by Judy Baca and four hundred teenagers: Rosie the Riveter from World War II is being sucked into a vacuum cleaner and a washing machine as she is deposited into a 1950s suburban home, alongside car, husband, and children? As World War II broke out, women were chastised by psychologists for spoiling their children with their doting presence. In order to encourage women's exodus from the home to bolster war efforts, psychological studies were used to make it appear that women could be better mothers by leaving the home, thus saving their children's character. When soldiers returned home in need of jobs, women were again upbraided by psychological studies that blamed increases in juvenile delinquency on women's being out of the home pursuing work. In Baca's method of mural painting, itself a process of community individuation, a group explores a period of history within a community and searches for metaphors that can convey the spirit and conflicts of that time. The viewer is not only initiated into seeing the hidden dynamics of a historical period, but is quickened to the task of inquiring what the metaphors are that forge the present. It provides an active process of penetrating the prevailing ideologies while at the same time involving both muralists and spectators in processes of symbolization that have been systematically eroded.

For communities to individuate, they, like individuals, need to recognize where they are identified with the status quo, reflect on these identifications, and grapple ethically with the morality of their position. Art forms such as collective dreaming activate what Jung called the transcendent function, mediating the known and the unknown, the visible and the invisible. Aurora Levins M. Lorales describes such collective dreaming as "the reservoir of our deepest understandings and desires and hopes, as essential as water."[10] To drink from this precious reserve we must leave open a space where our identifications are questioned and, further, where perspectives, experiences, and pieces of history that have been pushed into the margins can be retrieved and reintegrated into the known.

"Events forgotten reappear in dreams"

There are events in our lives that we cannot understand because we keep a part of what we know away from understanding. Susan Griffin reminds us that:

> Events forgotten reappear in dreams. And fragments of memory left in the mind cry out as if for some connecting knowledge. Unless of course another false order of events has been created from the fragments so that even the scent of memory is threatening.[11]

When members of a community have suffered greatly, their travail becomes traumatic when it exceeds what can be expressed or represented, when the means for such expression and representation are denied, or when such expression fails to find itself believed and witnessed. Philosopher Kelly Oliver describes Kristeva's idea of creating revolt through representation:

> Revolt becomes the way that "I" will express my specificity by distorting the nevertheless necessary cliches of the codes of communication and by constantly deconstructing ideas/concepts/ideological philosophies that "I" have inherited. This process of distorting and deconstructing is the way in which "I" make the cliches of culture mine; it is a way of belonging that counteracts alienation

from meaning and dominant culture. These distortions can be playful or angry, subversive or conservative, conscious or unconscious, but they must be creative and born from passion. They are ways of finding or creating the living social space that can support and open psychic space.[12]

"[P]sychic revolt, analytic revolt, artistic revolt," says Kristeva, "refers to a continuous questioning, of transformation, change, an endless probing of appearances."[13] She suggests that analysis be understood as an act of questioning, similar to the questioning that occurs in artistic experience. Indeed, this work of symbolization breaks open social and psychic space and can ignite renewal and regeneration.[14]

A dream that deeply affects us arises from some place outside of our usual knowings. It arrests our attention and orients us to its way of seeing. Its images place us in a world we cannot yet fully understand, often wordlessly posing questions to our being. When we think of "dream" in this way, images from many sources qualify as dreams—poetic images, song images, paintings, certain memories, photographs, pieces of news that haunt us. As archetypal psychologist James Hillman pointed out in *Suicide and the Soul*, we need to welcome even the most disturbing images when they visit us, as, in our relation to them, psychic energy becomes available.[15]

The poem "Strange Fruit" arose from such a haunting by an image. It was written by Abel Meeropol, a white, Jewish, New York high school teacher, communist sympathizer, poet, and songwriter, known for his adoption of the Rosenberg children after their parents' execution. One day he was looking through a Civil Rights magazine and came across a photograph of a particularly ghastly lynching of two African-American teens, Thomas Shipp and Abram Smith, in Marion, Indiana, in 1930. The faces of the crowd are deeply disturbing, particularly those of two young girls in the left corner who look happy and excited as though they were at a school prom. Like a nightmare image, it haunted him for days. From this haunting he first wrote a poem about it that was published in a teacher's union publication. Then he set it to music.

In 1939, when Billie Holiday took Meeropol's images of racial lynching in the South, "Strange Fruit," onto the nightclub stage, she broke her audience's set of expectations about the kind of song they would hear in such a setting. Samuel Grafton, a columnist for the *New York Post*, put it this way:

> It is as if a game of let's pretend has been ended and a blues singer who has been hiding her true sorrow in a set of love ditties had lifted the curtain and told us what it was that made her cry . . . [It was] a fantastically perfect work of art, one which reversed the usual relationship between a black entertainer and her white audience: "I have been entertaining you," she seems to say, "now you just listen to me."[16]

"Strange Fruit" is considered to be not only the first significant song of the Civil Rights Movement, but also the first representation of lynching in song. It has been called the "first unmuted cry against racism," a "declaration of war . . . the beginning of the Civil Rights Movement," one of the "ten songs that actually changed the world."[17]

Billie Holiday always demanded that people stop talking during the song, that waiters not serve, and that cashiers and busboys stop their activities. The room would go completely dark except for a single light on her face, creating a ritual space in which her white audience was asked to witness the living nightmare of the lynching of African-Americans. At the end of the song, the stage would go completely dark; Holiday would leave and not return for a bow. She wanted the images of the song to stick inside of her audience, doing their psychic work. The images performed a healing function in the community, bringing marginalized facts into consciousness through the soulful, difficult lyrics and disjunctive melody of the song. Holiday's mother worried about Billie singing this song, fearing it could bring her harm. Holiday is said to have told her mother she thought singing the song could make things better and that, when she died, she thought she would be able to feel this better state of affairs from her grave. Margolick, the biographer of this song, interviewed many who heard it in the early 1940s. He says,

> They credit it with helping awaken them to the realities of racial prejudice and the redemptive, ameliorative power of art. Whether they protested in Selma or took part in the March in Washington or spent their lives as social activists, many say that it was hearing "Strange Fruit" that triggered the process.[18]

Angela Davis wrote that "Strange Fruit" "put the elements of protest and resistance back at the center of contemporary musical culture."[19]

Part of the power of Holiday's singing of "Strange Fruit," according to Vernon Jarrett, was that she impressed her audience as

> someone who had also been wronged, as if she'd been lynched herself in some fashion or another . . . . To me, that was part of the whole lynch syndrome, the lynching of the body and the spirit together. That's the way her face looked when she sang that. All over this woman was the fact that "we're all taking a screwing, someone is messing with us, this is a [messed] up situation"—like she was psychoanalyzing herself and the black condition, telling us there was "no escape" signs up, regardless of how great you were.[20]

Members of New York's Theatre Arts Committee sent the lyrics of "Strange Fruit" to members of the U.S. Senate as Southern senators were about to filibuster anti-lynching legislation. Frank Bolden, a newspaper writer and a member of the Black elite, said the song was almost sacred; that listening to it was like sitting in church. Indeed, it provoked a form of sacred witness.

As testament to the subversive power of the image, Billie Holiday and Abel Meeropol were both questioned by the Committee on Un-American Activities about whether or not they had communist affiliation because of their singing and writing of "Strange Fruit." "Strange Fruit" exemplifies what Kristeva means by "revolt":[21] Through its subversive passion, its deconstructing representation, it created a social space in which the brutal expression of racism, lynching, could be taken out of the dark of night and placed in the spotlight to confront denial and to stimulate public witnessing. Its images addressed a need, psychic and communal.

Limit-acts and the imagination

In our lives, we come up against what Alvaro Vieira Pinto and Paulo Freire call "limit-situations," situations which block our freedom, and which are often initially experienced by us as fetters and insurmountable obstacles. Refusing to accept the usual idea of "limit," Vieira Pinto says that limit-situations can be seen not as where "impossibilities begin"—they are not "the frontier which separates being from nothingness, but the frontier which separates being from being more."[22]

In 2001, as a recent émigré to California from Boston, I found myself living in the dark shadow cast by the United States government's creation and maintenance of the U.S.–Mexico border, an embodied limit-situation that is stark in the misery it creates by extracting human labor to sustain privileged lifestyles that result in countless people remaining in poverty, often separating families and—as though that were not enough—taking the lives of many who, in desperation, try to cross this man-made border. I joined a work camp of 16 teenagers and eight adults sponsored by the American Friends Service Committee. We were invited to Maclovio Rojas, near the Tijuana border. The AFSC has developed a relationship of accompaniment[23] with Maclovio Rojas, helping with community projects and providing a witnessing presence to discourage ongoing assaults on the community by the Mexican government. Here I experienced a place where image work is central to discovering the other face of the limit-situation, where possibility breaks in on demoralizing life conditions.

In 1988, 25 women and their families migrated from Oaxaca to a dusty hillside area southeast of Tijuana, near the U.S.–Mexico border, to find work. Since the North American Trade Agreement (NAFTA), this area has spawned huge factories to produce American goods using cheap Mexican labor. The working conditions are notoriously poor, with inadequate safety precautions. Workers are poorly paid and are expected to work overtime, often for no further compensation except the retention of their jobs. In 2001, many young people worked for less than $1 an hour, receiving from $35 to $50 for a six-day week. More than half of the jobs are in *maquiladores*, with over one million *maquiladora* workers in Mexico as a whole. *Maquiladores*, or sweatshops, are foreign-owned assembly plants. The products they make do not flow back to the communities creating them. The components they assemble rarely come from Mexico, and their assembly does not profit the Mexican economy.

The families formed a land-squatter community, building their homes from cast-off American garage doors. They were banking on a Mexican law that gives such squatters the land on which they have lived after a certain number of years. Within

14 years, 1200 families settled in Maclovio Rojas. There is no governmental provision of electricity, sewer system, or clean water. Both electricity and water must be pirated from supplies running to neighboring *maquiladores*. Their story is emblematic of the human suffering United States policies have created at the border through the implementation of NAFTA. It is also emblematic of noble efforts to wrest dignity even in grossly inhospitable circumstances. Community dreaming and the art-making that flows from it are central to this effort. They are not sufficient, but they are key ingredients.

Their community is named after Maclovio Rojas Marquez, a Mixteca Indian from Oaxaca, who traveled with his family to the North, looking for agricultural work. In San Quintin, Mexico, he became the secretary general of the CIOAC (Central Independiente de Obreros Agrícolas y Campesinos), an effort to establish the first union in Mexico for farm workers to fight for decent working and living conditions. In 1987, when Maclovio Rojas was only 24, an anti-union grower contracted for his murder by having him run over by a car.

The community leaders at Maclovio Rojas struggle for their own existence, having suffered both being jailed and put under house arrest for their role in fighting the Mexican government's attempt to dislodge Maclovians from the land and their homes. While legally entitled to the land at this point, the value and desirability of the land have skyrocketed owing to the expansion of the *maquiladores* in this area. The neighboring Korean Hyundai plant, which makes cargo containers, is eager to annex the land in Maclovio Rojas, and the government would like it to do so.

Maclovians draw inspiration from the Zapatista movement in Chiapas that has encouraged communities to form cultural centers of resistance that can help to mobilize and support community self-determination and dignity. In 1995, the leader of the Zapatistas, Subcomandante Marcos, convened the first National Democratic Convention from a stadium stand called Aguascaliente—hot springs. Six months later, when the government betrayed the peace negotiations, it destroyed this site. Marcos then called for such cultural centers of resistance to be built in communities around the world.[24]

The people in Maclovio answered this call and began to build a community center in a small shed with the beginnings of a stage in an open area. Such sites of resistance have been called "public homeplaces." bell hooks describes public homeplaces in the African-American community as providing "the warmth and comfort of shelter, the feeding of our bodies, the nurturing of our soul. There we claimed dignity, integrity of being; there we learned to have faith".[25] In Bond, Weinstock, and Belenky's[26] discussion of public homeplaces, art-making is seen as essential to the expression of experience, to the welcoming of marginalized voices, and to the emergence of common dreams.

Manuel Mancillas and Michael Schnorr, of the Border Arts Workshop/Taller de Arte Fronterizo (BAW/TAF), enter the story as the public homeplace of the Aguascaliente began to emerge. Mancillas had met Maclovio Rojas Marquez before his death and believed he had a photograph of him. When he met some friends who told him they had spent the day in Maclovio working on the community center, he had the idea of offering to paint a mural of Marquez. He and Schnorr went to visit the community, who liked their idea.[27]

The BAW was created as a transborder partnership to work on issues around the U.S.–Mexico border. Like many public art projects, a lot of the community workshops they had run up to this point had not involved a long-term commitment to the community and had limited community participation. As they spoke with the Maclovians, they began to see a different possibility for their work, one of a collaborative partnership that could evolve over the long haul, that combined art-making with the ongoing social struggle of the community, linking people from both sides of the border to dream past the U.S. government's destructive border policies. They offered to help create further murals and to help build a larger community arts center where art and ceramic classes could be taught.

The three leaders of the community were arrested, and there was a 400-mile march planned to protest their imprisonment. Their involvement with the community became one of participant-witness to their struggle. The murals painted around the edge of the courtyard depict the struggle of the Maclovians for their land and homes, including scenes from the march of 400 of its citizens. On one of the interior walls, the Maclovians have painted "*luchamos por el derecho de una vivienda digna*" (we fight for the right to a dignified way of life). The murals are a form of what Aurora Levins Morales calls medicine history, a radical history which distills "a legacy of pride, hope and rebellion from ordinary people's lives," as opposed to imperial history which is used to strip hope and further agendas of domination. Such medicine history, she says, is medicine for the "cultural and psychological effects of poverty, enslavement, intense racism, and patriarchal colonial rule."[28] It resists the amnesia engendered by those attempting to escape accountability. As they involved young people in the design and execution of the murals, further images came forth. Mancillas stresses that these images were not born out of formal focus groups, but out of day-to-day living with the community and being involved in all facets of community life.

At the rear of the community there is a hilly area that is particularly susceptible to annexation by the *maquiladores*. To protect this land for the community, a plan was conceived to create a memorial for unidentified Mexicans who died trying to cross the border and a cemetery for them and Maclovians. The teenagers I traveled with had, the summer before, spent days constructing and painting white wooden crosses for each of the border's victims. This summer we returned to paint the wooden backdrop to the cemetery. Covered with yellow and red paint and sweat from working in the intense summer heat, these relatively privileged teens came close to lives quite different from their own, as each cross they painted symbolized a life needlessly lost owing to the hypocritical policies of the U.S. government. The cemetery is called the Pantheon of Maclovio Rojas. Artists of international renown have come to work on pieces of art that are gradually transforming this barren hillside. The fame of the international artists and the interesting work they are creating will hopefully give the government pause. To bulldoze a living museum known to people around the world, a memorial to Mexico's own citizens, and a graveyard would require an embarrassing show of brutality by the government. Here, art itself bears witness, where otherwise further encroachment by corporate capitalism would erase the community and its creative, persevering struggle for community individuation.

Psychoanalyst D.W. Winnicott spoke of the need for the analyst to provide a protected, safe, reliable, what he called "transitional space" in which experience can freely arise, a space that welcomes what is neither wholly private nor public, neither inner nor outer.[29] Having arrived at Maclovio Rojas in the dark, I was struck in the morning, when I woke up on the upstairs porch of the Aguascaliente, to see Maclovio Rojas looking at me, his image asking me and others to come into relation to the struggle of Maclovians. Like the analyst, images of such figures protect the space and invite the viewer to remember the struggle for what Freire calls "the vocation of humanization," to move from being objects of a culture we are passively used by to standing in opposition to dehumanizing processes, taking on the task of creating and claiming a different future.[30] The preservation in art of such figures in our moral imagination is critical. At an elementary school in the largely Latino Mission District of San Francisco, Cesar Chavez protects the asphalted play space of the children, reminding the children in English, Spanish, and Chinese: "Help me take responsibility for my own life so I can be free at last." On the right side of the mural, Dolores Huerta, who has continued Chavez's work, is cutting open a chain-link fence, helped by a mighty falcon near her right shoulder. She hands a ribbon to a girl that says "*Si Se Puede*," lending her example and encouragement to the children in the mural and to those playing beneath it.

In a public library in East Los Angeles, a portrait of Mary Bethune, the founder of the first college for African-Americans in the South, looks over the schoolchildren studying below, reminding them of the liberatory potential of their studies. Under the protective, watchful eye and embrace of a cultural father or mother, we are oriented by such images to the values incarnated in their living, as we pursue our own studying, playing, art-making, and activism.

"In dreams begin responsibilities"[6]: Prophetic dreaming and moral pilgrimage

Robin Kelley writes, "The map to a new world is in the imagination, in what we see in our third eyes rather than in the desolation that surrounds us."[31] Deborah Saunders, an African-American cultural worker and leader speaks of how she was helped to develop a prophetic voice.[32] Her grandmother would first ask her to still herself and to listen for the voice of God. Then, importantly, she would ask the child, "What did you hear?" Slowly, Saunders's life became a rhythmic motion orienting to the still, small voice of God, bringing her experience of it forth in community in relation to others' visions. She then worked through action with others to honor the prophetic voices and images. I had the deep pleasure of encountering such a prophetic image and witnessing the moral pilgrimage it inspired.

After 9/11, when the United States began bombing Afghanistan, Edith Cole, a woman in her 70s, sat one Sunday morning in Quaker meeting, feeling the deep sadness of the situation and asking for guidance for a way to be in relation to what was tragically unfolding.[33] Another woman rose to share something from her worship and used the metaphor of different ways to help someone who is drowning, such as throwing them a life ring or forming a human chain to help pull them from the water. Edith said she immediately recognized that this was the image she was waiting for. She grasped that this image of forming a human chain not only allows the recipient to be pulled to safety but also helps those in the chain to actively embody their concern as they witness the danger and difficulty of the drowning person. Through the eye of the image, she came to understand that she needed to find some way of responding to the war that would have not only the possibility of helping those in Afghanistan, but also that of helping those in the U.S. who were deeply disheartened and shocked by the bombing and occupation of Afghanistan and who needed to be in some form of human relationship with the Afghans.

Cole said she had no idea what this response would be, that it was the image of people forming a human chain, connecting across space amid difficulty, that oriented her. Her daughter had married a Pakistani, and Edith was due to visit them in Pakistan. She and a colleague and friend, Joe Franko, decided to go and visit the Afghan refugee camps to see what their needs might be. While there, one person mentioned the need for 1,000 blankets, another for food. But Edith could feel that these single acts were not the right embodiment of the image that was guiding her. At one point, she met with a group of women, and Joe met with a group of men. Both, however, given their histories as a school psychologist and as an educator, had been attuned to listening to the needs of schools for Afghan children. When they reconvened, they realized they had come away with different impressions. Joe had heard that there was no school for Afghan girls in the camps. He had given his card to a man who said he wanted to create one. Edith had heard there were three schools that had some girls. She decided that, on her next trip, she would take the 2,000 notebooks she had been asked for. She could then visit the schools and see for herself if they existed and if they had further needs.

The first school she visited on her next trip had 1,000 students, some of whom were girls. It was in fairly good shape, as were the other two schools she saw. At the last one, the principal asked her if she would like to see a very poor school that was really struggling. She said she did and found it was in yet another refugee camp. When she arrived, she saw some eroded mud walls, without a real roof and with the students exposed to the elements. Owing to the shortage of wood, the roof timbers had been taken long before by people travelling back to Afghanistan. The students had no notebooks or books. There were mainly boys. When she spoke with the principal, he said he had a dream of creating a school for girls. Edith immediately resonated with this dream and saw helping to create such a school as a way to activate the image of the human chain that guided her. She helped the principal write a proposal for a school for two hundred girls and six teachers that Edith would then bring back to America to seek funding for. As she was leaving, the principal said he had met someone else who might be helpful. He pulled out a card from his wallet, and it was Joe Franko's, her colleague, who had given it to him some months before. This confirmed her sense that, as Quakers put it, "a way had opened."

Within a year, there were four hundred girls at the school. Edith Cole and Joe Franko went back and forth four times a year to help in the development of the school and to hear its ongoing needs for support. Back home, they met with an advisory board of people who felt moved to witness and support their work, joining hands in the human chain Edith saw in her initial vision.

I saw in Edith's approach a confirming resonance with the approach we have developed at Pacifica Graduate Institute for depth psychologically oriented cultural and ecological fieldwork and research:

- Listening to the imaginal field for the image(s) that calls us, be it from dream, conversation, newspapers, art, poems, songs, movies;
- Honoring the images that haunt us through study, reflection, participation, and action;
- Participation with a given community so that one can begin to learn where, as Buechner puts it, our "deep gladness meets with the deep hunger of the world."[34] The particularity of our lives gives us each unique paths between the depths of who we are and engaged participation in community and ecological life;
- Preparing the ground so that the way can open requires a suspension of premature knowings, a careful listening to the dreams of the community, and an ability to patiently wait for a resonant chord that links individual and community life and action at their deeper levels;
- Once the opening has been found, a sustained careful listening informs our participation. Such participation can create solidarity and actions that support the unfolding of beloved community.

Depth psychology can use its sensitivities and practices to support the multiplicities of healings this time requires. As imaginal psychologists, we must use our abilities to ask people to dream and image in relation to the limit-situations we struggle with, and then to listen together to the emerging images in a way that bears witness.

Without public homeplaces to do such listening, we are each left alone to struggle with the images that haunt us. When Adolf Harash, a Russian psychologist, traveled to Chernobyl after the nuclear accident to offer trauma assistance, he was struck by the number of plant workers who reported that they had dreamed of the plant's malfunction, but had never discussed their dreams and fears with those close to them, let alone with the plant management, who, it was feared, would feel such forebodings to be almost unpatriotic.[35]

Without a witnessing community, the images that find us fall to the status of mere fantasy, for we fail to find relation to their catalytic, dynamic power. When our relationship with images falls into being a mere pastime, we sever ourselves from the regeneration they might otherwise provide. The depth of meeting the ethical demands of the image together in our ongoing living is replaced by the superficiality of being stimulated by an ongoing barrage of prepackaged images in commercials, television, and political discourse that aim to program our consumption and elicit our complicity while eroding opportunities for dialogue, debate, and public dreaming.

"The inexhaustible ovary of another way of being"

Danilo Dolci, the Sicilian poet and social activist who helped to free Sicily from the oppressive grasp of the Mafia in the 1960s, says, "perhaps the pollen of words penetrates the inexhaustible ovary of another way of existing."[36] Dreams, images, and the actions they can give rise to provide such pollen.

In December 2002, I traveled to the island of Guana in the British Virgin Islands to attend a small ecopsychology gathering, hosted by James Hillman. I met Professor Liao, an ornithologist and biologist in his 70s who works each day to restore and preserve a peaceable kingdom on Guana. His sculptures, poetry, and songs are woven together with paths he has created and newly planted trees to encourage breeding grounds for disappearing species of flamingoes and iguanas.

Liao was born into extreme poverty on Hainan Island in the South China Sea, at the same latitude as Guana. He witnessed horrifying atrocities during World War II, his neighboring village being doused with gasoline and set alight by Japanese soldiers, who then machine-gunned people fleeing the flames. Later, he witnessed the assaults perpetrated during the Cultural Revolution. He changed his name from what is translated as "Dung beetle" to Wei-ping, "safeguard for peace," an apt name for the life that was to unfold. As a child, he wanted above all else to learn, but had no money for school. He became a school janitor as an adolescent and gradually convinced the teachers that he should be given the chance to learn. He became a leading authority on the ecologies of Guangdong Province and Hainan Island, which were undergoing a serious crisis of erosion, with species dwindling. He met an American biologist, James Lazell, who was studying Guana Island, which not only turned out to be an island at the same latitude, but probably had the richest wildlife diversity of an island of its size in the West Indies, and perhaps in the world. It had many plant and animal species in common with Hainan Island. Liao understood that, if he studied Guana, he might be able to create a plan of restoration for Guangdong Province. Van Lare says that Liao "knew there was a symbiotic relationship between certain bird and tree species that influenced the temperature of the ground, which in turn influenced local rainfall." He knew trees provided the necessary link by anchoring topsoil and lowering the temperature. With only scrub vegetation, "the forest ecosystem—including the birds who nest in the trees and spread the trees' seeds—vanishes and is replaced by a hotter, drier local climate and an eroded landscape."[37] Liao studied Guana Island in the hope that it would teach him which birds and trees could be helpful in bringing back the forests of Guangdong and Hainan.

Guana too was beginning to erode, and so he also developed a plan to increase forest, bird, and plant species there. After going back and forth for a number of years, Liao made his home on Guana, combining biological study with ecological restoration and art. As he walks with visitors, the images in his poems, his Chinese songs, and hand-hewn sculptures are part of the ecology of the place. They are called forth by the landscape, but do not stand out from it. Their simple beauty is resonant with the beauty of the place itself. His acts of restoration, like our own, are responses to the way the world addresses him, and us.

Standing in his orchard garden, where he is familiar with each tree he has planted and sheltered until it could grow on its own, he shared that one day at dusk, as he was finishing his work he heard the words "I love you" coming from his own banana plant. His solidarity with the place has created a space to open where the trees and creatures address him as though in a dream, and where resonant images as expressed in his sculpture and poetry unfold to mark the community relationships that he nurtures.

These sculpted images, as well as the paths he has created and the trees he has planted, are akin to the idea of the Sabbath in Judaism. The Sabbath is thought of as a homecoming, to our source and to our destination, a time during which we become attuned to the ways in which Paradise is already upon us, to how existence is completed and fulfilled.[38] It awakens us to the latent possibility of such homecoming in each moment. In Hasidism, it is believed that heaven and earth are one, though moved apart. Buber says we were "created for the purpose of unifying the two worlds [through] holy living, in relationship to the world in which [we have] been set, at the place on which [we] stand."[39]

Our communities have need of pollination by images that bring us into creative relationship with the limit-situations of our time, that nourish us with the sense of the possible, that refresh our spirits, renew our hope. What is the image that haunts you, as the photo of the lynching of teenagers Thomas Shipp and Abram Smith haunted Abel Meeropol, which led to the writing of "Strange Fruit"? What is the history in your community that needs to be placed on a public wall to inspire and educate, to be retrieved from the processes of social amnesia? What are the limit-situations to which your particular being is attuned and on which dreams and imagination must be brought to bear? What is the dream or image that could provide a path for you in relation to others, to link your own well-being and liberation to that of others, like Edith Cole's image of linking hands in the face of drowning that led to the creation and nurture of the Afghan girls' refugee school? And, in your efforts to forge a bit of heaven on earth, what images might flow from psyche to grace our shared spaces, as Liao's wooden sculptures show our capacity to create in resonant relation to the rest of creation?

We have been too quick to use dreams to anchor our focus to the personal and the presumably collective or archetypal, sidestepping culture, community, and nature. Individualism's tropism to retreat to the narrow boundaries of an encapsulated self needs to be countered by a turn to the creation of what Thich Nhat Hanh has called "communities of resistance," public homeplaces where "people can return to themselves more easily, where the conditions are such that they can heal themselves and recover their wholeness," where they can come to see more clearly, where there is support for resistance to being "invaded, occupied, assaulted, and destroyed by the system."[40] Such communities are created and nurtured by image.

The moral pilgrimage that requires us—that our individuation requires—is best undertaken in the company of others. Those tutored in depth psychology have a critical role to play in the opening of public spaces to receive and work with image. While not letting go of our sensitivity to listen to images in relation to the personal life of the individual, we must not rest here. To do so silently colludes with the cultural forces that want us to accept this poor world as it is, where species are being extinguished, Indigenous communities erased, where racial and economic apartheid are accepted as inevitable. It is into this world that we must welcome the embers of image that are gifted to us and fan their glowing core with the breath of our attention and love, praying they will ignite and reorient our lives through the creative actions we undertake together in the light of their vision.

Indian author and activist Arundhati Roy shared, "Another world is not only possible, she is on her way. On a quiet day, I can hear her breathing."[41] If we listen together, we too can hear this other world breathing on the ember images that will mark our paths. We need only add our breath to hers.

Notes

1 Pablo Neruda, *Toward the Splendid City* (New York: Farrar, Straus & Giroux, 1972).
2 Kenneth L. Smith & Ira G. Zepp, Jr., *Search for the Beloved Community: The Thinking of Martin Luther King, Jr.* (Valley Forge, PA: Judson Press, 1998), 139.
3 Coretta Scott King, *My Life with Martin Luther King, Jr.* (New York: Puffin Books, 1969), 223.
4 Martin Luther King, Jr., *Where Do We Go From Here: Chaos or Community?* (New York: Bantam Books, 1967), 10.
5 Mary Watkins, "From Individualism to the Interdependent Self: Changing Paradigms in Psychotherapy," *Psychological Perspectives*, 27 (1992): 52–69.
6 C.G. Jung, *Collected Letters, Vol. I (1906–1950)*, ed. G. Adler (Princeton: Bollingen Series, 1992).
7 A.R. JanMohamed, "Some Implications of Paulo Freire's Border Pedagogy," *Cultural Studies*, 7, no. 1 (1993): 113.
8 Tod Sloan, *Damaged Life: The Crisis of the Modern Psyche* (New York: Routledge, 1996), 62–63.
9 Ibid., 63.
10 Aurora Levins Morales, *Medicine Stories: History, Culture, and the Politics of Integrity* (Cambridge: South End Press, 1998), 129.
11 Susan Griffin, *A Chorus of Stones: The Private Life of War* (New York: Anchor Books, 1992), 32, 53.
12 Julia Kristeva, *Revolt, She Said* (Los Angeles: Semiotext(e), 2002), 57.
13 Ibid., 120.
14 Kelly Oliver, *The Colonization of Psychic Space: A Psychoanalytic Social Theory of Oppression* (Minneapolis: University of Minnesota Press, 2004).
15 James Hillman, *Suicide and the Soul* (Dallas: Spring, 1964).
16 David Margolick, *Strange Fruit: The Biography of a Song* (New York: Harper Collins, 2001).
17 Quoted in Margolick, 4–5, 8.

18 Margolick, 6.
19 Quoted in Margolick, 7.
20 Ibid., 43–44.
21 Julia Kristeva, *Revolt, She Said*.
22 Quoted in Paulo Freire, *Pedagogy of the Oppressed* (New York: Continuum, 1989), 89.
23 Mary Watkins, *Mutual Accompaniment and the Creation of the Commons* (New Haven: Yale University Press, 2019).
24 Juana Ponce De Leon, *Our Word Is Our Weapon: Selected Writings of Subcomandante Insurgente Marcos* (New York: Seven Stories Press, 2002).
25 bell hooks, *Yearning: Race, Gender, and Cultural Politics* (Boston: South End Press, 1990), 41–42.
26 Lynne A. Bond, J.S. Weinstock, and Mary Belenky, *A Tradition That Has No Name: Nurturing the Development of People, Families, and Communities* (New York: Basic Books, 1999).
27 Manuel Mancillas, "Transborder Collaboration: The Dynamics of Grassroots Globalization," in *Globalization on the Line: Culture, Capital, and Citizenship at U.S. Borders*, ed. Claudia Sadowski-Smith (New York: Palgrave, 2002).
28 Aurora Levins Morales, 5.
29 D.W. Winnicott, *Playing and Reality* (New York: Routledge, 2005).
30 Freire, *Pedagogy of the Oppressed*.
31 Robin Kelley, "Finding the Strength to Love and Dream," *Chronicle of Higher Education*, June 7 (2002): B7–B10.
32 Deborah Saunders, Workshop on Prophetic Ministry, Southern California Quarterly Meeting, Society of Friends, Pacific Palisades, CA, 2003.
33 I became a contributor to Edith Cole's project and was so moved by the story she shared with those of us with whom she worked.
34 Frederick Buechner, *Wishful Thinking: A Seeker's ABC* (San Francisco: Harper, 1993).
35 Shared by Harash during dream conference hosted by Robbie Bosnak, Moscow, 1989.
36 Danilo Dolci, "Education, Creativity, and Development," in *Facing Apocalypse*, eds. V. Andrews, R. Bosnak, and K. Goodwin (Dallas: Spring, 1987).
37 P. Van Lare, *Guarding the Peace on Guana Island*. Unpublished manuscript, 2001.
38 Abraham Heschel, *The Sabbath: Its Meaning for Modern Man* (New York: Harper, 1951).
39 Martin Buber, *The Way of Man: According to the Teaching of Hasidism* (Secaucus, NJ: Citadel Press), 40.
40 Thich Nhat Hanh and Philip Berrigan, *The Raft Is Not the Shore: Conversations toward a Buddhist-Christian Awareness* (Maryknoll, NY: Orbis Books, 1975).
41 Arundhati Roy, "Confronting Empire," *Z Magazine*, retrieved from https://zcomm.org/znetarticle/confronting-empire-by-arundhati-roy

Part IV

Gender, sexuality, and the patriarchy

Introduction

"The essence of patriarchy is having and needing to have things in their places," writes Andrew Samuels. "It is characterized by order, perhaps rank, certainly discipline."[1] In patriarchy's search for certainties lies a hunger for power and authority. Patriarchy is an oppressive, discriminatory system that favors reductionistic, simplistic views of the world. Fixed categories, binaries, and gendered discourses all serve its claims to a comfortably knowable, controllable life. A psychological approach that accounts for the unconscious offers a stark contrast to patriarchy by challenging the convictions that come with it. Hillman defines psychoanalysis as "a work of knowing in the midst of feeling the unknown and unknowable, a self-limiting, self-inhibiting ethical discipline, casting doubt on certitude, bringing hesitation to irrelevant desire, and reflection to megalomania."[2] He declares his path:

> I am seeking to ground possibility in the impossible, searching for a way to account for the unknown in the still more unknown, *ignotum per ignotus*. Rather than explain I would complicate, rather than define I would compound, rather than resolve I would confirm the enigma.[3]

The two essays in this section seek to both complicate and confirm enigmas about sex and gender that are societal, cultural, political, and psychological, including Jungian. Both essays critique fixed oppositions and neat divisions, such as male and female or masculine and feminine, while advocating for a style of consciousness that acknowledges and celebrates multiplicity, diversity, and fluidity.

Jungian psychotherapist Claudette Kulkarni's "In the wake and shadow of 'the battle of the sexes': A new myth is arising," asks: What happens when individuals undertake the task of deconstructing, reinterpreting, or rejecting collective myths and dominant narratives? Assimilating her research in Jungian studies, philosophy, and social anthropology, Kulkarni analyzes the concept of opposites as Jung and many of his followers have employed it. She examines the historical evolution of ideas pertaining to opposites in Western thought and underscores the need to redefine them, and some of their implications, especially in the context of sex and gender. In search of a more flexible way of understanding "the problem of opposites,"

DOI: 10.4324/9781003325765-14

Kulkarni discusses the American myth of "the battle of the sexes," asserting that male and female are not opposites; masculine and feminine are socially constructed concepts that exist only in the imaginations of individuals.

Jordan Shapiro, an author and professor in gender, sexuality, and women's studies, whose work draws on archetypal psychology and phenomenology, picks up the same thread in "Private parts, public prejudice: Archetypes, gender essentialism, and American patriarchy," an essay that affirms that the American understanding of gender is now being renegotiated. Citing examples, Shapiro shows how the language of feminist and queer studies is going mainstream, and how the use of nonbinary pronouns is debated almost daily. Shapiro maintains that these deliberations are not only a political, cultural, and legal renegotiation, but also an unconscious and symbolic one. In providing a critique of Jungian theory, Shapiro sheds light on its binary archetypal typologies, cisgendered images of the soul, and a generally patriarchal understanding of symbolic life that contributes to the rhetoric of gender essentialism. He invites the depth psychology community to acknowledge that patriarchy is a primary infection at the site of the American psyche and to recognize the imperialist, white supremacist, capitalist, hetero-patriarchal footing on which many psychological theories stand. Shapiro urges Jungian and archetypal thinkers and analysts to pay close attention to current cultural transformations. "The American psyche is undergoing a chiropractic-style readjustment," he writes, and, although it may at times seem painful, he avows what amounts to a healing transformation. According to Shapiro, re-visioning anatomy, gender, sex, and sexuality matters not only for defining and/or informing individual and collective identities, but also for collective ideals, aspirations, and ideologies in the field of depth psychology, as well as in American society.

Using the lens of sex and gender, both Kulkarni and Shapiro show that the deconstruction of rigid theories and dismantling of oppressive systems are about open minds and open hearts. This openness is not only an outcome of psychological theory but also a requisite for it to recognize and celebrate the psyche's "inherent multiplicity," in Hillman's words, as well as "[the] innate diversity, both among individuals and within each individual."[4]

Notes

1 Andrew Samuels, *Jung and the Post-Jungians* (New York: Routledge, 2013), 229.
2 James Hillman, "Dreaming Outside of Ourselves," in *City & Soul* (Putnam: Spring, 2006), 345.
3 James Hillman, *Revisioning Psychology* (San Francisco: Harper Perennial, 1975), 152.
4 James Hillman, "Polytheistic Psychology and Religion," in *Archetypal Psychology* (Putnam: Spring, 2006), 40.

Chapter 10

In the wake and shadow of "the battle of the sexes"

A new myth is arising[1]

Claudette Kulkarni

This is a work in progress that, I hope, lays the groundwork for a more ambitious future work on the concepts of sex, gender, and opposites. For now, I will unpack these concepts (which are foundational to the myth of "the battle of the sexes") and examine their interactions with Jungian theory, with the goal of disrupting this old myth and painting a backdrop for the emergence of a new myth that *could* take us in different directions. In the spirit of Jung's assertion that "every psychology—my own included—has the character of a subjective confession"[2] and of Hans-Georg Gadamer's rehabilitation of "prejudice,"[3] I will, along the way, acknowledge "prejudices" I bring to this project.

As a Jungian, I am deeply fond of Jung. As a post-Jungian, I recognize his flaws. So, I resonate with Andrew Samuels's call for "a program of renewal"[4] from within and with Mark Saban's warning that analytical psychology "must itself continue to individuate" if it is "to outlive [Jung] . . . to remain alive and to continue to interact meaningfully with . . . the 21st century."[5] For me, this means critiquing Jung with an attitude similar to Foucault's toward Nietzsche:

> I am tired of people studying [Nietzsche] only to produce the same kind of commentaries . . . . The only valid tribute to thought such as Nietzsche's is precisely to use it, to deform it, to make it groan and protest. And if commentators then say that I am being faithful or unfaithful to Nietzsche, that is of absolutely no interest.[6]

I cannot say that being "faithful or unfaithful" to Jung is of "no interest" to me— actually, I always strive to be in dialogue with him in order "to make problematic what has been taken for granted, rather than to provide a new orthodoxy."[7] I would like to believe that this was Jung's intention as well.

"The" American psyche, myth, and imagination

I will not be making claims about "the" American psyche since asserting something about an entire nation has been negated by Samuels[8] and by advances in archaeogenetics. However, I do recognize that most Americans "inherit" (or otherwise

DOI: 10.4324/9781003325765-15

acquire) a set of beliefs which are shared by *some* others and packaged as myths/ metaphors purporting to convey what it means to be "American." These myths are assimilated fairly unconsciously—just from breathing the air or by absorbing them from family, friends, books, movies, and other media. In addition, when people are gathered in small but passionate groups (e.g., family, club) or organized around a common set of beliefs (e.g., religious, political), they may *identify with* a particular myth and even become *caught* in what Thomas Singer has called a "cultural complex."[9] Such a myth can become glorified, even sacrosanct, and its adherents (being Americans) may "circle the wagons"[10] to defend it. But others may see the same myth as reprehensible and reject its underlying claims—and (being Americans) try to replace it with a "new and improved" opposing myth.

Myth

A myth is a story or metaphor conveyed through cultural symbols and signs—a kind of collective dream or "projection of the collective unconscious."[11] It usually includes an emotional component and serves some societal *purpose(s)*— imparting moral lessons, recounting historical events, reinforcing social norms/ values, justifying cultural beliefs, and so on. Some myths are old and well established. Some are new: These usually emerge in reaction to social/cultural circumstances and are energized by movements of people offering new ideas and symbols about the topic at hand. According to Jung, new symbols come from the unconscious via the imagination and/or the transcendent function, though their source is never exclusively conscious or unconscious; rather, they "arise from the equal collaboration of both."[12]

Imagination

For social anthropologist Rodney Needham, all narratives rely on imagination for the "formation of images . . . contrivance, inventing, devising"[13] and "the evasion of constraints"[14]—ingredients needed to escape the limitations of ordinary life and "abandon ourselves to fictions."[15] In addition, anyone "under the sway of collective representations"[16] is even more likely to believe things that are clearly not true. Too often, all of this results in the triumph of imagination over reason, especially since products of the imagination are "properties of the unconscious" and thus "independent of the will."[17] In other words, we are "not so free and not so individual as we thought we were."[18]

Jung also associates imagination—an "irrational force of instinct"[19]—with the unconscious: It can operate without our consent, evade rational constraints, and turn unconscious material "into something like a substitute reality."[20] But he also sees imagination as the source of "every good idea and all creative work"[21]—not as "something *contrary* to reason, but something *beyond* reason."[22] Still, he too recommends caution: Sometimes we need imagination to break an impasse, but we must not forget that "the unconscious can produce something disastrous to us"—yet, we "must be careful not to prescribe to the unconscious—it may be that a new way is required."[23]

Clearly, imagination is a tricky faculty. It can take us where no one has gone before, but it can also lead us down the proverbial garden path to disasters, "alternative facts," and conspiracy theories. And someone immersed in one of its products (e.g., a myth) may be operating in the realm of the irrational and thus be impervious to rational arguments. Perhaps only a new myth can reach them.

The battle of the sexes

This old myth is *not* uniquely American. Nor is it a story. It is more a metaphor and cultural complex in which heterosexuality is taken for granted and relationships between men and women are *imagined* as inborn antagonisms between two biologically and psychologically "opposite" sexes. It assumes that males and females have "naturally" incompatible and "opposite" needs, desires, goals, and traits: "She" is emotional and irrational, willing to ask for help (or directions), and likes talking about feelings; "he" is forever reasonable and rational, refuses to ask for help (or directions), and avoids discussing feelings. She is passive, delicate, dependent, and collaborative with others; he is active, strong, independent, and competitive. She is monogamous, scheming, intent on trapping him into marriage, and uses sex to manipulate him; he is polygamous, straightforward, always sexually available to her, but cannot be expected to control his urges. And so on.

Of course, this is not an accurate portrayal of most men or women. It merely reflects what a society expects, allows, or even requires of them. It relies on essentialist and stereotypical ideas about males/men and females/women and on a murky conception of "opposites." However, even if my rendition of the myth is something of a caricature, I believe it represents what many Americans seem to believe (if only unconsciously); it certainly is what many banter about. In some ways, it is true and false: True as displayed in sexist jokes, parodies, acts of discrimination, harassment, and violence; and false in implying that men and women (including heterosexuals who supposedly love each other) are *so* different from each other that relationships between them are inevitably never-ending battles. In Jung's words: "Although man and woman unite they nevertheless represent irreconcilable opposites which, when activated, degenerate into deadly hostility."[24] Really?

To understand this myth more deeply, we need to examine its components—sex, gender, and "opposites"—concepts around which I have accumulated several prejudices in relation to Jungian theory: As a lesbian feminist Jungian, I am frustrated with its deep-seated sexism and heterosexism, and its reliance on "opposites" to explain almost everything. As a (retired) Jungian psychotherapist, I am frustrated by the harm such prejudices cause. As a post-Jungian, I am committed to dismantling aspects of Jungian theory that keep us shackled to a binary system—fabricated notions such as "feminine," "masculine," "contrasexuality," and "anima/animus."

Here are three "rhetorical" questions to keep in mind going forward: What kind of a world is it in which the metaphor for relationships between men and women is a battle?[25] How does dualistic thinking affect our perceptions of our world, ourselves, and others? How can we cultivate a more compassionate world?

Gender/sex

"Gender" and "sex" are concepts conceived by humans. They are *not* "natural," *not* prior to culture, *not* ontological. Rather, they represent "a cultural reality laden with sanctions, taboos, and prescriptions."[26] Many scholars address them separately, but gender theorist Judith Butler argues that separating them implies that sex is a "natural" given on which "gender" is culturally constructed.[27] And biologist Anne Fausto-Sterling believes that separating them is actually a mistake because we still do not know "whether [various] skills are inborn or learned" and because they are "knotted together in complex ways"[28]—hence she suggests using "gender/sex," which I am adopting. Although I will occasionally use these terms separately, each should be understood as *always* lurking in the shadow of the other.

History

Most people assume that the idea of two biological sexes with corresponding social roles has been around forever. However, historian Thomas Laqueur contends that, from antiquity through the seventeenth century, there was just a "one-sex" body—reflecting the traditional belief "that women had the same genitals as men except that . . . 'theirs are inside the body and not outside it.'"[29] So, for centuries, the "intensely gendered [and hierarchical] social order" was "profoundly dependent on cultural meanings"[30] (not biology). It was only in the eighteenth century that "sex as we know it was invented"[31]—that is, when scientists began searching for "discoverable biological distinctions"[32] between males and females. Ever since, researchers have *presumed* that there are "two stable, incommensurable, *opposite* sexes" based "on [biological] 'facts'"—thus making biology "the epistemic foundation for prescriptive claims about the social order."[33] The result of this fixation on differences has been that "negative data"—that is, "data that shows no regular differences between the sexes"[34]—was (and still is) not reported. So, "far from being an expression of natural differences," gender/sex obscures "the suppression of natural similarities."[35]

I am not contending that Laqueur's analysis is the only way to think about gender/sex—but it is a thought-provoking one. In addition, for me, the "one-sex" body resonates with aspects of Aristotle's ideas that I find helpful for thinking about gender/sex. Simplistically put,[36] for Aristotle, every individual entity (animate or not) is a "substance," and every substance is made up of "form" (that which is *essential* to making something what it is) and "matter" (the "accidental" physical material out of which it is made). Since males and females share the same (human) form, any differences between them can only be "accidental" differences in matter—for example, reproductive organs.[37] We will see below how this interacts with Aristotle's ideas about opposites and how the two together will prove useful.

Furthermore, some contemporary biologists believe that "the idea of two sexes is simplistic."[38] Sex development is more complex than previously thought. Advances in various technologies have revealed that "there's much greater diversity within male and female, and . . . [that] some people can't easily define themselves within the binary structure."[39] When one considers all of the factors involved in sex development (gene activity and mutations, hormone signaling, XX and XY cell variations, etc.) and assesses the resulting evidence (including the wide variety of "intermediate cases"[40]), it becomes clear "that sex is no simple dichotomy."[41]

In addition, ideas about gender/sex are filtered through a complex network of factors beyond biology (e.g., social norms, cultural beliefs, historical and political factors). Authors from many disciplines have testified to this—for example, social anthropologist Rodney Needham (who remarked on multiple cultures having more than two gender/sexes[42] and criticized the tendency to divide human attributes into "masculine" and "feminine" since "[t]he more factors we admit . . . the plainer it becomes that the conceptual pair man/woman is not a natural opposition"[43]); social theorist Simone de Beauvoir (who emphasized the forging power of culture: "One is not born, but rather becomes, woman"[44]); novelist and social theorist Monique Wittig (who saw "men" and "women" as "political categories"[45]); philosopher/activist Michel Foucault (who traced how social and political institutions became adept at "regulating sex through . . . public discourses"[46]); philosopher-gender theorist Judith Butler (who has written extensively about the *regulatory practices* of gender formation"[47] and the cultural construction of sex); psychologist Christopher Kilmartin (who has dissected various popular fictions about men); and educator-social psychologist Helen Haste (who calls for "an *anti-logos*"—"an alternative picture"—a different myth?—about gender/sex that can confront the received dualistic *logos* "in terms which undermine—and, ideally, replace—it"[48]).

Unfortunately, few Jungians have entered the fray. I particularly appreciate the pioneers who did—for example, Lyn Cowan, Andrew Samuels, Demaris Wehr, Christine Downing, and Peter Mudd. In general, though, many if not most contemporary Jungians continue to follow Jung in reifying supposed differences between females and males by claiming that women and men have "separate but equal" innate traits.

Jung on gender/sex

It is difficult to disentangle Jung's ideas on gender/sex from those about opposites. He did not really distinguish between sex and gender, but he did insist that males/men and females/women are innately opposite to each other. And, although he often claimed that he was not conflating "the feminine" with females/women or "the masculine" with males/men, he did so regularly.[49] His numerous preconceptions about "the masculine" and "the feminine"—some personal,[50] some cultural—were hypothesized by him into opposing "masculine" and "feminine" principles and then improvised into concepts such as anima/animus and contrasexuality—heterosexist ideas which seem devised to fit with what Samuels has called "gender certainty," a mindset which leads to "lists of antithetical [i.e., 'masculine'/'feminine'] qualities, each list yearning for the other list so as to become 'whole'"—lists that only serve to "hamstring us."[51] Samuels calls instead for some "gender confusion."[52] Perhaps that would help Jungians think differently about gender/sex and stop genderizing human qualities—none of which "belong" only to a particular gender/sex. I know many men and women (myself included) who do not recognize themselves in those lists. I'm sure you do, too.

My take on gender/sex

Even within this brief survey, we have encountered a number of authors who argue decisively that sex and gender are *not* "natural." So, it seems only reasonable to me that we keep an open mind about these categories and see where that takes us. Perhaps the following thought experiment might help: Divide all human beings into two groups, using *any* biological or psychological trait (aside from parts of the reproductive system). This will *never* result in one group of only males/men and the other of only females/women. Even if one tries to divide them according to genitals, there will always be some number of intersex people comprising a third group; some trans people refusing to be assigned to a group just because they have (or had) a particular body part that, for them, does not define who they are; and some nonbinary people who do not identify with either of the two boxes. Sure, you could take the authoritarian path and assign them to the box that fits with *your* prejudices, but then what would you have? Something like two internment camps. This would be the only way everyone could be made to fit into just two boxes.

The concept of opposites

What do you mean when you call two things "opposites" versus "different"? Do you mean the same thing every time? Have you ever asked anyone to explain what "opposite" means to them? Are "opposite sexes" analogous to "opposite sides of the street"? Are "opposites" always both mutually exclusive and exhaustive? Are opposing sports teams "opposites"? If you "oppose" a policy, does that make you the "opposite" of its supporters? Does dividing something in two make the two parts "opposites"? Obviously, a truly comprehensive exploration of this ambiguous concept would raise more questions than can be addressed here. Plus, the concept has a 3,000-year history in Western thought involving diverse disciplines, cultures, and languages. So, I must limit myself here to what might provide some context for "the battle of the sexes" and for a new emerging myth.

History

The concept of opposites in Western thought can be traced back to eighth-century BCE Greece, where it was used both literally—that is, spatially (e.g., opposite sides of a river or directions such as up/down, right/left)—and metaphorically. Its metaphorical use generated a profusion of different kinds of opposites: Complementary versus incompatible pairs, processes on a scale (e.g., hot and cold), opposing forces (e.g., rarefaction and condensation), arguments for the "unity of opposites," pairs of supposedly analogous hierarchical opposites (e.g., the Pythagorean table of opposites), and so on. The first methodical study of opposites was undertaken by Aristotle in the fourth century BCE. He identified four kinds of opposites, though the only truly relevant one for our purposes is "contraries"[53]— that is, the two "most different"[54] predicates (qualities, capacities, traits) that can be *said of* a "substance" (as defined above). For Aristotle, a "mark of substance is that it has no contrary. What could be the contrary of a primary substance, such as the individual man or animal? It has none."[55] (Or what would be the opposite of a book, or refrigerator, or tree?) So, I take this to mean that females and males cannot *be* opposites, that they are only "capable of admitting contrary qualities"[56] (e.g., reproductive organs).[57]

In spite of Aristotle's efforts, the concept of opposites continued to be used in assorted ways for two millennia without any effort to explicate it until C.K. Ogden's *Opposition* in 1932. Ogden, an eccentric British linguist, proposed classifying most opposites as either "the two extremes of the scale" or "the two sides of a cut."[58] Since Ogden, there have been several noteworthy studies of the concept's *use* in specific contexts—for example, Lloyd, Maybury-Lewis and Almagor, Drob, Saban—but Needham's *Counterpoint* is the only work I have found that comprehensively addresses the concept itself, though he came to the conclusion that the concept has "no attribute . . . that is both essential and distinctive . . . no intrinsic logical form . . . no proper definition, but instead only . . . dyadic relations holding between variables of many disparate kinds."[59] There is truth to this, of course, but that's the problem. How can we continue to use such an equivocal concept?

Jung on opposites

The concept of opposites was foundational to Jung's thinking and deeply rooted in his personal life,[60] though he was also influenced by various thinkers. At times, his thinking about opposites was not consistent—for example, he stated in a seminar that "in a certain sense, the notion of the pairs of opposites is a projection upon nature"[61] but, later in the same seminar, claimed that they were "a rule of nature."[62] Be that as it may, for Jung, opposites were "indispensable preconditions of all psychic life,"[63] the tensions between them providing the fuel of life without which consciousness, experience, and knowledge would be impossible. Jung does not appear to have undertaken a study of the concept itself. Rather, for him, it was "a heuristic principle always to seek for the opposite of every given trend."[64] Perhaps, this is what led to his finding (or assuming?) that "opposites" were everywhere.

In any case, for Jung, psyche's task was "to imaginatively integrate a whole host of oppositions"[65]—which could be a stormy process, like "two parties at war with one another"[66]:

> The psyche . . . is *a boiling cauldron* of contradictory impulses, inhibitions, and affects, and for many people the conflict between them is so insupportable that they even wish for the deliverance preached by theologians.[67]

A preferred path to "deliverance" for him was the transcendent function: An "irrational, instinctive function"[68] that combines "conscious and unconscious elements"[69] and mediates between the opposites by "bridging the yawning gulf"[70] between them. The confrontation of opposites "generates a tension charged with energy"[71] which may constellate the transcendent function and result in creating an "attitude which liberates from the pairs of opposites,"[72] a "living symbol"[73] that can reconcile the opposites,"[74] "a living, third thing . . . a new situation."[75] However, as Jon Mills notes, opposites can sometimes "resist reconciliation"[76] or sometimes "simply [be] held in tension . . . [and] allowed a co-existence."[77] Only sometimes do they become "transformed"[78] and, in Jung's words, "flow on with renewed power towards new goals."[79] For this to happen, Jung tells us, each of the opposites must "be allowed to have its say,"[80] both must "play their part,"[81] and the individual (and, by extension, the collective) must make an effort to understand the symbol's "meaning and purpose."[82] In other words, the transcendent function is not something magical. It is a Gadamerian hermeneutic process, a way of expanding consciousness by being "true to both sides of a conflict,"[83] a path we must be open to if we hope to catch sight of a solution.[84]

Jung's ideas about opposites mirror "the first law of thermodynamics which states that energy demands two opposing *forces*."[85] However, Jung did not restrict himself to physical forces when discussing opposites. Rather, he sometimes applied the concept to *entities* (i.e., Aristotle's "substances," such as males and females) and abstractions (e.g., "masculine" and "feminine"). In addition, as noted above, Jung often referred to pairs of opposites inconsistently—for example, as "never incommensurables,"[86] as "irreconcilable,"[87] as complementary, as needing to be brought together through compromise versus needing to be compartmentalized and "balanced,"[88] as behaving as if on "a scale,"[89] and so on—all of which echoes the concept's history, but does not clarify what Jung meant each time he used the concept, nor how it might have affected his theorizing.

My take on opposites

Dualistic divisions are generally simplistic and reductive. To understand our increasingly complex and changing world, I believe we need to consider more pluralistic and discriminating methods. This is not to say that opposites (or dichotomous division) are *never* useful or appropriate, just that we should be thoughtful, transparent, and explicit in our use of them. To that end, but because this is a work in progress, I can offer only some *tentative* and preliminary ideas about classifying various kinds of opposites:

- *Spatial*: Relationships between (a) physical features (e.g., opposite sides of a street) *or* (b) directions in space (e.g., up/down, right/left);
- *Logical*: (c) Contradictory statements (two statements which cannot both be true)—though certain contradictory statements (paradoxes) can both be true and false;
- *Physical forces*: (d) Natural forces that attract/repel/interact resulting in some type of physical action (e.g., positive/negative poles of magnets, clashing of hot/cold air) *or* (e) human forces physically facing each other on a field of battle or play (e.g., opposing armies or sports teams);
- *Psychic forces*: (f) People, energized by conscious/unconscious psychic forces, enacting a pair of opposites (e.g., adherents of opposing myths; though psychic in origin, such forces can result in physical actions);
- *Metaphorical*: (g) Pairs of concepts/predicates (e.g., light/dark, right/wrong, black/white) that can be explicated as opposites (scientifically, logically, etc.). Some might seem "self-evident," but all require some indication of what makes them "opposites."

Obviously, much still needs to be resolved in terms of further challenging, parsing, and defining each of these categories and subcategories, and of developing guidelines related to each, especially to the metaphorical use of opposites. But, hopefully, this constitutes a constructive first step toward elucidating the various uses of opposites.

Linking "gender/sex" and the concept of "opposites"

The results of these surveys of gender/sex and opposites may be encapsulated in a few *tentative* "axioms" that will provide a foundation for going forward:

- *Males and females are "substances" and, therefore, cannot be opposites*, though they can possess opposite or "contrary" predicates (qualities, capacities, etc.)—but so can two men, or two women, or two cats. The only predicates that can be attached to "sex" might be in the context of reproduction. But even then, why would having a few different body parts make two people "opposites" when they have numerous other body parts in common?
- *The terms "masculine" and "feminine" are invented concepts.* Aside from reproductive organs, there are no predicates that apply universally to *all* males but to *no* females (and vice versa);
- *Sex development is a complex process.* Current biological research indicates that the binary system is unable to accommodate the complications being detected;
- *The binary gender/sex system is increasingly being called into question*—by scientists, social theorists, philosophers, historians, psychologists, and so on and

by ordinary people (especially young people) who are, more and more, rejecting their assigned gender/sex in favor of identifying as nonbinary;[90]

- *There are various kinds of opposites.* Two (from the list above) will be pertinent to subsequent sections:

  - (f) Psychic forces being enacted by people holding opposing beliefs (e.g., adherents of our two myths);
  - (g) Pairs of concepts/predicates that distinguish two opposing myths.

Now, finally, it is time for the new emerging myth to show itself.

The rise of a new, still emerging, myth

New myths often demand new social norms. Butler tells us there are two kinds of social norms: Those "we cannot do without" because they "orient toward the common good"[91] and others which impose unnecessary and oppressive constraints. She urges us to distinguish between them since the former are "the norms that permit people to breathe, to desire, to love, and to live" while the latter are "those . . . that restrict or eviscerate the conditions of life itself" and make it "unlivable for some."[92]

Our current gender/sex system (reflected in "the battle of the sexes") *is* unlivable for many, including some who want to fit into the prevailing system of "opposite" sexes and some who do not. However, since "any excessively strong position brings forth its opposite,"[93] our current gender/sex system has also aroused a resistance: People who are enacting a new "opposite" myth (or *anti-logos*), one still emerging, that I am calling the myth of "a *nonbinary* world." Riki Wilchins, an early activist in the transgender movement, believes that the term nonbinary "will challenge everything we currently think about bodies, sexual orientation, and gender, almost all of which depends implicitly or explicitly on the binary."[94] Evidence of this can be found in the many discussions about pronoun usage in American media.[95]

For me, "nonbinary" refers to anyone who cannot, or will not, conform to prevailing dualistic gender/sex/sexuality norms. This encompasses a cornucopia of gender-bending movements and a wide range of people—not only those who identify specifically as "nonbinary," but also those who use other terms to indicate their rejection of the prevailing binary system: Transexual, transgender, drag queen, intersex, gender non-conforming, LGBTQIA+, and so on. Nonbinary people have been around since time immemorial, but it is only recently that changing societal attitudes and the internet have made it possible for them to come out of the closet, find each other, and feel safe enough to express themselves in books, blogs, lectures, online videos, and onstage performances and declare their preferred pronouns.[96]

Although I think of myself as solidly in the margins of this movement, I cannot claim to speak *for* it. Instead, I will try to sketch this myth by channeling one vocal nonbinary person: Alok Vaid-Menon, an American author, activist, and performance artist who, in a recent book, published in 2020, exhorts us to get *Beyond the*

Gender Binary. This tiny but remarkably evocative book does not literally recount a myth, but it does suggest features of an evolving myth and its community: "Self expression sometimes requires other people. Becoming ourselves is a collective journey."[97]

Vaid-Menon asserts that the problem is "the whole gender system"—a system that is "set up for [all of] us to fail"[98] and that uses many strategies "to make the gender binary system seem like a given, not a decision."[99] For example, it uses biology "to position trans and gender non-conforming people as artificial and everyone else as natural."[100] This is just

> a rhetorical strategy for a normative goal. There is absolutely no biological basis for why boys should not paint their nails or be sensitive and girls should not play football or be taken seriously for their ideas. This is not about science, it's about power.[101]

Vaid-Menon attests to the wide diversity of gender non-conforming people: From the intersex (examples of "human diversity"[102]), to the transgender (whether or not transitioning medically to another sex), to someone who might wear a dress and sport a beard, and so on. "There are as many ways to be nonbinary as there are non-binary people"[103] (just as for cisgender women and men). So, Vaid-Menon argues for "multiple genders" because

> [n]o one should be able to tell you who you are; that's for you to decide . . . . We don't consider remembering everyone's individual name a burden; we just accept that as the way things work. Gender should be the same way.[104]

Vaid-Menon *imagines* a future in which "boys can feel, girls can lead, and the rest of us can not only exist but thrive. This is not about erasing men and women but rather acknowledging that man and woman are [just] two of many."[105] They (Vaid-Menon's pronoun preference) hope for a time when "[o]bjects, emotions, and careers will not be 'masculine' or 'feminine,' [but] 'adventurous' or 'compassionate'" because we will be willing to cultivate "more precise language . . ., more just practices."[106] Think about "how much time and work it takes to sustain the gender binary. How much we have to repress—all the feelings and dreams we have to sacrifice" to accommodate gender norms.

> We sacrifice what they call feminine so that we can be masculine, and we sacrifice what they call masculine so that we become feminine . . . . It's exhausting. . . . What part of yourself did *you* have to destroy in order to survive in this world?[107]

At the end of their book, Vaid-Menon shares their own experience: "I was terrified that when I came into myself I would lose everything. Instead, I found myself."[108] They now *imagine* a world in which everyone can find themselves, a world that truly fosters individuation by acknowledging and even celebrating a proliferation of gender/sexes, a world that allows every individual to live a full and authentic life versus being pressured into conforming to oppressive social norms.

That's the world I would like to live in. Wouldn't you?

People of the old myth could learn many things from the people of the new myth (and their allies)—for example, that gender is not identical to sex, that basing gender/sex on "external reproductive organs leads to gray areas,"[109] that everyone has a right to feel free to explore gender/sex in a world that recognizes "not only . . . the complexity of gender, but . . . the complexity of the individual,"[110] and that "choices" around gender/sex include, but are not limited to, the option of identifying as male/man/masculine/he or female/woman/feminine/she. And perhaps people of the new myth have something to learn from the adherents of the old myth, but that can happen only if the adherents of both myths find ways to talk with each other.

When opposing myths collide

As everyone knows, our two myths are currently colliding—which was inevitable once the people of the new myth started demanding rights and social acceptance. This conflict is likely to continue for some time, given the polarized energy on each side: One insisting on conformity to a binary system that limits gender/sex to two innately opposite gender/sexes and the other demanding a pluralistic world in which gender/sex *non*conformity is the norm and all gender/sexes are free to thrive. They are like two armies/*forces* facing each other in battle.

But are they also "opposite" myths? I believe so. *On the side of our old myth* are people who are rigidly attached to traditional views of two gender/sexes in "battle." Some of them feel strongly enough about this to support discriminatory and oppressive legislation against nonbinary people (for example, the Human Rights Campaign reported that, in 2021, a record-breaking number of anti-LGBTQ laws were introduced into state legislatures across the U.S., and many were enacted into law).[111] Others campaign to ban books by nonbinary authors (for example: *Gender Queer* by Maia Kobabe and *All Boys Aren't Blue* by George M. Johnson).[112] And still others have engaged in violence against people who do not conform to gender/sex ideals. *On the side of the new myth* are people who believe that gender/sex is a fluid category and that there are more than two gender/sexes—possibly an *unlimited* number. They long for a time when people of whatever gender/sex are fully accepted as members of the communities they live in. In other words, the people of each myth are animated by the "most extremely different" ideas about gender/sex and *imagine* a world governed by contrary predicates: Solid/fluid, rigid/flexible, limited/unlimited, groupthink/individuality, exclusionary/inclusionary, and so on.

Not surprisingly, when two such opposing myths come face to face, we can expect the eruption of tensions that Jung warned us about (the "boiling cauldron") to result in battles, chaos, and polarization prior to any potential collaboration. At this point, resistance to the new myth is fierce, and the transcendent function is nowhere in sight. But Jung tells us what is needed:

> The living symbol cannot come to birth in a dull or poorly developed mind, for such a mind will be content with the already existing symbols offered by established tradition. Only the passionate yearning of a highly developed mind, for which the traditional symbol is no longer the unified expression of the rational and the irrational, of the highest and the lowest, can create a new symbol.[113]

In addition, much will depend on how the adherents of each myth use the powers of imagination and how they envision the "meaning and purpose" of the new myth: Is this Armageddon, or are we on the threshold of a potentially more egalitarian society? In any case, Jeffrey Kiehl suggests that we "create new stories around what is happening now" and *imagine* "the world that we would like to bestow on future generations"[114]—something I believe the people of the new myth are trying to do, while the people of the old myth, unfortunately, appear to be doubling down. Perhaps, ultimately, the solution might lie with the people of an intermediate myth—but, for now, we must deal with what we have.

This leads me to Kiehl's important reminder that *every* complex has "both positive and negative dimensions," and that "[t]he optimal situation is one in which both . . . poles of the dyad are active,"[115] so as to resist the one-sidedness that Jung repeatedly warned against. But what are these opposing dimensions of our myths? I have already suggested problematic aspects of our old myth (e.g., rigidity, restricted creativity, and an us/them attitude toward gender non-conforming people), but what about its beneficial side? Well, it promises social order, establishes predictable expectations, and, theoretically, minimizes gender confusion and anxieties about how to "pass" in one's assigned gender/sex and have a place in the social world. And what about the new myth? On the upside, it promises personal freedom and creativity, allows for unregulated individuality in relation to gender/sex, and promotes a pluralistic, inclusive, and accepting I/we attitude toward all gender/sexes. And its shadow side? Well, it could be seen as lacking in boundaries and promoting excessive fluidity, replacing gender certainty with uncertainty and confusion, and challenging everyone's sense of self/identity. Of course, such opposing dimensions are all in the eye of the beholder. Arguments can be made for and against both myths, depending on what kind of a world one would prefer to live in. But, regardless of the outcome, we are each being called to reckon with the possibilities.

Another consideration: Jung frequently referred to an archetype at the heart of every complex, and Kiehl contends that this "is true for cultural complexes as well."[116] Taking archetypes as Jung does (as "sources of energy"[117]), it seems to me that it is possible to see our two myths as sharing the same archetype (which likely intensifies their polarization)—perhaps something like the archetype of Self/Otherness. The people of the old myth see the "other" gender/sex as Other, as so different that relationships are like battles, each side trying to be in control in order to get their needs met (though they also seem to fear the end of the binary system). The people of the new myth see the "other" gender/sexes as part of humanity's diversity, *not* as Other; they applaud the multiplicity of gender/sexes as more livable than the binary system.

Reflecting on all of this, I am (like Kiehl) reminded of Jung's insight that "the symptomatology of an illness is at the same time a natural attempt at healing."[118] Though the clash of myths is not an illness, the sometimes-extreme emotional polarization displayed in the clashing seems to express a need for healing and evidence of a collective effort on the part of both opposing forces to come to terms with something new and still unknown, a new living symbol. At this point, it may all seem more polarized than collaborative and healing, but perhaps that is just what happens when new living symbols begin to show themselves.

Concluding ruminations

Will the tensions between the old and new myths be sufficient to constellate the transcendent function? Can the new myth help us realize another myth—that we are all created equal (a myth we have never lived up to and that is currently under enormous threat)? Is humanity ready to create a world in which women-of-whatever-kind and men-of-whatever-kind can imagine their relationships *as* relationships versus battles? To achieve all this, many things would need to change, including each of us. I believe the new myth could help us reimagine all of our relationships (regardless of gender/sex, sexuality, "race," religion, etc.)—but only if we heed Jung's words: "Where love reigns, there is no will to power; and where the will to power is paramount, love is lacking. The one is but the shadow of the other."[119]

In *Lesbians and Lesbianisms*, I wondered about the "meaning" of lesbianism and what lesbians might contribute to the collective. In that, I was inspired by Downing:

> To acknowledge that none of the ways we live our gendered lives is fully satisfying . . . is to recognize that others who choose different paths from our own do so on our behalf. They live for us as well as for themselves.[120]

I came to agree with her that lesbianism represents "a transcendence of reproductive love, a commitment to a different kind of co-creation"[121]—something that might assist in correcting the collective one-sidedness of compulsory heterosexuality and make possible "the transition from gender certainty to gender uncertainty."[122]

Now I find myself wondering the same thing about the nonbinary community: What previously (maybe still) unknown, unthought, unconscious "something" might it be carrying for the collective? Something about gender/sex/sexuality? Or love? Or diversity? Or what it means to be human? I don't know, but I am convinced that the new myth has something to teach us about ourselves, something that might help us make a better world.

In summary, I am not arguing *against* the idea that there may be differences be-tween males/men and females/women, just *in favor* of an *anti-logos* that rejects the received *logos* (the essentialist stereotypes, dualistic theories, hierarchical differ-ences) and concentrates instead on determining what differences there *actually* are, what their causes are, what they actually *mean*, how *significant* they might be (or not)—and that attends to *similarities* as well. All we really know at this point is that differences are not destiny, our ideas about gender/sex are not "natural" but shaped by many factors, males and females are more similar than different, and the con-cept of opposites is not quite as universal and self-explanatory as Jung presumed.

And I am not arguing against *concepts* of gender/sex as such, just against reduc-ing them to binaries, since these seem mostly to "function as othering mechanisms" that "provide the rationale for systems of domination"[123] which always benefit the dominant group. Instead, why not simply allow people to be themselves? Why not appreciate presentations-of-whatever-kind (vs. "gender") as just part of their persona—as something unique to them, though consisting of traits variously shared by others?

Finally, a few questions for my Jungian colleagues: Why not wonder about the overuse of undefined "opposites"? Why not (at least) question, challenge, rethink, or even (I would argue) abandon the use of concepts such as "feminine," "mascu-line," "contrasexuality," and "anima/animus"? Why not think about ideas such as "anima/animus" as aspects of the Shadow (qualities repressed to "pass" in one's socially assigned gender/sex), or as introjects of patriarchal norms,[124] or simply as a non-genderized soul? Using genderized terms merely legitimizes illegitimate concepts and prevents Jungian theory from individuating into the future (or even coming into the present)—not very different from recent rulings by the U.S. Su-preme Court that are taking us back to the eighteenth century; its conservative justices (who form a majority) follow a theory ("originalism") by which the Con-stitution must be interpreted strictly according to what the justices *speculate* was in the mind of its signers in 1787! Maybe the time has come, as Cowan suggested 22 years ago, "to throw out the petrified skeletons in the Jungian closet," things such as "[o]ppositional thinking, 'positive/negative' moralisms . . . masculine/feminine 'principles,'" and "the animus."[125] Undoubtedly, this will seem like "too much" for many Jungians and maybe "too hard" for most. But can we not at least *start* ques-tioning why Jungians are so attached to these terms? *Start* looking at the shadow side of these concepts? *Start* acknowledging the new myth? *Start* making the effort to understand its "meaning and purpose"? *Start* employing our imagination to ex-plore different ways of thinking (since "a new way" may be required)? And, most of all, *start* exploring different ways of thinking? *Start* wondering whether some of Jung's theories (his "subjective confession") might be just that, and not true for everyone and all times? While I respect concerns expressed by clinicians that we need to meet clients/others where they are (i.e., often within the prevailing frame-work), I do *not* believe that we need to collude with the binary system in order to do that. Rather, I think it is time for us to do the *opposite*—to refrain from reinforcing an oppressive system.

Notes

1 In remembrance of Lyn Cowan (1943–2022), a fellow traveler in critiquing the sexist/heterosexist aspects of Jungian theory. She has inspired me since we first met in 1983. I am forever grateful for the privilege of calling her my friend.
2 C.G. Jung, *Freud and Psychoanalysis. The Collected Works of C.G. Jung*, Vol. 4, trans. R.F.C. Hull (Princeton: Princeton University, 1961), para. 774.
3 For Gadamer, prejudices (what we bring to any situation) are preconditions of understanding: "The important thing is to be aware of one's own bias, so that the [other] can . . . assert its own truth against one's own fore-meanings"; Hans-Georg Gadamer, *Truth and Method,* trans. Joel Weinsheimer and Donald G. Marshall (New York: Continuum, 1993), 269.
4 Andrew Samuels, *The Political Psyche* (London: Routledge, 1993), 325–326.
5 Mark Saban, *"Two Souls Alas"* (Asheville: Chiron, 2019), 3.
6 Michel Foucault, quoted in Claudette Kulkarni, *Lesbians and Lesbianisms* (London: Routledge, 1997), 10.
7 Helen Haste, *The Sexual Metaphor* (Cambridge: Harvard University, 1994), 17.
8 Samuels, *Political Psyche*, 317–336.
9 In a cultural complex, everything fits into a "preexisting point of view," thinking is "*simplistic*" and "impervious to modification," and "emotions" are pronounced; Thomas Singer, *Cultural Complexes and the Soul of America* (London: Routledge, 2020), xxiii.
10 Phrase inspired by Jeffrey T. Kiehl, "A Tale of Two Cultures," in *Cultural Complexes and the Soul of America*, ed. Thomas Singer (London: Routledge, 2020), 266.
11 Jung, *CW8*, para. 325.
12 Jung, *CW6*, para. 821.
13 Rodney Needham, *Counterpoints* (Berkeley: University of California, 1987), 51.
14 Ibid., 59.
15 Ibid., 61.
16 Ibid., 62.
17 Ibid. 65.
18 Ibid., 67.
19 Jung, *CW5*, para. 30.
20 Jung, *CW11*, para. 793.
21 Jung, *CW6*, para. 93.
22 Ibid., para. 774. Italics added.
23 C.G. Jung, *Analytical Psychology*, ed. William McGuire (Princeton: Princeton University, 1989), 11.
24 Jung, *CW12*, para. 192.
25 Thanks to Michael Sipiora for the underlying question—"What kind of a world is it in which such things can happen?"—which he put to a Duquesne University class in the aftermath of Columbine. I have been asking it ever since.
26 Judith Butler, "Variations on Sex and Gender," in *Feminism as Critique*, ed. Seyla Benhabib and Drucilla Cornell (Minneapolis: University of Minnesota, 1987), 131.
27 Judith Butler, *Gender Trouble* (New York: Routledge, 1990), 7.
28 Anne Fausto-Sterling, *Sexing the Body* (New York: Basic Books, 2020), 270.
29 Thomas Laqueur, *Making Sex* (Cambridge: Harvard University, 1990), 4; quoting fourth-century bishop.
30 Ibid., 115.
31 Ibid., 149.
32 Ibid., 5.
33 Ibid., 6. Emphasis added.
34 Ibid., 9.
35 Gayle Rubin, quoted in Laqueur, 241.

36 For a detailed version, see Marguerite Deslauriers, "Sex and Essence in Aristotle's *Metaphysics* and Biology," in *Feminist Interpretations of Aristotle*, ed. Cynthia A. Freeland (University Park: Pennsylvania State University, 1998).

37 This *logical* argument contradicted the entrenched Greek belief that males were superior to females. Lloyd points out several times that Aristotle often opted to justify such beliefs, usually by "explaining" how males were perfect exemplars of form while females were imperfect variants. See G.E.R. Lloyd, *Polarity and Analogy* (Indianapolis: Hackett, 1966/1992). (Also, I should note that I approach Aristotle as I do Jung—with the intent of using him against himself.)

38 Claire Ainsworth, "Sex Redefined," *Nature*, 518: 288.

39 Ibid.; quoting research scientist.

40 Ibid.

41 Ibid., 290.

42 Needham, *Counterpoints*, 211.

43 Ibid., 212.

44 Simone de Beauvoir, *The Second Sex*, trans. Constance Borde and Sheila Malovany-Chevallier (New York: Vintage Books, 2011), 283.

45 Wittig, quoted in Butler, "Variations," 135.

46 Michel Foucault, *The History of Sexuality, Volume One*, trans. Robert Hurley (New York: Vintage Books, 1978), 25.

47 Butler, *Gender Trouble*, 16. Original italics.

48 Haste, 14.

49 For numerous examples, see Lyn Cowan, "Dismantling the Animus" (2000), Dismantling the Animus, jungpage.org

50 See Saban's excellent study.

51 Andrew Samuels, *The Plural Psyche* (London: Routledge, 1989), 97.

52 Ibid.

53 Aristotle, *The Complete Works of Aristotle: The Revised Oxford Edition, Vols. One* and *Two*, ed. Jonathan Barnes (Princeton: Princeton University, 1984), 11^b18–14^a25. The other three: *relatives* (e.g., half/double), *affirmatives/negatives* (logical contradictions), and *privatives/positives* (e.g., blind/sighted). Connell notes that privative/positive sometimes *seems* to apply to female/male, but admits "Aristotle never calls [female] a 'privation' of humanness or even maleness" (Sarah M. Connell, *Aristotle on Female Animals* (Cambridge: Cambridge University, 2016, 23). N.B.: Something worth noting, but beyond our scope: Some contraries have intermediates (e.g., white/gray/black) while some do not (e.g., numbers must be odd or even).

54 Deslauriers, 142.

55 Aristotle, 3^b24–26.

56 Aristotle, 4^a10–12. See Deslauriers' detailed discussion of these arguments.

57 Although, to "explain" the different reproductive functions performed by males and females, Aristotle invented "masculine" and "feminine principles" and declared that these principles were opposites (Deslauriers, 141; Connell, 68–69).

58 C.K. Ogden, *Opposition* (Bloomington: Indiana University, 1932/1967), 58.

59 Needham, *Counterpoints*, 235.

60 Saban analyzes this in detail.

61 Jung, *Analytical Psychology*, 72.

62 Ibid., 78.

63 Jung, *CW14*, para. 206.

64 Jung, *Analytical Psychology*, 77.

65 Sanford Drob, *Archetype of the Absolute* (Santa Barbara: Fielding University, 2017), 182.

66 Jung, *Analytical Psychology*, 85.

67 Jung, *CW9i*, para. 190. Emphasis added.

68 Drob, 189, quoting Jung in *The Red Book*.
69 Jung, *CW6*, para. 184.
70 Jung, *CW7*, para. 121.
71 Jung, *CW8*, para. 189.
72 Jung, *Analytical Psychology*, 10.
73 Jung, *CW6*, para. 828.
74 Jung, *Analytical Psychology*, 98.
75 Jung, *CW8*, para. 189.
76 Jon Mills, "Psyche as Inner Contradiction," *Continental Thought & Theory*, 2 (4): 72.
77 Ibid., 79.
78 Ibid.
79 Jung, *CW6*, para. 827.
80 Jung, *CW8*, para. 181.
81 Jung, *CW6*, para. 827.
82 Jung, *CW8*, para. 147.
83 Demaris Wehr, *Jung and Feminism* (Boston: Beacon, 1987), 33.
84 See Gadamer, 383–389.
85 Andrew Samuels, Bani Shorter, and Fred Plaut, *A Critical Dictionary of Jungian Analysis* (London: Routledge, 1986), 102. Emphasis added.
86 Jung, *CW8*, para. 406.
87 Jung, *CW12*, para. 192.
88 See Saban's discussion of this, 156–159.
89 Jung, *CW8,* para. 408.
90 For example: Dawn Ennis, "New Research Reveals Insights into America's Nonbinary Youth," *Forbes*, July 13, 2021; and Mercedes Leguizamon and Brandon Griggs. "More US Teens Are Rejecting 'Boy' or 'Girl' Gender Identities, a Study Finds," CNN, October 3, 2018.
91 Judith Butler, *Undoing Gender* (New York: Routledge, 2004), 207.
92 Ibid., 8.
93 Jung, *Analytical Psychology*, 77.
94 Riki Wilchins, "Foreword," in *Nonbinary*, ed. Micah Rajunov and Scott Duane (New York: Columbia University, 2019), xii.
95 For example: The National Institute of Health's article, "What Are Gender Pronouns? Why Do They Matter?" Office of Equity, Diversity and Inclusion (nih.gov).
96 Books such as *Nonbinary*, ed. Micah Rajunov and Scott Duane (New York: Columbia University, 2019); blogs such as "Non-Binary People 101," Love Is a Rainbow, n.d.; a lecture such as Jesse Lueck, "Walking through the World Non-Binary," TEDx Ranney School, May 9, 2018; videos such as Michelle Guzowski, "A Trans Bowler in Ohio Fights for Acceptance," PBS Docs, n.d.; and performances such as Jo Michael Rezes, "A Playful Exploration of Gender Performance," TEDx Tufts, December 15, 2020.
97 Alok Vaid-Menon, *Beyond the Gender Binary* (New York: Penguin Workshop, 2020), 25.
98 Ibid., 27.
99 Ibid., 36.
100 Ibid., 47.
101 Ibid., 47–48.
102 Ibid., 50.
103 Ibid.
104 Ibid., 45.
105 Ibid., 60
106 Ibid., 61.
107 Ibid., 61–62. Emphasis added.

108 Vaid-Menon, 62.
109 Rajunov and Duane, xvi.
110 Ibid., xv.
111 Wyatt Ronan, "2021 Officially Becomes Worst Year in Recent History for LGBTQ," Human Rights Campaign, May 7, 2021.
112 Marisa Dellatto, "'Unprecedented' Book Ban Attempts in 2021," *Forbes*, April 4, 2022.
113 Jung, *CW6*, para. 823.
114 Kiehl, 271.
115 Ibid., 267.
116 Ibid.
117 Jung, *Analytical Psychology*, 91.
118 Jung, *CW8*, para. 312; quoted in Kiehl, 270.
119 Jung, *CW7*, para. 78.
120 Christine Downing, *Myths and Mysteries of Same-Sex Love* (New York: Continuum, 1989), xvii.
121 Ibid., xxiv.
122 Kulkarni, 213.
123 Carole R. McCann, Seung-Kyung Kim, and Emek Ergun (eds.), "Introduction," in *Feminist Theory Reader* (New York: Routledge, 2021), 21.
124 Wehr, 18, 20.
125 Cowan.

Chapter 11

Private parts, public prejudice

Archetypes, gender essentialism, and American patriarchy

Jordan Shapiro

In late summer 2022, when I told friends and colleagues that I was excited about the fall semester of teaching at Temple University, some asked if I was worried about being canceled. "These days, if you say one thing wrong, your career is over," one acquaintance warned, "I don't know how anyone can teach in those conditions!" At the time, most folks weren't even aware that I had recently expanded my course offerings, joining the core faculty for Temple's Gender, Sexuality, and Women's Studies program. Had they known, their comments might've made more sense—especially because I'm a cisgender white man. Even without taking my identity into account, there would be good reason to expect derision. Social media overflow with negative memes about gender studies instructors. One popular video offers to teach students how to "fight back" and "undermine leftist orthodoxy and lies" espoused by their "liberal" professors.[1]

Worldwide, gender studies has become an overt target, often scapegoated and attacked as "postmodern neo-Marxism."[2] In Hungary, Viktor Orbán's government has withdrawn accreditation for all gender studies programs, falsely claiming that the discipline is based on ideology, not social science.[3] Likewise, Vladimir Putin considers progressive ideas about gender to be one of the "problems in Western society." In one instance, Putin said that the acceptance of gender nonconformity was a "pandemic" comparable to the coronavirus.[4] Defending the illegal annexation of Ukraine in September 2022, he used the word "satanic" to describe the idea "that there are supposedly some genders besides women and men."[5] He sees military action as a righteous solution to the perversions of gender studies. In the United States, attitudes can be similarly troublesome. Governor Ron DeSantis signed Florida's so-called Don't Say Gay Bill in early 2022, prohibiting any discussion of "sexual orientation" or "gender identity" in elementary schools.[6] Around the same time, the Wyoming State Senate passed a bill to defund "any gender studies courses, academic programs, co-curricular programs, or extracurricular programs" at University of Wyoming.[7]

From the left, these examples are seen as a right-wing effort to maintain a hegemonic and patriarchal gender binary, which has often been identified as "both function and feature" of white supremacy.[8] Progressives see Orbán's, Putin's, and DeSantis's anti-gender studies positions as examples of explicit misogyny, homophobia,

DOI: 10.4324/9781003325765-16

and racism. From the right, however, these leaders' actions are celebrated because some folks believe that postmodern thinkers such as Michel Foucault and Jacques Derrida were engaged in an identity-based revision of Marxist theory, which will inevitably lead to a Soviet-style, totalitarian redistribution of power and status.[9] To this end, the popular conservative writer Jordan Peterson—who claims a Jungian pedigree—evokes red-scare images of the Soviet gulag. He became one of the bestselling authors in the United States thanks to a viral video in which he argues that Canada's Bill C-16 (which prohibits discrimination based on gender identity and gender expression) represents an attack on free speech. Notice that both sides villainize the other for authoritarian inclinations. Both also dismiss criticism as an unconscious projection of their partisan opponent's own fascist intentions.

On U.S. college campuses, the controversy often extends beyond the gender studies classroom. University of Pennsylvania's transgender swimmer Lia Thomas sparked outrage and debate when she won the 2022 NCAA Division I Women's 500-yard freestyle competition.[10] Many people called her win illegitimate. Trans-exclusionary radical feminists (TERFs) called it sexist and misogynist—extolling the sanctity, necessity, and equality of sex-segregated sports. To my knowledge, none of them mentioned, or even seemed aware, of the long feminist fight for gender- and sex-integrated youth sports. Girls' teams only became popular in the 1970s after the American Little League Association lost a landmark court case and could no longer exclude girls from playing baseball. The association's solution was to create *softball* leagues. They hoped that separate, but equal, teams would subvert most girls' interest in playing boys' baseball.[11] To me, sex-segregated sports are inherently problematic not only because of their dubious history, but also because they masquerade as meritocratic equity despite regularly perpetrating systemic sex-identity discrimination—unequal funding, equipment, prestige, and so on. But, for other people, sex-segregated sports uphold and reinforce a comfortable and safe gender binary, both symbolically and practically. This is why, in at least 30 states, GOP-sponsored bills have been introduced to block trans individuals from participating in publicly funded school and extracurricular athletic leagues.[12] Despite clear federal nondiscrimination laws and legal precedent defining sporting leagues themselves as "public accommodations,"[13] folks continue to propose legislative measures to maintain the categories to which they are accustomed.

In the wake of the U.S. Supreme Court decision overturning *Roe v. Wade*, it is not hard to imagine that we are witnessing the early stages of yet another slight-of-hand political strategy. This one is presumably designed to misdirect our attention toward transgender folks—one of the most vulnerable affinity groups in America, four times more likely than cisgender people to experience violent crime.[14] The ultimate goal, however, may be to challenge some of second-wave feminism's major victories. The Civil Rights Act of 1964's prohibition on sex-based discrimination could be at risk, especially the established legal precedent for interpreting Titles VII and IX.[15] To understand why, recognize youth sports as one of the primary locations in which gender- and identity-based hierarchy is taught and reinforced. Sociologist Michael A. Messner has written at length about how sports play "a key role in the construction and stabilization of a male dominant, heterosexist system of gender relations." He describes how British school sports were originally designed "to socialize boys to a certain kind of 'manliness' whose raison d'être was the administration of domination over (mostly nonwhite) colonized people." He also explains how, on the other side of the pond, the "rapid rise and expansion of organized sport" in the United States at the beginning of the twentieth century can be "interpreted as the creation of a homosocial institution which served to counter men's fears of feminizaton in a new industrial society."[16]

With Messner's history of organized sporting leagues in mind, consider the current controversy around transgender athletes alongside Colin Kaepernick's famous Black Lives Matter protest. Kaepernick has been unable to secure employment in the NFL since taking a knee during the national anthem in 2016. Then-presidential-candidate Donald Trump called Kaepernick's protest "Total disrespect for our great country!"[17] "The Star-Spangled Banner" gave Trump a covert way to hint toward nationalism. Just like Orbán, Putin, and DeSantis, he could then easily associate identity-based activism with a socialist threat to democratic freedom. From a Jungian standpoint, efforts to conflate sports with patriotism should be interpreted as a reactionary compensation for a potential dissolution of persona-identity. If institutions of sport function as a nucleus of a white supremacist, cis-hetero-patriarchal hierarchy, then both Lia Thomas and Colin Kaepernick are not only challenging social norms but also threatening to interrupt the masculine fantasy of athletic meritocracy. Sports not only reflect American puritanical values such as competence, perseverance, teamwork, and determination, they also function to camouflage systemic discrimination, and prejudice as free-market-style fair play. Hence, disruptions on the field or in the pool are uniquely constellating because they are experienced as disruptions at the soul of hegemonic masculinity and white supremacy.

It's important to acknowledge, however, that the handwringing about gender identity, gender nonconformity, and gender studies isn't limited to the conservative side of the partisan political spectrum in the United States. Those who watch cable news may have also seen liberal pundits, such as Democratic political strategist James Carville, grumbling that "faculty lounge politics" hurts the left. Complaining about the gender-neutral term *Latinx*, Carville said, "Wokeness is a problem and everyone knows it . . . but they don't want to say it out loud."[18] He's hinting at exactly the same fears as Orbán, Putin, DeSantis, Peterson, and Trump: That gender studies (also, presumably, Latin American studies) is inherently coercive and totalitarian. Like my colleagues who thought I should be concerned with cancel culture, he seems to believe that "identity politics" are not really about amplifying marginalized voices, but rather about silencing established voices. Moreover, Carville suggests that the academy is elitist and tone deaf. By saying "everyone knows it," he implies that a majority of people in the United States are concerned that the common academic understanding of gender—which says that it is a social construct or, to use philosopher Judith Butler's term, a "regulatory fiction"[19]—has become too extreme. Carville is just plain wrong: It's not true that "everyone knows it." According to the Pew Research Center, only 38 percent of adults in the United States believe society has gone too far when it comes to thinking about issues of gender identity. While there are clear differences of opinion that track neatly with political-party (and religious) affiliation, it's age alone that makes the biggest difference. Young Americans, on average, are much more likely than their older compatriots (by almost 10 percent) to say society has either "not gone far enough" or has been "about right" on progress toward gender equity.[20]

It's these young Americans that I meet every day in the classroom. They are not novices when it comes to gender studies. For them, the language of feminist and queer theory is familiar. Terms such as "normative" and "intersectionality," once common only among career academics and political activists, have become part of young people's everyday discourse. Kids and teenagers call out fresh examples of institutional bias regularly. They've even criticized beloved celebrity superstars such as *Harry Potter* author J.K. Rowling, standup comedian Dave Chappelle, and actress Bette Midler. All three have been accused of making transphobic comments in recent years. Nobody should be surprised by young people's outrage; it is grounded in the kind of empathy that comes from direct experience with subjugated gender nonconforming individuals. In 2021, a Pew study found that 42 percent of adults in the U.S. were likely to know someone who was transgender. About one in four respondents (26 percent) said they knew somebody who prefers gender neutral pronouns, an astounding 18 percent increase since 2018.[21] Perhaps this also sheds some light on why social media platforms, dating apps, and video teleconferencing services, such as Zoom, have been proactive about inviting users to share their pronouns. These Silicon Valley tech giants are not only acknowledging that issues of gender inclusivity contour the popular zeitgeist, but also—and possibly even more revealing when it comes to cultural change—they're recognizing that gender pronouns provide a significant amount of valuable data for algorithmically targeted advertising.[22] Bottom line: Pronouns may still be controversial, but they are no longer a fringe issue; *they* was Merriam-Webster's word of the year in 2019, based on a remarkable 313 percent surge in online searches.[23]

These examples all make it clear that, in the U.S., our collective understanding of gender is undergoing a tense renegotiation. People stake out positions on both sides of the debate. But I feel ethically compelled to acknowledge that, while their stances may be binary, the issue is not. Neither gender nor genitals are binary, either scientifically or socioculturally. As esteemed science writer Emily Willingham explains,

In each of us, gender—the state of being, for example, a woman or nonbinary or transmasculine—is a fluid mosaic of "masculinity" and "femininity" as our society and culture define them. The term "sex" is perhaps the most misused, perceived as accurately representing a clear biological choice between only two options: male and female.[24]

While there's no denying that biologists regularly use the language of binary sex to describe reproduction and gene transmission, Willingham explains that

> biologists bring loads of sociocultural baggage to their research, to the categories they create, and to the organisms and features they place in those categories. Although these terms and the binaries they imply can be serviceable shorthand, they are not culturally unsullied, pure representations of nature's boundaries.[25]

In the current gender renegotiation, as in all epistemic revolutions, it will take time for the facts to disrupt the status quo. As Thomas Kuhn elucidated in his classic tome *The Structure of Scientific Revolutions*, even researchers are usually less concerned with "scientific progress" than they are with proving their ability to operate within the current accepted paradigm. We are all likely to focus, first and foremost, on using the equations, tools, and methodologies considered correct within our respective fields and disciplines. For archetypal psychology, descriptive metaphors and images are analogous to the equations, tools, and methodologies of the science lab. Kuhn documented how folks will outright refuse to abandon the familiar "exemplars" of "normal science" until there are so many unsolved puzzles, anomalies, and errors that the consensus must crumble. In this context, it means that, although the facts about sex and gender are indeed settled, we're still living through exactly the kind of sluggish "paradigm shift" that Kuhn became famous for describing.[26]

Settled or not, the current political, cultural, and legal conflicts around gender warrant attention. They are evidence that the American psyche is actively undergoing a chiropractic-style readjustment. It's painful now, but, ultimately, it will be a healing revision to the way anatomy, gender, sex, and sexuality can define and inform our individual and collective identities, as well as our ideals, aspirations, and ideologies. It's especially important that the depth psychology community be attentive to this paradigm shift because much of the current, troublesome rhetoric around gender essentialism is derived from Jungian archetypal theory.

Analytical psychology has always been wedded to binary archetypal typologies, cisgendered images of the soul, and a generally patriarchal understanding of symbolic life. In her 2002 book *Jung: A Feminist Revision*, Susan Rowland is direct about it, explaining that Jung uses the terms "masculine" and "feminine" in essentialist ways, collapsing "gender onto bodily sex."[27] To understand what Rowland means, look at how Jung describes *animus* and *anima*: "The animus corresponds to the paternal Logos just as the anima corresponds to the maternal Eros." He's quick to point out that Logos and Eros are just "conceptual aids," lest his readers take the terms too literally. But he does not offer a similar disclaimer when it comes to sex and gender binaries. Instead, he writes, "woman's consciousness is characterized more by the connective quality of Eros than by the discrimination and cognition associated by Logos." He calls Eros an expression of women's "true nature." For women, he says, "Logos is often a regrettable accident."[28] Susan Rowland explains how later Jungian thinkers, "evade the reductive nature of Jung's identification of sex and gender by claiming that the feminine and masculine principles are purely archetypal and available to both women and men."[29] Certainly, this is true for later thinkers. But it's hard to believe that Jung thought in any way that resembles this construction. Even when he explains that we can all have both feminine and masculine characteristics, he doubles down on some of the most familiar chauvinist stereotypes. "Men can argue in a very womanish way," he writes, "the question becomes one of personal vanity and touchiness (as if they were females)."[30]

Jung's is one among many psychological theories responsible for images of masculinity and femininity that buttress cultural convention, shape a collective understanding of the individual self, and contour the American psyche. I suppose it's possible that archetypal gender essentialism was once just esoteric theory, shared only among Jungian analysts and their clients, who may have been able to avoid letting injurious symbolism impact everyday experience in toxic ways. But, as Jung's theories have spread to mainstream consciousness and popular culture, his essentialist attitudes have been regularly used to validate problematic attitudes. To understand this point, recognize how sexism relates to misogyny. In her 2017 book *Down Girl: The Logic of Misogyny*, Kate Manne offers a useful framework. She draws a distinction: "Sexism wears a lab coat; misogyny goes on witch hunts."[31] What she means is that sexism has to do with ideology. It tries to justify inequality by asserting that there are inherent differences between sexes, so it's sexist when somebody argues that men and women are each naturally inclined toward certain societal roles, or that they're psychologically predisposed to specific behaviors. Whenever we abide the sexist fallacies of biological determinism, it implies that the fight against imbalance or discrimination is ultimately futile—that inequality is just the way things have always been, the way they're supposed to be. Hence, Manne says that misogyny, in contrast to sexism, has to do with "enforcing" and "policing." It manifests as actions, speech, and attitudes that maintain and fortify cisgendered men's privileged positions of power.[32] Simply put, sexism substantiates misogyny. Orbán's, Putin's, and DeSantis's political actions are all examples of misogyny supported by a sexist commitment to dichotomous gender symbolism.

Using Manne's framework, it's also easy to see how archetypal gender essentialism has contributed to misogyny by offering sexist corroboration for false ideas about gender difference. For example, Jordan Peterson told the *New York Times*, "It makes sense that a witch lives in a swamp" and "it makes sense that an old king lives in a desiccated tower." With similar rhetoric to Robert Bly's *Iron John* men's movement, Peterson uses a familiar archetypal binary—feminine Eros as moist and dissolute chaos, masculine Logos as dry and resolute order. He argues, "The people who hold that our culture is an oppressive patriarchy, they don't want to admit that the current hierarchy might be predicated on competence."[33] He believes that sexist symbolism is so natural and essential that it should be seen as justification for misogynist social and political structures. His argument may seem outlandish, but it is not atypical. The same inclination to let sexist archetypal gender essentialism function as the rationale for misogyny is found among many progressive thinkers with misguided means for accomplishing feminist ends. Susan

Rowland describes this attitude as "the rejection of masculine-dominated mono-theistic culture in favour [sic] of a 'return' to the divine as a great mother." She calls it "Jungian Goddess Feminism," explaining that it is "designed to empower the insecure female psyche."[34] Just think about all the new-age pop psychology books which elevate so-called divine feminine energy types. They rely on typical mythopoetic amplifications directly drawn from Jungian binaries. *Men penetrate; women encase. To be male is to enter and infiltrate; to be female is to hold and encompass.* These are symbolic fallacies that may have a visual correlation with anatomy, but have no relationship to psychology. Research has consistently shown that receptivity, nurture, and intuition are genderless. Likewise, emotion, empathy, and intimacy have nothing to do with genitals. Connective eros is not "woman-ish." As sociologist Raewyn Connell writes, "The broad psychological similarity of men and women as groups can be regarded, on the volume of evidence support-ing it, as one of the best-established generalizations in all the human sciences." Some may protest, thinking of all the articles they've read which claim research has substantiated certain differences. Headlines that bolster a gender binary may sell, but they're deceptive. In 2015, a survey of "106 meta-analyses, incorporating data from 12 million people," found that the bulk of studies concluding that there are identifiable gender-based differences in psychology relied on effect sizes that were small or close to zero.[35]

Jungian Goddess Feminists may not care what the research says about corporeal being because they approach gendered symbolism as what Susan Rowland calls "non-material pre-patterning in the unconscious."[36] But, if that's the case, then why use the terms feminine and masculine at all? Cataloging any psychological incli-nations according to gendered imagery reinforces false assumptions about innate differences between *two* anatomical types—which not only strengthens the sexist foundation for misogynistic attitudes, but also fails to acknowledge that a simple binary can't adequately represent the full spectrum of biological (or psychologi-cal) difference. Disparate unconscious archetypal images, structures, and voices may indeed constitute our cognitive experiences, but the characters in our minds only become gendered because we filter their images through a lifetime's worth of patriarchal lenses.[37]

One of the best examples of an unduly influential patriarchal lens is also an ex-ample of archetypal gender essentialism contouring mainstream consciousness—Joseph Campbell's monomyth. Look at how Campbell described the battle between hero and tyrant: "Whether he knows it or not, and no matter what his position in so-ciety, the father is the initiating priest through whom the young being passes on into the larger world."[38] He's talking about cognitive and social-emotional development in a general sense here. The hero's journey is not only about comparing folktales or archetypal patterns. It also metaphorically describes a supposedly healthy path to-ward psychological maturity. Notice that Campbell presumes the young hero to be male. There's no getting around the fact that it's really a boy's journey and it neces-sarily includes a confrontation with a dominant patriarchal authority figure—the father, the king, the tyrant, the wizard, the judge. Campbell lays out the archetypal rivalries: "the son against the father for the mastery of the universe, and the daughter against the mother to *be* the mastered world."[39] A binary, misogynistic hierarchy is built right into the monomyth. And therefore, according to Campbell, the archetypal battle between fathers and sons is an inescapable fact of real-life experience: Men are destined to compete for the alpha position in a gendered social hierarchy, which only has space for one dominant male authority, who has implicit sexual access to women's bodies. It reminds me of the way sociologist Michael Kimmel describes American manhood: As a competition to become "the biggest of wheels, the sturdiest of oaks, the most virulent repudiators of femininity, the most daring and aggressive."[40] With the monomyth, is Campbell simply observing an archetypal truth? Or is he perpetuating a sexist fallacy? It depends on your perspective.

Like the Goddess Feminists, Jungians and their self-help, pop-psychology disciples might argue that the monomyth's gendered images are products of the unconscious and, therefore, they don't correlate with physical anatomy or sex-based psychological dispositions. In which case, we should presumably understand the monomyth as a simple explication of the *generation gap*. From this perspective, Campbell's mythopoetic amplification of hero stories distills adolescent rebellion into a pure and essential structure. That's why it's so easy to recognize how the hero archetype is constellated in the Industrial Age fetish for innovation and the American obsession with political revolution. Think: *Drain the swamp, fight the deep state*, and *eliminate the political establishment*. Likewise, the same archetypal hero story is lurking in our business and professional preoccupation with technological disruption and it's in the capitalist consumer fixation on novelty: We Americans always want the newest, fastest, flashiest, and most powerful products. We aim to trade our aging goods for youthful replacements because all young heroes must eventually replace elderly fathers and kings—we expect the insurgent to become the establishment, we expect the margin to become the center. Undoubtedly, this is an archetypal inclination that humans sometimes have, but not always. The notion that this story constitutes a universally applicable psychological schema—an essential law of human nature that transcends cultural and historical context—comes directly from Sigmund Freud. And it's wrong. In fact, there are plenty more primary hero myths that tell a variety of other tales about fathers and sons—Abraham and Isaac, Odysseus and Telemachus, Shiva and Ganesha—but, because Freud chose Oedipus, and because Campbell grafted his multicultural survey of hero myths onto Freud's Oedipus complex, we continue to understand both child development and psychological transformation through the singular lens of patriarchal murderous ascendency.[41] Which means, no matter how you look at it, the monomyth constellates as toxic masculinity and lionizes the American image of manhood as the essence of heroism.

James Hillman praised Campbell's classic, *The Hero with a Thousand Faces*, describing it as heroic in and of itself. He wrote,

By recovering the myth of the hero and restoring myth itself to primary place in cultural importance, Campbell has protected the city from the nihilism of materialist science, from Christian otherworldly redemption, and from the tyranny of capitalist commodification of all values.[42]

It's an uncharacteristically positive take from Hillman, yet one that also fails to see the way Campbell's narrative of murderous ascendancy has transformed just about every niche of the highly commodified personal development industry, which was valued at $41.8 billion in 2021.[43] There is now a "Hero's Journey" book, retreat, or inspirational program for just about everything—writing, weight loss, leadership, spiritual transformation, marketing, branding, and more. Each promises a foolproof algorithm—a kind of supernatural aid; a secret code; a treasure map; a lightsaber to maximize engagement, success, fulfillment, and/or profit—each seems to be promising exactly the kind of "nihilistic materialism" and "otherworldly redemption" that Hillman referenced. Certainly, Hillman is correct that Campbell's work embodies "the heroic foundation of myth," as Campbell himself describes it.[44] This is evident in the way the once-revolutionary monomyth has now become nothing more than an ogre-king, promoting a problematic narrative of psychological transformation that's not only sexist and male-centric, but also binary, heteronormative, and misogynistic.

The cis-hetero-patriarchal binary is a primary infection at the foundation of the American psyche. It is a root cause of myriad psychological symptoms which archetypal psychologists often claim to "see through" while remaining blind to the imperialist, white supremacist, capitalist footing on which our theories stand. Like Thomas Kuhn's scientists, the depth psychology community remains wedded to traditional Jungian categories and resists an inevitable paradigm shift. Like Lia Thomas's and Colin Kaepernick's critics, we're afraid of revising archetypal gender because it feels safe and comfortable. Do we think that nonbinary imagery threatens to cancel the nucleus of our intellectual identities? If so, we need to know that there's nothing to fear. Normalizing, binary-gendered narratives limit people's sense of self-worth, restrict their imaginative possibilities, and constrain their psychological aspirations. Worse still, they marginalize all the unconscious figures that fail to conform with the patriarchal gender order. The future of depth psychology requires not only seeing archetypal imagery in gender nonconforming ways, but also analyzing how a constellated gender binary restricts a fluid understanding of psyche.

Notes

1 Young America Fountation, "FIGHT BACK: Here's How to Win against Your Liberal Professors." YouTube. June 4, 2021. Accessed September 8, 2022. www.youtube.com/watch?v=pFxktaL7zBc
2 Ben Burgis and Matt MsManus, "Why Jordan Peterson Is Always Wrong," *Jacobin*, April 24, 2020. https://jacobin.com/2020/04/jordan-peterson-capitalism-postmodernism-ideology
3 Andrea Pető, "Four Reasons Why Gender Studies Has Changed Because of Illiberal Attacks, and Why It Matters," Heinrich Böll Foundation, May 3, 2021.

4   Maite Fernandez Simon, "'A Woman Is a Woman, a Man Is a Man': Putin Compares Gender Nonconformity to the Coronavirus Pandemic," *Washington Post*, Dec. 23, 2021.

5   Matt Steib, "Putin Decries U.S. 'Satanism' in Bizarre Speech Annexing Parts of Ukraine," *New York Magazine: Intelligencer*, Sept. 30, 2022. https://nymag.com/intelligencer/2022/09/putin-decries-u-s-satanism-annexes-parts-of-ukraine.html

6   Jaclyn Diaz, "Florida's Governor Signs Controversial Law Opponents Dubbed 'Don't Say Gay'," National Public Radio, March 28, 2022. www.npr.org/2022/03/28/1089221657/dont-say-gay-florida-desantis

7   Funding was restored a few days later when the Wyoming House and Senate renegotiated to pass the state budget.

8   Ruby Hamad, *White Tears Brown Scars* (New York: Catapult, 2020).

9   Ben Burgis and Matt McManus, "Why Jordan Peterson Is Always Wrong," *Jacobin*, April 24, 2020. https://jacobin.com/2020/04/jordan-peterson-capitalism-postmodernism-ideology

10 Katie Barnes, "Amid Protests, Penn Swimmer Lia Thomas Becomes First Known Transgender Athlete to Win Division I National Championship," ESPN, March 17, 2022. www.espn.com/college-sports/story/_/id/33529775/amid-protests-pennsylvania-swimmer-lia-thomas-becomes-first-known-transgender-athlete-win-division-national-championship

11 Heath Fogg Davis, *Beyond Trans: Does Gender Matter?* (New York: New York University Press, 2017).

12 Katelyn Burns, "The Massive Republican Push to Ban Trans Athletes, Explained," Vox, March 26, 2021. www.vox.com/identities/22334014/trans-athletes-bills-explained

13 See *Marin v. PGA Tour, Inc.* (2000) and *Matthews v. National Collegiate Athletic Association* (2001) as referenced in Heath Fogg Davis's *Beyond Trans: Does Gender Matter?*

14 Mev Rude, "Trans People Four Times as Likely to Face Violent Crime as Cis," *Advocate*, March 23, 2021.

15 See *Bostock v. Clayton County, GA* (2019) in which the United States Supreme Court held that Title VII of the Civil Rights Act of 1964 protects gay and transgender individuals from sex-based discrimination.

16 Michael A. Messner, *Power at Play: Sport and the Problem of Masculinity* (Boston, MA: Beacon Press, 1992), 11–15.

17 Dan Cancian, "Everything Trump Has Said about NFL Kneeling So Far," *Newsweek*, June 8, 2020. www.newsweek.com/everything-donald-trump-said-nfl-anthem-protests-1509333

18 Sean Illing, "'Wokeness Is a Problem and We All Know It.' James Carville on the State of Democratic Politics," Vox, April 27, 2021. www.vox.com/22338417/james-carville-democratic-party-biden-100-days

19 Judith Butler, *Gender Trouble* (New York: Routledge, 1990).

20 Kim Parker, Juliana Menasce Horowitz, and Anna Brown, *Americans' Complex Views on Gender Identity and Transgender Issues*. June 26, 2022. www.pewresearch.org/social-trends/2022/06/28/americans-complex-views-on-gender-identity-and-transgender-issues/

21 Rachel Minkin and Anna Brown, "Rising Shares of U.S. Adults Know Someone Who Is Transgender or Goes by Gender-Neutral Pronouns," Pew Research Center, July 27, 2021. www.pewresearch.org/fact-tank/2021/07/27/rising-shares-of-u-s-adults-know-someone-who-is-transgender-or-goes-by-gender-neutral-pronouns/

22 Rena Bivens and Oliver L. Haimson, "Baking Gender into Social Media Design: How Platforms Shape Categories for Users and Advertisers," *Social Media + Society*, 2016. doi:10.1177/2056305116672486

23 Amy Harmon, "'They' Is the Word of the Year, Merriam-Webster Says, Noting Its Singular Rise," *The New York Times*, Dec. 10, 2019. nytimes.com/2019/12/10/us/merriam-webster-they-word-year.html

24 Emily Willingham, *Phallacy: Life Lessons from the Animal Penis* (New York: Avery, 2020), 11.

25 Ibid.

26 Thomas Kuhn, *The Structure of Scientific Revolutions: 50th Anniversary Edition* (London: University of Chicago Press, 2012).

27 Susan Rowland, *Jung: A Feminist Revision* (Malden, MA: Polity, Blackwell, 2002), 39.

28 C.G. Jung, *The Collected Works of C. G. Jung*, Vol. 9.2, trans. R.F.C. Hull (Princeton: Princeton University Press, 1969), 14.

29 Rowland, 45.

30 Jung, 15.

31 Kate Manne, *Down Girl: The Logic of Misogyny* (New York: Oxford University Press, 2018), 80.

32 Ibid.

33 Nellie Bowles, "Jordan Peterson, Custodian of the Patriarchy," *New York Times*, May 20, 2018: Section ST, 1.

34 Rowland, 47.

35 Raewyn Connell, *Gender in World Perspective*, 4th ed. (Cambridge, MA: Polity, 2021), 45.

36 Rowland, 48.

37 Jordan Shapiro, *Father Figure: How to Be a Feminist Dad* (New York: Little Brown Spark, 2021).

38 Joseph Campbell, *The Hero with a Thousand Faces* (Princeton: Bollingen/Princeton University Press, 1972), 136.

39 Ibid.

40 Michael Kimmel, "Masculinity as Homophobia: Fear, Shame, and Silence in the Construction of Gender Identity," in *Research on Men and Masculinities Series: Theorizing Masculinities*, by Michael Kaufman and Harry W Brod (Thousand Oaks, CA: Sage, 1994), 138.

41 Shapiro.

42 James Hillman, *Mythic Figures* (Putnum, CT: Spring, 2007), 339.

43 Grand View Research, *Personal Development Market Size, Share & Trends Analysis Report by Instrument (Books, e-Platforms, Personal Coaching/Training), by Focus Area, by Region, and Segment Forecasts, 2022–2030*. Market Analysis (San Francisco, CA: Grand View Research, 2022).

44 Hillman, 339.

Part V

Psychotherapy, citizenship, and cultural movements

Introduction

Youth, independence, development, progress, and futurism. As James Hillman sees it, in the United States, the psychological naivete evident in the worship of such ideas signals the intoxicating presence of the child archetype in the American psyche.[1] "Child archetype is by nature apolitical and disempowered," he writes. The result is a preoccupation with personal survival and success, narcissism, greed, false feelings of entitlement, psychic numbing, passivity, apathy, and more.[2] "Democracy depends on intensely active citizens, not children," Hillman warns.[3] The following four essays touch on many related themes, such as idealism and independence, while their authors raise questions about the meanings of responsibility, agency, and empowerment for citizens in society. The authors discuss the ways in which psychological activism is a necessity for cultural movements and revolutions that ensure the survival of democracy, diversity, and justice in the United States.

In "America's child," author and psychotherapist Thomas Moore writes about the need to analyze America and its psychological character—the country's puer spirit, inferiority complexes, violent history, narcissism, unacknowledged guilt, and psychological defenses. Using Jungian and archetypal insights that probe myths across cultures—from Krishna to Icarus and Narcissus—Moore examines both the positive and negative aspects of the child archetype. He underscores the importance of building a good, healthy relationship with the archetypal child. Only then can a balance be found to help America maintain its hopeful and idealistic state and creative imagination, while it learns to think critically and take responsibility like a grownup. At once a rich depth psychological exploration and cultural critique, Moore's piece serves as a touching and persuasive plea for the American nation to engage in self-reflection and therapy, which entails looking beyond self-narratives of democracy and goodwill, probing the dangerous relationship between innocence and violence throughout its history, wrestling with the country's foundational ideas and ideals, and living out its values in sincerity.

In the subsequent essay, "Archetypal psychology and fugitive democracy: James Hillman's political legacy," professor of psychology and clinical psychologist

DOI: 10.4324/9781003325765-17

Michael Sipiora provides an insightful analysis of James Hillman's political re-visioning of psychotherapy. Sipiora reasons that, while Hillman's project was to re-vision psychology, his work extended well beyond the clinical field, to citizenship and democracy. Hillman "called into question the unconscious assumptions of the disordered world that give rise to the suffering of citizens—the inextricably linked anguish of psychological repression and political oppression"[4]. Hillman trusted that a psychological citizen is someone who has awakened and can uphold a duty to protest the world's injustices and futilities. Sipiora demonstrates how, for Hillman, psychotherapeutic practices must not isolate and only address the inner world—such as personal dreams, memories, and fantasies—but also must work toward the cultivation of the citizenry, with an eye for the common good. Following both Hillman and political philosopher Sheldon Wolin, Sipiora critiques corporate capitalism, neoliberalism, and the American empire while retuning theories of the unconscious, democratization of the self, and pluralism to emphasize the empowerment of psychological citizens.

In "Swimming the wave: Occupying uncertainty and the OWS movement," Gustavo Beck, a Jungian and archetypal psychotherapist from Mexico, dives into capitalism and psychotherapy, putting forth an intimate and thoughtful account of 2011's Occupy Wall Street movement. Beck draws parallels between psychic and economic movements and exchanges and examines unconscious and systematic symptoms that manifest in each. He tends to images and addresses emotions such as fear, anxiety, and despair, which increase in the face of inequality and injustice. Through clinical and personal reflections, Beck keeps returning to unresolved questions, highlighting the inevitability of uncertainty and the importance of being able to surrender and learn to swim the waves as they come. He sees crisis as an opportunity that can raise awareness of one's unawareness and delve deeper into issues, thereby urging revolutions, both individual and social.

Mythologist Rebecca Armstrong turns to the movies in "*Nomadland*: Scanning the horizon of the American dream." Although upward mobility served as the North Star of the American dream for generations, for the last 40 years, social and economic indicators confirm that, for most, the dream is simply unattainable, she writes. Therefore, according to Armstrong, when the film *Nomadland* won the 2021 Academy Award for Best Picture, it showed how mobility, or life on the road, offered a proverbial happy ending, or the promise of new possibilities. Underlying the film's precarity is the American fixation on the myth of progress: The idea that individual and collective lives must follow a storyline that moves toward a happy conclusion. Armstrong turns to Joseph Campbell's theories on myths and symbols to examine the metaphysical and psychological function of the horizon as a symbol in the American psyche, in poetry, art, film, and religion, to show how living myths are essential for any society.

Engaging in political action and cultural movements requires, to borrow Hillman's words, "the courage of the heart to stand for its perceptions."[5] He writes:

I don't know how to do the right thing. I don't even know what's right. I have no answer. But I sure smell something wrong with the government. And, within the federal government, for which I pay, something is wrong with airport safety, airline prices, gas prices, car efficiency, income tax loopholes, agricultural supports, PACs, rail service, sabotage of the postal service unions and union busting, aid to schools, military pensions, veterans' hospitals, drug testing, remedial education, busing.[6]

Even though certain experiences can feel disagreeable or even oppressive, repetition means that individuals often become numb to these experiences and begin taking them for granted. In these instances, Hillman does not call for treatment plans, cures, or solutions, but for aesthetic responses—simply noticing the wrongness and expressing outrage or anguish. For Hillman, this is a matter of heart-awakening, a matter of integrity. Likewise, Moore, Sipiora, Beck, and Armstrong advocate for following emotional experiences and embodied responses to the social, cultural, and political realities that individuals witness, both material and symbolic. The authors beckon the American nation to follow the symptoms and trust the uncertainty and unknowns. They show that an empowered citizenry requires such honesty and courage above all else.

Notes

1 James Hillman, *Re-Visioning Psychology* (New York: HarperPerennial, 1992), 128.
2 For more on these kinds of collective psychic wounds, see Mary Watkins and Helene Shulman, *Toward Psychologies of Liberation* (New York: Palgrave Macmillan, 2008), 64–79.
3 James Hillman and Michael Ventura, *We've Had a Hundred Years of Psychoanalysis and the World Is Getting Worse* (San Francisco: Harper, 1993), 6.
4 Michael Sipiora, "Archetypal psychology and fugitive democracy: James Hillman's political legacy," in *Re-Visioning the American Psyche: Jungian, Archetypal, and Mythological Reflections* (London: Routledge, 2024), 213.
5 James Hillman, "Aesthetic Response as Political Action" and "Aesthetics and Politics," in *City & Soul* (Putnam: Spring, 2006), 145.
6 Hillman and Ventura, 103–104.

Chapter 12

America's child

Thomas Moore

On ancient maps, the place we know as America is labeled Terra Incognita, the Unknown Land. Even today it is a land that is difficult to know, with its high-minded values coupled with extreme violence and a history of social inequalities. It seems to believe in visionary values, yet typically it doesn't live them out. At times its leaders sound either cynical or uneducated in their country's history and philosophy. Individual people and families often display American values in their sweet and challenging lives, but the nation as a whole sometimes appears vacuous in its claims to democracy and good will. America is often like a child who plays with life and has a dire need to grow up.

As I write, the country suffers a plague of shootings of young children and of people happily watching patriotic parades and innocently enjoying themselves. Over three hundred mass shootings in 150 days! One wonders about the object of these attacks—children and the innocent. The backdrop to this violence is a serious political threat to democracy rising from profound psychological aberrations—bizarre fantasies, hysterical emotions, and moral vacancy. It's time to reassess who we are and to do the analysis in depth. A nation, like a person, has its own psychological profile and its own therapeutic needs.

In the case of a troubled person, we often begin by looking into his or her childhood. We can do the same with the country as a whole.

Early mapmakers also labeled America Mundus Novus, "The New World," another synonym for childhood. This emphasis on "new" may reveal something significant about the psychology of America even today. Beneath all of its sophisticated technology and communications, America is still in its psychological infancy.

C.G. Jung wrote one of his more original and radical essays on the archetype of the child, and many of his comments could apply to America. When Jung speaks of the eternal child, he doesn't mean one that lasts forever, but a youthful spirit that is essential and timeless. It isn't just that America hasn't been around long, but that its character is formed around a spirit of youth, which offers both strengths and difficulties.

America is a complicated place with a varied history and citizenry, and yet the spirit of the child or adolescent—youth in many forms—dominates. Before this

DOI: 10.4324/9781003325765-18

country can finally become an adult among other nations, it will have to embrace the child that lives deep in its heart. The psychological rule is: You can't strive for what you need before you deal with what you have. We don't want to get rid of the youthful spirit, but to deepen it.

Another rule: Image and reality interact. America's complicated handling of children and young people is connected with the archetypal child and youth that could be the source of the country's vitality. We can get hints about the archetypal core by noticing how the nation deals with actual young people. The picture is complicated, because we are sentimental about children and yet neglect them routinely. We also have to ask, why would an 18-year-old man shoot almost twenty children in a classroom? At a deep level, is this an attack on childhood or on education or something else? Could the archetypal child be the object of the rage?

Jung and the child archetype

Jung's lengthy essay on the child archetype was written as a companion piece to two essays on the divine child by Karl Kerényi, a Hungarian scholar of classical religion. Both Jung and Kerényi see that the child image takes us far beyond actual children. For both men, the image evokes the infancy of life itself. Kerényi, for example, writes about the *archai*, the Greek word for beginnings or origins. The image of the child points to the ever-flowing source from which life emerges. "The human being's organic being from which he continually creates himself . . . . To this origin, understood as the beginning of a new world-unit, the mythologem of the divine child points."[1]

This child image is not the same as the popular idea of the "inner child." The archetypal child is not just an aspect of personality but the very seed of life. It has a significant, positive role to play in developing the visionary side of the American citizen, as well as a negative potential that interferes with becoming adult. Paintings of the Madonna and child also hint at the *archai* by portraying the huge potential for life in the figure of the infant Jesus, who often holds a globe in his hand, a figure who grew up to offer a route to an alternative, transformed humanity.

This vast, mythic image of potency and potential also appears in the playful creativity of the child Krishna. According to a famous story, one day he was playing with friends and got mud in his mouth. The friends told his mother, Yashoda, who confronted her child. Krishna denied playing with mud, and Yashoda told him to open his mouth. His mother looked inside and beheld the entire universe—planets, mountains, oceans. She fainted at the sight. Again, the child has the *archai*, the seeds of life and the universe itself, inside it. In a similar way, Jung says the child image signifies beginnings and the future—seeds and atoms.

I might add a fragment from Heraclitus: "Life is a child playing a simple game. The power of life belongs to a child."

In America's story, you might glimpse this child spirit in Johnny Appleseed, Lewis and Clark, Susan B. Anthony, the Wright Brothers, Martin Luther King, Jane

Fonda, and so many others. Hear their stories and you behold seminal ideas about exploration, the expansion of human rights, life-changing inventions, racial progress, and alternatives to violence. You see the child seeds in movements toward a more advanced society, in athletic and artistic achievement. You see America as potential itself, keeper of the *archai*. America as promise, hope, experiment, and the opportunity to live freely.

Puer and senex

Jung's disciple, James Hillman, approached the archetypal youth from a somewhat different angle, emphasizing the puer in relation to the senex. *Puer* is Latin for a young person or sometimes an infant, as in the celebration of Christmas, when on Christmas Day the choir sings in Latin: "*Puer natus est nobis.*" A child is born to us. More often, the puer is pictured as an adolescent and there signifies the spirit of a teenager. Icarus and Narcissus are examples of the benefits and dangers of a youthful psyche, teenagers on risky journeys of transformation, whose stories can shed light on the role of youth in the American way of life.

The corresponding Latin word is *senex*, for the spirit of old age and maturity. A person having a strong senex spirit may enjoy authority, tradition, formality, structure, abstract thinking, and quantifications. In actual life, these two archetypal presences, puer and senex, may clash, so that, when people don't get along, it may not be personal antagonism as much as these dominants in them finding each other hard to take. An old person possessed by the senex spirit may automatically criticize young people, and a young person may have a low opinion of the elderly. People often note that, in America, old people don't get the respect they might have in other countries, a sign of the child or puer dominance.

Some people have a puer character, its spirit influencing much of who they are and what they do. They have trouble with romantic and steady relationships because they can't imagine settling down or being "stuck" with one person, job, or locality. They are on the move in many aspects of their lives and, generally, they like to move quickly. You see an attractive puer in movies with Paul Newman, and then you find out he loved to drive race cars.

A cure for the puer spirit, if indeed cure is the right word, is to find some senex influence that might add necessary complexity to the psyche. For America, this might mean taking its visionary ideals and its high-minded values more seriously. In speeches and slogans, these values are too airy and unreal. Politicians might understand that their bloated language for American ideals makes things worse. It would be better to be realistic and honestly find ways to put these values to work. This would be the senex–puer solution to exaggerated youthfulness.

Aiming high

In 1979, James Hillman published an anthology of articles on the puer aptly titled *Puer Papers*, in which he reprinted an essay, "American Icarus," by the Harvard psychologist Henry Murray, who was not an archetypalist in orientation and yet added some fascinating ideas and language to the discussion.[2]

He wasn't writing about the Icarus myth in the American character, but about a particular man who exhibited extreme traits and pathologies of a youth-dominated psyche. Some of his odd terminology—ascensionism, prospection, and cynosural narcissism—helps us further understand the puer.

Murray lists a number of activities that lure an "ascensionist," one prone to soaring high, including sky diving, circus acrobatics, and mountain climbing. People with this complex, he says, do these things as much for attention as the thrill of height. The puer's Icarian delight in rising and being high and visible is like Jesus ascending into heaven and the astronaut blasting off the Earth. It is a movement toward transcendence, achievement, and vision. It is characteristic not only of many typical Americans but of the country itself. It accounts for America's visionary stance in the world, its role as beacon for discovery and experiment, and its falls from grace.

But Murray's comment is helpful: The puer often soars for attention. We will explore this aspect when we come to the puer Narcissus.

Puer is a particular personification of spirit, and ascending is one of its main attributes. Murray adds the word "cynosural" to ascending, meaning of the North Star, a desire to be seen, coupled with a need to have followers, people who admire you and believe in you. America certainly has a cynosural compulsion in its psyche, which can show as an inherent quality of leadership as well as distaste for joining or following others.

Prospection, Murray's second puer attribute, is an orientation toward the future, including both a fear of falling (failing) and a craving for immortality. We see this focus on the future in American life, especially a constant preoccupation with technological advancement. America is not known for its attention to the past, and generally Americans are not informed about their history. A 2018 Woodrow Wilson National Survey showed that 37 percent of respondents said that Benjamin Franklin invented the light bulb, and 2 percent said that climate change was the cause of the cold war.[3] These are extreme displays of ignorance, of course, but they point to a greater failure to understand the importance of history.

Icarus and Narcissus

Let's turn now to specific types of puer psychology that have, as usual, their positive and negative potential. We can find puer figures depicted precisely in mythology.

Icarus wants to eavesdrop on the secrets of the gods in the sky and soars high on the wax wings Daedalus made for him. But, exposed to the heat of the sun, he comes crashing down. Puer reaches too high and crashes in depression and hopelessness. Many creative people are fired up by the puer spirit and begin excellent work, only to leave it unfinished in a box or drawer full of incomplete projects. Politicians may talk about American ideals at such a high level that they never find actualization in ordinary life. America is widely Icarian, reaching high but susceptible to painful failure and disillusionment.

America pursues fame and celebrity with a passion, but it doesn't take much pleasure in doing all the work needed for those goals. We pay attention to many famous people, but we don't seem to appreciate all the work that went into their achievements.

Narcissus, a different sort of puer, starts out as a cold, distant teenager who happens to see his image in a pond and discovers for the first time that he is lovable. This realization is transformative, and Narcissus turns from a cold, marble statue into a flower, a sign of his metamorphosis. If America is the least bit narcissistic—Murray's third category—this annoying symptom shows that it, too, needs to learn deep, hard-won, honest self-love. Like Narcissus, it needs a long moment of reflection and then transformation, discovering its deepest nature and then becoming more open-hearted and less belligerent.

People think of narcissism as excessive love of self, but as a symptom it is just the opposite. The narcissist doesn't feel self-acceptance or doesn't value who he/she is or what he/she does. Therefore, he/she goes too far in trying to coerce others to love and appreciate him/her. America's narcissism, too, the kind we notice in speechmakers forever claiming that America is the greatest nation on Earth, is, at base, anxiety about the country's worth. It is not grounded appreciation of the country, or we wouldn't have to make such big claims. The more you tout yourself, the less certain you are about your worthiness. America's history of slavery and other moral failings stain its image and give pause to those who praise it too highly.

Other countries find America's narcissism offensive, because, from their position, they can see the emptiness in its claims of superiority. Some people don't care what other countries think, but a strong identity is largely familial and communal. The narcissist will suffer seriously from loss of connection and community. Maybe Americans should be more concerned about how other people think of them.

Puer men and women often dream of flying, either in jet-powered planes or by the strength of their own flapping arms. They usually have several of the traits of a "flying," airborne personality. They may feel above ordinary life, detached, aiming high, or unlimited. They may be concretely involved in actual flying—as pilots, astronauts, makers of model planes, students of space travel and exoplanetary habitation—NASA plays a big role in the American psyche. They tend to be unrealistically ambitious, imagining great things for themselves, but usually they end up feeling frustrated because they can't turn their dreams into reality. They may talk too much about themselves, even when there isn't much of value to be said. They may betray the ugly truth that their ideals are often puffy and unrealized.

The mythic narrative of Narcissus offers an ultimate cure for the narcissism that afflicts America, both politically and in ordinary lives.

Columbus the puer

We find some of this puer psychology in America's tales of origin. Christopher Columbus, who has been demoted from his role of discoverer, created in part by Washington Irving, from founder of America to the highly deluded visitor to Cuba, the nearby islands, and Venezuela, typifies the puer adventurer. It makes little difference that his presence in the American story is largely inaccurate. It has served as a myth for many decades, as a central narrative about who we are.

By the accounts of the journals from his four voyages, it appears that he was a talented navigator but not a good leader. He pursued three objectives passionately: To find China, to get as much gold as possible for his monarchs in Spain, and to convert all the people he found in the new lands to Christianity. About China, for years he maintained the hope that he would find the mainland among the many islands he came upon in his first explorations. Like the typical puer, he couldn't ground his search in a more realistic appraisal of where he was, because his grand fantasies got in the way.

Columbus's celebrated "discovery" of America took place with illusions and grandiose expectations. Even after getting to know the locals and surveying the islands, he believed he was only a short sail from China. He is honored for having discovered America, but in truth he was the first European to land in Haiti, Cuba, and surrounding islands. He never set foot in North America. The puer's own image of himself often overshoots reality, and he lives in a bubble of exaggerated accomplishments.

The invaders, such as Columbus, felt justified in naming every place they "discovered" in their own fashion, ignoring the native people as if they were not cultured enough to matter. They felt fully justified in imposing their religion and belief system on the people, as well. All of this came under the delusion that their religion was correct and their authority and power God-given—a childish approach to both religion and exploration.

The myth of the child often unfolds in relation to the parents and, in many cases, involves a difficulty separating from the original family to become independent. Interestingly, in his journals Columbus seems torn between his own independent exploration of the lands and people he encountered and the wishes of the king and queen back in the old country. The monarchs wanted gold and converts, while he, in a typical puer/senex split, yearned to colonize exotic lands.

We might understand the limited geographical knowledge in Columbus's time and excuse him for thinking he was always on the edge of Asia, but, on one of his voyages, he became certain that he had found a pear-shaped geographical pathway to heaven. This fantasy took him to extreme heights in his view of himself and his mission. The puer person typically gets swept away by fantasies of glory and adventure, the more unrealistic the better, and America is not immune to such flights of imagination.

The New World, therefore, came into being in the midst of immature, literalistic views about religion, an approach that still keeps many Americans in a childlike worldview that inhibits the development of values and relationships. Americans are still susceptible to wild fantasies, illusions, and conspiracies and still have an odd connection to Columbus and his visions of a pathway to heaven.

To summarize, the child archetype that permeates the American psyche accounts for innocence, archaic seeds of potential, and a concern for the future. On the negative side, it also brings immaturity, emotionalism, undeveloped thinking, and a weak link to adulthood. These are strengths and challenges America has always had to face.

Therapy for the child and the puer

For all these problems with the puer spirit in the nation, we don't want to deal with it by trying to get rid of it. The puer spirit keeps us going toward our ideals and helps us accomplish the seemingly impossible. But, so as not to be swept away in fantasy and adventure, it needs to encounter the senex demand for hard work, realistic goals, and patience. For America, this means actually living out its vision in the real world, doing all the challenging work needed to bring its excellent expressed values to fruition. To merely claim ideals such as universal freedom and international peace is not enough. America has to work constantly and with sincere dedication toward these goals that, if actually lived out, would bring deep happiness.

Hillman recommended avoiding any pressure on the puer spirit. Rather, he said, help deepen it and connect it to other elements in the psyche where it will be somewhat tamed and made more subtle. One of those, of course, would be the senex. Bridge art and craft, imagination and wisdom, strong leadership and openness to other people or nations, a thrust into the future and appreciation for history. A more sophisticated puer mentality would solve old, serious problems.

Puer dreams are especially easy to spot and they can be revealing. A man once told me of a dream in which he was flying in a small plane over fields. He looked down and saw his family waving to him from the ground. He waved back and then flew higher and farther away. Whether it was his actual family down there, or an image about having a family, or simply the past, I didn't know. But he was clearly flying away from family members who wanted him. The dream appeared to offer him a remedy for his extreme puer tendencies—to get low enough to reconnect with family.

America has a sickness of soul, part of which is its Icarian habits and its North Star narcissism. These neurotic tendencies harm community life and create a feeling of malaise that people can't see. Their narcissism and Icarianism are too pleasant. They don't reveal that they are a sickness with harmful consequences. And the remedy may appear too subtle: Reflection, hard work, a community sense, ideas about morality, and the common life. The child attitude and the puer spirit offer much that defines America, but they also turn into sickness in need of therapy.

America, the wounded child

Jung writes: "'Child' means something evolving towards independence. This it cannot do without detaching itself from its origins: abandonment is therefore a necessary condition."[4] The mythic narrative of the child can inform a person, but also a corporation, an idea, or a community. A nation might be dominated by the child theme and evolve toward independence and manifest the qualities of a child who makes gradual and stumbling headway. It may have feelings of abandonment or even an orphan psychology, the feeling of having to go it alone and find its own way, without the guidance of a parental figure. Internally, there is no senex parental figure to mature and at times restrain a runaway child.

Bereft of a positive motherland and fatherland, America rests on an insecure foundation, psychologically speaking. On July Fourth we celebrate a long, bloody battle to be free of an Old World parent. The War of Independence may have freed the country politically, but it could also be seen as the cause of psychological limitations.

According to Jung, the abandoned child feels exposed and threatened. At the same time, it holds a cherished promise of a better future, a new life. For over a century, people in other lands have considered America a model of hope and possibility. Americans have accepted that image and hold it dear, except that, in the reality of everyday life, pragmatism often wins out over idealism. The shining image of America easily gets tarnished and rusty. The message of the Statue of Liberty becomes too much of a burden, and, instead of just not living up to its ideals, many people become cynical and give up any hope of being a beacon. The idea of America gets lost and is abandoned, along with a new imagination of how life can be.

America doesn't need to live like a child but rather to have sufficient child spirit to remain hopeful and idealistic. Most of the time, it may need an adult relation to the world and a sober understanding of its place on the globe. Its citizens need to be well educated and adequately refined. Extreme political positions, so much a part of its history, reveal a child's histrionics rather than an adult's reasonable version of leadership.

James Hillman's archetypal child

James Hillman also wrote about the archetypal child.[5] Among many other things, he says that this psychological child is often seen as natural and wild and in need redemption or salvation. People believe it should be baptized and educated, initiated solidly into family and society values, learning its rules and expectations, for it carries Original Sin, the human stain, and a primal, untamed spirit to be broken and restrained.

On the connection between the archetypal child and actual children, Hillman makes an interesting point:

> We do not know what children are in themselves, "unadulterated" by our need for carriers of the imaginal realm, of "beginning" (i.e., "primitivity", "creation"), and of the archetype of the child. We cannot know what children are until we have understood more the working of the fantasy child, the archetypal child in the subjective psyche.[6]

Adults are often split in their feelings about children: They may sentimentalize or they may express their rage and frustration. America could transform its sentimentality into solid feelings of love for the child and children and make real efforts to give children opportunities for security and the chance to grow up into educated and cultured human beings. This shift in attention, this deepening of the concept of child care and child rearing, would heal the inner split of the country, because a healthy archetypal child is the foundation for a healthy adult. In Hillman's words, they make a "tandem," one supporting the other.

By treating children more sincerely, we could heal the nation's archetypal child and in doing that provide a path for maturity. Americans might grow up and be more adult among the nations of the world. America's deep child nature is a gift that needs attention. As Jung said, the psychological child is about the future and possibility. It isn't entirely correct to say that we need the child in place before we can be adults. It's more that we need to give attention to both childhood and emotional maturity. Neglect the child, and we won't be able to grow up. Without a good relationship with the archetypal child, we will remain childish and cut off from our maturity (senex).

Go with the symptom

How could Americans accomplish this psychological advance toward maturity? The first step is to call upon a fundamental rule in archetypal psychology: Go further into the symptom, not against it. It may seem counterintuitive, but this approach wants to preserve the symptom rather than get rid of it. In general, we want to help others with their suffering, but the best way toward that goal is to stay with the symptom and see what it is asking for or where it is headed. What is it trying to accomplish?[7]

If our symptom is immaturity, then we don't want to force ourselves to be mature but to deepen our flirtation with the child figure. A symptom is a defense against a more solid experience of the theme, but it also points us in the direction of what we need. America shows many signs of immaturity, pointing to the possibility of possessing real innocence and a deeper manifestation of a child psychology. If we get the child right, the actual symptom, maturity, will more likely find its place. We don't go directly to a solution, a typical strategy, but let the symptom take us to its core.

In our symptoms and pathologies, we are trying to accomplish something that we can glimpse and find valuable, but there are inhibitions and obstacles. Americans may treasure the image of the child or the spirit of youth, but they also want to avoid being gullible and too innocent. The result is being half in and half out of childhood. Symptoms tend to be extreme manifestations of an otherwise moderate and effective way of being. Americans don't want to be taken advantage of by shadow figures who appear cleverer than they, and so, defensively, they steer away from the youthfulness that is natural to them, often looking tough the way a young person might try to be adult. The potential for vibrant and adventurous youth gives way to symptomatic childishness and ineffective attempts at maturity. Often there is the pose of adult wisdom, but a pose is simply one more clever form of defense.

One good strategy might be to actually believe in the ideals so often praised in American discourse: Equality for all, blind justice, providing a home for those without a home. To foster the natural childlike innocence in the American psyche, we could develop it into a mature innocence and then a fresh, open-hearted adult persona.

Let me focus on this last idea. Archetypal themes and images usually appear in *tandem*. The child archetype may evoke the mythic mother. Mother and child. In the sonnet by Emma Lazarus at the base of the Statue of Liberty is inscribed the phrase, "Mother of exiles." When people from around the world come to America for the first time, they are often inspired and comforted by this glorious statue and perhaps perceive the country as a motherland receiving them with assurance of freedom and opportunity. The statue—and America itself—welcomes people in need of a home. On the other hand, some black writers remind us that the origins of the statue involved the theme of freedom from slavery. The various themes that cloak Liberty are strong and no doubt have a place: The abolition of slavery, "mother of exiles," welcome to immigrants, and freedom of citizens.

But this sign of welcome runs up against other deep-seated passions, a fear or suspicion about the other, anyone from another place. In the case of "Liberty," the welcome also has to vie with sibling rivalry. If Liberty is the mother of exiles, she is also the mother of established, loyal citizens, and these two groups may well get caught up in the difficult, competitive clash. The mother of exiles is also the mother of settled citizens who may not want intruders.

The common resistance to immigrants among many Americans is understandable. It is a raw passion, unreflected, that doesn't want anyone else to be part of the family. We all might feel this at times in different circumstances. It is one of those raw emotions that requires maturity to soften. The symptom is deep feelings of annoyance with immigrants, while the goal of that symptom, its telos, may be to be more strongly dedicated to the American family, to feel a sense of belonging. If Americans appreciated the country and its history more, they might not get caught in the symptom of anti-immigrant passion. On the other hand, the anti-immigrant is a deep emotional complex and isn't affected much by ideas. It is as deep-seated as a child's insecurity about another taking his place in the family.

Anti-immigrant Americans don't have a philosophy of boundaries and identity; they don't like to hear people speaking any language other than English. They don't like food that is not familiar. They don't like unusual dress, hair styles, or skin tones. Their adversaries see these annoyances as absurd, but they should understand that these are all images, styles, and markers that speak louder than abstract ideas. What they might do instead of fighting the anti-immigrant is to have some understanding of those emotions and help America grow up.

An innocent's values

We are now close to our main theme: To be thoroughly American in the stream of values fought over for many decades, and even centuries, to see America not as a geographical place but a hope for the future of humankind, is to be part of a magnificent experiment in human living. But to betray those values through a cynical view of human life, thinking that these idealistic values are foolish childhood dreams, is to separate from the essence of America.

One of the central secrets of American success is to dare to speak for and live out the values associated with America from its birth; to avoid the cynicism that is rampant in modern life; to mean it when you say that America stands for equal opportunity, racial equality, gender freedom, and love of the land. To speak deeply and honestly for these values is to accept the youthful sincerity of America's history and to be in league with the many American leaders who gave their lives for these values. You won't find cynicism in Emily Dickinson, Ralph Waldo Emerson, or Walt Whitman. They took the American fantasy of a New World seriously and dedicated themselves to it.

This kind of sincerity comes in part from the child archetype, an innocence that doesn't manipulate or dissemble. It is a special version of "beginner's mind." It isn't always easy for an adult to achieve, because, as you grow up in this country, you become jaded and suspicious. You come to assume that America's values are not workable in the current world setting. You have to be harder and prepared to be taken advantage of. The child's vision becomes one you can still speak about in the abstract but can't take too seriously in the real world.

This is not to say that it is acceptable to be literally naive and innocent. The world does have corruption in it. But still the myth of idealistic youth has a place. We have to watch out for extremes in dealing with the puer spirit or the child archetype. Here is how Hillman puts it in general:

> On the one hand, one works to become mature, to put all childish things away, to develop out of infantalisms and *avidya* [misunderstanding] of ignorance. On the other hand, one is to become a child, for only into the child enters the kingdom of heaven, and the child should lead the psyche and be its "end."[8]

Modern Americans may be tempted to sink into cynicism and compensate by not taking life seriously enough. They don't educate themselves in politics and culture enough to have well-reasoned positions and to make good choices of leaders. Democracy works best when citizens use all their intelligence as voters. Some take positions based on passions and superficial analyses of the situation. Some just follow the customs of their families and regions. There may be little individuation in terms of political positioning.

The image the world has of America is a precious one, important for Americans and the rest of the world. People in other countries find hope in the illusion of

America, and people everywhere need hope amid the world's corruption. Earth does not evolve uniformly, so there are pockets of advancement here and there, among cultures and countries, regions and neighborhoods, families and marriages. If one finds the hope of peace and security in some place on the planet, that is enough to support a life of hope and trust. Even a sliver of novus mundus supports the old world.

The odd thing is that America is not the New World, but you can find it here. It appears like the flash of a lightning bug on a summer night. I am not talking about a moment of human sensitivity. You can find that anywhere. No, there is a specific kind of American humanizing that rises up from its history and ideals. It is not generic goodness; it is a specifically American love of people and of life.

In Jungian thinking, Liberty, presented so dramatically in the Statue of Liberty, is a form of anima. She is in our hearts and minds not just as an idea or concept, but as a quality of soul, a deep presence in the notion of America and in its citizens. This freedom is less visible and less open to formula or definition than the idea of liberty. She is a she, a feminine presence that defines us, when she is not lost or obscured. She is a value of soul—deep, pervasive, felt, enlivening, and softly enlightening. A torch, not a thunderbolt.

Jung compares the sparks in nature to the luminous eyes of fish underwater,[9] and to the eyes of God in an illustration by Hildegard von Bingen. I would say that there is a special American spark, that the United States has its own luminous sparks that emanate from its soul. Even if they are covered over by racism, greed, violence, and prejudice, they are still present and still inspire the world—perhaps not as much as in the past—to a particular set of ideals.

We aren't afraid of the future but want to be involved and recognized for our involvement in futuristic developments such as space travel or communications. This focus is not just a matter of historical unfolding but is related to our very essence. We are the future. We are the infant in Stanley Kubrick's *2001: A Space Odyssey.* Other cultures are the concern of gerontology, while we are engaged in youthful explorations of the yet unknown.

The therapy of America

So, the question remains, how can America recover its health? How can it turn its pathology of cultural immaturity into its strength? From Jung and Hillman we get the rudiments of a plan.

First, we go with the symptom. We do not get caught up in a program of self-improvement but rather take a subtle, sometimes paradoxical approach that respects the symptom at the same time that it understands the suffering and negativity brought on by the symptom.

Americans are not known for a love of ideas or deep thought. In the media, serious conversations are rare and usually focus on actions, political strategies, or personalities. To live American ideals and keep them in mind requires some knowledge of American history and ideas. But there are emotional factors involved.

It isn't necessarily that you have to make a break in your relations with your family, but ease the bond that keeps your identity tied to the family mindset, enough to become a person in your own right. Jung calls this individuation. Hillman adds that we could reach a point where we enjoy the individuation of all creatures and things, allowing them their lives, free of our anxious control. We are back with Liberty in New York Harbor, enjoying differences and feeling satisfaction as other people and the things of the world have their own experiences and identities.

Second on our list of therapeutic steps is Jung's warning against "regressive restoration of the persona," which is basically a defense against life moving ahead into its future. We feel anxiety about the unknown in the next step forward, and so we retreat into what we know and with what we feel safe. We long for the "good old days" and try to restore the old ways and "traditional values."

Americans need to step back and see the larger picture, the ideas and ideals of their nation, not just personal concerns. That way we keep democracy in mind and remember all the courageous sacrifices so many outstanding Americans have made to this developing nation. You can't be satisfied with your small opinions and personal satisfactions. America is a huge ideal and a mammoth experiment in human freedom and communal living. If we forget that and live as though everything is about us, the American experiment will certainly fail, and it could fail soon, before we know it.

We are young. So be it. Let our youth be the solution to an adult's self-directed pragmatism and a child's unrealistic hope. But let us be young in a way that, in every instance, invites an adult to be present. Let's become more sophisticated by being both young and old.

Conclusions

So, let me summarize this exploration of the child myth that determines America's character in many ways. We are still terra incognita, we were delusionally discovered by a puer Columbus, we have had a history of explorers and adventurers and pioneers, we have sustained a veneer of innocence even during slavery, the slaughter of buffalo, the extermination of our native people, and the war in Iraq, among others. Yet the mythic child always lies at the bottom, showing through diverse displays of shadow.

We enjoy a child archetype, largely creative and beneficial, but also a child shadow and negative emotional complex. We are brimming with vitality and creativity but also immature in the extreme and coyly play the role of the innocent. We have an Icarian impulse to aim high and a narcissism that typically gets in the way of honest communication and real community, especially with other nations with regard to immigrants.

All of this could resolve in constructive ways, but the resolution will not come naturally—that is, unconsciously. We have to understand ourselves better and make a serious effort to be more solid in our ideas and speech. In a multitude of ways, we have to grow up, all the while preserving our deep child potential and our puer imagination.

Notes

1 C. Kerényi, "Prologomena," in *Essays on a Science of Mythology*, trans. R.F.C. Hull (Princeton: Princeton University Press, 1959), 8.
2 James Hillman, ed., *Puer Papers* (Irving, TX: Spring, 1979), 77–99.
3 Patrick Riccards, "National Survey Finds Just 1 in 3 Americans Would Pass Citizenship Test," *Woodrow Wilson National Fellowship Foundation News*, Oct. 3, 2018. woodrow. org/news/national-survey-finds-just-1-in-3-americans-would-pass-citizenship-test/
4 C.G. Jung, "The Psychology of the Child Archetype," in *The Collected Works of C. G. Jung*, vol. 9.1, trans. R.F.C. Hull (Princeton: Princeton University Press, 1980), para. 287.
5 James Hillman, "Abandoning the Child," in *Loose Ends* (Zurich: Spring, 1975), 5–48.
6 Ibid., 10.
7 Patricia Berry, "Defense and Telos in Dreams," in *Echo's Subtle Body* (Dallas: Spring, 1982), 8–95.
8 James Hillman, *Loose Ends*, 40.
9 C.G. Jung, "Flying Saucers: A Modern Myth," in *Civilization in Transition*, trans. R.F.C. Hull, 2nd ed. *Collected Works*, Vol. 10 (Princeton: Princeton University Press, 1975), 404.

Chapter 13

Archetypal psychology and fugitive democracy

James Hillman's political legacy

Michael P. Sipiora

Introduction

In these dire times for American democracy, the work of archetypal psychologist James Hillman is of political consequence and an inspiration for a socially engaged practice of psychology.[1] While his project was to re-vision psychology,[2] Hillman's vision extended beyond that discipline to the world at large, including a worried attention to democracy, specifically "individuality in a democracy . . . and the life of the citizen."[3] He called into question the unconscious assumptions of a disordered world that gives rise to the citizen's suffering—the inextricably entwined suffering of psychological repression and political oppression. His political legacy resides in a conception of the psychological citizen whose "special role" is the "awakening and refining of aesthetic sensitivity" and whose duty is to protest against injustice, ugliness, and senselessness.[4] This is the telos of both his challenge to psychotherapy to prepare a "cell of revolution"[5] as well as his "therapy of ideas" in the "public arena."[6] "The daimon of my destiny,"[7] he said, led him to be a "Platonistic man of the spirit who at the same time would be a democratic citizen and polytheistic liberal in soul."[8] Crucial to Hillman's polytheism is his defense of "the metaphorical discourse of myth" out of which it arises.[9]

Hillman's fundamental concern with the psychological—the soul—shares an inherent kinship to political philosopher Sheldon Wolin's overriding concern with the nature of the political. As scholars, both sought to rescue their disciplines from the reductions of scientific method and restore the prominence of ideas in their respective fields. Both took on the role of public intellectual in their shared concern for democracy and opposition to American empire. The political import of Hillman's work is amplified when taken in relation to Wolin's notion of "fugitive democracy,"[10] specifically, its requirements of both a democratization of the self and the cultivation of the citizenry's capacity to engage in deliberations which concurrently recognize diversity and are informed by a sense of the common good. While not by itself sufficient to engender these necessities, a re-visioned psychology is nonetheless politically relevant, as well as socially and personally therapeutic, when aligned with the awakening of a distressed citizenry to the possibilities of genuine democratic participation.

DOI: 10.4324/9781003325765-19

Hillman's leftist politics go back to his student days at Georgetown University and travels in Mexico before World War II, through his time as a correspondent in Europe after the war, and extending to his support for Progressive Party presidential candidate Henry Wallace in 1948. Biographer Dick Russell notes that Hillman's "interest in politics fades" when he immerses himself in classical studies at Dublin's Trinity College en route, ultimately, to his Jungian training and psychology doctorate in Zurich.[11] While reflections on the role of the citizen appear in Hillman's writings from early to late, his 1970s proclamation of the "renaissance of a psychology that returns psychic reality to the world"[12] marks an arc in his thinking about the soul and "political psychology."[13] "Politics," he will contend "is psychology: depth psychology is also a depth sociology; to go truly deep is to go the soul of the world."[14]

Late-stage capitalism, neoliberalism, and American empire

"A rule of archetypal psychology . . . [is to] 'start right where you are.'"[15] Where we are, Hillman and Wolin agreed, is in the throes of the American empire.[16] In his public address "Farewell to Welfare," Hillman expressed outrage at "Unbridled late-stage capitalism euphemistically called the 'free market economy,'"[17] and he flat out described it as a "runaway nightmare."[18] He cautioned:

> Beware of taking capitalist free-market economics as a science, or as a progressively developing system, or as equivalent with and necessary to our American Dream of political democracy. The economy that rules our lives is also a morality, a psychology, and even a monotheistic belief that converts all values into its one bottom line.[19]

These sentiments echo what he asserted in *Kinds of Power*, a book specifically addressed to the business community. There he claims that "Business, as defined by the ideas of Western Capitalism, has become the fundamental force in human society."[20] Business ideas have penetrated and then colonized most of American life, public and private. They have become "internalized" and rule "by psychological means."[21] Indeed, because they are "so unquestioningly and universally accepted, it is the Economy where," according to Hillman, "the contemporary unconscious resides and where psychological analysis is most needed."[22]

Unconsciousness, Hillman reminds us, "is exactly what the word says: what is least conscious because it is most usual, most familiar, most everyday. That is the daily round of business."[23] In naming the "Economy" as the collective's unconscious today, he means that the values of capitalism, the practices of market economics, and the ideas of business are, without our direct awareness, the operative modes of sense-making that guide us in virtually all areas of life. Repressed in this unconsciousness are any valuations with which to envision the social, political, and historical realities of everyday life, leading to the disruption of that business-defined daily life by the symptomatic return of those realities that have been repressed. "The psyche," Hillman asserts, "is literalized in economics . . . . All value reducible to cost. Cost efficiency as decisive."[24] The oppressive reign of reality defined in terms of business both correlates with the economic injustice that is widespread today and is testified to by the ever-widening gap between the "haves" and the "have nots," the ugly state of our civil life, as well as the accelerating climate crisis that threatens us locally and across the planet.

This everyday unconsciousness is at the core of neoliberalism, in which a market mindset rules all and manifests in the "privatization of the public sphere, deregulation of the corporate sector, and the lowering of income and corporate taxes, paid for by cuts to public spending."[25] "Reaganomics gone global" as Naomi Klein succinctly sums it up.[26] But trickle-down isn't happening. Quoting U.S. Senator Bernie Sanders, "There is something profoundly wrong when the top one-tenth of 1 percent owns almost as much wealth as the bottom 90 percent, and when 99 percent of all new income goes to the top 1 percent."[27] It is no surprise, as Hillman noted, that "the therapists in the trenches have to face an awful lot of the social, political, and economic failures of capitalism."[28] He acknowledges that individual therapy is necessary, but it can never be sufficient as the "core" of the "malaise" is "collective and only secondarily individual."[29]

Far from being equivalent to political democracy, "unbridled late-stage capitalism" and its neoliberal reduction of everything to market values do equate, in Hillman's view, to the domestic scene of the American empire.[30] "If you are for the American republic, the Bill of Rights, the Declaration of Independence," he wrote in *We've Had a Hundred Years of Psychotherapy—And the World's Getting Worse,* "if you are for these things you are against the American empire."[31] Recognizing that the republic requires an active citizenry, he notes that "the sort of democracy envisioned by our founding documents . . . derives from a populace of keenly and lively imagining persons."[32] In the American empire, on the other hand, the unconscious reign of economics produces a dysfunctional society where, as Hillman saw things in the 1990s, hyperindividualist members are "psychically numbed but are still reliably functioning as workers and consumers."[33] "The task of the consulting room," ventured Hillman, "is in part to keep the pores open to what goes on in the empire. The job of psychotherapy is to keep one *suffering* the decline of the republic."[34]

And so too it is in Wolin's view of the United States as an "inverted totalitarianism" in which government serves the corporate economy,[35] unlike traditional totalitarianism—Nazi Germany, for example—in which the state controls the economy and fosters political fanaticism. Beginning in the late twentieth century,

Life in the highly integrated advanced capitalist states became more economically determined and its politics, popular culture, educations, and intellectual life more subordinate to economic mandates and imperatives . . . The economic rules all domains of existence.[36]

Out of this leveling to economy arise political arrangements in which public functions are increasingly privatized and corporate interests direct the exercise of state power. Concomitant with this, and likewise in the interest of corporate capitalism, is the production of "human beings unfitted for democratic citizenship: self-interested, exploitive, competitive, striving for inequalities, fearful of downward mobility."[37] Left vulnerable to what Franklin D. Roosevelt's vice president, Henry Wallace, decried as "intolerance, bigotry and the pretension of invidious distinction,"[38] the citizenry is "ripe material for fascist leadership"[39] of the very kind that directed Nazi totalitarianism, about whose American version he warned in the 1940s.

What is "lost" in this situation is the political.[40] For Wolin, the political is

an expression of the idea that a free society composed of diversities can nonetheless enjoy moments of commonality when, through public deliberations, collective power is used to promote or protect the well-being of the collectivity.[41]

In our time, the political is forgotten in the instrumentalism and proceduralism of technological society, dissipated by the illusions of consumer culture, fractured by the resurgence of deep-seated racism, suppressed by the machinations and manipulations of global corporations, and—important to add—obliterated by psychology's propagation of atomic individualism. No wonder that "the political," according to Wolin, "is episodic, rare."[42]

Facing both the powerful resources of longstanding corporate dominance and the current rise of a reactionary populism, the democratic state is imperiled. Recognizing democracy's historical record as a comparatively uncommon and not too successful form of state government,[43] Wolin contends that

democracy needs to be reconceived as something other than a form of government: as a mode of being which is conditioned by bitter experience, doomed to succeed only temporarily, but is a recurrent possibility as long as the memory of the political survives.[44]

Fugitive democracy, as he names it, is that mode of being, of the people's collective being, in which there is a remembering of the political in the midst of empire:

A moment of experience, a crystallized response to deeply felt grievances or need on the part of those whose main preoccupation—demanding of time and energy—is to scratch out a decent existence. Its moment is not just a measure of fleeting time but an action that protests actualities and reveals possibilities.[45]

Democratic moments are scattered throughout the history of the American republic, moments when there is an emergence of solidarity in establishing civic bodies, trade unions, or community organizations; moments of popular uprising in support of civil rights, women's rights, and worker's rights; contemporary moments of widespread protest against war, nuclear armament, and environmental destruction.

Near the end of *Democracy Incorporated*, after a compelling, detailed explication of the emergence of inverted totalitarianism, Wolin specifies the demands democracy makes on the citizen:

> The survival and flourishing of democracy depends, in the first instance, upon the "people's" changing themselves, sloughing off their political passivity and instead, acquiring some of the characteristic of demos. That means creating themselves, coming-into-being by virtue of their own actions. While it cannot be emphasized too strongly that democracy requires conditions—social, economic, and educational—the democratization of politics remains merely formal without the democratization of the self. Democratization is not about being "left alone," but about becoming a self that sees the value of common investments and endeavors and finds in them a source of self-fulfillment . . . . To become a democrat, is to change one's self.[46]

Both the "democratization of the self" as becoming a different kind of self and people's acquiring the "characteristic of demos"—that is, a sense of themselves as a political community—are psychological matters not only because they involve individual and collective transformation but, more significantly, because of their pertinence, in Hillman's view, to "how the soul can be in the world and in the best manner fulfilled."[47] Just as a soulless world is comprised of only material facts and instrumental procedures, a soulful world is the condition for the emergence of meaning in the deepening of events into experiences; for the realities of love, mortality, and religious experience; and for the experience of reality as not merely factual but also as metaphorical and symbolically meaningful.[48]

An idea of therapy and the democratization of the self

The first allegiance of depth psychology, Hillman maintained, is to pay attention to what is disclosed in symptoms. Yet he came to believe that "neither Freud nor Jung had imagined far enough, fundamentally enough, into the disorder of the world of concrete things, government institutions, commercial practice—the physical, political, and economic unconscious—these symptoms and these pathologies."[49] He realized that his patients' symptoms revealed issues that ran deeper than their individual lives and he followed what these symptoms disclosed all the way into the world to those matters of importance that condition and transcend the personal. Listening to patients' symptoms discloses layers of meaning in which personal narratives are intertwined with the rise of social media, the ups and downs of the housing and job markets, racial and gender discrimination, the fluctuations of the economy, changing demographics, cultural trends, technological transformations of the workplace, the skyrocketing cost of health care and education, climate change, the shifting political scene, and the like.

Here begins Hillman's entreaty to therapy. He argues that, if we put aside our individualistic biases and dare run symptoms to ground, if we track them through their entanglement in the personal to their ultimate sources, we end up face to face with the disorder of the polis. We confront the disarray of the civic realm that is the place of the demos, "We the People," as a political community.

Hillman's political revisioning of psychotherapy as preparing a cell of revolution relies on two moves. The first, just mentioned: Follow what is disclosed in patients' symptoms to the conditions of life in which they are embedded. That the therapy "room should be a cell of revolution . . . means it should be very aware of the political and social world that people are in."[50] "The job of therapy, in part," Hillman contends, "becomes one of keeping you acutely conscious of the dysfunctional society."[51] This is the reverse of what psychology typically does in its "vicious"[52] reduction of all affect and cognition to the realm of "the private and the personal."[53] For example, psychotherapy's insidious conversion of realistic fears and reasonable anger into internal anxiety and pathological depression turns us away from the actual conditions of our distress as we become captives of our dysfunctional inner children. Hillman would have us turn the other way and return to the life-world whose disturbances evoke our emotional responses. "Therapy might imagine itself," he suggests "investigating the immediate social causes"[54] making "the link between the personally felt needs and the soul's clamor for the invisible values that sustain the soul's life—and that link is political."[55] Hillman called for

> each therapist's room to become a cell of revolution, heresy, and beauty rather than a globule of self-improvement; a place where imagination moves from building castles in sand to constructive visions for the real city; a place of outrage at social injustice rather than adaptation; a place of mourning over ecological destruction rather than of working through depression; a place of shame over failed participation in the present rather shame over past abuses to oneself; and of cosmic involvement rather than of transference and countertransference.[56]

However, acute awareness of social disfunction can fuel the fires of fascism no less than feed the flame of democracy. As the inequities wrought by neoliberal policies have worn thin, populist fears have broken through psychic numbness. "The current American identity as victim," Hillman contends, "is the tail side of the coin whose head brightly displays the opposite identity: the heroic self-made 'man' carving out destiny alone and with unflagging will."[57] The country's predominate mindset of extreme individualism and competitive self-interest, cultivated in no small part by conventional psychology, generates the expectation of individual control; if we aren't in control, if we can't cope, it means there is something wrong with us—we are failures or become victims. The stage is set for "Trumped-up magnificoes" offering an illusory ideology of "Making America Great Again."[58]

Thus, Hillman's second move, as Wolin concurs, is absolutely crucial for democracy. That is the movement from the self as highly individualistic, competitive, and supremely self-interested to a relational understanding of the self. Hillman came to this conclusion relatively late in his thinking. Just as he came to recognize that his "metaphysical speculations [had] bewitched" him "toward the world,"[59] he came to "some severe doubts about [the] individualistic ontology that was [his] faith and remains the faith of psychotherapy in general."[60] He came to understand that his Jungian notion of an individuated center of one's being was itself a kind of relational self, an interiorization of community, his Zurich community, living and dead, in which he was increasingly "unable to differentiate individuation from alienation" and "which reflected a social, political context which, [he], immersed in individualism, then did not recognize."[61]

Ultimately, Hillman came to recognize that the hyperindividualism propagated by most psychology was a "disease";[62] that the individualistic kind of self both reflected and reproduced the repressions and oppression of a disordered world. Bolstered by "the religion of individualism, [and] the belief in consumerism,"[63] this self is inherently patriarchal, racist, white-minded, and colonial. Long subject to critique as distinctive to Western modernity, this atomistic kind of self is the dwelling place of the heroic ego, Hillman's foil in *Re-Visioning Psychology*. Caught up in relentless coping, struggling to stay in control, and anesthetized in its consuming, the individualistic self "is supported and promoted by our economics, our entertainment, our refrigeration, our modes of communication and transportation, and of course, our medications"[64]—and, maybe most crucially, by our whole system of education, our technically oriented education that serves economy at the expense of the arts and humanities, an education in calculation without imagination—neither aesthetic nor moral—that serves as indoctrination into a "sociopathic society of manipulations."[65] Without the attention to critical though and language engendered by a humanities education, we fall prey to an endemic "anesthetized stupidity," lacking the means to cultivate a nuanced and reflective engagement in our lives.[66]

The alternative to the self-contained individualism, in general terms that apply to most of the world's cultures, is that the "self is communal,"[67] some variety of a relational self: a kind of self that sees, experiences, enacts itself in and through its inherent connection to and interactions with others, things, places, living entities—in short, the world. Despite "the world view of individualism [having] become our mythology. . . . for millennia this was not the case. Tribal culture, even high cultures such as the Egyptian, do not, did not, live in an individualistic *Weltbild*."[68] Western individualism's sense of an autonomous, willful ego contrasts sharply with the majority of cultures in which "a human being is imagined less as a central agent . . . and more as a field in flux in which friction between figures requires rituals of reflective questioning."[69] Instead of looking for one's true voice found deep inside one's subjectivity, "the human being in these other cultures reflects contested voices and is imagined always in a nexus of relations."[70]

Hillman's particular relational conceptualization of "a self *among*, not a self apart"[71] is that of the "self as the interiorization-of-community."[72]

[A] re-imagin[ing] the idea of Self as the focus or locus of visitations and semi-permanent residential inhabitants both dead and alive, both older than ourselves and not yet born, both of this world and other worlds—and interiorizations as well of the various communities to which we give allegiance in daily life.[73]

"Interiorization," as Hillman uses the term, is not a process of introjection into an encapsulated subjectivity but rather a connecting and appropriating of something as having an essential significance such that I am bound to it and it constitutes a part of me. Interiorization is an intimate communion that gives meaning to the specific relatedness that constitutes a particular self.

Further, Hillman is not "literalizing community"; instead, he is intending toward Alfred Adler's *Gemeinshaftsgefühl*, a social feeling that fictionalizes many goals, many literal political activities, as retorts for [that] . . . feeling, where object libido can be intensified, differentiated, manifested. Throughout one *imagines* oneself as a citizen where discourse about Self and reading of this Self and its actions is conceived always within a context of *Gemeinshaftsgefühl*.[74]

Gemeinshaftsgefühl, most often translated as "community feeling" or "social interest," is our participation in the commons manifest both as empathy, cooperation, and respect for others in our concrete engagements and as our investment in the ideals of communal life. While an innate capacity, Adler recognized that social interest requires development through the process of education. As Hillman notes, in the arts and humanities, "imagination is awakened and trained by confrontations with the great moral dilemmas" of the human condition.[75] Not to be literally identified with any specific social community, *Gemeinshaftsgefühl* exists as an ideal, an aspiration whose reference always remains the inspirational perfection of humanity.[76]

Hillman identifies it "with our ordinary English word 'common,' as the village green in my New England hamlet was once a common for all bodies, human and nonhuman, to take part in common, to care for in common, to enjoy in common."[77] The founders of the republic knew it, in John Adams's words, as a "positive Passion for the public Good."[78] It is the way one makes sense of the relations in terms of which imagines oneself and gains satisfaction in one's labors and political activities; it is invaluable to the democratic sensibility necessary to people making sense of themselves as a community.

Hillman's two moves coalesce in the context of attending to symptoms: "Interiorizing of community means taking in, noticing, attending to what actually engages me and enrages me. The environment is now the mirror and insight is now outrage."[79] Leaving the therapy room, patients go back into the world as what Hillman calls psychological citizens. Such citizens are now more inclined to see and understand their good as inseparable from, or at least connected to, the common good; they are more likely to understand their interests as not independent of the commons but as conditioned and informed by communal interests. This is the aspect of democratization that Wolin refers to as "the 'people' . . . creating themselves, coming-into-being by virtue of their own actions."[80] These actions, for Hillman, are citizens' aesthetic responses, responses which themselves constitute a "psychological activism."[81] Hillman claims "the special role for the psychological citizen is the awakening and refining of aesthetic sensitivity,"[82] an awakening that "counters our anesthetized numbing."[83]

In broad terms, an aesthetic sensibility is "the appreciation of the inherent intelligibility given in the qualitative patterns of events . . . [a] response in which judgment always inheres."[84] As a qualitative, meaning-laden apprehension, the terms of this sensibility are values, not in the abstract but in the most concrete configuration, there in our experience; values such as beauty, justice, and destiny that comprise the cosmological principles that Hillman says more "accurately qualify the 'poetic basis of mind'"[85] essential to his revisioning of psychology and that he will offer as the "foundation for an ecological psychology."[86] "Civic courage in an ecological age," he argued, "means not only demanding justice, but also an *aesthetic justice* and the will to make judgements of taste."[87] It is the kind of sensibility to which Bob Dylan refers in his Nobel Prize lecture:

> I had principles and sensibilities and an informed view of the world. And I had had that for a while. Learned it all in grammar school. *Don Quixote, Ivanhoe, Robinson Crusoe, Gulliver's Travels, Tale of Two Cities,* all the rest—typical grammar school reading that gave you a way of looking at life, an understanding of human nature, and a standard to measure things by.[88]

While Dylan's reading may not be typical or at the grammar school level, it reflects an education in the arts and humanities which teaches the grammars of imagination that school an aesthetic sensibility and develop social interest as a "standard to measure things by."

"A citizen's duty," for Hillman, is "to awaken and stand for his and her aesthetic responses . . . above all, to work to protest actively against ugliness wherever it appears, or threatens to appear."[89] And he is adamant that saying "no" to what is ugly, unjust, or senseless is not conditional on having a full-blown solution. Its condition is citizens thoughtfully evaluating their civic engagements and critically reflecting on their social connections within the context of life in community with its shared freedoms and responsibilities. It is precisely in these terms that "Our aesthetic response to ugliness restores our responsibility as citizens."[90]

For Hillman, the role of the psychological citizen is patterned on the very kind of engagement employed in psychotherapy itself—a critical sense-making that sees through to deeper meanings, to the configuration and value of relationships, and ultimately to a sense of what makes us human. In response to the "anesthetized stupidity" of hyperindividualism, psychotherapy can prepare a cell of revolution;[91] it can be an agent of democratization. When therapy offers patients self-understanding as relational selves, it leads to citizens being concerned for the commons. When it promotes patients' critical thinking that follows symptoms into the world, psychotherapy can lead to citizens' protest. When therapy encourages patients' imaginative participation in the common good, it can lead to citizens being aesthetically engaged in their communities—Hillman's version of that Wolin describes as a "citizen-participant."[92] Such engagement includes any and all activities that serve the common good, and, as Hillman remarks, they "could be to collaborate in the physical improvement of your township, to protect regionalism and biodiversity, to insist on art education in schools, to support conservation of good buildings."[93]

Hillman proposed a "responsive environmentalism" that advocates personal engagement in local communities, in programs inspired by ethical and aesthetic visions; a "long-term vision of the common good invites that wider participation and broader comprehension which can overcome the rancor of partisan opinion."[94] Likewise, Wolin observes that "Demotic rationality is rooted in a provincialism where commonality is experienced as everyday reality and 'civic spirit' is unapologetic."[95] Accordingly, the possibilities of democratic participation are "most likely to be nurtured in local, small-scale settings."[96] This being so, equally important is the recognition that the establishment of multiple, necessarily diverse, local "democratic citizenries" cannot sufficiently address the crises that confront us.[97] In order that these citizenries might, ventures Wolin, come together and check, even redirect, state power, "requires serious changes in the quality of public discussion."[98]

Therapy of ideas and acquiring characteristics of demos

Crucial to the citizen's aesthetic response is the informed view of the world and human nature that Dylan, Hillman, and Wolin associate with an education which includes the arts and humanities. This is the kind of education which cultivates, as has been noted, the social interest essential to the self as the interiorization of community. Tragically, it is the kind of schooling that is most lacking in the current reduction of education to job training and the affairs of the commons to business transactions. Without the retrieval of a public discourse which includes terms such as empathy, solidarity, and responsibility, citizens have little chance of "acquiring some of the characteristic of demos."[99] It is in response to this situation that Hillman saw culture itself as in need of therapy. Like his patients, he too was led to attend to the world as a psychological citizen.

The practice of psychotherapy not being sufficient to the distress disclosed in the consulting room, Hillman turned to a cultural psychology enacted as a therapy of ideas. "Dysfunctional ideas in the world . . . claim our psychological care today."[100] He explained:

I have more and more shifted my psychological practice from the individual psyche in the consulting room to the wider psyche in the public arena, and its deeper roots in root ideas. I call my work now a therapy of ideas rather than a therapy of persons.[101]

In *Re-Visioning Psychology*, Hillman followed Plato in asserting that ideas are the eyes of the soul, that reflection through ideas is the soul's "habitual activity."[102] Based on his wide-ranging scholarship in the humanities as well as his clinical acumen, Hillman practiced therapy on the root ideas—self, world, and nature; money, power, and war; childhood and aging—that condition the quality of contemporary life. He brought cultural psychological attention to the family, immigration and refugees, pornography, streets, ceilings, and, most prominently, the city itself. In this practice, we have the other dimension of Hillman's political legacy—his work as a public intellectual. As Hillman says, "we must go where the soul is sick and where the unconscious most darkly and thickly reigns: the *polis*."[103]

To be clear, Hillman's public undertakings—from those connected to the Men's Movement in addressing the loss of community, to the bestselling *The Soul's Code* and *The Force of Character* which offered reimaginations of childhood and aging, to his efforts in articulating an ecological psychology, to the multiple talks given to audiences outside academia—are a far cry from pop psychology's peddling of positivity, self-help, and mindfulness. Instead, Hillman's practice as a public intellectual, as well as his scholarly pursuits, belongs in a tradition that he himself identifies with the speech of the soul, rhetoric. "The improvement of the quality of life," he often noted, "depends on a restoration of a language which notices the properties of bodies, the qualities of life" and that "lead[s] back to the Renaissance insistence on rhetoric."[104] The rhetors of the Renaissance served as maestros of culture who provided instruction on personal character and civic virtue based on their studies of the humanities. Likewise, Hillman's therapy of ideas was based in depth psychology in its intimate connection to the humanities, and his instruction—offered in the academy and in the city—was on how to see through whatever was taken literally in order to genuinely notice (*notitia*) the qualities of life.[105] Literalism, for Hillman, was the "enemy" ensconced in the "isms" that "clamp the mind and heart into positivistic science (geneticism and computerism), economics (bottom-line capitalism) and single-minded faith (fundamentalism)."[106]

Just as a critical seeing-through of "individualism" is crucial to therapy's participation in the democratization of the self, Hillman's therapy of the idea of "the Economy" is critical to a retrieval of democratic sensibilities. Breaking us out of the numbness that besets life in late-stage capitalism was a primary rhetorical task of Hillman's therapy of ideas. Disturbing our complacency, he called out our suffering of the decline of the American republic. And his cultural therapeutic practice was to attend deeply to what that suffering discloses. His work in the polis was to see through the literalisms at the root of the conditions—social, economic, and educational—identified by Wolin as necessary for democratization. In so doing, he opened the possibility of other modes of discourse; he introduced aesthetic terms that had been repressed in our economic unconsciousness; he offered the principles of beauty, justice, and destiny. "With them," he argues, "psyche finds itself in a moral, aesthetic, and intentional cosmos, and psychology becomes the study of the ways phenomenon, including human beings, measure its place in the world."[107] In this vision, the *sensus communis*, the communal sense of things, includes an aesthetic sensibility that entails being drawn to beauty and repelled by ugliness; a fitting sense of justice and of outrage at injustice; and an intuition of destiny in differentiating what meaningfully lays claim on us from the senselessness that disturbs us.

The overarching political aim of Hillman's work—both as a psychologist and as a public intellectual—was to liberate the citizen's keen and lively imagination from subjugation to reliable functioning, to awaken the citizen's capacity for social interest from its hibernation in hyperindividualism, and to cultivate the citizen's concern for the common good that makes of people a demos. Crucial to all three, and essential to archetypal psychology, is Hillman's "insistence on the mythical polytheistic perspective."[108] Polytheism inspires a pluralistic imagination that can help keep outrage at injustice from falling prey to the enticements of fascist populism and demagogic manipulation. While not a "guarantee [of] freedom from political tyranny, yet for psychological reasons," ventured Hillman, "it's worth considering."[109]

Political pluralism

Unlike a religious polytheism that takes its gods literally as objects of worship, in Hillman's polytheistic psychology, the "Gods are *imagined*" within the metaphorical discourse of myth.[110] They "are imagined as the formal intelligibility of the phenomenal world, allowing each thing to be discerned for its inherent intelligibility and for its specific place of belonging in this or that kosmos [ordered pattern or arrangement]."[111] Polytheism means that there are multiple ways in which we imagine, and are imagined by, the world and our being in it. Even then, with polytheism taken as "modes of experience" or "cosmic perspectives," it is not the particular "theism" that Hillman advocates which is crucial to his political legacy.[112] His is undoubtedly the polytheism of the ancient Greeks, and he cites its differentiated sophistication and enduring significance in the Western imagination in which democracy appears. No less important, he recognizes, is an acknowledgment of the "genocidal and cultural catastrophes"[113] wrought by the "white supremacy"[114] embedded in this imagination. Accordingly, in relation to the current globe-spanning reach of American psychology, Hillman argues that "rather than applying the epistemology of Western understanding to the alien, the tribal, and nontechnological cultures, we would let their anthropology (their stories of human nature) be applied to ours."[115]

What then is essential is the "poly" of polytheism: A pluralism—which comes of a metaphorical seeing-through of the literal—that recognizes the inherent multiplicity of experience, the perspectival character of understanding, and the polysemic nature of truth. This is the style that gives things a "pagan feeling . . . a style that welcomes myth, personification, fantasy, complexity, and especially humor, rather than the singleness of meaning that leads to dogma."[116] Likewise, noting Wolin's "pagan appreciation of a deep plurality of being,"[117] William E. Connolly observes that the

linkages between polytheism, plurality, and commonality . . . express in embryo a Wolinesque tendency to downgrade questions about divine source, transcendental ground, final end or contractual basis of authority, justice, legitimacy, and membership in favor of a living, immanent, and engaged politics of commonality.[118]

Wolin refers to "political polytheism against political monotheism" in discussing Montesquieu's conception of "political society as a concatenation of differences—of moral beliefs, religious customs, local practices, class structures, economic systems, and geography."[119]

This same concern is expressed in Hillman's conception of the pluralism recognized in founding the American republic:

The differing individual imaginations manifesting themselves as differing religious concerns, geographical loyalties, philosophical commitments, and economic goals must be fundamentally affirmed, not dissolved in the ogre's cauldron called America, the Melting Pot. The founding documents assume the inalienable differences of imagination in the citizenry, and so the Constitution had to provide means for negotiating differences—elective, judicial, legislative—as well as be amended by a Bill of Rights.[120]

Two centuries later, a fuller embrace of diversity must necessarily come into play when considering citizenship in a multicultural polity. Just as the Founding Fathers' acknowledgment of individual rights needed to be further amended—specifically the Thirteenth, Fourteenth, and Nineteenth Amendments—Hillman's work needs to be amended to acknowledge and attend to differences of race and gender and their inalienable claims on the imagination.

Polytheism, pluralism, and a polyvalent conception of truth are necessary to both ensure that the varieties of imagination are "fundamentally affirmed, not dissolved" and to "negotiate" between them in the service of the common good. Without pluralism, political discourse succumbs to "the singleness of meaning that leads to dogma."[121] It is in the negotiating between multiple truths that the theism in Hillman's polytheism matters politically:

> For archetypal psychology, pluralism and multiplicity and relativism are not enough: these are merely philosophical generalities. Psychology needs to specify and differentiate each event, which it can do against the variegated background of archetypal configurations, or what polytheism calls gods, in order to make multiplicity both authentic and precise.[122]

Education in the arts and humanities, as previously discussed, is essential to cultivating an aesthetic response which can discern the "archetypal configurations" that differentiate multiple truths, and critically articulate varying senses of beauty, justice, and destiny (Hillman's cosmological principles) in terms of their soulful value. Such discernment empowers dialogue between these on the basis of their authenticity in relation to the common good.

Wolin reminds us that the local not only carries the potential of an active citizenry but also the demagoguery that populates the current political landscape: "[T]he Klan, militiamen and -women, neo-Nazis, Protestant fundamentalists, would-be censors of public and school libraries, champions of the 'original Constitution.'"[123] Indeed, outrage at neoliberal politics and corporate economics has, as noted earlier, awakened many voices from their "anesthetized numbing."[124] Polytheism is antidote not to the appearance of racial prejudice and antidemocratic dogmas, but to their pretense of upholding singular truths. Wolin recognizes the "political value" of these reactionary dogmatists "not as bearers of truth but as provocateurs whose passionate commitments can arouse self-consciousness in the public, stimulating the latter to become aware of what they believe and of the mixed legacies that compose a collective inheritance."[125]

Political polytheism engenders the kind of pluralistic public discourse in which an awakened citizenry may possibly come to terms with its "mixed legacies" and potentially engage in deliberations that, while acknowledging diverse beliefs and concerns, can come to agreement on the commonweal. This is no small feat, given the existence of multiple citizenries with shifting identities, diverse sensibilities, and varying notions of what best serves the general welfare. Indeed, pluralistic discourse faces the ever-present challenge of transcending its own diversity in "seeking out the evanescent homogeneity of a broader political."[126] The requisite confluence of plurality and commonality is indeed rare, momentary, and quickly dissipating, and yet the political is like the soul, a matter of deepest human concern. Hillman notes with agreement that "When Aristotle says that we are by *nature* political," he means that "the structure and purpose of human kind is political."[127]

Conclusion

Wolin's envisioning of fugitive democracy provides the context in which Hillman's revisioning of the psychological assumes contemporary political form. Hillman's notion of the psychological citizen enlivens fugitive democracy with an aesthetic, cosmological sensibility, the "aesthetic-affective dynamics that fall outside Wolin's range of vision."[128] In bringing this sensibility into play, archetypal psychology tends to a citizenry capable of political engagement from polytheistic, cosmological perspectives. "Democracy," as Wolin would have us conceive of it, "is a political moment, perhaps the political moment, when the political is remembered and recreated."[129] The psychological citizen's protest against the injustices of empire carries the memory of the American republic. The import of Hillman's work is to obligate psychology's service to recreating the conditions for democracy. Patients are served by a practice of psychotherapy, "a post-self-centered therapy," that goes beyond attending to their individual distress.[130] Restoring their identity as citizens, it engenders a relational sense of the self and cultivates an aesthetic sensibility infused with a passion for the common good. Likewise, the public is served by the practice of a cultural therapeutics that offers critical reflection on the ideas that animate our collective life. By seeing through the literalisms that generate collective unconsciousness and individual powerlessness, a therapy of ideas serves to open a space for political discourse and civic engagement.

At this moment in our nation's history, Hillman's legacy could not be more relevant. While not in itself sufficient to bring about democratization, the practice of psychology, by therapists and public as well as academic intellectuals, can and should address the political conditions that give rise to people's distress; can and should empower people to address these conditions as psychological citizens. To do less, no matter with good intentions, risks collusion with empire and betrayal of the soul.

Notes

1 Earlier versions of this essay were delivered at the 12th Annual Conference, APA Division 32, Society for Humanistic Psychology, 2019, and at the Jungian Psychology and the Human Sciences Conference, International Association for Jungian Studies (IAJS), 2021.
2 James Hillman, *Re-Visioning Psychology*, reissue (New York: William Morrow, 1997).
3 James Hillman, *The Soul's Code: In Search of Character and Calling* (New York: Ballantine Books, 2017), 286.
4 James Hillman and Michael Ventura, *We've Had a Hundred Years of Psychotherapy—And the World's Getting Worse*, revised ed. (New York: HarperOne, 2009), 125.
5 Hillman and Ventura, *We've Had a Hundred Years*, 125.
6 James Hillman, *City and Soul: Uniform Edition of the Writings of James Hillman*, vol. 2, ed. Robert Leaver (Washington, D.C.: Spring, 2021), 372.
7 Hillman, *Soul's Code*, 271.
8 James Hillman, *Egalitarian Typologies versus the Perception of the Unique* (Washington, D.C.: Spring, 1986), 1.

9 James Hillman, *Archetypal Psychology: Uniform Edition of the Writings of James Hillman*, vol. 1 (Washington, D.C.: Spring, 2021), 14.

10 Sheldon Wolin, "Fugitive Democracy," in *Fugitive Democracy: And Other Essays*, ed. Nicholas Xenos, reprint (Princeton: Princeton University Press, 2018), 100.

11 Dick Russell, *The Life and Ideas of James Hillman: Volume I: The Making of a Psychologist*, 1st ed. (New York: Arcade, 2013), 192.

12 Hillman, *City and Soul*, 27.

13 James Hillman, "Notes on White Supremacy: Essaying an Archetypal Account of Historical Events," *Spring* (1986), 29.

14 Hillman, *City and Soul*, 101.

15 James Hillman, " . . . And Huge Is Ugly: Zeus and the Titans," in *Mythical Figures: Uniform Edition of the Writings of James Hillman*, vol. 6, 1st ed. (Washington, D.C.: Spring, 2007), 144.

16 While recognizing Wolin's distinguishing between empire and inverted totalitarianism, I am following Hillman in using the term "American empire" loosely to depict late-stage capitalism and its undermining of the American republic.

17 Hillman, *City and Soul*, 376.

18 Ibid., 387.

19 Ibid., 384.

20 James Hillman, *Kinds of Power: A Guide to Its Intelligent Uses* (New York: Crown, 1997), 3.

21 Ibid., 4.

22 Ibid.

23 Ibid.

24 Hillman, *City and Soul*, 300.

25 Naomi Klein, *This Changes Everything: Capitalism vs. The Climate* (New York: Simon & Schuster, 2014), 72.

26 Naomi Klein, "Our Environmental Future: Connection, Collaboration and Caution," Keynote address, Pacific Standard Series, May 17, 2017, the Granada Theatre, Santa Barbara, CA.

27 Bernie Sanders, *Our Revolution: A Future to Believe In*, 1st ed. (New York: Thomas Dunne Books, 2016), 120.

28 Scott London, "On Soul, Character and Calling: A Conversation with James Hillman," scott.london, http://scott.london/interviews/hillman.html

29 Hillman, *Kinds of Power*, 14.

30 Hillman, *City and Soul*, 376.

31 Hillman and Ventura, *We've Had a Hundred Years*, 235.

32 Hillman, *City and Soul*, 88.

33 Ibid., 144.

34 Hillman and Ventura, *We've Had a Hundred Years*, 235.

35 Sheldon Wolin, *Democracy Incorporated: Managed Democracy and the Spector of Inverted Totalitarianism—New Edition*, revised ed. (Princeton: Princeton University Press, 2017), 15.

36 Sheldon Wolin, *Politics and Vision: Continuity and Innovation in Western Political Thought—Expanded Edition*, revised ed. (Princeton: Princeton University Press, 2016), 566.

37 Wolin, *Politics and Vision*, 597.

38 John Nichols, *The Fight for the Soul of the Democratic Party: The Enduring Legacy of Henry Wallace's Anti-Fascist, Anti-Racist Politics*, 1st ed., first printing (Brooklyn: Verso Books, 2020), 80.

39 Nichols, 60.

40 Sheldon Wolin, "Fugitive Democracy," 111.
41 Ibid., 100.
42 Ibid.
43 As is often said, "democracy is too simple for complex societies and too complex for simple ones." Wolin, "Fugitive Democracy," 111.
44 Ibid.
45 Wolin, *Politics and Vision*, 603.
46 Wolin, *Democracy Incorporated*, 289.
47 Hillman, *Soul's Code*, 274.
48 See the discussion of "soul" in Hillman, *Re-Visioning Psychology*, x.
49 Hillman, *City and Soul*, 49.
50 London, "On Soul, Character and Calling."
51 Hillman and Ventura, *We've Had a Hundred Years*, 235.
52 Hillman and Ventura, 11.
53 Hillman, " . . . And Huge Is Ugly,"150.
54 Hillman and Ventura, *We've Had a Hundred Years*, 38.
55 James Hillman, "Figuring the Future," in *Philosophical Intimations: Uniform Edition of the Writings of James Hillman*, vol. 8, ed. Edward S. Casey (Washington, D.C.: Spring, 2021) 272.
56 Hillman, "Figuring the Future," 243–44.
57 Hillman, *Soul's Code*, 6.
58 Ibid., 32.
59 Hillman, *City and Soul*, 50.
60 Ibid., 110.
61 Ibid., 109.
62 Ibid., 53.
63 Ibid., 370.
64 Ibid., 144.
65 Ibid., 92.
66 Ibid., 89.
67 Hillman, *Kinds of Power*, 162.
68 Hillman, *City and Soul*, 368.
69 Hillman, *Kinds of Power*, 194.
70 Ibid.
71 Hillman and Ventura, *We've Had a Hundred Years*, 43.
72 Ibid., 40.
73 Hillman, *City and Soul*, 114.
74 Ibid., 59–60.
75 Ibid., 91.
76 Randolph Severson remarks: "What Adler consistently stressed throughout his long career was the civilizing function of social interest. The development of social interest heightens all the civic interests. What then is the content of social interest? Its content is symbolic. *Gemeinschaftsgefühl* is topoi, a piece of rhetoric, an image, a symbol." Randolph Severson, *Dance Steps with Alfred Adler: An Interpretive Soul Psychology* (Benson, NC: Goldenstone Press, 2015), 45.
77 Hillman, *City and Soul*, 106.
78 Gordon Woods, *Friends Divided* (New York: Penguin Books, 2018), 115.
79 Hillman, *City and Soul*, 60.
80 Wolin, *Democracy Incorporated*, 289.
81 Hillman, *City and Soul*, 146.
82 Hillman and Ventura, *We've Had a Hundred Years*, 125.

83 Hillman, *City and Soul*, 206.
84 Ibid., 40.
85 Ibid., 211.
86 Ibid., 207.
87 Hillman and Ventura, *We've Had a Hundred Years*, 126.
88 Bob Dylan, "Nobel Lecture" (2016 Nobel Lecture in Literature, Los Angeles, CA, June 5, 2017). The Nobel Foundation. www.nobelprize.org/prizes/literature/2016/dylan/lecture/
89 Hillman, *City and Soul*, 193.
90 Ibid., 206.
91 Ibid., 89.
92 Wolin, *Democracy Incorporated*, 186.
93 Hillman, *City and Soul*, 193.
94 Ibid., 335.
95 Wolin, *Democracy Incorporated*, 289.
96 Ibid., 291.
97 Ibid., 290.
98 Ibid., 291.
99 Ibid., 289.
100 Hillman, *Kinds of Power*, 15.
101 Hillman, *City and Soul*, 372.
102 Hillman, *Re-Visioning*, 117.
103 Hillman, *City and Soul*, 153.
104 Ibid., 42.
105 See Hillman's discussions of "notitia as that capacity to form true notions of things from attentive noticing" (*City and Soul*, 41); and Edward S. Casey, "Introduction," in James Hillman, *Philosophical Intimations: Uniform Edition of the Writings of James Hillman*, vol. 8 (Washington, D.C.: Spring, 2021).
106 James Hillman, *The Force of Character: And the Lasting Life* (New York: Ballantine Books, 2000), xxiv.
107 Hillman, *City and Soul*, 212.
108 Hillman, *Re-Visioning*, 222.
109 Hillman, *Kinds of Power*, 193.
110 Hillman, *Re-Visioning*, 169. Original italics.
111 Hillman, *Archetypal Psychology*, 43.
112 Hillman, *Re-Visioning*, 169.
113 James Hillman, "Notes on White Supremacy: Essaying an Archetypal Account of Historical Events," *Spring* (1986), 33.
114 Ibid., 27.
115 Hillman, *Soul's Code*, 31.
116 Hillman, *Archetypal Psychology*, 147.
117 William E. Connolly, "Politics and Vision," in *Democracy and Vision: Sheldon Wolin and the Vicissitudes of the Political*, ed. Aryeh Botwinick and William Connolly (Princeton: Princeton University Press, 2001), 12.
118 Ibid., 7.
119 Sheldon Wolin, "E Pluribus Unum: The Representation of Difference and the Reconstitution of Collectivity," in *The Presence of the Past: Essays on the State and the Constitution* (Baltimore: Johns Hopkins University Press, 1990), 131.
120 Hillman, *City and Soul*, 88–89.
121 Hillman, *Archetypal Psychology*, 147.
122 Hillman, 141.
123 Wolin, *Politics and Vision*, 604.
124 Hillman, *City and Soul*, 206.

125 Wolin, *Politics and Vision*, 604.
126 Wolin, *Democracy Incorporated*, 112.
127 Hillman, "Figuring the Future," 389.
128 Stephen White, "Three Conceptions of the Political: The Real World of Late Modern Democracy," in *Democracy and Vision: Sheldon Wolin and the Vicissitudes of the Political*, eds. Aryeh Botwinick and William Connolly (Princeton: Princeton University Press, 2001), 181.
129 Wolin, *Fugitive Democracy*, 111.
130 Hillman, *City and Soul*, 58.

Chapter 14

Swimming the wave

Occupying uncertainty and the OWS movement[1]

Gustavo Beck

Psycho-economics: Movement and exchange

Psyche moves, and it operates through exchange. The entire discipline of depth psychology and psychotherapy is, in fact, built around the notion of movement: Professionals in the field speak of psychodynamics to describe how instinctual or libidinal energy moves and travels within our psychic structures, as well as to study how it is exchanged among individuals and members of groups or societies. We have theories of motivation that study the motors that propel or hinder human patterns of behavior. Consequently, psychotherapy also rests on movement and exchange: "What brings you here? What can I do for you?" asks the psychotherapist. "I don't understand how I ended up in this place; I don't like my life, I wish it would be different," says the patient. Our interest as depth psychotherapists focuses to a very large extent on what moves humans, as well as on how they move and why they stop moving. We are constantly looking for the ways in which psychic energy is mobilized, and for the blueprints that map these libidinal exchanges, which occur both intrapsychically and interpersonally. We sometimes even refer to this mobilization of energy as psychic economy(!). And this psychic economy is, according to our theoretical framework, what powers our conduct and relationships. A patient usually comes to therapy precisely when motion is interrupted, when his or her libidinal interactions are either absent, calcified, or moving in a direction that is not to his or her liking. Jungian analyst Rafael Lopez Pedraza goes as far as stating that "psychic movement lies not only at the core of psychotherapy, but also of life." [2]

Like psyche, economic systems move and are based on exchange. And here we need to understand "economic system" in its most basic definition—a structure that regulates the trading and management of energy and resources, in the form of food, objects, gifts, ideas, goods, actions, and so on. Human communities have always been built around the act of trading, which is to say that they have always moved through exchange. Nowadays, of course, just as psyche has libido, economic systems have money. Strictly speaking, in fact, *psyche is an economic system through which energy moves at certain rhythms using certain routes and generating certain effects*. And again, just as there are professionals who dedicate

DOI: 10.4324/9781003325765-20

their lives to studying how psychic energy moves through the personality structures of a given individual, there is another set of specialists who dedicate their lives to building financial models, to predict how money will travel from hand to hand, from company to company, from nation to nation—from system to system. And of course, finally, just as a patient can enter into shock when facing a personal crisis, the entire world becomes paralyzed when the balance in the movement of our financial trading system is disturbed. Patients suffer depression, their anxiety level rises, and some go as far as falling into psychotic states; on the other hand, stock markets lose points, currencies depreciate, inflation increases, and homes run low on commodities—or, in many cases, on food.

The movement of the Occupy Movement

An important manifestation of this psycho-economic movement and exchange began in New York City's Zuccotti Park, which witnessed, in September 17, 2011, the first demonstration of what since has become one of the most impressive social uprisings in the twenty-first century: Occupy Wall Street (OWS). OWS was the first chapter of what we now know as the Occupy Movement, a protest movement that emerged as a response to the economic inequality, social injustice, and corporate abuse that stem from certain aspects of the free market and the capitalist system. Inspired by the Arab Spring, the Tahrir Square protests, and the Spanish Indignados (Indignants), the movement advocated in favor of economic policies and social measures that promote equality and fairness. In the original Declaration of the Occupation of New York City, the "occupiers" described their starting point as follows:

> As *one people*, united, we acknowledge the reality: that the future of the human race requires the cooperation of its members; that our system must protect our rights, and upon corruption of that system, it is up to the individuals to protect their own rights, and those of their neighbors; that a democratic government derives its just power from the people, but corporations do not seek consent to extract wealth from the people and the Earth; *and that no true democracy is attainable when the process is determined by economic power*. We come to you at a time when corporations, which place profit over people, self-interest over justice, and oppression over equality, run our governments.[3]

After this statement followed a list of everything "they" (the corporations) have done—"taken our houses," "held students hostage with tens of thousands of dollars of debt on education," "continuously sought to strip employees of the right to negotiate for better pay and safer working conditions," "poisoned the food supply," "perpetuated inequality" . . . the list is quite long. The inequity denounced by these statements was also present in the political slogan that the movement used as a banner: "We are the 99 percent." People were angry, on both sides of the conflict.

Protests continued, governments retaliated, media covered the events, academics discussed the issues, and people in the streets articulated and defended their opinions on the matter every day.

A decade later, looking back at the OWS movement, one cannot help but imagine it, together with the Arab Spring and the Spanish Indignants, as a catalyst in more ways than one. Initially, it might be interesting to wonder how these protests might have paved the way for other civil rights and activism movements—notably Black Lives Matter in the United States and many feminist and environmental movements all around the globe. On the other hand, it is striking to notice that, parallel to the rise of activism on many fronts, we have also been witness to an increasingly polarized political landscape where conservative agendas that sometimes border on fascism are being pushed with much force. Greed has certainly not disappeared. If anything, it seems that, during the past decade, the 1 percent has doubled down. The landscape appears simultaneously much more hopeful and much more hopeless. There are more people fighting back against social, gender, racial, economic, and environmental injustice, but despair, fear, and anxiety are also more palpable. Today, as the world tries to leave behind a seemingly never-ending pandemic, while also facing the prospect of escalating wars and nuclear anxiety, we are left again with a financial system that, at least from the perspective of the everyday person, seems to be collapsing. Might it be that the OWS movement was sensing, ten years ago, the initial stages of the crisis that we face today, or at least the initial crisis as felt in the apparently invincible United States of America?

In any case, the Occupy Movement was certainly moving something—but what, exactly? What was moving the movement and what was the movement moving? That is the central question of the following essay.

Moving from, into, and out of economic and psychic uncertainty

I am not an economist. Therefore, this text will not speak of the technical subtleties of the capitalist system, or of the specifics of financial models or the logic of money. Rather, it will be concerned with the archetypal and psychological implications of the word "economy" in the context of the Occupy Movement. Additionally, in spite of being a professional psychologist, I have no interest in emitting a psychological interpretation of a financial phenomenon, essentially for two reasons. Firstly, it would seem rather useless; as much as I appreciate depth psychology, our financial crisis deserves much more than a psychological interpretation, which would be insufficient at best and self-indulgent at worst. Secondly, my concern for the financial crisis is not merely theoretical. My disclaimer about not being an economist is meant to clarify that mine is not a technical argument; nevertheless, like any other inhabitant of the planet, I participate in the financial system—I pay rent, go to the supermarket, buy clothes, and have a job. Therefore, this text wants to address the disturbances in the economy of psychological and financial fields, but, rather than doing so as a psychologist or an economist, I wish to do it from the perspective of a reflective witness and an active participant. I am writing this from the vantage point of someone who, whether he likes it or not, whether he wants to or not, takes part in these problems and is involved in this issue. So, these are not the interpretations of a psychologist or an economist, but the musings of a psychological and economic being who, through innumerable exchanges every day, is somehow participating in whatever movements are currently happening in our world. Put more simply, I write because something moves me to write, and because I wish to exchange ideas with people who are also involved in the ongoing crisis. For our problems continue: Relentless inflation, skyrocketing interest rates, energy insufficiency, abortion bans, racial injustice, nuclear threats, mass shootings, and an increasingly unsettling uncertainty. Conversations are becoming more and more polarized, and dialogue does not abound. Yet, the accentuated crisis only makes evident one simple fact: We are all in trouble, even if some of us feel more troubled than others. This is why, in this text, bibliographical quotations and theoretical inferences will, on purpose, be as absent or basic as possible. As I write this, I am nothing more than another *homo economicus* swimming in this vast, unexplainable sea of financial systems. I can feel how social and economic undercurrents overpower me and am simply trying to find the proper swimming stroke to plunge into the movements, past, present, and future. Maybe, as I swim, I will find a fellow troubled soul with whom I can converse, connect, and collaborate. Perhaps this might contribute to the continuation of movement.

Movement and exchange

So, let our first two strokes consist of an initial survey of how each side of the conflict understood what happened during OWS, and the environment in which it happened.

On the one hand, we had the OWS website (www.occupywallst.org), which described itself as the "online resource for the growing occupation movement happening on Wall Street and around the world." There was a brief section that described both the website and the Occupy Movement. The word with the most mentions in the text was *movement*. It spoke about an "occupation movement" and a "people-powered movement" and described the web page as "an affinity group committed to doing technical support work for resistance movements."[4]

On the other hand, we had Wall Street, home to the New York Stock Exchange (NYSE), the heart of economic trading in the United States (and, therefore, one of the most important financial centers in the entire globe). But what exactly takes place there? Although the web page has since been modified, at the time there was a section in the NYSE's official "Company Overview" where one could find a brief operational description of the company. In this text, the most repeated word was *exchange*, its first appearance being in the subtitle of the text: "NYSE Euronext— Powering the Exchanging World."[5]

The endeavor of the present text then is to dive into the economic ocean using two basic strokes—the notions of movement and exchange. The NYSE emphasizes exchange, OWS underlines movement, and both agree in the economic nature of the issue. For this text, these three terms are simply different avenues of entrance into the same phenomenon: They are, in fact, inseparable. Economic systems, after all, move through exchange. In any system, when there is an imbalance in the exchange of energy or resources, the movement of the system is disturbed, and we call that an economic crisis. This is valid for *any system*—financial, environmental, social, or psychological, as we will see below. The question then becomes: What is the relationship between movement, exchange, and economics—between the swimmer's arms and the movement of the ocean? And (outside financial discourses) what would be the implications of a conflict in movement, a problem with exchange, or a crisis in the economy? What if our left arm was cramping, or if the tide arose all of a sudden? Also, does the swimmer influence the ocean at all? Do we have any agency outside the decisions we take regarding our own path? Is it naïve to imagine that our swimming can impact the tides?

When we speak about movement or exchange, be it psychological, economic, social, cultural, or otherwise, it is important to ask a few questions. To remain content simply with the fact that something moves or that something is being exchanged is problematic, particularly if we neglect reflection and lose sight of the spirit of the movement and the exchange. A good swimmer is constantly aware of the movement of his or her body, the movement of the ocean, and the interaction between those movements. It seems important, therefore, to reflect about the Occupy Movement and its original circumstances in order to find what moved it, and to ask ourselves if some ripples of such movement can still be felt today. More specifically, what I am interested in is the subject and the place of Occupy, so that I can speculate about its intentionality and possible teleology. If I resort to my work as a psychotherapist, I can put it like this: When patients sit in front of me, I am interested in *who* they are and in *where* they are standing at this point in their life. By knowing this, I can begin to speculate about what *drives* their emotional and behavioral patterns and thus what brings them to therapy, as well as where the therapy might be heading. In this case, we are setting out to explore the *who* and the *where* of the Occupy Movement in order to decipher *what was in fact moving it*. The more I understand the cycles of the moon, the shifts in water temperature, and my own particular characteristics as a swimmer, the deeper I can penetrate the ocean.

The "where" of the movement

To start with location seems appropriate. Where were we swimming when the OWS movement came to be? Let us test the waters. The movement should be situated—that is, we should ask ourselves *where the occupation took place*. This allows us, firstly, to make some general observations. Speaking in clinical terms, the fact that the Occupy Movement emerged in Zuccotti Park and that it concentrated its attacks on Wall Street (and therefore on the NYSE) was *symptomatic*—in other words, the location tells us something about the movement, it reveals some of its inner logic and manifests the conflicts and tensions present in the situation. As *symptom*, Zuccotti Park speaks to the specificities of OWS. Why not Times Square? Why not the White House or the Capitol? Why not Disneyland or the Las Vegas Strip? Why not Kabul, Bagdad, Guatemala City, or Nairobi? The assumption seems to be that it is in Wall Street where the problem lies—the NYSE is the lair of the 1 percent, so to speak, or at least their operational center. If we consider that, five years later, the United States would elect one of the most divisive presidents in its history, and that such a president came from New York and essentially used money and economic success as one of his main banners, we can see that the occupiers were indeed onto something.

By choosing this spot as their meeting point, OWS implied that the enemy was to be found in the financial realm. There are at least two important issues that derive from this. The first one can be summarized in a brief thesis that has been building up in the previous pages: OWS is a *movement* that denounces the shortcomings of our contemporary *exchange* system. Here I remind the reader, once more, that, when I use the words "movement" and "exchange," I do so in the broadest of senses. If we phrase it more simply: One of the things the Occupy Movement set in motion (and probably one of the things by which it was set in motion) was the need to examine our exchange patterns. The problem, then, is economic; speaking psychologically, it stems from the hardening and ossification of the structures through which our libidinal exchanges take place. By "libidinal exchanges," I am simply referring to the way in which energy moves among people and communities, be it in the form of human relationships, actions, emotions, thoughts, money, and so on.

Here, OWS, inadvertently, might have been pointing at another, deeper and larger, problem: If we extrapolated this to realms other than the financial, would it not be important to ask ourselves how these neurotic patterns of exchange take place in the interactions between individuals, communities, societies, and nations or between aspects of each of our psyches? How fair is the libidinal trade within our own personalities? How does equality factor in the emotional economics of our relationships? How democratic are our psychic exchanges with other members of our communities? And, most importantly, how does the fairness, equality, and democracy (or lack thereof) translate into our positions regarding the exchange patterns in social and cultural levels—between races, social classes, nations, genders, and so on? In our daily psychological and economic lives, who are we exploiting, and how are we being exploited?

Examining every way in which all of us participate in harmful exchange patterns, not only financially but also culturally, socially, interpersonally, and intrapsychically, is extremely important and implies much more than just an "application" of the OWS logic to individual or family life: Performing this analysis is a recognition that individual neuroses and family dynamics display the same damaging patterns as the NYSE and free markets do. It implies acknowledging that, as swimmers, we are participating in the movement of the ocean; our swimming strokes do move the ocean, even if their comparatively small effect on its movement can go unnoticed. In financial terms, we suffer the consequences of an unfair trading system, but, as consumers (and a reminder here that psychotherapy is also embedded in capitalist systems and is thus part of consumerist culture), we are active—maybe unconscious—participants in its movement. Corporations might be pointed at as a very clear expression of oppressive patterns, and it is good they are targeted, but, if we forget that the issue at hand is not only the stockholders' greed, but also our outdated patterns of exchange—not only financial exchange, but also emotional exchange, intellectual exchange, behavioral exchange—we run the risk of missing much of the value that OWS brought. The message here is that *all of us participate in the unfair, dictatorial, and oppressive exchange patterns that find very high levels of expression in Wall Street.* This may provide a much more differentiated vision of the movement, which was more than just a forward charge against an oppressive structure (an attempt at bringing Wall Street down). No, we can't simply charge the wall, because we are part of the wall, part of its substance and configuration. The movement, then, wished to collapse the wall, *but came from within the wall.* We must not forget that. We are, in fact, still in the wall, even if the wall has more cracks now. Just as there is no being outside psyche, there is no being outside Wall Street, no being outside the economy.

The second issue that becomes important when we situate the movement is somehow related to this forgetfulness about our participation in the issue. On the OWS website, we could read the following slogan: "The only solution is World Revolution." The Occupy Movement was often described as global, or as a worldwide phenomenon. This was a somewhat beautiful idea, but also highly misleading, and signaling this is important because the fantasy of it being global was part of Wall Street logic. So, let us be clear: The Occupy Movement was first and foremost located in the United States and in Europe. The vast majority of assemblies were located in those two geographical zones. The rest were located in developed countries that either have a very marked European influence (such as Australia or South Africa) or have relatively strong economies (such as Brazil). The protests taking place in developing countries were few, and the numbers of attendees were much smaller. If anything, we might argue that the way in which OWS "spread" around the globe was analogous to the way in which U.S. ideas about capitalism and democracy have traditionally spread among developing countries—condescendingly and violently. Condescendingly because the logic of globalization ignores that most developing countries have been experiencing the strife that is now being felt in developed countries for decades, and violently because they neglect that such strife is at least partially a result of American and European colonialism. Uncritically imagining the world as globalized carries with it the shadow of colonialism.

If we combine the two issues raised by the "where" of the movement—the theme of exchange and the global fantasy—then we are obligated to ask some more questions. How does this illusion of being global (which brings with it the assumption that, because something happens in the developing countries of the world, it is in fact happening in the entire world) relate to social and psychological patterns of exchange? If this movement truly pertained to the entire world, how did psychic energy move between New York protesters in Zuccotti Park, Sudanese refugees in Ethiopia, and the marginalized peoples who inhabit the favelas in Sao Paolo? Did this movement and exchange of psychic energy mirror in any way the movement and exchange of financial resources between these peoples? Was everyone really involved? And, if everyone was involved, was everyone equally involved? How do we account for (and deal with) the inequalities among those who are fighting for equality? This brings us to the next question: Who was occupying?

The "who" of the movement

The Occupy Movement was, theoretically, a collective movement. In a certain sense, this is accurate; after all, it did advocate in favor of solidarity and "collective thinking." However, the fact that its actions occurred collectively (in several countries simultaneously) and somehow pointed in the same direction should not make us forget that, within that collective, there were individuals, with individual personalities, individual intentions, and individual motivations. All might unite under the banner of being the 99 percent, but to assume that this 99 percent is looking for the same thing—or moving in exactly the same fashion—is somewhat naïve. A 45-year-old father of three who joins the movement after losing his job will have a very different vision than a 20-year-old political science major who joined because he finds Slavoj Žižek's ideas fascinating and inspiring. Furthermore, was the Spaniards' motivation the same as the New Yorkers' or the Egyptians'? That the movements were connected is undeniable, much like all our psychic structures are, but does this necessarily mean that they were driven equally or evenly by *one* impulse? The Gulf of Mexico is certainly connected to the Arctic Ocean and the Dead Sea, but they behave very differently, and, even within their own systems, each of these bodies of water has innumerable particularities and specificities. The fact that they communicate and have common characteristics, and even problems, does not necessarily imply that their needs are exactly the same.

We could also pose the question in this way: We say that the movement was generated by the 99 percent—but the 99 percent of what? What is our reference point, our universe or our ocean, so to speak? Was it 99 percent of Americans, of Europeans, of males, females, of the middle class, of professionals? Was it 99 percent of the world? Of course it was not. Yes—speaking of the 99 percent was a rhetorical resource, a figure of speech that did make a very important point (the almost impenetrable omnipotence of the economic elite—the so-called 1 percent)—but this figure has to be looked into if we are to clarify the nature of the movement. Even if we take the top 1 percent of the United States as a reference point, we run into trouble, for, given the polarization in the United States at the moment, it would even be difficult to say that the top 1 percent is a monolithic block. Are they all Trump supporters, for instance? Doubtful. However, from the viewpoint of the rest, there is certainly a perception that the elite do work in unison when it comes to protecting their privilege. So, the top 1 percent is in itself a tense, dynamic whole.

On the other hand, if our frame of reference is the world, let us speak about percentages. First of all, let us take the top 1 percent out; once that is done, we have the 99 percent. Of this 99 percent, the bottom 40 percent receive 5 percent of the entire world's income. Most of these people, evidently, live in developing countries where the Occupy Movement had very little, if not no, presence. To this we can add that 75 percent of the world's income goes to the upper 20 percent. And 80 percent of the world's population lives on less than $10 a day—all this since long before the 2008 financial crisis.

So, how did the "Declaration of Occupation" relate to the bottom 40 percent? The bottom 40 percent did not lose their homes, because most of them did not own one to begin with; they were not held hostage by thousands of dollars of debt on education, because most of them did not even finish elementary school and certainly have no access to loans or credit; they were not deprived of the right to negotiate for better pay and safer working conditions, because most simply need a job and cannot afford the luxury of negotiation; their food supply was not poisoned, because they have no consistent food supply; and they certainly did not feel the perpetuation of inequality, because, for them, inequality has been the perpetual state since long before inequality was an issue for those who were not at the very bottom.

The two points to keep in mind here are that (1.) we are all indeed encompassed by the inequality of a system (even the top 1 percent, I would argue) and (2.) there are inequalities within inequalities. I had an aunt who used to jokingly say: "You know darling, in this world everyone is created equal, but some people are created more equally than others." It is crucial that we do not forget this; otherwise, it is easy to establish divisions that might be real, but have been chosen arbitrarily. That is, the line between the 1 percent and the 99 percent exists, but using this line as a starting point for a movement is a *choice*—more importantly, a choice originally made in New York City. There are thousands of divisions; why choose this one? Why not the one between the top 60 percent and the bottom 40 percent, or between men and women, or between Europe and Latin America? The fact that we *chose* this division in particular is also a symptom: It also points at the specific way in which OWS imagined oppression and injustice. As a Mexican, I would pose it like this: The framing of the issue, in which the division between the 1 percent and the 99 percent was put in the center and implicitly universalized, is a quintessential expression of the way in which the U.S. culture operates, imposing (often with good intentions) its own ideas on other cultures and countries. On the other hand, my own tendency to be drawn to this framing is part of my own neurosis as a Mexican upper-middle-class man. I was raised to idealize the United States and to seek assimilation into its culture.

My intention here is not to discredit the movement—not at all. The purpose of this differentiation is to signal the movement's complexity. Returning to the wall metaphor: As we said, the wall is moving from within, but it is not the entire wall that is moving, just one section of bricks, the ones that are uncomfortable enough to notice something is wrong, but comfortable enough to do something about it. The top 1 percent will not want to change, obviously, but the bottom 40 percent (one might even say the bottom 80 percent) is too busy surviving and does not have the time to think about inequality, much less to denounce it. It is, thus, up to those in the middle to engage more actively in the uncomfortable initial stages of transformation. This might become clearer if we return to our psychotherapy analogies.

Symptomatic movement

In depth psychotherapy, whatever manifestly brings the patient to the consulting room tends to end up being less central than it appeared to be in the beginning. When people start psychotherapeutic processes, they (we) usually have a complaint, or, in technical terms, a symptom. In other words, they are experiencing something being wrong in their lives. Patients come feeling anxious or depressed, having relationship problems, or feeling frustrated because they are not where they imagine they should be. From the perspective of depth psychology, however, this symptom usually points at a much larger (economic/psychically economic) crisis. The manifest conflict is the way into the crisis, the former being simply a visible and partial aspect of the latter. In this sense, OWS, the indignation of a large section of the middle class in developed countries, the housing crisis in the United States, unemployment in Spain, or (to include my context) the drug wars in Mexico were symptoms, but not the actual issue. They are all manifestations of something that is moving, connected but contingent to their specific location and population. They are peripheral issues, and, although their being peripheral does not make them less important, recognizing them as such is crucial because, as is the case with any symptom, assuming that when they go away the conflict will be solved is a tempting but dangerous move.

Symptoms, however, are there for a reason. It is common that a patient who comes in with depression is actually suffering from an identity crisis that threatens his or her marital illusions, professional goals, political convictions, or social status. That is what characterizes the start of depth psychotherapy—a crisis in meaning. Suddenly, whether we realize it or not, the system that supported our identity—that validated our self-image and gave coherent sense to our thoughts, feelings, and actions—breaks down. It becomes insufficient or outdated. But this breakdown, of course, cannot be processed (or even experienced) in its entirety by any person's conscious ego; it is simply too complex, too painful, and too threatening. Psychologically speaking, this is why we generate a symptom: To have something that is painful enough to get us moving, but bearable enough to allow us to move. In this case, the economic struggle of the 19 percent who stand between the top 1 percent and the bottom 80 percent is the symptom.

A symptom, then, is not the core issue, but rather *a way in*, the arrow pointing toward the core issue; in post-Jungian terms, it wants to be *seen through* to reveal the archetypal pattern behind it. This is what an economic crisis is, both financially and psychologically: A disturbance in the balance of the patterns of exchange (monetary or libidinal) that derives in certain painful manifestations. The patient divorces his or her spouse, or the citizen is evicted; these are very serious issues that should be addressed in themselves, but, when we enter a process that gives an economic context to that issue (when we go into depth psychotherapy or join a protest in Zuccotti Park), then it is no longer about the divorce or the eviction, but about what these phenomena are indirectly manifesting. In clinical terms, symptoms point to a much larger conflict that has two vital characteristics: It is *unconscious* and *systemic*. The depths of a psychic or financial economic crisis—the aspect of the crisis that reveals how it is present in *every aspect of a system*—are by definition outside the scope of any individual's consciousness, particularly that of the individual suffering the symptom. Once more: The conflict that underlies the symptom is too complex and painful to be fitted into our frames of reference. So, let us ask the uncomfortable question: What underlies this particular symptom? What were the undercurrents of this particular movement? What was actually moving those who protested to become outraged at inequality, to occupy, and to write about occupation?

I think it is fair to say that, at this point, we have seen certain aspects of the symptom unfold. We now have a clearer sense of its underlying dynamics and hold a deeper and wider awareness of the problem. In the past ten years, the breakdown has continued, and protests have multiplied and expanded to address other equally important issues that were already present (perhaps more implicitly or tangentially) in Zuccotti Park.

The "what" of the movement

As clinicians, the only thing to do is follow the symptom and see where it takes us—we swim the wave. When it is truly followed, the process is filled with suffering, for it will involve letting go of many (sometimes all) of those identifications that gave meaning to the life of the patient. In other words, as the wave moves and crashes, the entire psychological economy of the patient's personality is reconfigured, and that reconfiguration, rewarding as it might be, involves multiple movements (examining neurotic emotional patterns, reliving hurtful memories, confronting dark aspects of our personality) that are often much more difficult to endure than the pain of the initial symptom. Pursuing this process, however, can revolutionize a person's life and redefine his or her place in the world.

In the case of OWS, this means that, although stabilization of the American economy might have been good enough for U.S. citizens at the time, or the apparent amelioration of the drug war might have been temporarily sufficient for

Mexicans, or the resolution of the credit crisis might have calmed Europeans down for some time, stopping there only took care of some *symptoms*. It did not truly affect the *underlying economic crisis* that sustained them. Today, of course, the symptoms have returned and they are back with a vengeance. They still need to be heard. As we have said, this movement was pointing at a problem in our patterns of exchange at every level. If we extend our view of this crisis of exchange into its emotional, intellectual, and cultural aspects and look into its *unconscious* and *systemic* aspects, then it becomes much more complex, initially because it becomes both intrapsychic (psychological) and interpersonal (social). And here the words "unconscious" and "systemic" are also used in a very basic fashion: They refer to the collective aspects of the conflict (and the movement) that remain hidden, unseen, or unspoken.

It is important not to confuse the symptom with the spirit of the movement. The symptom was what detonated the movement at a conscious level: It triggered deliberate protest and reflection. But the movement that emerged back in 2011 was much more complex than the housing crisis, unemployment, or drug dealing. Divorce consciously brings the patient to the therapist's office, but it is not only her or his marriage that is moving—her or his entire psyche is. Similarly, the abuse perpetrated by the top 1 percent and the problems of the developed-world middle class were what started the movement, but the spirit of the movement involved an economic system that (unlike the protests) did include every inhabitant of the planet. Not everyone occupied, but everyone suffered the consequences of financial oppression. The bottom 40 percent, however, could not protest, essentially because they lived in survival mode. If OWS was to be truly revolutionary, then, it had to reach these usually hidden social consequences of our financial economic system. If this movement was to truly move us, it had to operate both within and without—it had to awaken both inner and outer (psychological/emotional and social/political) movement in all of us who participated in it. The patient cannot expect to resolve his or her relationship issues if he or she does not touch his or her fears of attachment, need to control, and an innumerable set of variables that intervene in his or her crisis. Thus, the entire psychic economic system has to be examined. It is no wonder that, today, the crisis often feels worse, and that more people are engaged in protesting on many fronts.

And here is where the true challenge emerges. In order to reach the 40 percent, we have to ask ourselves uncomfortable questions: Are we truly emancipated from Wall Street logic? Back in 2011, how were we part of Wall Street? Where in the wall did we stand? What was pushing us to move? Did we want to bring the financial system down or simply to change it so it becomes more comfortable? More comfortable for whom? How fair were the policies in our family? How democratic was our local community? How did we all participate in oppressive or dominating patterns that mirror those of the 1 percent? How did our purchasing of this or that product enable child labor, civil wars, or extreme poverty? How far were we willing to go in the reconfiguration of our economic system—not just of the aspects of the economic system of which we are aware, but of the economic system as a whole? If we were patients in the consulting room, would we have simply wanted to calm our anxiety, or did we really want that anxiety to reconfigure our way of life? And has any of this changed today?

In retrospect, these questions give us cause to be both optimistic and pessimistic. It seems clear that there is an increasing awareness of the ways in which unfair economic systems underlie the most pressing issues of our times—the climate crisis, racial justice, women's rights, refugee care, and so on. On the other hand, this heightened awareness has also brought with it starker sociopolitical polarization, possibly associated, among other things, with higher levels of anxiety and fear around economic collapse. In some ways, the psychic movement that started with OWS has kept on moving, and many have done a very good job at keeping up with its pace. Still, the continuing unfolding of this movement has also placed us deeper in trouble. If I continue with the therapeutic analogy, I might say that we are at that stage where the patient starts to resent the therapeutic process, for it has landed him or her in a much more uncomfortable place than the original symptom.

Thus, we find ourselves in the midst of exploring our neurotic patterns of exchange, and at this point the best course is to follow the movement through and simply trust it. If we are to participate in true and radical transformation, we now need to fully immerse ourselves in our psychological and economic neurosis. We must remember that the neurosis existed long before the patient entered the consulting room, just as poverty existed long before OWS; the crisis is simply an opportunity to go deeper into the issues, and it is this deepening that can really create a revolution, both individually and socially. By revolution, here I mean a change in the economic system, a radical shift in the way the energy moves through psyche, community, nation, globe, and so on. This shift, however, would signify a challenge to our identity: Everything that validates our psychological, social, financial, and cultural standing would be put to the test. It is not an easy or pleasant process. Back in 2011, the question was whether or not we were willing to follow the movement; today, however, the situation is even more pressing. Today, the question is whether we will consciously swim the wave or will be dragged by it against our will.

Occupying uncertainty and swimming the wave

We can recognize the symptom (the financial crisis) and respond to it (with the Occupy Movement); we can even acknowledge that there are much deeper and broader invisible patterns that move a movement, and that it is these underlying dynamics that need to be addressed (or at least acknowledged, experienced, and related to) once we have seen through the symptom. But the problem is that a movement such as OWS—and, more specifically, the spirit of a movement and the energy that underlies it—is too complex to understand. There are too many variables, too many possible levels of analysis, and too many conflicting realities.

Furthermore, even if we were capable of comprehending the entire movement, it is likely that confronting it fully would be too shocking and painful. In that sense, this problem might actually be a hidden blessing. If we were aware of all its implications, odds are we would be scared off rather easily. If I were truly and completely aware of every force, creature, or situation that could overpower me while I swam in the ocean, odds are I would jump out almost immediately. Challenging Wall Street, after all, implies challenging one of the pillars of our lifestyle, even if that pillar is, at the moment, more oppressive than supportive.

Whatever it was that moved the Occupy Movement remains ungraspable; there is no way of knowing why it moved or what it was precisely that moved it. What we do know is that it kept moving, and that its movement has us now swimming in deeper waters. If the landscape of 2011 was bleak and unpredictable, what we see around us in the early 2020s has reached levels of uncertainty that many of us have never experienced in our lifetimes. Psychologically, however, this does provide a silver lining, for uncertainty can force us into continuous engagement with conflict and with the world. Drawing another parallel with psychotherapy, I quote James Hillman:

> I have come to think that the *uncertainty* about what the patient and I are really there for is in fact what we *are* there for. [. . .] I believe the patient and I are kept in psychotherapeutic analysis because *it* keeps us there in all sorts of ways [. . .] we simply cannot grasp why we are engaged in psychotherapy, what it is, whether it is going well or even going on at all, or when it is over.[6]

If we knew why we were in therapy, the process would become a rigid pursuit to re-solve the symptom, the problem "that brought me here," and that would close many more doors than it would open. As strange as it might sound, it is our unknowing that keeps us moving forward and remaining open to new possibilities. In fact, the only thing that the 99 percent do share is this ignorance of what moves economic systems. Not everyone lost his or her home, not everyone is buried in debt, and not everyone lost a job. But everyone, *absolutely everyone*, is subject to a system the functioning of which remains mostly foreign to any kind of understanding. I would argue, in fact, that this applies also to the top 1 percent.

Acknowledging this uncertainty about what moves our psychic and financial economic systems is, in fact, what would allow us to truly make a movement global; it would help us go beyond the confrontation between the 1 percent and the 99 percent and realize that we can only be "one people" (as the Occupy declaration stated) if we include the 100 percent in both the problem and the response to the problem. Oddly enough, it is this lack of understanding that truly unites us, whether we like it or not and whether we are aware of it or not. It is this unknowing of the economic system and this impossibility of operating outside of it that actually make us a global community. Then, to pick up again on the wording of the declaration, we would find out that "true democracy" can in fact be attainable when "the process is determined by economic power," for what hinders democracy is not power itself, but the monopolizing, unbalance, and unevenness in the movement of such power, which result from psychologically outdated, socially shortsighted patterns of exchange in which all of us participate.

OWS was a symptom of a financial and psychological crisis of exchange. Following it led us to realize that we all participate from oppressive and unjust patterns of exchange, and that a true transformation would imply both to recognize that we are part of the Wall Street logic and to renounce to that logic (which in many ways supports our lifestyle and consequently is much more difficult than one might think). Surrendering to the psychic, communitarian, and social drive that powered the Occupy movement might lead us to a genuine shift in our worldview. The reason for this is that such power does not belong to corporations or to protesters; this power is autonomous and has its own intention. It is the ocean itself—with its currents, its saltiness, its density, its tides—that pulls us in, pushes us out, or keeps us afloat. What this power is, no one truly knows. We have ideas, hypotheses, and some rudimentary mapping. But again: not knowing it is important. Relating to the movement, reflecting actively about it and acting reflexively within it, was much more important than understanding it. It is crucial to remain aware that this problem, *that this economic conflict in which we all involved*, is much more complex than we can possibly imagine, that it generates suffering that does not even occur to us, and that it costs lives of people that we do not even know. It is this awareness of our unawareness that can move us from the visible symptom to the unseen conflict—from being detached witnesses to becoming conscious participants.

The challenge posed by the Occupy Movement, from this perspective, was to amplify our experience of occupation, to expand it beyond the confines of our own convictions and beliefs. The possibility that opened up for us was precisely to allow our personal and particular positions to be contained (and moved) by a collective movement. Instead of attempting to understand and frame a movement through our individual knowledge, we had the quite rare opportunity to allow our individual knowledge to swim and move alongside other individual knowledges, all contained within a movement that none of us understood and that we therefore could not control.

Today, more than a decade later, the waters are deeper, and the tides are more violent. The political landscape feels dangerous, wars escalate uncontrollably, the climate crisis threatens human survival, and economic systems are collapsing again. Uncertainty now often leads to anxiety, and anxiety to fear. But fear, perhaps because of its close relationship with instinct, is also an agent of movement. And, in these dark waters, where not-knowing has become a quite natural state of being, one is fearful, uncertain, and freed from the compulsion to understand. In this state, understanding and reflection can only be accomplished through action and relationship—through a different type of movement and exchange.

For one can only learn to swim if one is *in* the water, and one can only understand the motion of the ocean once one is caught in the movement of the wave.

Notes

1 An earlier version of this essay was previously published in *Occupy Psyche: Jungian and Archetypal Perspectives on a Movement*, ed. Jordan Shapiro and Roxanne Partridge (Lexington, KY: The Journal of Archetypal Studies, 2012), 89–111.
2 Rafael López-Pedraza, *Hermes and His Children*, 4th ed. (Einseldein: Daimon Verlag, 2010), 7.
3 "Declaration of the Occupation of Wall Street." NYC General Assembly, accessed December 10, 2011. www.nycga.net/resources/declaration/. Emphasis mine.
4 "About," Occupy Wall Street, accessed December 10, 2011. www.occupywallst.org
5 "Company Overview," NYSE Euronext, accessed December 10, 2011. http://corporate.nyx.com/en/who-we-are/company-overview
6 James Hillman, *Healing Fiction* (Putnam, Spring, 1983), 86.

Chapter 15

Nomadland

Searching the horizon for the American dream

Rebecca Armstrong

Movies and the American dream

Movies have an uncanny way of letting us know what is currently and perennially important to us. Like all works of art, they reflect both our conscious beliefs and our unconscious fears and desires. I was thus surprised and somewhat discomfited when *Nomadland*—which tells the story of a woman financially driven to abandon her house and neighbors for a life on the road in an old van—won Best Picture at the 2021 Oscars.[1] Holding up this work above the rest makes a statement about Americans and the American culture that deserves further exploration. This essay is an attempt to do just that.

While Homo sapiens might be an aspirational title, Homo narrans is an observable one; we are creatures who live by story, and all great stories begin in one of two ways—"A person goes on an unexpected journey" or "A stranger comes to town." The great American myth, in its infancy, certainly emphasized the first of these two themes; no one got to America except through a long journey. Whether you were a Siberian nomad who'd followed the reindeer herds too far east and ended up being caught out by the hostile incursions of the last ice age, circa 13,000 BCE, and had to wend your way along the kelp highway of the Pacific coast into the Americas, or were a more recent European fed up with the limited economic prospects or hostile religious incursions of church and state during the last millennium, you had to turn your face toward a horizon which took you well beyond the limits of the known and thrust you into the wild unknown.

In fact, many European Americans need look back only a generation or two to find their immigrant ancestors, family wanderers brave enough to leave behind what they had, spurred on by nothing more than hope and a willingness to risk danger. If this much of our cultural story features the nomad, the wanderer, the one who has left home as the hero of the story, why is it that we see all around us such animosity toward those who are unhoused? Why do we take the "not in my back yard" attitude when it comes to building affordable housing?[2] Why do we make laws that deprive the homeless of a place to sleep or restrict their right to enjoy the common spaces of our cities? How can we celebrate on screen the likes of Charlie Chaplin's Little Tramp, Robin Williams' Fisher King, Alan Ladd's Shane, or even

DOI: 10.4324/9781003325765-21

famous fictional characters such as Captain America, Tony Stark, or Robin Hood—homeless heroes all—and yet, if we saw them camping outside our front door, we would call the police? What is at the dark heart of such conflicting views?

Words used for the homeless are varied, suggesting the range of feelings stirred up by thoughts of the unsettled: Vagrant and vagabond come from the Latin *vagari*, to wander—a simple, descriptive term, but the words have denigrating overtones. Derelict, displaced, dispossessed, destitute are derived from relinquished, abandoned, or forsaken and share a deep sense of loss around homelessness. Hobo, bum, drifter, tramp, transient, itinerant, loafer are terms from the Great Depression in the United States and are all seen as derogatory. Rover, traveler, wayfarer, rambler are romanticized words drawn from folksong and story—the carefree, handsome stranger who woos the women and inspires envy in the land-bound men. Pilgrim, wanderer, sojourner are terms with spiritual overtones and connote a different kind of movement, one that is more deliberate, even if still unpropertied.

Etymologically, *nomad* comes from the Greek or Latin *nomas* and refers to the wandering herdsmen and tribes of Arabia, such as the Bedouins, whom we shall hear more about later on. This word is significant in that it has none of the derogatory connotations of the earlier terms. A nomad has the distinction, historically, of being born into that lifestyle, not falling or being thrown into it through misfortune. Therefore, a nomad need not be pitied. It is not by accident that David Manner and Tsugio Makimoto chose the word "nomad" for their book on the rise of a new class of tech workers who choose glamorous venues around the world in which to pursue their careers.[3] They did more than describe a new method of making money: They defined a new way of making a life. In the film *Nomadland*, the idea of the freedom to choose is of deep import to the elder nomads.

Everything can hang on a name, as Fern—the lead character played by Frances McDormand—lets us know. Fern is at a sporting goods store sneaking a nap when she bumps into McKenzie, a student whom she tutored some years earlier. Fern is delighted when McKenzie can still recite by heart some of the lines from Shakespeare's *MacBeth*, but is disconcerted when the teenager asks about Fern's homelessness. Fern's response is quick and assertive: She is not homeless but merely "houseless." Throughout the film, Fern continues to insist that she has *chosen* the nomadic life, but it is also obvious that for many nomads, including Fern, this life was forced upon them through economic necessity. They couldn't afford to live in any other way.

But it is not merely economics that creates the tension—it is not just a case of the haves and the have-nots—but also the meaning of freedom in America. The myth of the American dream includes both the little house on the prairie *and* the wide-open road, two forms of being at home in the world. This film paints a landscape where both ideas must try to come to terms with each other, and the individuals who have identified with one side or the other must also wrestle with their ambivalence. By using *Nomadland* as the focal point of these ambivalent feelings, we may be able to learn something important about the American myth here in the twenty-first century.

Nomadland at the intersection of genres

Cultural meaning and the messages of how we should behave and what we should strive for are always carried in sacred stories, and movies carry these sacred stories to the public. Movies frame our experience of reality and show us how to respond to it. One of the most popular genres in film is the post-apocalyptic film. Like the favorite fairy tales that have been passed down from the Bronze Age, these movies carry our anxieties about the biggest monsters and demons we know we still must face. If we survey the last 100 years of American cinema, there are roughly three types of dangers that our movies constantly warn us of:

• The dangers from without in the form of attacking aliens;
• The dangers we are to each other in the form of annihilating strife;
• The dangers from within in the form of pestilence, pandemics, and political and economic panics.

These movies help us rehearse imaginatively what our response might be in such a situation, like imaginary dry runs of what we could see ourselves doing if such a disaster were actually to occur. As such, films are tools for schooling us about what skills, knowledge, and virtues are essential for Homo sapiens to exercise if we are to survive. This is why I believe *Nomadland* exerted such a pull upon Americans in 2021, at the apex of the COVID-19 pandemic.

In the year 2021, Americans' collective dread conjured up many dark places from the past. Warnings of economic failure in view of the massive layoffs pulled into memory haunting images from the Great Depression—now almost a century behind us. The scars from that disaster shaped the generations who lived through it and the next generation who received the memories from their parents. Scenes of Hoovervilles lurk uneasily behind contemporary photos of homeless encampments in Los Angeles or San Francisco. *Nomadland* is not merely a glimpse into a possible American future, but a parable about how we are coping with such realities right now.

Nomadland straddles an unusual triad of genres: It is partly a documentary-like portrayal of American life; partly a new cinematic version of apocalypse; and partly an old-fashioned Western. It is a new twist on the uniquely American genre of "the wild, wild west"—with Fern taking on the character of Shane, or Jeremiah Johnson, or one of Clint Eastwood's iconic loners. Don't let the absence of a gun and holster deceive you; the film makes clear that Fern is pitting herself against the settled culture to hold the high ground as a traveling sage, communal judge, dispenser of quiet diplomacy, gadfly of the social conscience who rides off into the sunset (or sunrise) and disappears into the horizon at the conclusion of her visitation.

Fern's character aligns not only with the loners of the great Westerns, but even more so with Mel Gibson's character of the *Mad Max* movies, or Hans Solo of *Star Wars*, or Neo of *The Matrix*—the latest of the American Western heroes who roam the fringes of society, attempting to uphold some form of personal ethics in the face of complete social breakdown. *Nomadland* is a type of the new movie genre of the neo-Western.

The symbol in society

A flourishing society will have a flourishing story, according to Joseph Campbell's theory, a living mythology that serves four functions—metaphysical, cosmological, social, and psychological.[4] In the absence of a flourishing mythology, there will be an upwelling of unconscious attempts to find a new mythic image to live by, a new symbol system that will take on the functions necessary for the society to survive. The role of the artist, the poet, the playwright, the filmmaker is to bring to consciousness those latent symbols of the new vision.

According to Campbell, the functions played by myth and symbol are these:

1. The metaphysical function awakens a sense of awe and wonder by lifting the veil of the physical world to reveal the mystery of being in such a way that we are reconciled to what is;
2. The cosmological function is satisfied when we are given a story about the universe that corresponds with what we know rationally, but still inspires us with its grandeur;
3. The sociological function weaves a moral infrastructure for social relations that we can live with, willingly sacrificing personal goals for the greater good of the whole;
4. The psychological function instructs the individual on how to live life through its different stages, finding meaning and satisfaction at each waypoint, and then making a graceful exit without despair.

Symbols work with the cultural myth to evoke the powerful feelings that tie individuals back—*re-ligare*—to the shared story. A living mythology satisfies the religious need for coherence and direction. But the symbols only work in the way they are intended if they have the quality of being "transparent to the transcendent"—as Campbell summarized the idea of Karlfried Graf Dürckheim.[5] The tendency is to read symbols literally, which makes them opaque. Campbell's favorite example of this problem is the literalization of the virgin birth story in Christianity, where the insistence on a physical *virgo intacta* misses the point entirely and draws attention away from the metaphoric meaning, in which all human beings may participate, to focus belief at the level of physical proof, which is always the death knell of a symbol.

The American myth is supported by the great story of the Wild West, and one of the critical symbols of that story is the image of the horizon. The physical grandeur of the wide expanses of the American western landscape magnificently serves the metaphysical function of mythology— that which inspires awe and wonder— which then provides for the psychological function of myth—that which guides and directs the individual path by virtue of its power to command us in things of ultimate concern.

Symbols must be used because not all members of a society have the privilege of encountering the sacred for themselves directly. Moses went to the mountaintop alone, but he came back with stone tablets and the story of a burning bush. These would provide grist for a tremendously vital myth that would serve the Hebrew people and satisfy the social, psychological, and metaphysical functions for generations. Likewise, the bold explorers who came back with stories of the American West and its awe-inspiring horizons were followed by the poets and painters who would find ways to symbolize that soul-shaking experience so that it could speak to the deep heart of those who had never seen it for themselves. The success of those symbols is apparent in the steady stream of human beings who have sought the promise of the western horizon *in spite of* danger, difficulty, and distance.

Amplifying these symbols of the American dream was the work of the artists, writers, and poets who carried the torch of a romanticized nationalism that reached its zenith in the heady days of the Hudson River School painters of the early to mid-1800s. Thomas Cole, Albert Bierstadt, Frederick Church, Thomas Moran, and George Innes all picked up the themes of the transformed religious view of Nature—no longer was wilderness the residence of demons and symbolic of heaven's outcasts, as it had been in the Middle Ages; it was now the new representation of God's grandeur, largesse, and generosity to humankind.[6]

The deism of the Founding Fathers and the agreement among our most revered philosophers and poets—Ralph Waldo Emerson, Henry David Thoreau, Walt Whitman—made the wilderness of the West a backdrop not for Hieronymus Bosch's version of the inferno, but for the new paradise where the American pilgrim could find salvation. As Estwick Evans proclaimed:

> How great are the advantages of solitude! How sublime is the silence of nature's ever-active energies! There is something in the very name of wilderness, which charms the ear, and soothes the spirit of man. There is religion in it.[7]

The origins of the Hudson River School painters, alongside the influential works of Emerson and Thoreau, guided the trajectory of the American imagination in its new spiritual path. As humanities scholar Max Oelschlaeger wrote,

> Thoreau, as with the Hudson River School, invites us to find a sense of meaning, of direction and purpose in life through immediate contact with the living creatures, the vicissitudes of the seasons, and the varied textures of the earth.[8]

It is impossible to miss the intentionality of artists such as Cole, Bierstadt, Durand and others whose massive canvases filled entire walls in galleries in order to inspire the sense of awe that would bring viewers into that aesthetic arrest which invites an experience of the sublime or the numinous. The religious impulse to worship that which is infinitely more powerful had come from the awe inspired by the starry heavens and the orderly rounds of sun, moon, and planets during the epoch Campbell calls the way of the celestial lights. The grand cathedrals with their rounded domes and rigid symmetry spoke to the perfection of that conception of the divine. Bringing the sacred down to Earth was made easier by the grandeur of the American West, for the experience of standing in front of the Grand Canyon can have as great an effect of awe and wonder as any cathedral ever built—perhaps even more for the modern mind, which has been steeped in evolutionary science for several generations. When Americans wanted to locate God outside after generations of inside, the landscape made that possible.

Nomadland returns us with full force to the raw grandeur of the American West: Into the sullied and ragged edges of dying towns, Amazon warehouses, beet processing factories, and Walmart parking lots, burst the undimmed glories of the Western landscape, horizon still beckoning, still a symbol of promise.

The horizon as symbol

The horizon is an imaginary line and, as such, it has served as the basis for many a metaphor that requires a division of one zone into two, or a meeting of two domains. As a line, the horizon is often used to mark a boundary. The limits of our current understanding might be referred to as the horizon of our knowledge. If we want to expand our knowledge in some area, we often say we "expand our horizons" or "broaden our horizons."

While our conscious perception of the horizon is very often a straight line, the horizon itself is much more properly conceived of as a sphere. While a line suggests progression, a sphere suggests completion. To contemplate the horizon is to put oneself in the picture of wholeness where, even unconsciously, we are supported by the symbolism of integrity and unity. Horizon gazing is a form of western meditation.

It is very interesting that the horizon is most often used for imagining into the future. This is not accidental but is hardwired in the biological origins of horizon gazing. The "refuge and prospect theory" of Jay Appleton[9] (related to an earlier idea called "savannah theory") suggests that, given our long ancestral history on the African savanna, we are especially suited to and desirous of geographical locations that provide us some form of safety—that is, *refuge*—that ideally has protection at our back in the direction that we are not looking at, such as a cave, as well as a view toward the horizon—that is, *prospect*. This ideal setting means that we are aware of any predators who might be approaching, as well as prospecting for our dinner, as we survey the herds out in the distance.

For the nomads in their caravans or RVs, like the ones in *Nomadland*, the prospect and refuge formula is ideally preserved. The safety of one's vehicle provides the cave, and the view through the window or the windshield provides the prospect. The concept of horizon as promoting future focus is hardwired into this savanna theory, since the future focus of most primitive Homo sapiens, as well as many of their contemporaries, finds that food and the prospect of it in the foreseeable future tend to occupy a rather large amount of brain space. When the stomach is satisfied, however, the future focus continues to hold us fascinated, and we gaze outward into the space we are moving into with the curiosity of the hunter-gatherer.

We are often not consciously focused while we are gazing at the horizon, for one of the curious facts of this soft focus is that it pulls us into that daydreaming state where conscious and unconscious thoughts rise up to swirl together in a creative vortex birthing the seeds of new possibilities. The horizon is, thus, a kind of incubator for the imagination. Symbols that work in this way on both conscious and unconscious levels are powerful catalysts for shaping what the new vision will be. And the ability to speculate about the future is one of the most important signs of the endurance of hope in the human psyche. A complete disinterest in the future—especially for an American—is tantamount to an admission of despair. The person who has absolutely no interest in what might happen tomorrow has given up hope.

The American dream is founded upon the hope for a better future—in a sense, it is its *raison d'être*. Of all the various reasons given by early European migrants for leaving the known world for the unknown, the hope for a better future was the spoken or unspoken foundation for every other ambition. They endured the long ocean voyage where the watery western horizon beckoned with that promise. They left the eastern seaboard to push deeper into the new territory, lured by the western horizon and its promise of more land, more freedom, and more opportunity.

As the movie *Nomadland* now shows us, some of those who have been pushed out of the comfort of a stationary retirement are once again seeking the comfort of the horizon, moving mainly westward to the open spaces along the highways that travel up and down the spine of the American Rockies. During one of the scenes in the film, Fern is visiting her sister, Dolly, and is challenged by her sister's friend on her homeless status. The friend argues that homelessness is a problem and something to be fixed; Fern reiterates her claim that to be without a house is not the same as being "homeless," and that she has chosen her status. Dolly jumps in to support her, declaring that Fern and the other nomads are the latest incarnation of the great American pioneers, crossing the country in their covered wagons, something to be admired rather than lamented. An awkward silence follows.[10]

Nomads and the experience of the numinous

During the television series *The Power of Myth*, Bill Moyers posed the question to Joseph Campbell: "Are we seeking the meaning of life?" Joseph Campbell shot back, unexpectedly, "I don't think that's what we're seeking at all; I think what we're really seeking is the experience of being alive."[11] This curious distinction makes sense to those who have followed the important arguments of the twentieth century, particularly among the existentialists such as Nietzsche, and the emphasis on pure being or becoming or beingness.

Campbell explains this critical distinction in one of his earlier works. In his essay "The Symbol without Meaning," he urges the reader to recognize the importance of letting go of the fruitless search for "meaning" which many people grip with the stubbornness of an unruly dog. Campbell suggests we follow the track of thought until thought drops away from language, and language itself dissolves, and points to the fact that so many religious rituals and spiritual practices have the goal of releasing the human mind, rather than focusing it. Campbell goes on to say:

> In the simplest terms, I think we might say that when a situation or phenomenon evokes in us a sense of existence (instead of some reference to the possibility of an assurance of meaning) we have had an experience of this kind . . . When this occurs, our own reality beyond meaning is awakened (or perhaps better: we are awakened to our own reality beyond meaning) and we experience an affect that is neither thought nor feeling but in interior impact . . . We have had, for an instant, a sense of existence: a moment of unevaluated, unimpeded, lyric life—antecedent to both thought and feeling; such as can never be communicated by means of empirically verifiable propositions, but only suggested by art.[12]

Campbell identifies this experience with that kind articulated by Rudolf Otto in *The Idea of the Holy*, which he calls a numinous encounter with the *"mysterium tremendum."*[13] It is this evocative phrase that Campbell returns to again and again to emphasize the real goal of the metaphysical function of myth. In one of his most devastating critiques, Campbell asserts that

> [T]here is a precise relationship between the format or stature of the psyche and the quantum of immediate experience that one is capable of sustaining and absorbing and that the training and shaping of the mandala-conditioned psyche of the incomplete man of the agriculturally based societies has simply unfitted him for the reception of the full impact of any *mysterium tremendum* whatsoever.[14]

If not the agricultural human, then who has the necessary stature to receive the numinous vision? Campbell claims, "It must be clear by now that a certain relationship is indicated here between the courage of the Paleolithic Hunter and his individualism and his willingness to face unprotected the spiritual experiences available to our race."[15]

Campbell's critique of "the mandala-conditioned psyche of the incomplete man of the agriculturally based societies" juxtaposed to the "courage of the paleolithic hunter and his individualism" may make uncomfortable listening for us. Are we not more fully developed as agriculturally based societies than the "primitive" hunter-gatherers? We have been conditioned to believe so. And yet that belief is not universally shared. Award-winning author Jared Diamond boldly inquires whether the agricultural revolution has actually been a good thing for human beings:

> Are twentieth century hunter-gatherers really worse off than farmers? Scattered throughout the world, several dozen groups of so-called primitive people, like the Kalahari bushmen, continue to support themselves that way [through hunting and gathering]. It turns out that these people have plenty of leisure time, sleep a good deal, and work less hard than their farming neighbors . . . Thus, with the advent of agriculture the elite became better off, but most people became worse off. Instead of swallowing the progressivist party line that we chose agriculture because it was good for us, we must ask how we got trapped by it despite its pitfalls.[16]

And, if we dare to ask how we got trapped by it, we may find ourselves staring into the shadows of the human psyche where the urge to abandon the quest is always at war with the horizon of hope. The fourteenth-century Muslim historian Ibn Khaldun theorized about the mistrust between the Bedouin nomads, who "go alone into the desert, guided by their fortitude, putting their trust in themselves," and the inhabitants of the settled city-states of Arabia, who are "accustomed to luxury and to indulgence in worldly desires." In his magnum opus, *The Muqaddimah*, Khaldun writes:

> [S]edentary life constitutes the last stage of civilization and the point where it begins to decay. It has thus become clear that the stage of sedentary culture is the stopping point in the life of civilization and dynasties.[17]

By way of explanation, he describes the number of times that cities have been attacked and then ruled by nomad warriors who want to enjoy the ease and pleasure available in the settled life, but how this very lifestyle then erodes the characteristics of strength, stoicism, and courage that enabled them to survive the harsh demands of nomadic life, leaving them vulnerable to be overrun and ruled by the very tribes they used to be part of. This is what drives settled peoples' fear and distrust of the nomads: At a species-deep level, we know this cyclical nature of domination and submission, and that the price of luxury, sloth, and indolence is ultimately to become weak and overpowered by a leaner, meaner, and hungrier adversary. The settled despise the nomads because they remind them of their less cultured origins, but fear them because they are a reminder of the settled society's ultimate doom.

The American adventurer Estwick Evans seems to have intuited the difference between the softness of settled life and the exhilaration of nomadism for, in 1818, he strode out into the wilderness during "the season of snows" in order to find "the pleasure of suffering, and the novelty of danger."[17] He later recalled:

> I wished to acquire the simplicity, native feelings, and virtues of savage life, to divest myself of the factitious habits, prejudices and imperfections of civilization

. . . and to find amidst the solitude and grandeur of the western wilds, more correct views of human nature and of the true interests of man.[18]

Campbell's mandala-conditioned human differs from the Paleolithic hunter in
the manner that social anthropologist Claude Lévi-Strauss refers to when he speaks
of the difference between the raw versus the cooked. A mandala-circumscribed society has prepared or "cooked" life's raw experiences for its members so that they
do not encounter life in its terrifying reality, but always through the prepared lens
of some facet or other of their social matrix. In the film of that name, *The Matrix*—
another iconic cinematic cultural mythology—reality has been so cooked that the
juice of life itself has all but been cooked out of it.

It is in this context of an overcooked-to-the-point-of-lifelessness cultural mythos that Campbell soberly predicted that, unless we could find the "fearless self-
sufficiency of our shamanistic inheritance,"[19] we would likely succumb to the
terrifying emptiness of a wheel without a hub.

The horizon is intimately connected to the greater symbolic image of the planetary curve of outer space—the rim of Earth or moon or planet over which we peer
into the fathomless eternity of space. The famous NASA Earthrise photo of 1968
was heralded by Campbell as the defining new icon for the mythic imagination in
which merely terrestrial maps no longer suffice, and the sacred center is anywhere
and everywhere.

Is the center the earth? Is the center the moon? The center is anywhere you like.
The chosen center may be anywhere. The holy land is no special place. It is
every place that has ever been recognized and mythologized by any people as
home.[20]

American movies such as *2001: A Space Odyssey* show again and again that
iconic curve of a planet or moon over which we see the vastness of outer space.
All of *Star Trek* and *Star Wars* and Marvel and the *Avengers* films participate in
serving up this image to hungry eyes. In fact, almost all of the *Star Wars* films begin and end with some kind of horizon imagery locating the viewer multiple times
in the new sacred posture where "prospect" is the universe itself, and "refuge"
may be nothing more than an elaborate tin can whirling in space. "Space, the final
frontier" intones the opening sequence to the original *Star Trek* television series,
as viewers careen through vast reaches of outer space. But an intimate version of
this symbol is available to every citizen willing to leave the confines of the cooked
urban life and seek out the raw and lonely byways where a far-distant horizon is
still possible.

The way of the nomad is the stark reminder that the characteristics which are
native to the lifestyle of the wanderer are what propelled our species to roam into
every part of the planet and find a way to survive and then thrive. For some, whatever our citified selves may feel about the people of the road and their itinerant existence, we need what they have, and the symbol of the horizon is there to provoke

and evoke the call to adventure that will take us toward the deepest reaches of inner space where we can grow ourselves a whole person, not condemned to be eternally a small cog in a great wheel, but to have within our individual psyche the entire sphere of existence.

The archetype of a new hero

Myth is the collective dream that holds people together; symbols are the images that unite the individual with the numinous experience that animates the myth; archetypes define the kinds of characters that inhabit those myths.

An enduring version of the American dream upholds the idea that anyone can pull themselves up by their bootstraps to become a success. It is an article of faith inside this version of the myth and has as great a holding power as the tautology that the doctrine of the elect had on the Protestant religion in colonial America. That religious doctrine insisted that if God loved you it would be reflected in your prosperity, making prosperity itself the proof of God's love, and its absence the proof of God's displeasure. That idea has bled through to the American myth that still holds sway and propels Americans to reject safety nets for the poor and, directly related to our inquiry, legislates vindictive solutions around homelessness in America. Any countervailing story that suggests that poverty has systemic origins is routinely rejected since it does not fit into the storyline.

The danger of accepting the systemic view is that it would threaten the core of the dream, which is that individuals have the power to transform their situations *in spite of* all the prevailing conditions that may be arraigned against them. At the crux of the American dream is the need to believe in individual agency that supersedes the structures of oppression. It is easy to see why that story is hard to kill: It is a story that is a lifeline of hope to those seeking a better life. Where there is no hope, the dream dies.

For a growing demographic of Americans, the dream is deteriorating. Linda May, a character in *Nomadland* who plays herself in the film, explains to Fern that she started working when she was 12 years old and continued to work while raising two daughters, and yet, when it came time to retire, her social security was only about $500 a month. That's why she took to the life of a nomad in her van. For a minimum wage earner, this is not an unusual situation to end up in, although it is not possible to survive anywhere in the U.S. on $500 a month, factoring in rent on top of food, medicine, and other necessities.

Nomadland: Surviving America in the Twenty-first Century, the documentary book by Jessica Bruder, paints a much grimmer and realistic picture of how individuals' initiative fares against the economic system that is imposed on them. *Nomadland* the movie paints a gentler picture. It does not shy away from addressing the economic realities, but it keeps alive the story of individual initiative and capacity to succeed in the face of overwhelming odds. In other words, it is a true hero journey and, as such, fits into our imaginative beliefs about heroes as the ones who make it through the road of trials.

The next two decades in America will be dominated by older women as, in the great surge of 75 million baby boomers, for every 75 men over the age of 65, there are 100 women.[21] Fern is thus, in a tangible sense, the face of the future. By embracing her choice of the nomadic life, Fern is offering herself as an imaginative bridge to every one of the viewers of that film to be able to see themselves making that choice; meaning that we must find within ourselves that same level of courage, daring, grit, determination, and hopefulness which Fern exhibits by her very existence. Although for many it may be the road not taken, it forces us to look inside and question whether we have those characteristics still latent within us, should the need arise.

Given pandemics and global warming, it is not unthinkable that our species is right now facing some of those calamities which we had thought to be confined to movies and science fiction books. *Nomadland* is an unconscious attempt to call back from memory those ancient strengths of our ancestral hunter-gatherers so admired by Joseph Campbell. In the face of Fern, one can quite easily find these characteristics. Frances McDormand, who plays Fern, is a brilliant actress, but she is also an American woman who may innately carry within her that inborn characteristic, that pioneering spirit of stoic strength, once spoken of by Tocqueville when he remarked, "If I were asked to what the singular prosperity and growing strength of that people ought mainly to be attributed, I should reply: to the superiority of their women."[22]

Almost every scene of the movie gives us another opportunity to witness Fern's grit, determination, self-reliance, and willingness to absorb the shocks and rudeness of daily life while still remaining above the surface of despair. Even her name, Fern, evokes the organic resilience of one of the longest-surviving life forms on the planet, a herbaceous perennial that has withstood millions of years of shocks and changes to habitat.

But Fern is not merely treading water. She is making powerful choices in what seem to be circumstances that offer very little choice, and so the choices that are made resound with a special significance. In the movie's plotline, the key dramatic moment arrives near the very end of the film when Fern is offered the opportunity to move in with Dave, a gentleman friend who is sincere in his affection for Fern and has made it clear he'd like her to come live with his extended family. At a family Thanksgiving in northern California we see their warm welcome to her. After dinner, Dave's daughter-in-law asks Fern about her old house in Empire, Nevada. Fern starts to brush it off by saying the house was nothing much, but then stops herself and becomes more honest. She admits that it was a special place because the view from the house, which was on the very edge of town, stretched all the way to the mountains on the horizon. There was nothing in our way, she recalls.

Later, Dave urges her again to stay and settle down with him. The camera follows Fern in a silent walk around the slumbering household in the early morning hours after the Thanksgiving feast, her eyes traveling over the memorabilia of family life, her fingers lightly touching the furniture in the piano room where she watched father and son share a musical interlude the night before. And yet, before the sun is fully up, she is back in her van, headed toward the open road.

In the very next scene, we find her at the coast, standing on a stone outcrop facing the vast horizon of the Pacific Ocean. A dark and brooding sky pelts cold rain into her face, but she tears off her woolen hat and flings her arms out in a wide embrace to the expanse of wind and water. A huge smile illuminates her face as she leans back to take in the rain. She is aware that she has made a choice, and we are left to contemplate the magnitude of that choice. She has rejected the safety and comforts of home and family for the uncertain adventure of solitary wandering and is exhilarated by that choice.

The very next scene jumps forward in time to Fern walking by herself in another setting of the early hours of the morning, among a group of nomads slumbering at the turn of a new year. Fern walks alone through the camp waving a single sparkler, calling out gently "Happy New Year" to her adopted tribe. The implication is clear: It is better to live a life that is truly your own than be an appendage in a more secure system, but one in which your identity is eroded. Fern has chosen to be fiercely loyal to her own life, to continue to create and explore her own culture-of-becoming, rather than exist in a culture that is not her own.

Certain people arrive at a time in their life where they carry the sense of form forward in a self-sustaining culture. These are the folks who know what they love and have ordered their lives around hierarchies of personal value. They are the ones who initiate traditions for themselves and are committed to their own fancies. They may be of few words, but their speech has stature. Their actions may be spontaneous, but they are never chaotic. There is an abiding sense of coherence, of a life curated with care and intention. They are not necessarily the culture bearers of the existing society, but cultural creators of a new conscience, a new sensibility for their tribe. They are no longer being enculturated into the common stock; they are now contributors at the highest level to the potentiality of the commons. This is precisely the role that Fern takes up in *Nomadland*; she is an incarnation of a new archetype whose image arises like a dark but brilliant silhouette against the setting sun of the American dream.

In the final scene of the film, Fern returns to her old hometown, Empire, and walks through her abandoned house. She stands for a moment by the kitchen sink, gazing out at the view that she had described earlier. The snow-speckled scrubland stretches away as far as the eye can see, to sweep up at the far horizon into mist-covered mountains. She opens the back door and stares for a moment into that vast stretch of emptiness. The barest flicker of a smile dances across her face, and then she strides through the opening in the fence toward the mountains. Seamlessly, the scene shifts, and we're still looking at those mountains, but this time from the back of Fern's van—the call of the road is now the song of her soul and, quite possibly, the true soundtrack of the American dream.

Notes

1 Academy of Motion Picture Arts and Sciences, "The 93rd Academy Awards, 2021," Oscars.org, 2021, www.oscars.org/oscars/ceremonies/2021

2 Harry Simon, "Towns without Pity: A Constitutional and Historical Analysis of Official Efforts to Drive Homeless Persons from American Cities," *Tulane Law Review*, 66, no. 4 (1992): 649–51.
3 Tsugio Makimoto and David Manners, *Digital Nomad* (Chichester, UK: Wiley, 1997).
4 Joseph Campbell, *The Masks of God. Volume 2: Oriental Mythology* (New York: Penguin, 1976).
5 Joseph Campbell, *The Hero's Journey: Joseph Campbell on His Life and Work* (Boston: Element Books, 1999), 40.
6 See Albert Bierstadt, *Among the Sierra Nevada Mountains, California,* 1868, Smithsonian
   American Art Museum. Wikimedia Commons.
7 Estwick Evans, *A Pedestrious Tour, of Four Thousand Miles: Through the Western States and Territories, During the Winter and Spring of 1818: Interspersed with Brief Reflections Upon a Great Variety of Topics . . .*, reprint (Concord, NH: Joseph C. Spear, 1819), 202.
8 Max Oelschlaeger, "Emerson, Thoreau, and the Hudson River School," in *Nature Transformed* (National Humanities Center, May 2008).
9 Jay Appleton, *The Experience of Landscape* (New York: Wiley, 1975).
10 Chloé Zhao, *Nomadland* (Screenplay, January 12, 2019), 66.
11 Joseph Campbell, *The Power of Myth* (New York: Knopf Doubleday, 2011), 5.
12 Campbell, "Symbol without Meaning," in *The Flight of the Wild Gander: Explorations in the Mythological Dimension—Selected Essays, 1944–1968* (New York: Viking Press, 1969), 151.
13 Rudolf Otto, *The Idea of the Holy; an Inquiry into the Non-Rational Factor in the Idea of the Divine and Its Relation to the Rational*, trans. John Harvey (New York: Oxford University Press, 1968), 12–13.
14 Campbell, "Symbol without Meaning," 189.
15 Ibid.
16 Jared Diamond, "The Worst Mistake in the History of the Human Race," *Discover Magazine*, 1987.
17 Evans, *A Pedestrious Tour . . .*, 102.
18 Ibid.
19 Campbell, "Symbol without Meaning," 189.
20 Joseph Campbell, *The Inner Reaches of Outer Space: Metaphor as Myth and as Religion*, vol. 2 (New World Library, 2002), 18.
21 Mark Mather and Lillian Kilduff, "The U.S. Population Is Growing Older, and the Gender Gap in Life Expectancy Is Narrowing," Population Reference Bureau, February 19, 2020.
22 Alexis de Tocqueville, *Democracy in America* (Chicago: University of Chicago Press, 2000), 576.

Index

Page numbers followed by "n" refer to notes.

For Product Safety Concerns and Information please contact our EU
representative GPSR@taylorandfrancis.com
Taylor & Francis Verlag GmbH, Kaufingerstraße 24, 80331 München, Germany